rick stein's *seafood*

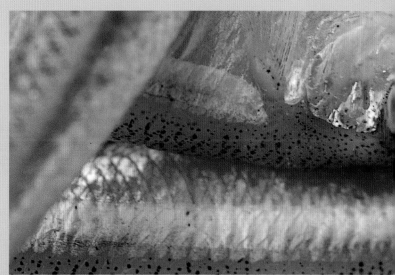

stein's
seafood

BBC
BOOKS

photography by
james murphy

Published by BBC Books, an imprint of Ebury Publishing
A Random House Group Company

The Random House Group Limited Reg. No. 954009

Addresses for companies within the Random House Group can be
found at www.randomhouse.co.uk

First published in hardback in 2001
Paperback edition published in 2006

The Random House Group Limited supports The Forest
Stewardship Council (FSC), the leading international forest
certification organisation. All our titles that are printed on
Greenpeace approved FSC certified paper carry the FSC logo.
Our paper procurement policy can be found at
www.rbooks.co.uk/environment

Commissioning Editor: Vivien Bowler
Project Editor: Rachel Copus
Art Director: Lisa Pettibone
Designer: Paul Welti
Home Economist: Debbie Major

Set in RotisSemiSans light
Printed and bound by Printer Trento S.r.l., Italy

ISBN 978 0 563 53417 4 (Hardback)
30 29 28 27 26 25 24 23 22 21
ISBN 978 0 563 49347 1 (Paperback)
20 19 18 17 16 15 14 13 12 11

contents

chapter five
soups, stews
and mixed
seafood 100

MIX
Paper from
responsible sources
FSC® C015829
www.fsc.org

introduction

A FEW YEARS AGO I heard that the old fish market on the quay in Padstow was going to be pulled down, as it was crumbling into the harbour, and a new big shed was to be built to house the fishmongers and chandlers who traded in the old building.

The plans for the new building showed a first floor above the fish shops that was to be used for storage. I discovered that most of the businesses didn't actually need this space, so I persuaded the architects to put in windows and design a seafood school there for us that overlooks the harbour and the estuary beyond. It has round windows at one end and the other end, which has a view of the harbour, is all glass. A large pine table, seating 20, stands right next to the glass, so that you can watch the fishing boats as you eat lunch. There are 10 work areas, each with light hard-wood units, blue worktops and stainless-steel cookers and fish-patterned tiles behind. The curved ceiling is covered in planks and painted light blue, like the hull of a fishing boat, and the floor is of light wood. It's very modern in feel and is the perfect space for teaching fish cookery.

We produce a course manual, which is bound in a loose-leaf file. It contains recipes, cooking and preparation techniques and includes a description of all the fish and shellfish we use in the school. That manual is the origin of this book. I thought a book that contained detailed information on how to buy and store fish, then prepare and cook it, together with hundreds of good photographs showing not just important techniques such as filleting, but also step-by-step cooking and serving methods would be of real benefit to everyone. I decided to include a section on good equipment and essential ingredients, plus a chapter describing not only British fish, but all the best fish around the world, together with observations on their eating qualities. I have added a section of all my favourite seafood recipes plus many that I have written just for this book.

buying fish

My recipes are generally rather simple and require the excitement of truly fresh fish to make them shine. Buying the freshest fish is therefore essential. I worry that my recipes will not work as well if people only have the average fish counter at a supermarket to rely on. But even faced with a limited selection of fish there's always going to be something good to buy. The cardinal rule is to be flexible; most of my recipes can be made with lots of different fish and I have given alternatives for many recipes. Large John dory, for example, can be used instead of brill or turbot, monkfish dishes can be made with swordfish. Rather than slavishly going for the fish in the recipe, choose the best-looking fish on the counter and use that. Go for the brightest eye, the most sparkling skin. Like wine tasting, it's easier to make a judgement of quality by contrasting one fish with another.

look particularly for the following signs of quality:

- EYES: these should be clear and bright, not cloudy and sunken or blotched with red.
- SKIN: the skin should be shiny and vivid. Colours such as orange spots on plaice, the green and yellow flecks on cod and the turquoise, green and blue lines on mackerel should be bright and cheerful. Slime on fish is a good sign.
- FINS: these should be clearly defined and perky, not scraggy and broken.
- GILLS: the gills should be a startling lustrous pink or red, moist and a delight to the eye, not at all faded or brown.
- SMELL: fresh fish doesn't smell of fish, just of the sea. It should be appetizing; something you want to eat, not something the odour of which you hope will disappear when you cook it. It won't.

- FEEL: good-quality fish should be firm. Obviously some fish is softer than others, but all fish goes slack and feels flabby as it goes stale.

farmed fish

Farmed fish have one advantage over wild: freshness can be perfectly controlled as the fish are kept alive until they are ordered. Otherwise the quality is not quite as good as that of wild, mainly because the fish tend to be sold when they are too small and the flavour has not had a chance to develop. There are signs, however, that fish may be allowed to mature in the future and as long as the fish are fed nothing to rid them of any of their flavour before they are dispatched, the quality can be excellent. Salmon are harvested in larger sizes but there is a vast difference between the best and worst. If you can select your cut from a whole fish you will notice that the top-quality fish are much sleeker and firmer than the cheaper ones, which are stubby and quite often have truncated fins – an indication of overcrowding in the fish pens. When buying prepared fillets of salmon, look for firm flesh and leave the flabby stuff alone.

filleted fish

It's harder to tell the freshness of fish fillets because there are fewer indicators to go by. But, as with whole fish, fillets should look bright and shiny. The flesh should be white, pink or off-white depending on the species. Fillets that are going stale will have a yellow – or worse – a brown tinge about them. Fresh fillets should be firm to the touch and should not smell.

A simple rule I follow when buying fillets is to ask myself if I would like to eat them raw, sliced and served as the Japanese dish sashimi, with wasabi and soy.

storing fish

Domestic fridges are not ideal for storing fish as they are set at about 5°C and fish should be stored at 0°C. If possible, you should use the fish the day you buy it, but if you must store it for a short time, put the fish in a shallow dish or tray, then wrap the container in cling film and place it in the coldest part of the fridge.

defrosting frozen fish and shellfish

Always defrost fish in the fridge, on plenty of kitchen paper, or in a colander set over a bowl, so that it doesn't end up sitting in water into which it will leech out lots of its flavour.

buying crustaceans

Lobsters and crabs are sold either live or cooked. They are never sold dead and uncooked because the flesh deteriorates very quickly and becomes mushy and tasteless. Cooking stops this process. Live lobsters or crabs should be obviously alive, with clear signs of muscular activity, whether aggressive waving of the claws in crabs or snapping of the tail in lobsters. Claws, tails and legs should not be dangling limply.

Whether cooked or raw, crustaceans should feel heavy for their size as this is an indication of good muscle quality. Compare the weights of two similarly sized lobsters or crabs by weighing them in each hand and opt for the heavier as it will have more meat.

It's hard to get consistent quality in cooked lobsters or crabs because you are dependant on your fishmonger as the cook. How much salt, if any, did he or she use? How long did he or she cook the crustaceans for? What was the quality like before cooking? It's really a question of sticking to a fishmonger who you know and trust.

prawns

Prawns are sold either raw or cooked and can be bought whole with their heads still on or as tails, which can be bought either peeled or unpeeled. Prawn tails are better value for money than whole prawns, but whole prawns are usually better quality. The shells preserve the flavour and, once removed, can be used to make nice stocks and flavoured oils.

Prawns are normally sorted by size and sold by the average number per kilogramme. If the fishmonger is offering approximately 20–25 prawns per kilogramme the prawns will be large enough for most purposes. The lower the number of prawns per kilogramme, the bigger the prawns and the more expensive they will be.

With the exception of local catch, the majority of prawns available will be frozen. 'Fresh' prawns will almost always have been frozen and then defrosted at their destination. Prawns freeze well, but do not travel well chilled, which is why they are usually boiled at sea if they are not to be frozen. Like lobsters, prawns deteriorate after death and become soft and tasteless very quickly. Unless they are local, or I can get them still alive, I always prefer to buy frozen raw prawns of the best quality as it gives me complete control.

Once the prawns are defrosted they deteriorate quickly. So when buying 'fresh' make sure the prawns feel firm, that the shells are taut, intact and not dull looking. Make sure too that they smell fresh – definitely not of ammonia – and avoid any that have signs of darkening or black spots around the head.

dublin bay prawns

These prawns, also known as langoustines or scampi, are more like lobsters and care should be taken if buying them raw as, like raw prawns, they deteriorate rapidly (see notes, above). When buying cooked langoustines, give the tails a flick; there should be some spring left in them, indicating the muscle was in good condition when the prawn was cooked.

buying live shellfish

All uncooked shellfish whether living in two shells (bivalves) or one (univalves) should be alive before cooking.

The shells of bivalves, such as oysters, cockles, mussels and clams, should be closed or should close when tapped or squeezed together. Broken shellfish and those that don't close should be discarded. It's advisable not to buy from a batch where many of the shells are open because it's a sign that they have been out of the sea too long and won't taste fresh.

Univalves such as whelks, winkles and abalone are alive if you can see the creature moving inside the shell, if the shell moves, or if there is foam on the opening of the shell.

Live shellfish that you buy from a fishmonger, will have health certification. If you are gathering your own, be aware that they can present a health risk if taken from a polluted area. Shellfish taken from the seashore are safer than those found in estuaries and harbours because any pollution is likely to be diluted by the open sea but whenever gathering your own shellfish it is advisable to ask for advice locally.

cleaning and storing shellfish

Wash shellfish in cold water to remove sand and mud and scrape away any barnacles or weed. With mussels, remove the threads that attach the mussel to the rocks just before cooking. They don't keep well once this has been removed.

Shellfish can be stored for a few days in the bottom of a fridge covered with seaweed or a damp cloth.

how much fish and shellfish to buy

As a rule of thumb, you will be able to eat slightly less than half the weight of any whole fish you buy. Lobsters, crabs and prawns will give you much less, about one third of the weight you buy.

For whole fish, therefore, a 240 g (8½ oz) fish is about right for a first course, a 400–500 g (14–18 oz) fish will be generous for a main course. Good portion sizes of fillet are 100 g (4 oz) for a first course and 175 g (6 oz) for a main course.

The minimum size of lobster per person should be 500 g (1 lb 2 oz) for a whole one, 400 g (14 oz) for half a larger one. For crabs I would suggest 500 g (l lb 2 oz) of whole crab per person.

useful equipment for fish cookery

- KNIVES – a large cooks' knife with a 25 cm (10 inch) blade for chopping and cutting lobsters in half • A thin, flexible-bladed filleting knife that will allow you to feel both the fillet and bones whilst using • A small-bladed 7.5 cm (3 inch) knife for opening raw clams etc. • A very sharp, long-bladed knife for thinly slicing salmon, smoked salmon and tuna
- A FISH KETTLE – for poaching not only salmon, but other fish such as sea bass and coral trout too. It can also double-up as a steamer
- A DEEP-FAT FRYER – these are thermostatically controlled and are therefore safer to use than ordinary pans and are essential for fish cookery
- A FISH SCALER – you can use a knife, or even a scallop shell, but this makes the job much easier
- A FISH SLICE
- A CONICAL STRAINER, LADLE AND FINE SIEVE – vital for straining soups and stocks
- A PESTLE AND MORTAR – for making harissa and charmoula, for example
- KITCHEN SCISSORS – for cutting off fins
- A LOBSTER PICK
- FISH PLIERS or TWEEZERS – for pin boning
- WINKLE PICKERS (very fine, short skewers or long pins) – for removing winkles and whelks from the shell

- LOBSTER CRACKERS – for lobsters and crabs
- A LARGE, HEAVY-BASED FRYING PAN – with a well-seasoned surface
- A PETAL STEAMER – for steaming fish and vegetables
- A FISH-SHAPED WIRE CLAMP – for barbecuing
- A PAIR OF LONG-HANDLED TONGS
- A CLEAVER AND MALLET – for portioning whole turbot
- A RIDGED CAST-IRON GRIDDLE
- A WOK OR DEEP CHEFS' PAN
- A LARGE SHALLOW PAN WITH A WELL-FITTING LID – for steaming and braising
- A THERMOMETER
- A LARGE ROASTING TIN – for baking whole fish
- A FOOD PROCESSOR – for making light work of soups, mayonnaise, purées and pastes
- CHEAP, WOODEN CHOPSTICKS and a SUSHI MAT – for home-smoking fish
- A VERY LARGE SAUCEPAN – for cooking crabs, lobsters and langoustines

a few handy storecupboard ingredients
- A bottle of Pernod or Ricard
- A dry white vermouth such as Noilly Prat
- Some fennel herb, growing in the garden, or in a pot
- Capers
- Vinegar – sherry, white, red and balsamic
- Fennel seeds, crushed dried chilli flakes, coriander seeds, cumin seeds, ground turmeric, paprika, cayenne pepper
- Thai fish sauce (*nam pla*)
- Saffron

- Good quality anchovy fillets in olive oil
- A well-flavoured extra-virgin olive oil
- Roasted sesame oil
- A block of tamarind pulp
- A bottle of dark soy sauce
- Good-quality, whole black olives
- Maldon sea-salt flakes
- Some good-quality dried pasta
- A jar of sun-dried tomatoes in olive oil
- A few dried porcini mushrooms
- Sichuan peppercorns
- Chinese salted, fermented black beans
- Dried, fine rice noodles

a note about the recipes in this book

The recipes in this book are grouped under the following categories: Soups, Stews and Mixed Seafood; Large Meaty Fish, Skate and Eels; Large Round Fish; Small Round Fish; Flat Fish; Crustaceans; Molluscs and other Seafood. Some of these need explaining. By small round fish I mean any fish under 550 g (1¼ lb) i.e. a fish that would feed one person. Large round fish are larger than 550 g (1¼ lb) and less than 5 kg (11 lb) i.e. fish that could be cooked whole, but will sometimes be filleted and any fish larger than 5 kg (11 lb) that will always need to be filleted, being too large ever to cook whole. By large meaty fish I mean fish such as tuna, shark and swordfish, which will always be sold in steak or fillet form. Skate and eels also usually come ready prepared.

chapters 1/4

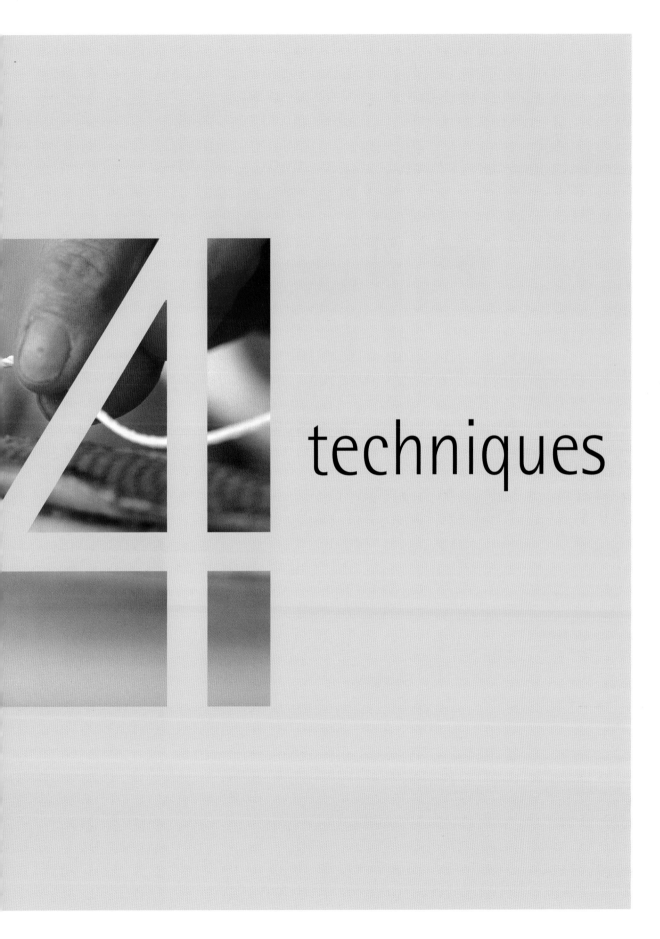

4 techniques

techniques
chapter 1

preparing fish

technique 1

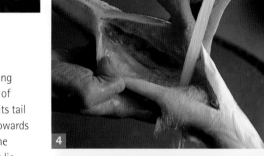

1 Work under cold running water or over several sheets of newspaper. Grip the fish by its tail and scrape it from the tail towards the head, working against the direction in which the scales lie, using a fish scaler or the blade of a blunt, thick-bladed knife.

2 Cut away the dorsal, pelvic and anal fins using a strong pair of kitchen scissors.

3 Slit open the belly of the fish from the anal fin up to the head and pull out the guts.

4 Cut away any remaining pieces of gut left behind in the cavity with a small knife and then wash it out with plenty of cold water.

scaling and gutting small round fish for the barbecue

BARBECUED WHOLE SEA BASS (for full recipe see pages 163–4)

5 Slash the flesh of each fish 4 or 5 times down each side. Rub it with oil and season with a little salt and pepper.

6 Season the inside of the gut cavity and then push in a small bunch of fennel herb.

7 Put the fish into a wire clamp and close it up. Barbecue them for 6–8 minutes on each side, sprinkling the fish with some Pernod just before turning.

8 When the fish are cooked through and the skin is crisp and golden, sprinkle them with a little more Pernod and serve with some fennel mayonnaise (see page 224).

preparing small oily fish for grilling

SPLIT HERRINGS WITH SALSA (for full recipe see page 158)

3 Alternatively, slit the fish open along the belly, all the way down to the tail, and pull out the guts with your hand. Wash the cavity clean.

1 Rub off the scales with your thumb, then rinse the fish under cold running water.

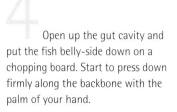

2 Cut off the head and discard. If you want to remove the guts without slitting the fish open, give the belly a gentle squeeze. Trap the exposed guts under the blade of a knife and drag them out.

4 Open up the gut cavity and put the fish belly-side down on a chopping board. Start to press down firmly along the backbone with the palm of your hand.

5 Continue pressing firmly all along the backbone until the fish is completely flat.

6 Turn the fish over and pull away the backbone, snipping it off at the tail end with scissors. Remove any small bones left behind in the fillet with fish pliers or tweezers. Season inside and out and then push back into shape.

7

8

7 Cut the tomatoes into small dice. Finely chop the garlic, roughly chop the parsley and rinse the capers. Mix all the ingredients together in a bowl with some seasoning.

8 Grill the fish under a high heat for 2 minutes on each side. Serve with a good spoonful of the salsa alongside.

skinning and pan-frying a whole flat fish

DOVER SOLE À LA MEUNIÈRE (for full recipe see page 181)

(for full recipe see page 181)

SKINNING
AND
PAN-FRYING
A WHOLE
FLAT FISH

1 Using a pair of kitchen scissors, cut away the frills from either side of the fish, close to the edge of the flesh. Snip off all the other little fins.

2 Make a shallow cut through the skin across the tail end of the fish with a sharp knife. Push the tip of the knife under the skin to release a small flap that you can get hold of.

3 Dip the fingers of your left hand in some salt and grab hold of the tail. With your other hand, take hold of the skin using a tea towel and, in one swift, sharp movement, pull the skin away along the entire length of the fish. Repeat on the other side.

4 Dip the skinned fish into some seasoned flour, making sure that it becomes well coated on both sides.

5 Lift up the fish and pat it on either side to remove the excess flour.

making a *beurre noisette*

Discard the frying oil from the pan and wipe it clean. For each fish add 20 g (¾ oz) unsalted butter and allow it to melt over a moderate heat (1). When the butter starts to turn light brown and smell nutty (2), add 1 teaspoon of lemon juice (3) and ½ tablespoon of chopped parsley. Immediately remove from the heat and quickly pour over the fish.

6 For each fish, heat 1 tablespoon of sunflower oil in a large, well-seasoned or non-stick frying pan. Add the fish, lower the heat slightly and add 7 g (¼ oz) unsalted butter pieces.

7 Leave to fry for 4–5 minutes over a moderate heat until richly golden on the underside. Carefully turn the fish over and cook for a further 4–5 minutes.

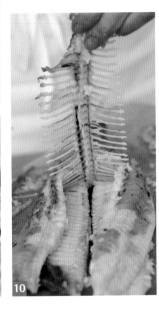

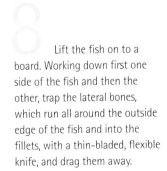

8 Lift the fish on to a board. Working down first one side of the fish and then the other, trap the lateral bones, which run all around the outside edge of the fish and into the fillets, with a thin-bladed, flexible knife, and drag them away.

9 Now run the knife down the centre of the fish and gently ease the fillets away from the bones, but leave them attached along the outside edge of the fish.

10 Take hold of the bones at the head end and carefully 'unzip' the fish. The bones will come away cleanly and the fillets will fall back into place.

11 Transfer the fish to a warmed serving plate and slightly part the fillets at what was the head end so that you can just see the underlying fillets. Spoon over some *beurre noisette* and serve.

filleting a large round fish and grilling thick fish fillets

COD WITH RED WINE SAUCE (for full recipe see page 126)

FILLETING
A LARGE
ROUND FISH
AND GRILLING
THICK FISH
FILLETS

1 Scale the fish and then remove the head by cutting diagonally just behind the gills on both sides from under the pelvic fin around to the top of the head. This will retain all the fillet.

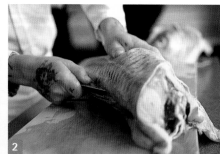

2 Starting at the head end, cut through the skin slightly to one side of the backbone along the whole length of the fish, using a sharp, thin-bladed, flexible knife.

3 Return to the head end and gradually cut the fillet away from the bones, keeping the blade as close to the bones as you can. When you reach the rib cage, if the bones are thick, continue to cut close to them until the fillet comes free. However, if the bones are fine, cut through them and remove them from the fillet with fish pliers or tweezers afterwards.

4 As you near the tail end, get the whole blade of the knife under the fillet, rest the other hand on top of the fish and cut the remainder away in one clean sweep. Turn the fish over and repeat on the other side.

5 Remove the thick bones from the fillets with fish pliers or tweezers.

6 Trim up the edges of each fillet and cut away the thinnest part of the belly flap. Cut the rest of the fillet across into portion-sized pieces weighing between 175 g (6 oz) and 225 g (8 oz).

7 For the sauce, sauté some finely chopped vegetables and spices in butter over a high heat until well browned.

8 Add some red wine, stock, sugar and a pinch of salt and simmer until well reduced and concentrated in flavour.

9 Strain the sauce through a fine sieve into a clean pan. Bring it back to a simmer and whisk in a little *beurre manié* to thicken. Adjust the seasoning if necessary.

10 Brush each portion of cod with melted butter and season on both sides with salt and pepper. Grill under a high heat, skin-side up, for 8 minutes. Serve on some cooked puy lentils, with a little of the sauce spooned around.

filleting small round fish for poaching

MACKEREL WITH MINT AND BUTTER SAUCE (for full recipe see page 158)

TWO WAYS OF
FILLETING
SMALL ROUND
FISH

1 With the back of the fish facing you, make a cut behind the back of the head, down to the backbone, using a sharp, thin-bladed, flexible knife.

2 With the knife still in place, turn it towards the tail and start to cut away the fillet. As soon as the whole blade of the knife is underneath the fillet, put your other hand flat on top of the fish and cut it away in one clean sweep, keeping the knife as close to the bones and as flat as possible.

3 Lift off the fillet, turn the fish over and repeat the process.

4 Make a hollandaise-style sauce: put the egg yolks, water and a sherry vinegar reduction into a large heatproof bowl. Rest it over a pan of simmering water and whisk vigorously until pale and voluminous. Remove the bowl from the pan and whisk in some clarified butter, lemon juice, seasoning and chopped mint.

5 Poach the fillets in simmering lightly salted water for 3 minutes, turning them over halfway through. Then lift them out and allow the excess water to drain off. Serve with the warm butter sauce.

filleting small round fish for stuffing

HERRING RECHEADO (for full recipe see page 160)

1 Remove the head of the fish. Start to cut away the top fillet until you can get the whole blade of the knife underneath it. Rest a hand on top of the fish and cut the fillet away from the bones until you are about 2.5 cm (1 inch) away from the tail.

2 Turn the fish over and repeat on the other side.

3 Pull back the top fillet and snip out the backbone close to the tail with scissors. The fillets will still be attached by the tail.

4 Spread the cut face of one fillet with a little masala paste, then put the fish back into shape.

5 Tie the fish in two places with string. Grill or barbecue for 3 minutes on each side.

preparing flat fish for grilling

GRILLED, SCORED PLAICE WITH ROASTED RED PEPPER

(for full recipe see page 178)

1 Remove the lateral bones that run through the frills and part way into the flesh of the fish by cutting very close to the underlying fillet with scissors.

2 This will remove the frills and about 1 cm (½ inch) of the adjacent flesh.

3 Score the fish on both sides like the veins of a leaf using a sharp knife.

4 Grill or roast a red pepper until the skin is black and blistered all over. Leave to cool, break in half and remove and discard the stalk and seeds. Peel off the skin and cut the flesh into very small dice.

5 Make a marinade with the roasted red pepper, some red chilli, garlic, oregano, olive oil, lemon juice, salt and pepper. Pour it over the fish and work it well into the cuts with your fingers. Leave for 1 hour. Grill the fish, dark-side up, under a high heat for 7–8 minutes.

24

preparing flat fish for deep-frying

GOUJONS OF LEMON SOLE (for full recipe see page 180)

1 To fillet the fish, cut around the back of the head, down to the backbone, using a sharp, thin-bladed, flexible knife. Then make a cut down the centre of the fish, from head to tail.

2 Starting at the head, slide the knife under one fillet and carefully cut it away, keeping the blade as flat and as close to the bones as possible. Remove the adjacent fillet, then turn the fish over and repeat.

3 Lay the fillet skin-side down, with the narrowest end facing you. Hold the tip of the skin with your fingers and, angling the blade of the knife down towards the skin and working it away from you, start to cut between the flesh and the skin. Firmly take hold of the skin and continue to work away from you, sawing the knife from side to side, keeping the blade close against the skin until the fillet is released.

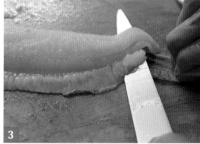

4 Trim the frills away from the edge of the skinless fillet to give it a neat finish.

5 Slice the fillets diagonally into goujons about the thickness of your little finger.

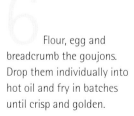

6 Flour, egg and breadcrumb the goujons. Drop them individually into hot oil and fry in batches until crisp and golden.

cutting large flat fish into steaks

TRONÇONS OF TURBOT WITH SAUCE VIERGE

(for full recipe see page 182)

1 Cut away the frills of the fish with scissors, then cut close around the back of the head, down to the backbone, so that you retain as much of the fillet as you can. Cut through the backbone using a cleaver and mallet and then cut away the head.

2 Cut through the flesh along the backbone of the fish, down to the bone, with a sharp knife. Cut through the bone with the cleaver and mallet and then finish cutting the fish in half with the knife.

3 Cut each half into portion-sized tronçons, cutting through the backbone when necessary with the cleaver and mallet.

cutting large round fish into steaks

Scale the fish and trim off the fins with scissors (1). Wash out the cavity with plenty of cold water (2). Cut the fish across, through the backbone, into steaks about 4 cm (1½ inches) thick, using a large, sharp knife (3).

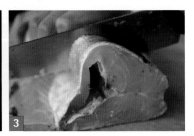

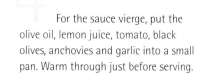

4 For the sauce vierge, put the olive oil, lemon juice, tomato, black olives, anchovies and garlic into a small pan. Warm through just before serving.

5 Mix together some olive oil, chopped rosemary, thyme and bay leaf, crushed fennel seeds and peppercorns and some sea salt flakes in a small roasting tin. Add the tronçons of turbot and turn them once or twice to coat.

6 Put the tronçons dark-side down into a smoking-hot ovenproof frying pan and sear until the skin has taken on a good colour. Turn them over, transfer the pan to the oven and roast for 8–10 minutes. Add chopped parsley and seasoning to the sauce vierge. Lift the fish on to warmed plates and spoon around some of the sauce.

PREPARING
DIFFERENT
CUTS FROM A
WHOLE
SALMON

cutting escalopes from a salmon fillet

ESCALOPES OF SALMON WITH SORREL SAUCE (for full recipe see page 141)

1 Fillet the salmon as described for cod on page 20. Put the fillet skin-side down on a board with the narrowest (tail-end) pointing towards you. Angle the blade of the knife down towards the skin and start to cut between the skin and the flesh, keeping the blade as close to the skin as you can. When the released fillet starts to get in the way, fold it back, take a firm hold of the skin and continue.

2 Remove the pin bones, which lie hidden in the flesh down the centre of the fillet; run your thumb along the line of bones in the opposite direction to which they are lying – they will then stand proud of the flesh. Pull them out with fish pliers or tweezers, or by trapping them between the point of a small, sharp knife and your thumb.

3 Put the fillet skinned-side down on to a board. Hold a long, thin-bladed knife at a 45-degree angle and cut the salmon into large 5 mm (¼ inch) thick slices called escalopes.

4 Brush the escalopes with oil, season and grill under a high heat for 30 seconds until only just firm. Arrange on top of the sorrel sauce and garnish with a little more chopped sorrel.

preparing a pavé of salmon

PAVÉ OF SALMON

(for full recipe see page 142)

1 Put the fillet skinned-side down on to a board. Remove the thinnest part of the belly flap and then neaten up the edges of the fillet with a sharp knife. Now cut the fillet across into neat rectangular pieces known as pavés (slabs), each weighing about 175 g (6 oz).

2 Lightly oil and season the pavés and put skinned-side down on to a smoking-hot ridged cast-iron griddle. Cook over a high heat, pressing them down gently now and then with a palette knife, until they have taken on rich golden bar marks underneath.

3 Sprinkle over some wine, leave them to cook for a few more seconds and then turn.

4 Cook on the other side for just 30 seconds or so, then remove the griddle from the heat and let them continue cooking in the residual heat of the pan for another 30 seconds. The salmon will remain quite rare inside. Serve on top of the roasted vegetables with the warm red wine vinegar and fennel seed *sauce vierge*.

PREPARING
THIN-BODIED
AND
ELONGATED
FISH FOR
GRILLING AND
GRIDDLING

filleting thin-bodied fish for grilling

JOHN DORY WITH LEEKS (for full recipe see page 169)

1 Make a cut around the back of the head and under the sharp, bony gill flaps with a sharp, thin-bladed, flexible knife.

2 Snip off all the spiny fins with strong scissors.

3 Lay the fish on a chopping board and run the tip of the knife vertically all around the outside edge of the fish, close to the raised ridge of sharp little spines.

4 Flatten the blade of the knife slightly and start to cut the fillet away from the underlying bones, keeping the blade of the knife as close to them as you can. The fillet from this side of the fish will come away in one piece. Turn the fish over and repeat on the other side.

5 Neaten up each fillet by cutting away the belly flap, then cut each fillet diagonally across into two similar-sized pieces. Brush with melted butter, season and grill skin-side up for 4 minutes.

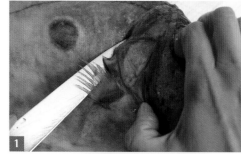

to assemble the dish

Griddle the blanched leeks until nicely marked on both sides. Arrange them in the centre of each plate (1) and put the John Dory fillets on top (2). Add the halved soft-boiled eggs and drizzle over some of the vinaigrette (3). Scatter over some Parmesan shavings and serve.

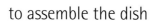

preparing elongated fish for griddling

SALAD OF GRIDDLED GARFISH (for full recipe see page 167)

1   Don't bother to gut small fish. Cut around the back of the head with a sharp, thin-bladed, flexible knife.

2   Turn the blade of the knife towards the tail and start to cut away the fillet, keeping the blade as flat against the bones as you can.

3   As soon as the whole blade of the knife is under the fillet, rest your other hand on top of the fish and cut the fillet away in one clean sweep, down towards the tail. Turn the fish over and repeat on the other side.

4   Make a marinade of olive oil, lemon juice, thyme, lightly crushed fennel seeds, chilli flakes and some seasoning.

5   Brush some of the marinade over both sides of each fillet and leave for 5 minutes to allow the flavours to permeate the fish a little.

6   Heat a flat or ridged cast-iron griddle until smoking hot. Add the garfish fillets and cook them for 1–1½ minutes on each side. Transfer them to a plate to stop them cooking any further.

7   Arrange the fish fillets and strips of sun-dried tomato in amongst some mixed baby salad leaves. Deglaze the pan with the leftover marinade and a little sherry vinegar. Spoon over the salad and around the outside edge of the plate.

a special technique for preparing gurnard

PAN-FRIED GURNARD WITH SAGE AND GARLIC (for full recipe see page 175)

2 Turn the blade of the knife horizontally towards the tail and take the dorsal fin in the other hand.

4 Cut through the backbone where it joins the back of the head but not right the way through the fish.

1 Place the fish belly-side down on a chopping board. Make a shallow vertical cut just behind the head of the gurnard, where the spines of the dorsal fin begin.

3 Slice just under the skin through the bones of the dorsal fin, right the way along the entire length of the fish and lift them away.

5 Push your thumbs underneath the skin on either side of the head and pull it away slightly.

preparing whiting for deep-frying whole

MERLAN FRIT EN COLÈRE (for full recipe see page 166)

2 Push a cocktail stick up through the soft part of its under-mouth, through the tail and out through the top of the head. Season the fish inside and out with salt and pepper.

1 Scale, gut and trim the whiting. Twist the fish into a circle so that the tail goes into its mouth.

3 Coat the fish well on all sides in seasoned flour, then knock off the excess.

6 Take hold of the head in one hand and the body of the fish in the other, and pull the head down towards the belly.

7 As soon as the head becomes free, use it to help pull away the skin from the body of the fish.

8 Pull the skin off the whole fish and right over the tail.

9 Pan-fry the prepared fish in a little oil and unsalted butter until golden. Remove to a plate and wipe the pan clean. Melt the remaining butter, add a little garlic and the whole sage leaves and cook gently for 30 seconds. Add some lemon juice and seasoning and pour over the fish.

4 Dip the floured fish in beaten egg, making sure that it is well covered.

5 Finally, coat the fish in fresh white breadcrumbs, pressing them on well to make sure that it gets well covered with a thick, even coating.

6 Deep-fry the fish one at a time at 160°C (325°F) for 5 minutes until crisp, golden and cooked through.

skinning a whole skate and roasting the wings

ROASTED SKATE WINGS (for full recipe see page 123)

ROASTED SKATE WINGS (for full recipe see page 123)

SKINNING A
WHOLE SKATE,
REMOVING
THE CHEEKS
AND
ROASTING THE
WINGS

1 Put the skate on to a large chopping board. Using a sharp, thin-bladed, flexible knife, make a cut 2.5 cm (1 inch) behind the nose, right the way through the fish. Cut around both sides of the head and then down either side of the backbone, to the tail. Separate the head from the backbone and tail and set aside. Discard the rest.

2 Separate the two wings where they are joined at the nose and deal with them one at a time.

3 Push the tip of the knife under the skin at what was the nose end to release a large flap that you can get hold of. Turn the wing over and release a flap on the other side.

4 Grab hold of the flap of skin with fish pliers and start to tear it away from the surface of the wing.

5 Once you have released a small amount, hold the wing down with a tea towel and sharply tear the skin away completely using the pliers. Turn the wing over and remove the skin from the other side, then repeat with the second wing.

6 Trim about 2.5 cm (1 inch) away from the thinnest edge of each wing.

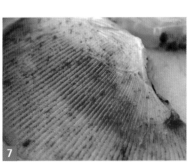

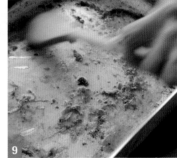

7 Dry the skate wings on kitchen paper and then sprinkle them on both sides with some paprika and coarsely crushed black pepper.

8 Lightly brown the wings in some butter in a small roasting tin on top of the cooker. Season with salt and transfer to the oven to roast for 10 minutes.

9 Lift the roasted skate wings on top of the plated chilli beans. Deglaze the roasting tin on top of the cooker by adding a little sherry vinegar and chicken stock and stirring with a wooden spoon to release all the juices which have baked on to the base of the tin.

10 Strain the juices through a fine sieve into a clean pan, season to taste and then spoon over the skate wings.

removing skate cheeks

Lay the head dark-side down on a board and pull back the jaw to open up the mouth (1). Slice diagonally under the jaw down towards the nose (2) and remove the mouth piece which will have the skate cheeks attached (3). Cut around the spherical cheek meats with the tip of a small sharp knife and remove (4). These will still have a small piece of bone in the very centre which you can remove if you wish (5), but they are easier to get out once the cheeks have been cooked.

skinning freshwater eel for stir-frying

STIR-FRIED EEL (for full recipe see page 125)

SKINNING
FRESHWATER
EEL FOR
STIR-FRYING

1 Cut through the skin around the back of the head with a small sharp knife.

2 Using fish pliers, pull away about 2.5 cm (1 inch) of skin from all the way around the head.

3 Hang the eel up by the head, with a meat hook or a piece of string, from something very secure and with plenty of room in which to work. Take a second pair of pliers, grab hold of some skin on either side of the eel and start to pull it away.

4 As soon as the skin starts to come away more cleanly, firmly and steadily pull it down towards the tail. As you near the tail it will start to get a little harder, but just give it a vigorous final tug and it will come away completely, over the tail.

5 To fillet the eel, lay it on a chopping board and cut off the head. Using a sharp, thin-bladed, flexible knife, make a shallow cut along the backbone of the fish, just above the line of bones. Start to cut away the fillet, keeping the blade of the knife as close to the bones as you can.

6 As soon as you can get the whole blade of the knife under the fillet, rest your other hand on top of the fish and cut the fillet away in one clean sweep, down towards the tail. Turn the eel over and repeat on the other side.

7 Cut the eel fillet diagonally into 2.5 cm (1 inch) wide pieces.

8 Put the pieces of eel into a bowl and add the cornflour and a pinch of salt. Toss together so that the eel gets well coated in the cornflour.

9 Heat a wok over a high heat until smoking hot. Add the sesame oil, garlic, ginger and chilli and stir-fry for a few seconds.

10 Add the black bean paste, quickly followed by the eel pieces. Stir-fry for 1 minute and then add the rice wine, soy sauce and water and stir-fry for 2 minutes until the eel is cooked through.

11 Add the spring onions, stir-fry for 1 minute and then tip out onto a warmed serving dish and serve with some steamed rice.

techniques
chapter 2

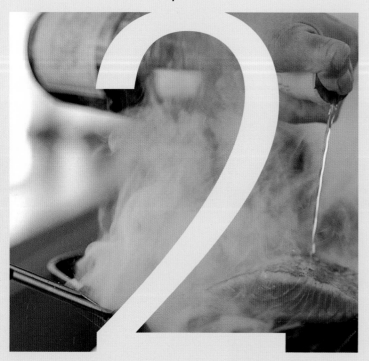

cooking fish

technique 19

1 Make a court-bouillon in a fish kettle. Add the salmon, bring back to a gentle simmer and leave it to poach for 16–18 minutes. Then lift it out using the trivet, rest it on the sides of the kettle and allow the excess liquid to drain away.

2 Lift the fish on to a serving plate. Make a shallow cut through the skin along the backbone and around the back of the head.

3 Starting at the head end, peel back and remove the skin. Carefully turn the fish over and repeat on the other side.

technique 20

1 Put some milk, or a mixture of milk and water, into a large shallow pan and add some bay leaves, onion and black peppercorns.

2 Bring to the boil, add the smoked haddock or smoked cod fillets and bring back to a gentle simmer.

poaching whole fish in a court-bouillon

POACHED SALMON (for full recipe see page 144)

4 To serve, run a small knife down the length of the fish between the 2 fillets. Gently ease them apart and away from the bones.

5 Lift off the fillets in portion-sized pieces, then turn the fish over and repeat. Serve with mayonnaise, cucumber salad and new potatoes.

poaching fish fillets in milk

3 Poach the fish for 3–4 minutes until it is firm to the touch and the flesh has turned opaque, then remove. If serving in one piece, peel back and discard the skin. Otherwise, leave on a plate until cool enough to handle, then break into large flakes, discarding the skin and bones.

poaching fish in oil

1 Fillet the fish as described on page 20 and then skin the fillets as described on page 28. Cover both sides of the fish in a thick layer of salt and leave for 10 minutes, then rinse well and dry on kitchen paper.

2 Prepare a bed of aromatic vegetables on which to put the fish; gently cook some sliced onion and garlic in olive oil until very soft but not coloured, then add some bay leaves, lemon slices and thyme.

3 Lay the fish fillets in a single layer on top of the vegetables.

4 Pour over some inexpensive olive oil so that the fish is completely covered. Place the pan over a low heat and slowly bring the temperature of the oil up to 100°C (212°F) – this will take about 15 minutes. Remove the pan from the heat and leave the fish to cool in the oil. Then remove the fillets, drain off the excess oil and use to make *tonno con fagioli* on page 118, for example.

poaching fish in oil at low temperature

HALIBUT POACHED IN OLIVE OIL (for full recipe see page 183)

1 Pour a thin layer of inexpensive olive oil into a shallow pan just large enough to take the fish in a single layer. Add the pieces of seasoned fish to the pan and add enough oil to just cover.

2 Place the pan over a low heat and allow it to heat very slowly until it reaches 55–60°C (130–140°F). Agitate the fish very gently with a fish slice now and then so that the oil and the fish heat evenly.

3 When the oil reaches temperature, poach the fish for 15 minutes, taking the pan on and off the heat when necessary to maintain the correct temperature.

4 When the fish is cooked it will be firm and opaque and will have a meltingly tender texture.

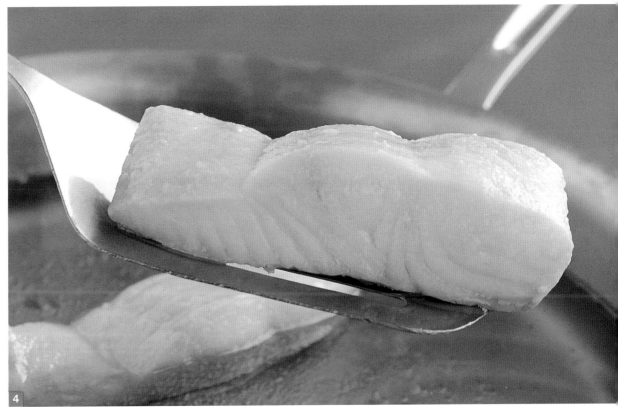

braising a whole large flat fish

MYRTLE'S TURBOT (for full recipe see page 182)

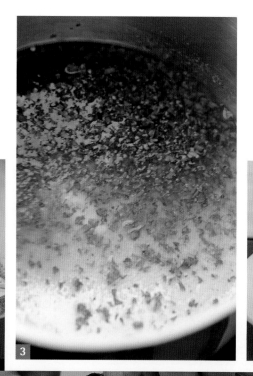

1 Cut through the dark skin, all the way around the fish, close to the frill-like fins. This will make it easy to remove before serving and prevent it from splitting during cooking.

2 Season the fish lightly and place it in a large roasting tin with just enough water to stop it sticking – about 600 ml (1 pint). Braise, uncovered, in a hot oven for 30 minutes.

3 Prepare a sauce with some melted butter and chopped *fines herbes* to which you can add the reduced cooking juices when the fish is done.

4 Transfer the fish to a warmed serving dish and carefully remove the top skin. Reduce the remaining cooking juices to a few tablespoons and add to the pan of herb butter.

5 Pour the sauce right over the fish and take it to the table to serve.

6 Remove portion-sized pieces of the top fillets by sliding a palette knife under and lifting them off the bones.

7 Lift off the bones to give you access to the two bottom fillets.

braising fish fillets

BRAISED SEA TROUT (for full recipe see page 149)

BRAISING
FISH FILLETS

1 Melt a generous amount of butter in a shallow pan large enough to take the fish fillets in a single layer. Add some sliced carrots, celery and leeks.

2 Stir the vegetables well, cover with a well-fitting lid and 'sweat' (cook gently in their own steam) over a medium heat for about 3 minutes until beginning to soften. Then uncover and add some dry white wine.

3 Next add some chicken stock and bring to a gentle simmer.

4 Cook the vegetables gently in an uncovered pan until almost all the liquid has evaporated but the vegetables are still moist. This makes a well-flavoured base or 'fondue' on which to rest the fish.

5 Lay the fish fillets skinned-side down on top of the 'fondue' and sprinkle with some seasoning and finely shredded basil leaves. Cover once more with the lid and simmer gently for 8–10 minutes or until the fish is just cooked through.

6 Carefully lift the fillets off the 'fondue' with a fish slice and put them on to warmed serving plates.

7 The fish will have released some liquid back into the vegetables, so increase the heat and simmer rapidly until it has reduced once more and the sauce is glistening. Add some more butter and shake the pan until it has amalgamated with the vegetables. Season to taste with a little lemon juice, salt and pepper, spoon over the fish and serve.

cooking fish in a steamer

STEAMED GREY MULLET (for full recipe see page 171)

1 Pour about 2.5 cm (1 inch) of water into the bottom of a shallow pan with a well-fitting lid. Put a petal steamer into the pan, bring the water to the boil and then lay the prepared fish on the steamer.

2 Sprinkle the fish with some julienned fresh ginger. Cover with the lid, reduce the heat to medium and steam for 10–12 minutes.

3 Carefully lift the fish off the steamer on to warmed plates and scatter over some sliced spring onions. Make a sauce with some of the steaming juices and some soy sauce and pour it over the fish.

4 Heat some sesame oil in a small pan. Add some thinly sliced garlic, leave to sizzle for a few seconds and then pour straight over the fish.

steaming fish over seaweed

BLACK BREAM STEAMED OVER SEAWEED (for full recipe see page 164)

1   Spread some washed bladderack seaweed over the base of a large shallow pan with a well-fitting lid.

2   Add about 300 ml (10 fl oz) water, put the prepared and seasoned fish on top and cover with the lid.

3   For the sauce, sweat some sliced fennel, onion and garlic in butter until soft. Add the stock, white wine and seasoning and simmer gently until the liquid has evaporated and the vegetables are very tender. Cool slightly, scrape into a liquidizer and add the Pernod, lemon juice and egg yolks. Blend until smooth.

4   With the machine still running, gradually add melted butter to make a smooth hollandaise-like sauce.

5   Pour the sauce into a bowl and add some chopped fennel herb and seasoning to taste. Keep warm.

6   Place the pan of fish over a high heat and, when steam starts to escape from under the lid, lower the heat and steam for 5 minutes. Take the uncovered pan to the table to serve if you wish, so that everyone can appreciate the smell when the lid is lifted.

TWO WAYS OF
COOKING FISH
IN THE OVEN

roasting whole large fish in the oven

BAKED SEA BASS WITH ROASTED RED PEPPERS (for full recipe see page 148)

1 Cut five or six shallow, diagonal slashes along the length of the prepared fish, first in one direction and then the other so that it becomes marked with a series of crosses.

2 Turn the fish over and repeat on the other side. This will help the heat to get through to the centre of the fish more quickly.

3 Arrange the vegetables over the base of a large roasting tin and bake for 30 minutes until par-cooked.

4 Put the fish on top of the vegetables, sprinkle it with oil, sea salt and pepper and rub these well into the slashes. Return to the oven for 35 minutes or until the fish is cooked through to the backbone. The temperature next to the bone should measure approximately 50°C (120°F).

gently cooking fish fillets in the oven

TETSUYA WAKUDA'S CONFIT OF SALMON (for full recipe see page 144)

Cut a thick piece of skinned salmon fillet across into four 65–90 g (2½–3½ oz) pieces. Turn them in a marinade of grapeseed and olive oil, ground coriander, white pepper, garlic, thyme and basil and leave for 2–3 hours.

Lift the pieces of fish on to a tray sprinkled with some finely chopped vegetables – these prevent the fish from coming into contact with the hot baking tray.

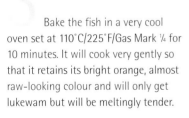

Bake the fish in a very cool oven set at 110°C/225°F/Gas Mark ¼ for 10 minutes. It will cook very gently so that it retains its bright orange, almost raw-looking colour and will only get lukewam but will be meltingly tender.

BAKING FISH
IN CASINGS

baking fish in a pastry casing

SALMON EN CROÛTE (for full recipe see pages 140–1)

1 Prepare 2 evenly sized thick pieces of skinned salmon fillet (see page 28). Spread the inner face of 1 fillet with the flavoured butter and lay the second fillet on top.

2 Put one sheet of rolled puff pastry on to a greased baking sheet and place the salmon in the centre. Brush a wide band of beaten egg around the salmon.

3 Roll out a second piece of pastry into a rectangle roughly 5 cm (2 inches) larger than the first one and lift it on top of the salmon.

4 Press the pastry tightly around the outside of the salmon, taking care not to stretch it or trap in too much air; this might cause the pastry to shrink and the parcel to pop open when it's cooking. Then press the edges of the pastry together very firmly.

5 Neatly trim the edges of the pastry and mark all the way round with a fork – this will help ensure an even better seal. Decorate the top of the pastry with 'scales' using an upturned teaspoon. Chill for 1 hour, then brush with egg and bake at 200°C/400°F/ Gas Mark 6 for 35–40 minutes. Serve cut into slices.

baking fish in a salt casing

SEA BASS BAKED IN A SALT CRUST (for full recipe see page 150)

1 Mix about 1.75 kg (4 lb) of cooking salt with 2 egg whites. The mixture will look very much like wet sand.

2 Spread a thick layer of the salt mixture over the base of a shallow ovenproof dish or tin and put the fish on top.

3 Completely cover the fish with the remaining salt mixture, making sure that there are no gaps. Don't worry if the tails are still exposed. Bake the fish in a hot oven set at 200°C/400°F/Gas Mark 6 for 20 minutes.

4 Remove the fish from the oven and crack the top of the salt crust with the back of a large knife. Lift away the crust so that you can carefully lift out the fish.

5 Put the fish on to a serving plate. Make a shallow cut through the skin along the backbone and behind the head of the fish.

6 Pull the skin away from the top of the fish and lift off the 2 fillets. Turn the fish over and repeat on the other side. Serve with the lemon sauce and potato confit.

baking whole fish in foil

WHOLE SALMON BAKED IN FOIL WITH TARRAGON

(for full recipe see page 140)

BAKING FISH
'EN PAPILLOTE'

1   Put a prepared salmon into the centre of a large sheet of foil which has been brushed with lots of melted butter.

2   Bring the edges of the foil up around the sides of the fish and scrunch it together at either end to form a canoe-shaped parcel. Carefully lift the parcel on to a large baking sheet.

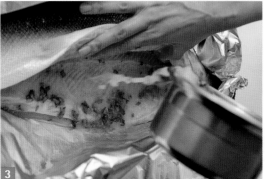

3   Pour a mixture of melted butter, tarragon, white wine, lemon juice and seasoning into the cavity and over the top of the fish. Bring the sides of the foil parcel together over the top of the fish and seal really well to make a loose, watertight parcel. Bake in a hot oven at 220°C/425°F/Gas Mark 7 for 30 minutes.

4   Remove the fish from the oven and open up the parcel. Carefully lift on to a serving plate and serve as described on pages 38–9 (technique 19).

baking fish fillets 'en papillote'

HAKE EN PAPILLOTE

(for full recipe see page 135)

1 Cut out four 38 cm (15 inch) squares of greaseproof paper and foil. Put the foil squares on top of the paper ones and brush the centres with olive oil. Put 3 pieces of oven-roasted tomato slightly off-centre on each one, sprinkle with basil and top with the pieces of seasoned hake.

2 Bring the other side of the square over the fish so that all the edges meet. Starting at one end of the opening, fold over about 1 cm (½ inch) of the edge, doing about 4 cm (1½ inches) at a time. Work your way all around the edge to make a semi-circular parcel. Then go around again to make an even tighter seam.

3 Give the folded edge a good bash with a rolling pin. Put the parcels on to a baking sheet and bake in a very hot oven at 240°C/475°F/Gas Mark 9 for 15 minutes.

4 As the fish cooks, the steaming juices will make the tightly sealed parcels puff up. Remove them from the oven, quickly transfer them to a warmed serving dish and take them to the table.

5 Slit open the parcels with the tip of a sharp knife.

6 Pull back the paper and foil from the baked fish.

7 Lift the fish and tomatoes on to warmed plates and pour over the cooking juices from the parcel. Spoon around a little tapenade and serve.

technique 33

making a fish stew

CACCIUCCO (for full recipe see page 102)

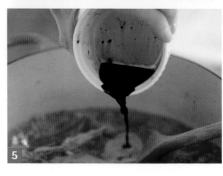

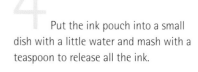

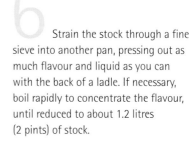

1 Prepare and fillet the whole fish (see pages 22 and 30). Clean the squid, reserving the ink sac (see page 92, steps 1–6) and remove the meat from the cooked lobster, reserving the shell (see page 76). Cut the fish fillets across into 4 cm (1½ inch) wide pieces. Cut the lobster meat into small chunks.

2 Make a well-flavoured stock for the base of the stew. Sauté some finely chopped onion, carrot and celery in olive oil until lightly browned. Add the red wine and lobster shell and boil vigorously for 3–4 minutes.

3 Add some chopped tomatoes, fresh bay leaves, red chillies and water and bring back to the boil.

4 Put the ink pouch into a small dish with a little water and mash with a teaspoon to release all the ink.

5 Add the ink to the pan and leave the stock to simmer for 45 minutes.

6 Strain the stock through a fine sieve into another pan, pressing out as much flavour and liquid as you can with the back of a ladle. If necessary, boil rapidly to concentrate the flavour, until reduced to about 1.2 litres (2 pints) of stock.

7 Slice the body pouch of the squid into rings. Heat some olive oil in a flameproof casserole in which you can finish the stew. Add the squid, some garlic and whole sage leaves and fry quickly until lightly golden. Lift on to a plate. Cook some prepared mussels with a little wine or water in a large covered pan until just opened (see page 88, steps 1–4). Tip into a colander and reserve the cooking liquor.

8 Pour the stock and mussel liquor into the casserole and bring to the boil. Add the pieces of fish and simmer for 2 minutes.

9 Add the lobster meat, mussels and squid and simmer for 1 minute until heated through. Put 2 slices of the olive-oil-baked ciabatta into the bottom of large soup plates, ladle over the stew and serve.

DIFFERENT
WAYS WITH
SMALL FRY

deep-frying small fry

DEEP-FRIED WHITEBAIT WITH LEMON AND PERSILLADE

(for full recipe see page 166)

1 Wash the whitebait, then drain through a colander and shake well. Dry on kitchen paper. Tip into a bowl of flour seasoned with cayenne pepper and salt.

2 Toss the whitebait in the flour until they are all well coated. Drop a large handful of fish into the frying basket and shake off the excess flour.

3 Lower the basket of fish into hot oil and fry for 2–3 minutes until crisp and golden.

4 Remove the basket from the oil and drain the fish briefly on kitchen paper. Repeat. Tip them on to a warmed serving dish, sprinkle with the persillade and serve with lemon wedges.

grilling small fish

GRILLED SMELTS (for full recipe see page 160)

1 Thread the prepared smelts on to bamboo skewers which have been left to soak in cold water for about 1 hour. Lay them on a lightly oiled baking tray.

2 Sprinkle them with olive oil, salt and pepper and grill under a high heat for 2 minutes until cooked through.

3 Lift the fish on to warmed plates and sprinkle with a finely chopped mixture of lemon zest, rosemary, parsley, garlic, green olives and capers. Drizzle a little oil around the plate and serve.

removing bones from small whole fish such as anchovies

Pinch the head between your thumb and forefinger and pull it off, taking the guts with it. Pinch along the top edge of the fish and pull out the backbone. The flesh is so soft it will come away easily. Open the double fillets out flat and proceed with the recipe. (For instructions on marinating anchovies in chilli, lemon and garlic, see full recipe on page 161.)

making fish quenelles

POACHED QUENELLES OF GURNARD

(for full recipe see page 174)

(for full recipe see page 174)

MAKING FISH
QUENELLES

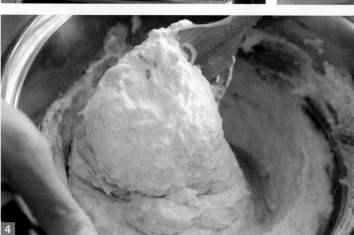

1   Everything must be as cold as possible before you start. Put the fish pieces, bread, milk and butter paste, egg, lemon juice and nutmeg into a food processor.

2   Blend the mixture for at least 1 minute so that everything breaks down to form a very fine paste.

3   Transfer the mixture to a bowl and sit the bowl in a slightly larger one of well-iced water. Add the cream a little at a time, beating vigorously between each addition.

4   The finished mixture should be light and quite thick in texture. Cover and chill for 30 minutes.

5 Bring some lightly salted water to a gentle simmer in a wide shallow pan. Mould the mixture into quenelles using two wet dessertspoons: take a heaped spoonful of mixture on to one spoon and scoop the mixture on to the other one by tucking the front edge of the empty spoon under the back edge of the mixture on the front one. Do this two or three times until you achieve a nice rugby-ball-shaped quenelle with a slight ridge running along the top. Drop them off the spoon into the water and poach gently for 3–4 minutes, turning them over half-way through.

6 Remove with a slotted spoon and drain briefly on a clean tea towel. Transfer them to individual gratin dishes and pour over the prepared prawn sauce. Grill under a very high heat for 1 minute or until lightly browned.

techniques
chapter 3

preparing raw, smoked and cured fish

1 Flavour the cooked Japanese sticky rice with a sweet and salty vinegar mixture; add it gradually, lifting and folding the rice, so that it takes on a glossy sheen.

2 Wet your hands with lightly vinegared water and mould a 20 g (¾ oz) ball of rice mixture into a small rectangular block.

3 Cut the slices of fish into small rectangles slightly larger than the tops of the blocks of rice. Put a very small dot of wasabi paste on to your finger.

Keta
The Japanese name for the large orange-red eggs of the salmon.

making sushi NIGIRI SUSHI (for full recipe see pages 105–6)

4 Spread the wasabi along the underside of each piece of fish or along the top of the blocks of rice.

5 Lay the pieces of fish on top of the blocks of rice and press down lightly.

6 Slit open the underside of the cooked prawns down to the tail and spread the cut face with wasabi.

7 Open the prawns out flat, lay on top of the blocks of rice and press down lightly.

8 Spoon some keta on to the remaining blocks of rice. Arrange the sushi on each plate and serve with some pickled ginger and the dipping sauce.

preparing monkfish for serving raw

CEVICHE OF MONKFISH (for full recipe see page 155)

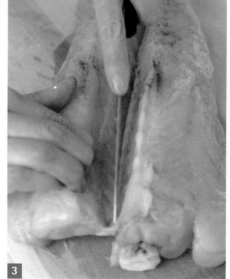

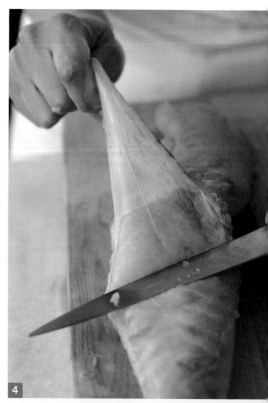

1 First remove the skin from the monkfish tail. Put the tail belly-side down on a board. Release and pull back some of the skin at the wider end of the tail so that you can get a sharp, flexible-bladed knife underneath to cut through the fine dorsal spines.

2 Grab hold of the wider end of the tail in one hand and the skin in the other and briskly pull it away, down over the tail.

3 Remove the 2 fillets by cutting along either side of the thick backbone with a sharp, thin-bladed, flexible knife, keeping the blade as close to the bone as you can.

4 Pull off the thin membrane that encases the fillets, releasing it with the knife where necessary.

5 Cut the fillets across into thin slices and put them into a large shallow dish.

8 Add some extra virgin olive oil and seasoning to taste and mix once more. Serve with thinly sliced avocado.

6 Squeeze over enough lime juice to cover all the fish. Cover and refrigerate for 40 minutes, during which time the fish will turn white and opaque.

7 Lift the fish out of the lime juice and mix with some thinly sliced red chilli, red onion, tomato and chopped coriander.

preparing tuna carpaccio (for full recipe see page 117)

Wrap the tuna in cling film so that it takes on a neatly rounded shape. Freeze until very firm but not completely frozen; this will make it easier to slice thinly. Unwrap the tuna (1) and slice very thinly using a sharp, long-bladed knife (2). Arrange the slices over the base of each plate and sprinkle with olive oil, sea salt and black pepper (3). Add some thinly shaved parmesan (4). Pile some rocket leaves into the centre and serve (5).

hot-smoking fish

CHAR-GRILLED LIGHTLY SMOKED ARCTIC CHAR (for full recipe see page 151)

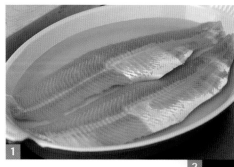

1 Put the skinned fish fillets into a light brine and leave to cure for 20 minutes.

2 Put a 2.5 cm (1 inch) layer of hardwood sawdust into the bottom of a wok and rest 6 wooden chopsticks over the top to act as a platform. Place the wok over a high heat until the sawdust begins to smoke. Then reduce the heat to low.

3 Rest a sushi mat (or something else that is permeable and will allow the smoke through) on the chopsticks and lay the fillets of fish on top. Cover the wok with a lid and smoke the fish for 3–4 minutes.

4 Uncover the wok and lift out the sushi mat and fish. With a palette knife, carefully lift the fish off the mat and on to a board. Cut into 4 even-sized pieces.

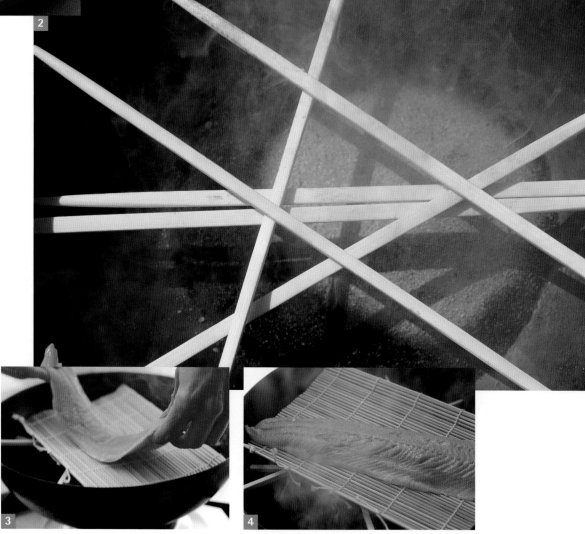

5 Make a dressing of finely chopped shallot, chopped chives, olive oil, vinegar and salt.

6 Brush the pieces of smoked Arctic char with some olive oil.

7 Heat a ridged cast-iron griddle until smoking-hot. Place the pieces of fish diagonally on to the griddle and cook for 30 seconds on each side or until lightly marked by the ridges. Spoon a little dressing into the centre of each plate, put a piece of the fish on top and serve warm.

hot-smoking fish in a box smoker

A box smoker is a small metal box with a tight-fitting lid. Inside a base plate sits directly above a methylated spirit burner. 1½–2 tablespoons of hardwood sawdust are sprinkled over the plate and the fish is cooked when the smoking has stopped. If the fish is left to cool in the smoker, the smoked flavour is stronger. Box smokers are ideal for small, cleaned, trimmed and slashed whole fish weighing between 175 g (6 oz) and 450 g (1 lb), such as mackerel, herring and trout, and 100–350 g (4–12 oz) steaks or pieces of thick fish fillet such as salmon, cod, sea bass, barramundi, snapper and tuna. The fish can be eaten hot or cold.

a scandinavian cure for salmon

GRAVLAX (for full recipe see page 143)

1 Put one unskinned salmon fillet skin-side down on to a large sheet of cling film. Thickly cover the cut face of the salmon with a mixture of chopped fresh dill, salt, sugar and crushed white peppercorns. You can cover this with another salmon fillet if you wish.

2 Tightly wrap the fish in 2 or 3 layers of cling film and lift it on to a large shallow tray.

3 Place a chopping board on top of the fish and weigh it down. Refrigerate for 2 days, turning it every 12 hours so that the briny mixture bastes the outside of the fish. Replace the board and weights each time.

4 Unwrap the salmon and place it on a board. Slice on a 45-degree angle with a very sharp, long-bladed knife into very thin slices.

5 Carefully lift off the almost see-through slices as you cut them. Arrange a few slices on each plate and serve with the traditional horseradish and mustard sauce.

salting fresh cod

BRANDADE DE MORUE (for full recipe see page 130)

1 To salt your own cod, pour a 1 cm (½ inch) thick layer of salt over the base of a shallow plastic container. Put a thick piece of unskinned cod fillet on top and cover with another thick layer of salt. Cover and refrigerate overnight.

2 The next day, lift the now rigid piece of cod out of the salt and rinse under cold water.

3 Put it into a large bowl and cover with lots of fresh water. Leave to soak for 1 hour.

4 Commercially produced salt cod will be almost completely dried out and needs much longer soaking. Rinse off the excess salt and leave to soak in lots of cold water for 24–48 hours, depending on its thickness, changing the water now and then.

5 To make the brandade, drain the soaked cod and remove the skin and bones. Simmer gently in water for 5 minutes, then lift out, drain well and put into a food processor.

6 Bring a mixture of double cream, garlic and olive oil to the boil in a small pan.

7 Add the hot cream mixture to the fish, turn on the machine and blend to a thick, smooth paste. Season to taste with lemon juice and pepper, spoon the mixture into a warmed dish and garnish with some croûtons, black olives and chopped parsley. Serve warm.

DIFFERENT
USES FOR
FISH ROE

using caviar in a sauce

GRILLED MULLOWAY WITH ASPARAGUS AND A CREAM AND CAVIAR SAUCE

(for full recipe see page 145)

1 Prepare a sauce of reduced fish stock, vermouth and cream. Brush portion-sized pieces of mulloway fillet with melted butter, season and grill skin-side up for 7–8 minutes. Lightly steam some asparagus until tender.

2 Arrange the asparagus in the centre of warmed plates and put the mulloway fillets on top.

3 Reheat the sauce and stir in some lemon juice and 1 teaspoon of caviar. Season to taste and then spoon around the outside of the plate.

sautéeing fresh roes

PAN-FRIED HERRING MILT ON TOASTED BRIOCHE

(for full recipe see page 159)

1 Dust the herring roes lightly in seasoned flour.

2 Melt some butter in a frying pan and, as soon as it begins to foam, add the roes.

3 Fry them over a medium-high heat for 2 minutes, turning once, until lightly golden.

4 Spoon the roes on to warm toasted brioche and serve with some dressed salad leaves, beurre noisette (see page 18) and capers.

making taramasalata

(for full recipe see page 130)

Scrape the roe away from the thick outer skin with a knife (1). Put the roe, soaked bread, garlic, onion and lemon juice into a food processor (2) and blend to a smooth paste. With the machine still running, gradually add some olive oil as you would for mayonnaise. Spoon the mixture on to a shallow plate and garnish with some lemon wedges, black olives and chopped parsley (3).

techniques
chapter 4

4

preparing and cooking seafood

techniques 46a and 46b

1 To butterfly peeled prawns, remove the head if necessary and peel off the shell leaving the last tail segment in place (see page 72). Make a deep cut down the back of each prawn with a small sharp knife, about halfway down into the meat. Pull out the intestinal tract if dark and visible.

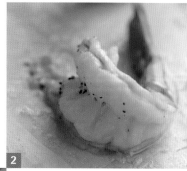

2 Brush the prawns with oil or melted butter, season and lay them on their sides on a lightly oiled baking tray. Grill for 2 minutes until cooked through.

technique 47

2 Toss the prawns in a lemon chilli marinade and leave for 20 minutes. Then stir in a tandoori marinade and leave for a further 20 minutes.

1 Make 3 little slits in either side of each unpeeled prawn, between the segments of the shell. This will allow the marinade to penetrate the shells and flavour the meats.

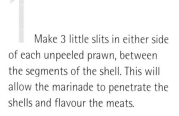

butterflying raw prawns for grilling

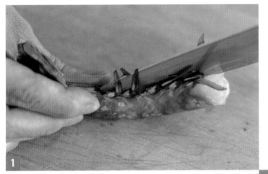

2 Open up the prawns and lay them with the meat facing uppermost on a lightly oiled baking tray.

1 To butterfly prawns in the shell, remove the head if necessary (see page 72) and put the tail belly-side up on a board. Cut each prawn in half through the shell to within 1 cm (½ inch) of the tail.

3 Brush them with oil or melted butter, season and grill under a high heat for about 2 minutes until cooked through.

marinating raw prawns for the barbecue

TANDOORI PRAWNS (for full recipe see page 200)

4 When the barbecue is really hot, place the skewers on the rack.

3 Thread the prawns on to metal or soaked bamboo skewers, piercing them just behind the back of the head and down through the tail.

5 Barbecue the prawns for 2 minutes on each side until cooked through and nicely coloured. Serve with the katchumber salad.

preparing raw prawns for curries and stir-fries

PRAWN CALDINE (for full recipe see page 197)

(for full recipe see page 197)

PREPARING
RAW PRAWNS
FOR CURRIES
AND
STIR-FRIES

1 Hold the body of the prawn in one hand and firmly twist off the head with the other. Save the heads for making stock if you wish.

2 Break open the soft shell along the underbelly of each prawn and peel it away from the flesh. You can leave the last tail segment of the shell in place for some recipes.

3 Run the tip of a small sharp knife along the back of the prawn and pull out the intestinal tract if dark and visible, but this is not always essential.

4 Mix the prawns with a little vinegar and salt and set to one side. Heat some oil in a medium-sized pan, add some sliced onion, slivered garlic and chopped ginger and fry gently for 5 minutes until softened.

5 Grind some turmeric, black pepper-corns, coriander seeds, cumin seeds and white poppy seeds together into a powder. Add to the softened onion and fry for 2 minutes to cook out some of the raw flavours.

6 Add some coconut milk, tamarind water and water and bring to a simmer.

7 Add some seeded and finely shredded mild green chillies and salt. Simmer for 5 minutes.

8 Add the prawns and simmer for 3–4 minutes until they are only just cooked through and still moist and juicy inside.

9 Stir in some more shredded green chillies and chopped coriander.

10 Spoon into warmed bowls and serve with some steamed rice.

cooking langoustine

GRILLED DUBLIN BAY PRAWNS WITH A PERNOD AND OLIVE OIL DRESSING

(for full recipe see page 190)

COOKING
LANGOUSTINES

1 Bring some salted water or the prepared shellfish bouillon (see page 223) to the boil in a very large pan.

2 Add the langoustines to the pan and bring back to the boil.

3 Cook the langoustines for 2–5 minutes, depending on their size. Leave to cool.

4

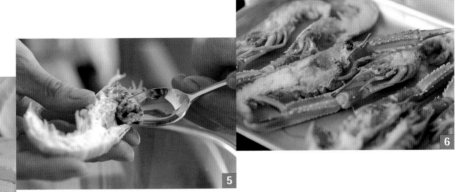

4 Put each langoustine belly-side down on a board and cut it in half lengthways.

5 Scoop out the creamy contents of the head (the tomalley or liver) with a teaspoon and mix it with the prepared dressing.

6 Arrange the halved langoustines cut-side up on a baking tray and brush with melted butter. Grill for 1–2 minutes until heated through. Arrange on warmed plates and spoon over the dressing.

PREPARING AND COOKING SEAFOOD

technique 50

REMOVING
THE MEAT
FROM A
COOKED
LOBSTER

removing the meat from a cooked lobster

LOBSTER THERMIDOR

(for full recipe see page 194)

to cook a lobster from raw

Put it into the freezer 2 hours before cooking; this will kill it painlessly. Bring a large pan of heavily-salted water to the boil (i.e. 150 g/ 5 oz of salt to every 4.5 litres/8 pints of water). Add the lobster and bring back to the boil. Cook those up to 750 g (1½ lb) for 15 minutes and 1.25 kg (2½ lb) for 20 minutes. Remove and leave to cool.

1 Put the lobster belly-side down on to a board and make sure none of the legs is tucked underneath. Cut it in half, first through the middle of the head between the eyes. Then turn either the knife or the lobster around and finish cutting it in half through the tail.

2 Open it up and lift out the tail meat from each half.

3 Remove the intestinal tract from the tail meat.

4 Break off the claws and then break them into pieces at the joints. Crack the shells with a knife.

5 Remove the meat from each of the claw sections in as large pieces as possible.

6 Remove the soft greenish tomalley (liver) and any red roe from the head section of the shell with a teaspoon and save. Pull out the stomach sac and discard.

7

8

9

Sprinkle with some finely grated Parmesan cheese and grill under a high heat for 4 minutes until the lobster meat has heated through and the cheese is golden.

7 Cut the tail meat into smaller pieces and evenly distribute the tail and claw meat between the two shells with any roe. Transfer the cleaned half-shells on to a baking sheet.

8 Make a fish stock and cream reduction (see page 194). Stir the tomalley into the sauce. Spoon about 3 tablespoons of the sauce into each half-shell.

removing the tail meat in one piece

Pull the tail away from the head (1). Turn the tail section over and cut along either side of the flat belly-shell with strong scissors (2). Lift back the flap of shell (3). Lift out the tail meat (4). Remove the intestinal tract either by cutting the tail into thin slices and removing it from each slice with the tip of a small sharp knife or by running the knife down the back of the meat and removing it in one piece.

1

2

3

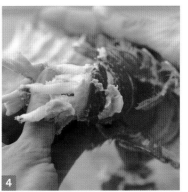

4

PREPARING AND COOKING SEAFOOD

techniques 51 and 52

CUTTING UP
RAW LOBSTER
FOR STIR-
FRYING AND
GRILLING

cutting up raw lobster for stir-frying

LOBSTER WITH GINGER, SPRING ONIONS AND SOFT EGG NOODLES (for full recipe see page 193)

1 Kill the lobster painlessly as described on page 76. Cut it in half and remove the stomach sac and intestinal tract as described on page 79, steps 1 to 3. Cut each tail half into 3 pieces.

2 Chop the claws from the head and cut each one into 2 pieces through the joint. Crack the shells with a large knife.

3 Snip off the antennae close to the head with scissors and discard.

4 Cut off the feeler-like legs as close to the shell as you can with scissors and discard also. Then cut each head section into 2 pieces.

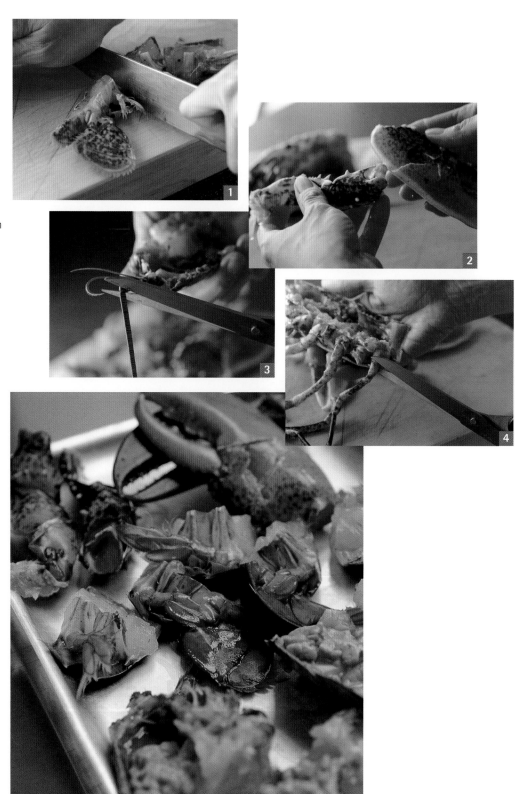

halving a raw lobster for grilling

GRILLED LOBSTER WITH FINES HERBES (for full recipe see page 192)

1 Kill the lobster painlessly as described on page 76. Lay the lobster belly-side down on a board and cut it in half.

2 Remove the stomach sac, a slightly clear pouch which will now be in half, from the head section of each half.

3 Remove the intestinal tract from the tail section.

4 Put the lobster halves on to a baking tray and brush the meat with melted butter. Season with salt and pepper and grill under a medium-high heat for 8–10 minutes.

5 Prepare a sauce of fish stock, Thai fish sauce, lemon juice, butter and chopped *fines herbes*. Spoon over the cooked lobster and serve.

PREPARING AND COOKING SEAFOOD

technique 53

REMOVING
THE MEAT
FROM A
COOKED CRAB

4

removing the meat from a cooked crab

to cook a crab from raw

Turn the crab on to its back with its eyes facing you. Drive a thick skewer between the eyes into the centre of the crab. Then lift up the tail flap and drive the skewer down into the centre of the body. When the crab is dead its legs will go limp. Bring a large pan of heavily-salted water to the boil (i.e. 150 g/5 oz salt to every 4.5 litres/8 pints of water). Add the crab and bring back to the boil. Cook those up to 550 g (1¼ lb) for 15 minutes, 900 g (2 lb) for 20 minutes, 1.5 kg (3¼ lb) for 25 minutes, and any larger for 30 minutes. Remove and leave to cool.

1 Put the crab back-shell down on to a board and break off the claws.

2 Break off the legs, taking care to remove the knuckle joint too.

7 Scoop out the brown meat from the centre of the body section with a teaspoon and keep it separate from the white meat.

8 Cut the body section in half using a large knife.

9 Remove the white meat from all the little channels with a crab pick.

3   Lift up and break off the tail flap.

4   Push the blade of a large knife between the body and the back shell and twist the blade to release it.

5   Place your thumbs on either side of the body section and press firmly upwards until it comes away.

6   Pull the feathery-looking gills, known as the dead man's fingers, off the body and discard.

10   When all the meat has been removed you should be left with a hollow and much lighter piece of shell.

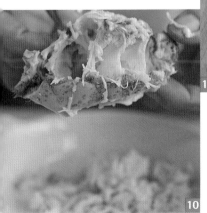

11   Crack the shell of the claws with the back of a knife and remove the meat. Remove the thin piece of bone concealed within the meat of the pincers. Break the shell of the legs with crackers and hook out the white meat with the crab pick.

12   Put the back shell on to a board with the eyes and mouth facing you. Press on the little piece of shell located just behind the eyes until it snaps. Lift out and discard the mouth piece and stomach sac.

13   Scoop out the brown meat from the back shell (which is sometimes quite wet and sometimes more solid) with a spoon and add it to that from the body.

making crab cakes

MARYLAND CRAB CAKES (for full recipe see page 187)

3   Fold this through the crab meat, taking care not to break up the lumps of crab too much, then stir in some parsley.

4   Shape the mixture into eight 7.5 cm (3 inch) patties. Put them onto a plate, cover and chill for at least 1 hour to help them firm up.

1   Add some finely crushed cracker crumbs to the white crab meat to absorb any excess moisture in the meat.

2   Make a binding mixture of beaten egg, mayonnaise, mustard, lemon juice, Worcestershire sauce and some seasoning.

6 Add the crab cakes and fry them over a medium heat for 2–3 minutes on each side until crisp and golden.

5 Pour some clarified butter into a well-seasoned or non-stick frying pan and leave it to get hot.

7 Lift 2 cakes into the centre of each warmed plate and spoon around some of the tarragon butter sauce.

how to prepare soft-shell crabs

SAUTÉED SOFT-SHELL CRABS WITH GARLIC BUTTER
(for full recipe see page 188)

Cut straight across the face, about 5 mm (¼ inch) behind the eyes to remove the eyes and mouth. Push your finger into the opening and hook out the stomach, a small, jelly-like sac. Turn the crab over and pull off the little tail flap. Turn it back over and lift up the sides of the soft top shell and pull out the dead man's fingers, or gills. They are now ready to cook.

preparing raw crabs for steaming or stir-frying

STEAMED CRAB WITH LEMONGRASS DRESSING (for full recipe see page 184)

PREPARING
RAW CRABS
FOR STEAMING
OR STIR-
FRYING

1 Kill the crabs as described on page 80. Then put each crab back-shell down on a board and break off the tail flap. Break off the claws close to the body.

2 Chop the body section of the crab in half (but not all the way through the back shell) with a large knife.

3 Grab hold of the legs and gently tug on them to pull the body sections away from the back shell. Use a knife as an added lever if necessary, but they should come away quite easily, with the legs still attached.

4 Turn each piece over and pick off the feather-like gills (dead man's fingers). Discard the back shells or save them for making stock.

5 Cut the claws in half at the joint. Crack the shells of each piece with a hammer or the back of a large knife.

6 Bring about 2.5 cm (1 inch) of water to the boil in a wide shallow pan. Pile the pieces of crab on to a petal steamer, lower it into the pan and cover with a well-fitting lid. Steam for 8 minutes.

7 Uncover the pan of now cooked crab pieces and lift out the petal steamer.

8 Transfer the crab to a serving dish and spoon over the prepared lemongrass dressing.

EXTRACTING
THE FLAVOUR
FROM
CRUSTACEANS
FOR SOUPS

using crab shells and meat for making a bisque

SHORE CRAB BISQUE (for full recipe see page 101)

1 Wash the crabs well under running water. Prepare them and cook in a pan of well-salted boiling water (see page 80) for 2 minutes, then drain.

2 Chop up the crabs very roughly with a large knife into smallish pieces.

3 Add the crab pieces and a splash of cognac to a pan of lightly sautéed vegetables.

4 Fry the crab pieces for 3–4 minutes, stirring now and then, until all the liquid has evaporated.

5 Add some tomatoes, tomato purée, white wine, tarragon and fish stock to the pan. Bring to the boil, lower the heat and leave to simmer, uncovered, for 30 minutes.

6 Briefly liquidize the soup in batches until the shells have broken down into pieces about the size of a fingernail. It should not be completely smooth. Then strain through a conical sieve into a clean pan.

7 Press as much liquid as you can from the debris with the back of a ladle and then discard everything that is left in the sieve.

8 Strain the soup once more through a fine sieve to remove the finer debris. Bring it back to the boil, and reduce a little to concentrate the flavour if necessary. Add some cream and season to taste with lemon juice, cayenne pepper and salt.

making a clear crab soup

SEAFOOD IN A CRAB AND GINGER BROTH

(for full recipe see page 104)

1 Flavour a pan of chicken stock with fresh ginger, lime zest, lime juice, lemongrass, chilli and Thai fish sauce. Add the pieces of prepared crab (see page 84) and prawn shells.

2 Bring the stock to the boil, cover and leave to simmer gently for 25 minutes, to extract the flavour from the crab.

3 Strain the stock into a clean pan and leave it to cool. Meanwhile, remove the meat from the crab claws and set aside.

4 Add some very finely chopped inexpensive white fish fillet, such as coley, some thinly sliced leek and 2 egg whites to the cooled stock.

5 Return the pan to a medium heat and whisk steadily until the mixture comes back to the boil. Then stop whisking immediately and leave to simmer very gently for 5 minutes, during which time a crust will form on the top of the soup.

6 Slowly pour the stock through a muslin-lined sieve into a clean pan. Finally, let the crust slide into the sieve and leave until all the liquid has dripped through. Briefly cook the prawns, some thinly sliced monkfish and some prepared vegetables in the clarified stock. Finish with some noodles and the reserved crab meat.

clarified soups and stocks

As the fish and egg whites cook and coagulate, they will entrap all the fine particles in the stock. When the crust is parted it should reveal a crystal clear stock underneath.

PREPARING
MUSSELS AND
CLAMS FOR
COOKING AND
SERVING RAW

cleaning and steaming mussels

MOULES MARINIÈRE

(for full recipe see page 213)

1 Wash the mussels under plenty of cold water. Discard any that are open and won't close up when lightly squeezed. Pull out the tough fibrous beards or 'byssus' protruding from between the tightly closed shells.

2 Then knock off any barnacles with a large knife and give the mussels another quick rinse to remove any little bits of shell.

3 Put the mussels into a very large pan with the butter, finely chopped onion and white wine. Make sure that there is plenty of room in which the mussels can move around. If the pan is overcrowded, those at the bottom of the pan will overcook before the heat can reach those at the top, so never more than half-fill the pan.

4 Cover and cook the mussels over a high heat, shaking the pan vigorously every now and then, for 3–4 minutes until they have all just opened.

5 Immediately remove the pan from the heat and spoon the mussels into warmed deep bowls, discarding any that have remained closed. Add the parsley to the juices in the pan and pour them back over the mussels.

opening mussels for serving raw

Push the tip of a small knife between the shells on the straighter side. Run the tip all around the edge (1). Ease back the top shell (2) and run the tip of the knife around its inside edge to release the meat, taking care not to tear the flesh. Pull back the top shell (3) and snap it off if you wish.

removing the meat from large clams

NEW ENGLAND CLAM CHOWDER

(for full recipe see page 204)

1 Wash the clams under plenty of cold water. Put them in a single layer into the bottom of a large shallow pan and add a little water.

2 Cover the pan with a well-fitting lid and cook over a high heat for 2–3 minutes or until the clams have opened just enough for you to get them out of the shells. You don't want to cook them completely.

3 Remove the clams from the pan, reserving the liquor if it's required, and leave them to cool slightly. Then slide a small sharp knife into each shell and cut through the two muscles on either side near the hinge, which hold the two shells together.

4 Remove the meats from the bottom shells and chop them into small pieces.

preparing small clams for serving raw

CLAMS WITH SAUCE MIGNONETTE (for full recipe see pages 204–5)

1 Slide the long sharp edge of a small knife between the two tightly closed shells, on the opposite side to the hinge.

2 Draw the blade of the knife back so that only the tip is inside the clam. Run just the very tip of the knife right the way around the edge of the shell so as not to damage the meat inside. You will eventually feel the resistance give way.

3 Run the blade around the top inside edge of the clam to release the meat from the top shell. Carefully pull back the top shell so as not to damage the meat, releasing it where necessary if still attached. Release the meat from the bottom shell and snip off the shell if you wish.

4 Arrange the clams on a plate of crushed ice and seaweed and serve with the sauce spooned over.

preparing scallops and searing

SEARED SCALLOPS WITH IBÉRICO HAM (for full recipe see page 215)

1   Wash the scallops to remove any sand and weed from the shells. Hold a scallop in one hand, with the flat shell facing uppermost, and slide the blade of a sharp, thin-bladed, flexible knife between the two shells.

2   Keeping the blade of the knife flat against the top shell, feel for the ligament that joins the meat of the scallop to the shell. Cut through it and lift off the top shell.

3   Pull out the frilly 'skirt' and black stomach sac which surrounds the white scallop meat and pink coral. Rinse away any sand from inside the shell.

4   Slide the knife under the scallop meat, keeping the blade close to the shell, and cut it away. Pull off and discard the small white ligament attached to the side of the scallop meat.

5   Rub the base of a non-stick frying pan with cold butter. Set the pan over a high heat and, when the butter starts to smoke, add the scallops. Sear them for 2 minutes on each side, pressing down on them lightly with a palette knife so that they take on a good colour. Keep warm.

6   Transfer the scallops to the plates of ham and salad leaves. Remove the pan from the heat, add some sherry vinegar and scrape up all the browned residue from the base of the pan. Return the pan to the heat and whisk in some butter, chopped parsley and seasoning. Spoon the dressing over the scallops and salad leaves and serve.

opening oysters

WARM OYSTERS WITH BLACK BEANS, GINGER AND CORIANDER (for full recipe see page 213)

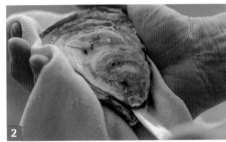

1 Wrap one hand in a tea towel and hold the oyster in it, flat shell facing uppermost. Push the point of an oyster knife into the hinge, located at the narrowest point.

2 Work the knife back and forth quite forcefully until the hinge breaks and you can slide the knife in between the two shells.

3 Twist the point of the knife upwards to lever up the top shell and locate the ligament that joins the oyster meat to it. It will be slightly right of the centre of the top shell. Cut through it with the knife and lift off the top shell. Keep the bottom shell upright so as not to lose any of the juices, although for this dish you need to pour away half the juices.

4 Release the oyster meat from the bottom shell and pick out any little pieces of shell. Arrange the oysters on a heatproof serving platter covered in a thick layer of rock salt and sprinkle with some ginger. Grill under a high heat for 3 minutes. Sprinkle the cucumber, coriander and chive mixture into each shell, spoon over the black bean dressing and serve warm.

PREPARING
SQUID FOR
STIR-FRYING

preparing squid for stir-frying

STIR-FRIED SALT-AND-PEPPER SQUID (for full recipe see page 221)

1 Hold the squid's body in one hand and the head with the other and gently pull the head away from the body, taking the milky white intestines with it.

2 Remove the tentacles from the head by cutting them off just in front of the eyes. Discard the head and separate the tentacles if they are large.

3 Squeeze out the beak-like mouth from the centre of the tentacles and discard it.

4 If you want to retain the ink sac, look amongst the intestines for a very small, pearly white pouch with a slight blue tinge and carefully cut it away.

5 Reach into the body and pull out the clear, plastic-like quill.

6 Pull off the two fins from either side of the body pouch. Then pull away the brown, semi-transparent skin from both the body and the fins. Wash out the body pouch with water.

7   Insert the blade of a sharp, thin-bladed, flexible knife into the opening of the body pouch and slit it open along one side. Open it out flat and pull away any left-over intestines and membrane.

8   Score what was the inner side with the tip of a small sharp knife into a diamond pattern, taking care not to cut too deeply. Then cut it into 5 cm (2 inch) pieces.

9   Heat a dry wok over a high heat until smoking. Add a little oil and a handful of the prepared squid and constantly move the squid around the sides of the pan for 2 minutes until it has taken on a light golden-brown colour. Repeat with the rest of the squid.

10   Add some of the roasted Sichuan pepper and salt mix, red chilli and spring onions and toss together briefly. Serve with the prepared dressed salad.

preparing octopus and tenderizing in the oven

OCTOPUS, PEA AND RED WINE STEW (for full recipe see pages 217–8)

2 Pull away and discard the entrails. Remove the bone-like strips sticking to the sides of the body.

1 Turn the body of the octopus inside out.

3 Locate the stomach sac, which is about the size of an avocado stone, and cut it away.

7 For the stew, gently sauté some garlic and shallots in olive oil until soft and lightly coloured.

9 Lower the heat and simmer until almost all the liquid has evaporated.

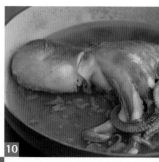

8 Add some red wine, sugar and halved plum tomatoes and bring to the boil.

10 Remove the octopus from the oven and lift it out of its cooking juices on to a chopping board. Reserve the juices.

94

4 Wash the octopus well inside and out and then turn the body right side out again. Press out the beak and soft surround from the centre of the tentacles and cut it out with the tip of a small knife.

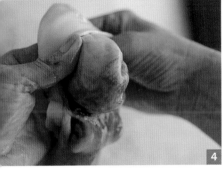

5 Put the prepared octopus into a shallow casserole dish.

6 Pour over some olive oil, cover with a well-fitting lid and cook in a cool oven set at 150°C/300°F/ Gas Mark 2 for 2 hours until very tender.

11 When it is cool enough to handle, cut it across into small chunky pieces. Stir the octopus pieces, the reserved cooking juices and a little extra water into the red wine and shallot reduction.

12 Simmer for 15–20 minutes until the liquid has reduced once more. Add the peas and simmer for a further 5 minutes. Stir in some chopped parsley and seasoning and serve drizzled with a little extra olive oil.

95

cleaning cuttlefish

SALAD OF RAW CUTTLEFISH

(for full recipe see page 219)

1 Cut off the tentacles, just in front of the eyes. Remove the beak-like mouth from the centre of the tentacles and discard.

2 Separate the tentacles and pull the skin from each one.

3 Pull the tough skin away from the body section.

4 Run a sharp knife down the centre of the back and lift out the cuttlebone.

5 Open up the body pouch. Locate the pearly white ink sac in amongst the entrails and remove it carefully. Remove and discard the rest of the entrails and head.

6 Wash the body well and then cut it in half lengthways. For serving raw, slice each piece across into very thin slices.

7 Arrange the tomatoes and cuttlefish strips on each plate. Squeeze over a little lemon juice, sprinkle with sea salt flakes and coarsely ground black pepper. Drizzle with olive oil and garnish with a few rocket leaves.

preparing sea urchins

PASTA WITH SEA URCHIN ROE, LEMON AND PARSLEY (for full recipe see page 218)

1 Wrap one hand in a tea towel and hold the sea urchin in it with the mouth (the soft part in the centre) facing uppermost. Push one blade of a pair of scissors into the mouth and cut around it to release a 5–7.5 cm (2–3 inch) disc of shell. Alternatively, cut a 2.5 cm (1 inch) slice of the sea urchin with a large serrated knife.

2 Lift away the disc of shell and pour away any liquid from inside the urchin.

3 Pull out all the black parts from inside the shell, leaving behind the small clusters of orange roe.

4 Scoop out the individual clusters of roe with a teaspoon, keeping them as whole as possible. Add them to the hot cooked pasta and turn over gently once or twice. The residual heat will be sufficient to lightly cook the roe.

chapters 5/12

2 recipes

recipes

chapter 5

soups, stews and mixed seafood

classic fish soup with rouille and croûtons

SERVES 4

900 g (2 lb) mixed fish such as gurnard, conger eel,
    dogfish, pouting, cod and grey mullet
1.2 litres (2 pints) water
85 ml (3 fl oz) olive oil
75 g (3 oz) each roughly chopped onion,
    celery, leek and fennel
3 garlic cloves, sliced
Juice of ½ orange plus 2 pared strips of orange zest
200 g (7 oz) can chopped tomatoes
1 small red pepper, seeded and sliced
1 bay leaf and 1 sprig of thyme
Pinch of saffron strands
100 g (4 oz) unpeeled North Atlantic prawns
A pinch of cayenne pepper
Salt and freshly ground black pepper

FOR THE CROÛTONS:

1 mini French baguette
Olive oil for frying
1 garlic clove
25 g (1 oz) finely grated Parmesan cheese
½ quantity Rouille (see pages 224–5)

1 Fillet the fish as described on pages 14 and 20 and use the bones
with the water to make a fish stock (see page 222).

2 Heat the olive oil in a large pan, add the vegetables and garlic and cook
gently for 20 minutes until soft but not coloured. Add the orange zest,
tomatoes, red pepper, bay leaf, thyme, saffron, prawns and fish fillets. Cook
briskly for 2–3 minutes, then add the stock and orange juice, bring to the
boil and simmer for 40 minutes. Meanwhile, for the croûtons, thinly slice
the baguette and fry the slices in the olive oil until crisp and golden. Drain
on kitchen paper and rub one side of each piece with the garlic clove.

3 Liquidize the soup, then pass it through a conical sieve into a clean
pan, pressing out as much liquid as possible with the back of a ladle.
Return the soup to the heat and season to taste with the cayenne, salt
and pepper.

4 Ladle the soup into a warmed tureen and put the croûtons,
Parmesan cheese and rouille into separate dishes. To serve, ladle the
soup into warmed bowls and leave each person to spread some rouille
on to the croutons, float them on their soup and sprinkle them with
some of the Parmesan cheese.

brandade and haricot bean soup with truffle oil

SERVES 4

175 g (6 oz) dried haricot beans, soaked in cold water
   overnight
450 g (1 lb) Fresh Salted Cod (see pages 67 and 227),
   soaked
600 ml (1 pint) creamy milk
6 garlic cloves, sliced
120 ml (4 fl oz) olive oil
300 ml (10 fl oz) double cream
1 tablespoon truffle oil
Chopped flat-leaf parsley, to garnish

1 Drain the beans and put them into a saucepan with 900 ml
(1½ pints) of water. Bring to the boil, then cover and simmer for 1 hour,
or until they are very soft and just starting to break apart. Drain,
reserving the cooking liquor.

2 Drain the salted cod and put it into a large saucepan with the milk.
Bring to a simmer and cook for 4–5 minutes or until just done. Lift the
cod out on to a plate and, when it is cool enough to handle, break it
into flakes, discarding the skin and any bones. Reserve the milk.

3 Put the flaked fish into a liquidizer with the garlic. Heat the oil and
cream together in a small pan until boiling, then add to the fish with

the beans and blend together until smooth. With the machine still
running, gradually add the reserved milk.

4 Return the soup to the pan and reheat gently but do not let it boil.
Add a little of the bean cooking liquor, if necessary, to obtain a good
consistency. Ladle the soup into 4 warmed soup bowls, drizzle over the
truffle oil and garnish with a little chopped parsley.

shore crab bisque (see technique 57, page 86)

SERVES 4

900 g (2 lb) shore crabs, washed
50 g (2 oz) butter
50 g (2 oz) each finely chopped onion, carrot and celery
1 bay leaf
2 tablespoons cognac
4 tomatoes
1 teaspoon tomato purée
75 ml (3 fl oz) dry white wine
1 sprig tarragon
1.75 litres (3 pints) Fish Stock (see page 222)
4 tablespoons double cream
A pinch of cayenne pepper
2 teaspoons lemon juice
Salt and freshly ground black pepper

1 Bring a large pan of well-salted water to the boil. Add the crabs,
bring back to the boil and cook for 2 minutes. Drain, leave them to cool
slightly and then chop up roughly with a large knife.

2 Melt the butter in a large heavy-based pan and add the chopped
vegetables and the bay leaf. Cook for 3–4 minutes without letting
them brown.

3 Add the crabs and the cognac and cook until all the liquid
has evaporated.

4 Add the tomatoes, tomato purée, wine, tarragon and stock. Bring to
the boil and simmer for 30 minutes.

5 Briefly liquidize the soup in batches until the shells have broken
down into pieces about the size of your fingernail.

6 Strain the soup through a conical strainer into a clean pan, pressing
out as much liquid as you can with the back of a ladle. Then pass it once
more through a very fine sieve.

7 Bring the soup back to the boil, and reduce a little to concentrate
the flavour if necessary. Then lower the heat, add the cream, cayenne
pepper and lemon juice and season to taste with some salt and pepper.

BRANDADE AND HARICOT BEAN SOUP WITH TRUFFLE OIL

cacciucco (see technique 33, page 54)

SERVES 8–10

1 loaf of ciabatta

150 ml (5 fl oz) olive oil

5 garlic cloves, peeled and thinly sliced

450 g (1 lb) uncleaned, medium-sized squid

1 x 900 g (2 lb) John Dory, filleted (see page 30)

1 x 1.5 kg (3 lb) gurnard, filleted (see page 32)

900 g (2 lb) thick, unskinned cod fillet

1 x 450 g (1 lb) cooked lobster

1 large onion, peeled and chopped

1 large carrot, peeled and finely chopped

2 celery sticks, finely chopped

300 ml (10 fl oz) red wine

400 g (14 oz) can chopped tomatoes

2 bay leaves

2–3 medium-hot red Dutch chillies, slit open lengthways

2.4 litres (4 pints) water

6 sage leaves

900 g (2 lb) mussels, cleaned (see page 88)

50 ml (2 fl oz) dry white wine

Salt and freshly ground black pepper

1 Pre-heat the oven to 200°C/400°F/Gas Mark 6. Cut the ciabatta into 1 cm (½ inch) thick slices. Put on to a shallow baking tray and drizzle with about 2 tablespoons of the olive oil. Bake in the oven for about 10–12 minutes or until crisp and golden. Remove and rub both sides of each piece with one of the peeled cloves of garlic. Set aside.

2 Clean the squid (see page 92), reserving one of the ink sacs. Slice the pouches across into rings and separate the tentacles. Slice the fish fillets into 4 cm (1½ inch) thick slices. Remove the meat from the lobster (see page 76) and reserve the shell. Season everything lightly.

3 Heat half of the remaining olive oil in a large pan. Add the onion, carrot and celery and fry for about 8 minutes until just beginning to brown. Add the red wine, the lobster shell, tomatoes, bay leaves, red chillies and water. Mash the reserved ink sac with a little water, add to the pan, bring everything to the boil and leave to simmer for 45 minutes.

4 Strain the stock through a sieve into another large pan, pressing the debris against the sides of the sieve with a ladle to extract as much flavour and liquid as possible. You want to have about 1.2 litres (2 pints) of well-flavoured stock. If there is any more, bring it back to the boil and boil rapidly for a few minutes until reduced to the required amount and well concentrated in flavour. Season to taste.

5 Put the remaining olive oil, sage leaves and garlic in a large clean pan and heat gently until they are beginning to sizzle. Add the squid

CACCIUCCO

and fry for 2 minutes or until lightly browned. Remove the squid and keep warm.

6 Put the mussels into a large saucepan with the white wine, cover and cook over a high heat for about 3 minutes until they have opened. Tip into a colander and reserve the cooking liquor.

7 Add the prepared stock and pieces of fish to the pan in which you fried the squid, bring to the boil and simmer for 2 minutes. Add the lobster meat, squid, mussels and all but the last 2 tablespoons of the mussel cooking liquor and simmer for 1 minute.

8 Take the pan of Cacciucco to the table with the crisp olive-oil ciabatta and serve.

bouillabaisse

SERVES 8–10

85 ml (3 fl oz) olive oil

2 medium onions, roughly chopped

White part of 2 leeks, cleaned and roughly chopped

4 celery sticks, thinly sliced

2 fennel bulbs, thinly sliced

10 garlic cloves, chopped

2 pared strips of orange zest

900 g (2 lb) plum tomatoes, skinned and chopped

½ medium-hot red Dutch chilli, seeded and chopped

1 teaspoon saffron strands

2 sprigs thyme

4 bay leaves

3.4 litres (6 pints) Fish Stock (see page 222)

3.5 kg (7 lb) mixed fish (suggested fish: a selection of
weever fish, monkfish tail, conger eel, red gurnard,
John Dory, Mediterranean grouper, dogfish, bream,
red mullet, bass and grey mullet)

750 g (1½ lb) mussels, cleaned (see page 88)

1 teaspoon chopped fennel herb or fennel bulb tops

1 teaspoon chopped oregano

1 teaspoon thyme leaves

2 tablespoons Pernod

750 g (1½ lb) cooked lobster or spiny lobster pieces in
the shell, cooked langoustines or prawns

2 tablespoons extra virgin olive oil

Cayenne pepper (optional)

Salt and freshly ground black pepper

½ quantity Rouille (see pages 224–5), to serve

FOR THE CROÛTONS:

Olive oil for frying

12 thin slices French bread

2–3 whole garlic cloves

1 For the croûtons, heat the oil in a frying pan, add the slices of bread and fry on both sides until golden brown. Drain briefly on kitchen paper, then rub one side of each piece with a garlic clove. Keep warm in a low oven.

2 Heat the oil for the bouillabaisse in a very large, deep pan. Add the onions, leeks, celery, fennel and garlic. Cook for 4–5 minutes until soft. Season with some black pepper and add the strips of orange zest, tomatoes, chilli, saffron, thyme, bay leaves and stock. Bring to the boil and boil for 10 minutes.

3 Add the firmer fish to the pan first, such as the conger eel, dogfish and monkfish. Bring back to the boil and simmer for 3 minutes. Then add the softer fish, return to the boil and simmer for another 2–3 minutes. Add the mussels, fennel herb, oregano, thyme leaves and Pernod and boil for 1 minute. Finally add the cooked shellfish and heat through.

4 Carefully lift the fish and shellfish out of the soup on to a large warmed serving dish. Keep warm. Strain the soup, return to the pan and add the extra virgin olive oil. Boil rapidly until it has concentrated and emulsified into a rich well-flavoured broth. Check the seasoning and add a little cayenne pepper if you wish.

5 To serve, scatter the croûtons over the soup and add a dollop of rouille.

mussel, cockle and clam masala

SERVES 4

2 tablespoons sunflower oil

1.75 kg (4 lb) mixed mussels, cockles and small clams,
cleaned (see pages 88–9)

2 tablespoons roughly chopped coriander

FOR THE MASALA PASTE:

1 tablespoon coriander seeds

1 teaspoon cloves

2 tablespoons cumin seeds

2 medium onions, quartered

8 large garlic cloves

50 g (2 oz) fresh root ginger, chopped

A walnut-sized piece of seedless tamarind pulp

1 teaspoon turmeric powder

3 medium-hot red Dutch chillies, chopped

2 tablespoons red wine vinegar

40 g (1½ oz) creamed coconut

1 For the masala paste, heat a dry heavy-based frying pan over a medium-high heat. Add the coriander seeds, cloves and cumin seeds and cook until they darken slightly and start to smell aromatic. Tip into a spice grinder and grind to a powder. Put this mixture and all the other paste ingredients into a food processor and blend until smooth.

2 Heat the oil in a large pan, add the spice paste and fry for a few minutes until it starts to separate from the oil.

3 Add the mussels, cockles and clams, cover and cook over a high heat for 3–4 minutes, shaking the pan now and then, until they have all opened.

4 Add a little water if there is not quite enough sauce, season with a little salt if necessary, then add the chopped coriander. Spoon into warmed bowls and serve.

seafood in a crab and ginger broth (see technique 58, page 87)

SERVES 4

2.5 cm (1 inch) fresh root ginger

2 limes

1.7 litres (3 pints) Chicken Stock (see page 222)

1 lemongrass stalk

1 red birdseye chilli, cut in half lengthways

1 tablespoon Thai fish sauce (*nam pla*)

1 tablespoon light soy sauce

8 headless raw prawns

4 x Asian blue swimming crabs or
   1 small cooked brown crab

15 g (½ oz) rice vermicelli noodles

100 g (4 oz) monkfish fillet, very thinly sliced

2 spring onions, cut into 5 cm (2 inch) pieces and finely
   shredded lengthways

25 g (1 oz) bok choi, cut into 2.5 cm (1 inch) pieces

25 g (1 oz) beansprouts

Coriander leaves, to garnish

TO CLARIFY THE STOCK:

100 g (4 oz) piece of coley or other inexpensive white
   fish, skinned and finely chopped

1 small leek, cleaned and thinly sliced

2 egg whites

TO SERVE:

1 tablespoon each of mint and coriander, chopped

2 birdseye chillies, thinly sliced

2 tablespoons rice wine vinegar or white wine vinegar

1 Peel the ginger, reserving the peel, and cut into very thin slices. Remove a strip of zest from one of the limes with a potato peeler, then squeeze the juice from both limes.

2 Pour the chicken stock into a large pan and add three-quarters of the sliced ginger, the ginger peel, the strip of lime zest and the lime juice, the outer leaves of the lemongrass, the birdseye chilli, fish sauce and soy sauce. Gradually bring to the boil.

3 Meanwhile, prepare the crabs as described on page 84. Peel and devein the prawns, reserving the shells (see page 72).

4 Add the crab legs, body and back shell, but not the claws, to the boiling stock with the prawn shells. Bring back to the boil, cover and simmer very gently for 25 minutes, adding the claws after 20 minutes.

5 Pour the stock through a large sieve into another large pan, discarding all the solids except for the crab. Leave the stock to cool.

Meanwhile, remove the white meat from the claws, legs and main body of the crab (see pages 80–1) in pieces as large as possible.

6 To clarify the stock, add the coley, leek and egg whites to the pan and whisk steadily over a medium heat until the mixture boils. Stop whisking immediately, lower the heat and leave to simmer very gently for 5 minutes.

7 Line a fine sieve or conical strainer with a double sheet of muslin and rest it over a clean pan. Carefully pour the stock into the sieve and leave until all the liquid has dripped through. The stock is now ready to use.

8 Bring a pan of lightly salted water to the boil. Add the noodles, remove from the heat and leave them to soak for 2 minutes. Drain and set aside. Finely chop the remaining ginger and half the remaining lemongrass.

9 Bring the stock up to a very gentle simmer, then add the prawns, monkfish, ginger and lemongrass and cook gently for 1 minute. Add the noodles, crab meat, spring onions, bok choi and beansprouts and simmer for 30 seconds, then remove from the heat.

10 Mix the mint and coriander together in one small bowl and the chillies and vinegar in another.

11 Divide the noodles between 4 large soup plates and then ladle the soup over them. Garnish with the coriander leaves and serve with the chopped herbs and chilli vinegar, instructing your guests to season their soup to their own taste.

miso soup

SERVES 4

7 g (¼ oz) dried mixed seaweed (e.g. dulse, wakame,
   agar agar and white moss)

50 g (2 oz) piece of thick cod fillet, skinned

3 prepared scallops (see page 90)

1 tablespoon white miso paste

7 g (¼ oz) baby leaf spinach

7 g (¼ oz) mizuna leaves

2 spring onions, thinly sliced on the diagonal

2 button mushrooms, thinly sliced

FOR THE DASHI (STOCK):

1.2 litres (2 pints) water

5 cm (2 inch) square of dried kombu seaweed

3 tablespoons bonito flakes

1 Drop the dried mixed seaweed into a large bowl of cold water and leave to rehydrate for 8–10 minutes. Drain.

2 For the dashi, put the water and the dried kombu into a pan and slowly bring to a simmer. Strain immediately, return the liquid to the

pan, bring back to a simmer and add the bonito flakes. Bring to the boil, then remove the pan from the heat and allow the flakes to settle for 1 minute. Pour the dashi through a very fine or muslin-lined sieve into a clean pan.

3 Cut the cod into 2.5 cm (1 inch) cubes and then into very thin slices. Slice the scallops horizontally into very thin slices. Drain the seaweed.

4 Bring the dashi back up to a gentle simmer. Mix a ladleful of the hot liquid into the miso paste until smooth. Return the mixture to the pan and add the scallops and cod. Cook for 30 seconds, then add the drained seaweed, spinach leaves and mizuna and simmer for a few seconds only.

5 Ladle the soup into bowls and garnish with the sliced spring onions and mushrooms. Serve immediately.

sashimi of sea trout, brill and scallops

SERVES 4 AS A STARTER

**100 g (4 oz) skinned sea trout fillet, taken from a
   small fish**
100 g (4 oz) skinned brill fillet, taken from a small fish
**4 prepared scallops (see page 90), weighing about 25 g
   (1 oz) each**
1 tablespoon wasabi paste
Long chives, to garnish

FOR THE SOY DIPPING SAUCE:

1 cm (½ inch) peeled fresh root ginger, very finely diced
2 spring onions, finely chopped
Finely grated zest and juice of ½ lime
40 ml (1½ fl oz) dark soy sauce
40 ml (1½ fl oz) water

1 Cut each piece of sea trout and brill across into slices 5 mm (¼ inch) thick, angling the knife blade at 45 degrees as you do so and keeping the fish fillets in shape.

2 Remove the corals, if any, from the scallops and slice each scallop horizontally into 2 or 3 discs. Divide the fish between 4 plates and place a small amount of wasabi paste alongside.

3 Mix all the ingredients for the soy dipping sauce together and pour into 4 small bowls or ramekins. Place on each plate next to the fish, garnish with the chives and serve.

nigiri sushi (see technique 37, page 60)

SERVES 6 (MAKES APPROXIMATELY 30 PIECES)

6 small raw, unpeeled prawns
1 x 40–50 g (1½–2 oz) piece of thick tuna loin
1 x 40–50 g (1½–2 oz) thick piece of skinned salmon fillet
1 x 40–50 g (1½–2 oz) skinned lemon sole fillet
A little wasabi paste
6 teaspoons keta (salmon roe)

FOR THE STICKY RICE:

375 g (12 oz) Japanese sticky rice
600 ml (1 pint) cold water
2 tablespoons caster sugar
6 tablespoons rice vinegar
1 teaspoon salt

TO SERVE:

4 tablespoons Japanese dark soy sauce
1 tablespoon mirin
25 g (1 oz) Japanese pickled ginger

1 For the sticky rice, put the rice into a large bowl, pour over cold water and run the grains through your fingers, changing the water now and then, until the water stays relatively clear. Drain the rice and put it into a pan with the 600 ml (1 pint) cold water. Bring to the boil, boil for 1 minute and then reduce the heat to low and simmer, uncovered, for 10 minutes. Remove from the heat, cover with a lid and leave undisturbed for 10 minutes. Meanwhile put 4 tablespoons of the rice vinegar, the sugar and salt into a small pan and heat gently until the sugar has dissolved. Pour into a bowl and leave to cool.

2 Turn the cooked rice out into a large shallow tray and gradually add the vinegar mixture, gently lifting and folding the rice, so that as it cools it takes on a nice sheen. Transfer to a bowl and cover with cling film, but do not refrigerate.

3 To stop the prawns from curling when you cook them, push a cocktail stick or fine bamboo skewer just under the shell, from the head, along the under-belly, down to the tail. Drop them into lightly salted, boiling water and simmer for 3 minutes. Drain, drop them into cold water and leave to cool. Pull out the sticks, peel the prawns as described for raw prawns on page 72, steps 1 to 3, and then make a cut along the under-belly down to the tail, part-way into the flesh so that you can open them out flat.

4 Cut the tuna and salmon into thin slices and then cut all the fish into small rectangles, measuring about 6 x 3 cm (2½ x 1¼ inches).

5 Mix the remaining 2 tablespoons of rice vinegar with 225 ml (8 fl oz) cold water. Wet your hands with the vinegared water and mould a 20 g

(¾ oz) ball of the rice into a small block, slightly smaller than the piece of fish. Do not squash the rice together too hard.

6 Smear one side of the tuna, lemon sole and salmon slices and the cut face of the prawns with a very small dot of wasabi paste. Lay each piece of fish and the prawns, wasabi-side down, on top of each block of rice and press down lightly. Spread the top of the last remaining blocks of rice with wasabi and spoon 1 teaspoon of keta on to each.

7 To serve, mix the soy sauce and mirin together and divide between 6 dipping-sauce saucers. Arrange the sushi in the centre of each plate. Put a little pile of pickled ginger and a small dipping saucer of the sauce to the side and serve.

laksa (malaysian seafood and noodle soup)

SERVES 4

8 unpeeled raw headless prawns
5 tablespoons vegetable oil
900 ml (1½ pints) Chicken Stock (see page 222)
100 g (4 oz) prepared small squid (see page 92)
175 g (6 oz) flat rice noodles
100 g (4 oz) beansprouts
400 ml (14 fl oz) can coconut milk
2 teaspoons palm sugar or light muscavado sugar
1–1½ teaspoons salt

FOR THE LAKSA SPICE PASTE:

3 medium-hot dried red chillies
25 g (1 oz) dried shrimps (optional)
2 lemongrass stalks, outer leaves removed and core finely chopped
25 g (1 oz) cashew nuts
2 garlic cloves, chopped
2.5 cm (1 inch) fresh root ginger, chopped
1 teaspoon turmeric powder
1 small onion, chopped
1 teaspoon ground coriander
3 tablespoons water

FOR THE GARNISH:

5 cm (2 inch) piece of cucumber, cut into fine matchsticks
1 tablespoon chopped coriander
1 tablespoon chopped mint
4 spring onions, thinly sliced
1 medium-hot red Dutch chilli, thinly sliced across into rings

1 For the laksa spice paste, put the dried red chillies and dried shrimps, if using, into a bowl, cover with warm water and leave to soak for 15 minutes. Drain, put into a food processor with the rest of the ingredients and blend to a smooth paste. Set aside.

2 Peel the prawns (see page 72) and de-vein if necessary.

3 Heat 1 tablespoon of the oil in a pan, add the prawn shells and fry for a few minutes until lightly browned. Add the chicken stock, bring to the boil and simmer for 10 minutes.

4 Meanwhile, cut along one side of the squid pouch and open it out flat. Score the inner side into a diamond pattern with the tip of a small short knife (see page 93), then cut into 2.5 cm (1 inch) squares and set aside.

5 Strain the stock and discard the prawn shells. Heat the remaining oil in a clean pan, add the spice paste and fry gently for 5–6 minutes, until it smells very fragrant and the spices are separating from the oil. Add the stock, bring to the boil, cover and simmer for 20 minutes.

6 Bring a pan of salted water to the boil. Add the rice noodles, take the pan off the heat and leave to soak for 4 minutes. Add the beansprouts and leave for another minute, then drain well.

7 Add the coconut milk to the stock and simmer for 3 minutes. Add the prawns, squid, sugar and salt and simmer for 4 minutes.

8 Divide the noodles between 4 large warmed soup bowls. Spoon over the hot soup and garnish each bowl with some cucumber, coriander, mint, spring onions and red chilli.

chickpea, parsley and salt cod stew

SERVES 4

350 g (12 oz) dried chickpeas
750 g (1½ lb) Fresh Salted Cod (see pages 67 and 227), soaked
1 x 75 g (6 oz) potato, peeled
85 ml (3 fl oz) olive oil
8 garlic cloves, finely chopped
1 teaspoon dried chilli flakes
4 plum tomatoes, roughly chopped
3–4 tablespoons chopped flat-leaf parsley
Salt and freshly ground black pepper

1 Cover the chickpeas in water and leave them to soak overnight.

2 The next day drain the chickpeas and pour over enough fresh water to cover them by about 5 cm (2 inches). Bring to the boil, add the

CHICKPEA, PARSLEY AND SALT COD STEW

seafood and white bean stew (cassoulet) with salt cod, garlic and toulouse sausage

SERVES 6

175 ml (6 fl oz) olive oil
225 g (8 oz) toulouse sausage, cut into 2.5 cm (1 inch) pieces
A pinch of dried chilli flakes
550 g (1¼ lb) dried haricot beans, soaked in cold water overnight
6 garlic cloves, finely chopped
2 bay leaves
2 sprigs thyme
900 ml (1½ pints) Chicken Stock (see page 222)
225 g (8 oz) Fresh Salted Cod (see pages 67 and 227), soaked
350 g (12 oz) squid, cleaned (see page 92) and cut into thin slices
225 g (8 oz) monkfish fillet, cut into 2.5 cm (1 inch) pieces
100 g (4 oz) coarse, fresh white breadcrumbs
1 tablespoon chopped parsley
Salt and freshly ground black pepper

peeled potato and simmer until tender, adding hot water now and then if necessary to make sure they stay just covered. Drain and set aside, saving the cooking liquid.

3 Drain the salted cod, drop it into a pan of boiling water and simmer for 6–8 minutes or until just cooked. Drain and, when cool enough to handle, flake the flesh into large pieces, discarding the skin and any bones.

4 Heat the olive oil in a large pan, add the garlic and chilli flakes and cook for a minute or two without browning. Add the tomatoes, chickpeas and potato, which should be broken up into small pieces with the back of a wooden spoon. Add a little of the cooking liquid from the chickpeas and 300 ml (10 fl oz) of water and simmer for 20–30 minutes, until the stew has reduced and thickened a little. Gently fold in the salt cod and parsley and season liberally with freshly ground black pepper. Taste the stew for salt but you probably won't need any.

ALTERNATIVE FISH

All fish from the cod family, such as haddock, hake, pollack or coley, are pleasant to eat when salted. I think the cheaper the fish, the more appropriate it is for salting. Pollack, for example, is much better salted than as a fresh fish.

1 Pre-heat the oven to 150°C/300°F/Gas Mark 2. Heat 120 ml (4 fl oz) of the olive oil in a large casserole, add the sausage pieces and chilli flakes and fry for 4 minutes, until the sausage is lightly browned.

2 Drain the beans and add them to the casserole with 4 of the chopped garlic cloves, the bay leaves, thyme sprigs, 600 ml (1 pint) of the chicken stock and some freshly ground black pepper. Cover with foil or a well-fitting lid and bake for 1½ hours, until the beans are tender and most of the liquid has been absorbed.

3 Drain and skin the prepared salted cod and cut it into 2.5 cm (1 inch) pieces. Heat a little of the remaining oil in a frying pan over a high heat and sear the squid and monkfish in it, in batches if necessary, until nicely browned. Stir them into the cooked beans with the salted cod, the rest of the chicken stock and a little more seasoning to taste. Increase the oven temperature to 200°C/400°F/Gas Mark 6.

4 Put the breadcrumbs into a bowl and rub in the remaining oil. Stir in the remaining garlic, the chopped parsley and a little salt and pepper. Spread this over the top of the beans, return to the oven and cook, uncovered, for 30 minutes, until crisp and golden.

soups, stews and mixed seafood

bourride of red mullet, brill and fresh salted cod

SERVES 4

225 g (8 oz) unskinned red mullet fillet

225 g (8 oz) unskinned brill fillet

225 g (8 oz) Fresh Salted Cod (see pages 67 and 227), soaked

2 tablespoons olive oil

1 medium onion, chopped

1 small leek, cleaned and chopped

½ fennel bulb, chopped

4 garlic cloves, chopped

2 pared strips of orange zest

2 tomatoes, sliced

1 bay leaf and 1 sprig thyme

1.2 litres (2 pints) Fish Stock (see page 222)

1 quantity Aïoli (see page 224)

½ teaspoon salt

Chopped parsley, to garnish

FOR THE CROÛTONS:

2 tablespoons olive oil

4 x 2.5 cm (1 inch) thick slices French bread, cut on the slant

1 medium-hot red Dutch chilli, seeded and finely chopped

4 sun-dried tomatoes in oil, drained and chopped

1 Cut all the fish into 50 g (2 oz) pieces.

2 To make the croûtons, heat the oil in a frying pan and fry the bread slices on both sides until crisp and golden. Drain briefly on kitchen paper and keep warm. Mix the chilli and sun-dried tomatoes together in a bowl and stir in 1 tablespoon of the aïoli. Spread the mixure on to the croûtons.

3 For the bourride, heat the oil in a large pan. Add the onion, leek, fennel, garlic and orange zest and fry gently without colouring for 5 minutes.

4 Add the tomatoes, bay leaf, thyme, fish stock and salt. Bring to the boil and simmer for 30 minutes.

5 Add the fish pieces and simmer gently for 5 minutes. Then carefully lift them out on to a warmed serving dish and keep warm.

6 Strain the cooking liquor through a fine sieve into a clean pan, pressing out as much liquid as you can with the back of a ladle.

7 Put the aïoli into a bowl and whisk in a ladle of the cooking liquor. Stir the mixture back into the pan and cook over a low heat until slightly thickened. Do not let it boil.

8 Pour the sauce over the fish and sprinkle with the chopped parsley. Serve with the croûtons and some plain boiled potatoes, if you wish.

cotriade

SERVES 8

1.5 kg (3 lb) mixed unskinned fish fillets such as cod, hake, haddock, brill, John Dory, gurnard, sea bass, grey mullet, mackerel and herring (one type of fillet needs to be oily)

900 g (2 lb) new potatoes, halved

unsalted butter, for brushing

450 g (1 lb) mussels, cleaned (see page 88)

Salt

FOR THE COURT-BOUILLON:

2 carrots, chopped

1 leek, cleaned and chopped

2 celery sticks, chopped

1 fennel bulb, chopped

½ onion, chopped

2.4 litres (4 pints) water

Pared zest and flesh of ½ lemon

2 garlic cloves and 1 bay leaf

150 ml (5 fl oz) dry white wine

2 tablespoons Pernod

6 black peppercorns

15 g (½ oz) salt

100 g (4 oz) crème fraîche

50 g (2 oz) fennel herb (stems and leafy fronds)

FOR THE SORREL AND ANCHOVY BUTTER:

10 sorrel leaves

4 salted anchovy fillets in olive oil, drained

100 g (4 oz) unsalted butter, softened

1 Cut each type of fish fillet into 8 even-sized pieces. For the sorrel and anchovy butter, put the ingredients into a food processor and blend until smooth. Spoon the mixture into the centre of a large sheet of cling film and shape into a roll 4 cm (1½ inches) thick. Wrap and chill in the fridge or freezer until firm.

2 For the court-bouillon, put all ingredients but the crème fraîche and the leafy fronds of the fennel herb into a large pan, bring to the boil and simmer for 30 minutes.

3 Strain the court-bouillon into a clean pan, bring back to the boil and boil rapidly until reduced by half. Add the crème fraîche and all but

1 sprig of the fennel fronds and simmer for 5 minutes. Strain once more, return the pan to the heat, add the potatoes and bring back to the boil. Simmer for 15 minutes or until the potatoes are tender.

4 Pre-heat the grill to high. Brush the oily fish fillet (such as the mackerel or herring) with the melted butter and season on both sides with some salt. Put skin-side up on a lightly buttered baking tray.

5 Put the mussels and a splash of the court-bouillon into a large pan, cover and cook over a high heat for 3–4 minutes until they have opened. Tip the mussels into a colander set over a bowl. Cover the mussels and keep warm. Pour all but the last tablespoon of the cooking liquor back into the court-bouillon and bring it back to the boil.

6 Poach the remaining fish fillets in batches in the court-bouillon for 3 minutes, turning half-way through, until just firm; they will continue to cook after you have removed them. As each batch is cooked, lift out and keep warm. When cooking the last batch, grill the oily fish for 3 minutes.

7 To serve, divide the fish fillets attractively between 8 warmed plates. Arrange the mussels and potatoes around the fish. Pour over just enough of the court-bouillon to half-cover the fillets.

8 Unwrap the butter and cut it into thin slices. Put 2 slices on to each plate and serve.

a meurette of lemon sole with beaujolais

SERVES 4

750 g (1½ lb) unskinned lemon sole fillets
Butter, for brushing
25 g (1 oz) Beurre Manié (see page 227)
1 quantity Persillade (see page 166)
Salt and freshly ground black pepper
FOR THE SAUCE:
25 g (1 oz) butter
50 g (2 oz) each of finely chopped carrot, celery, leek and onion
1 tablespoon brandy
1.2 litres (2 pints) Chicken Stock (see page 222)
½ bottle Beaujolais
1 bay leaf
1 sprig thyme
FOR THE GARNISH:
25g (1 oz) butter
24 shallots, peeled

A large pinch of sugar
1 rindless rasher smoked back bacon
225 g (8 oz) button mushrooms, wiped and quartered
FOR THE CROÛTONS:
2 medium-thick slices white bread
2 tablespoons sunflower oil
A small knob of butter

1 For the sauce, melt the butter in a medium-sized saucepan, add the chopped vegetables and fry over a medium-high heat until they are lightly browned. Add the brandy and, as soon as it has evaporated, add 900 ml (1½ pints) of the chicken stock, the wine, bay leaf and thyme. Bring to the boil, lower the heat and leave to simmer for 30 minutes. Strain the stock through a fine sieve into a wide sauté pan. Bring to the boil and boil rapidly until reduced to about 350 ml (12 fl oz) and well concentrated in flavour.

2 Meanwhile, for the garnish, melt half the butter in a small pan. Add the shallots and the sugar and cook until nicely browned. Add the rest of the chicken stock and simmer until the shallots are tender. Then turn up the heat and boil rapidly until the stock has reduced to a thick sticky glaze, shaking the pan every now and then so that the shallots become coated in it. Cover and keep warm. Cut the bacon across into short thin strips. Melt the rest of the butter in another pan, add the bacon and fry gently until golden. Add the mushrooms and cook for 2–3 minutes until they are soft. Season to taste and keep warm.

3 For the croûtons, cut the bread into eight 2.5 cm (1 inch) discs using a pastry cutter. Heat the oil in a frying pan, add the butter and the discs of bread and fry until golden on both sides. Lift out on to kitchen paper and keep warm.

4 Pre-heat the grill to high. Brush the lemon sole fillets on both sides with melted butter, season with salt and pepper and put on to a lightly buttered tray or the rack of the grill pan. Grill for about 2–3 minutes until cooked through.

5 Meanwhile, whisk the beurre manié into the stock, a small piece at a time, and simmer for 2–3 minutes until the sauce has thickened. Adjust the seasoning if necessary and then whisk in the persillade.

6 To serve, put the sole fillets on to 4 warmed plates and garnish with the shallots, bacon and mushrooms. Spoon the sauce over the fish and serve, scattered with the croûtons.

a ragoût of seafood with lemon and saffron

SERVES 4

A good pinch of saffron strands

8 unpeeled large raw prawns

2 x 50–75 g (2–3 oz) skinned lemon sole fillets

8 baby carrots, scraped and trimmed

8 very small florets of broccoli

8 French beans, trimmed and halved

8 mussels, cleaned (see page 88)

4 prepared scallops (see page 90)

100 g (4 oz) chilled unsalted butter, diced

Salt and freshly ground black pepper

Maldon sea-salt flakes, to garnish

FOR THE VEGETABLE NAGE:

½ lemon

1 fennel bulb

1 large onion, peeled

4 celery sticks

A handful of button mushrooms

½ teaspoon salt

1 teaspoon black peppercorns

2 bay leaves

3 sprigs thyme

½ teaspoon fennel seeds

300 ml (10 fl oz) white wine

A RAGOÛT OF SEAFOOD WITH LEMON AND SAFFRON

1 For the vegetable nage, pare the zest off the piece of lemon and then cut away and discard all the bitter white pith. Cut the flesh across into slices. Roughly chop all the vegetables and put them into a pan with the lemon zest and flesh, salt, peppercorns, herbs, fennel seeds and enough water to cover. Bring to the boil and simmer for 20 minutes. Take the pan off the heat and add the wine. Cover and leave to cool for 2 hours.

2 Strain the nage and pour 1.2 litres (2 pints) into a wide-based pan. (Freeze the rest for later use.) Add the saffron, bring to the boil and boil rapidly until it has reduced to 120 ml (4 fl oz). Transfer to a small pan and set aside.

3 Peel the prawns, leaving the last tail segment in place (see page 72). Cut each lemon sole fillet diagonally across into 4 pieces.

4 Drop the vegetables into a pan of boiling salted water, bring back to the boil, drain and then plunge into cold water to set the colour. Drain once more.

5 Prepare one stacked or two separate steamers (see pages 46–7). Put all the blanched vegetables on to one plate and the prawns, lemon sole, mussels and scallops on to another. Steam the vegetables for 3 minutes and the fish for 3–4 minutes. Keep everything warm while you make the sauce.

6 Drain all the cooking juices from the plate of fish into the reduced stock. Bring back to the boil and then whisk in the butter, a few pieces at a time, until you have a smooth, emulsified sauce. Season to taste with some salt and pepper.

7 Arrange the seafood and vegetables on 4 warmed plates. Spoon over the lemon and saffron sauce and serve sprinkled with some sea-salt flakes.

ALTERNATIVE FISH
Lobster, oysters, langoustines and freshwater crayfish.

gratin of seafood

SERVES 4

450 g (1 lb) unpeeled cooked North Atlantic prawns

½ onion, roughly chopped

65 g (2½ oz) butter

1 tablespoon cognac

600 ml (1 pint) Fish Stock (see page 222)

50 ml (2 fl oz) white wine

2 tomatoes, roughly chopped

900 g (2 lb) mussels, cleaned (see page 88)

2 shallots, finely chopped

20 g (¾ oz) plain flour

150 ml (5 fl oz) double cream

1 tablespoon chopped parsley

Juice of ½ lemon

8 prepared scallops (see page 90)

175 g (6 oz) skinned haddock fillet, cut into small chunks

100 g (4 oz) button mushrooms, sliced

100 g (4 oz) fresh white crab meat

100 g (4 oz) Gruyère, Emmenthal, fontina or Jarlsberg
    cheese, coarsely grated

¾ teaspoon paprika

A pinch of cayenne pepper

Salt and freshly ground black pepper

1 Peel the prawns, reserving the heads and shells (see page 72). Fry the onion in 15 g (½ oz) of the butter until soft. Add the prawn heads and shells and cognac and fry for 1–2 minutes. Add the fish stock, wine and tomatoes, bring to the boil and simmer for 20 minutes.

2 Add the mussels to the pan, cover and cook over a high heat for 3–4 minutes. Tip into a large sieve set over a bowl. If there is any less than 600 ml (1 pint) of stock, make it up with a little fish stock; any more and you need to boil it once more until it is reduced to the required amount. Remove the mussels from their shells and set aside with the peeled prawns. Discard everything else in the sieve.

3 Fry the shallots in another 25 g (1 oz) of the butter until soft. Add the flour and cook for 1 minute, stirring. Gradually stir in the stock, bring to the boil, then add the cream and simmer very gently for 10 minutes, until the sauce coats the back of a wooden spoon. Add the parsley and season to taste with some lemon juice, salt and pepper.

4 Pre-heat the grill to high. Melt the remaining butter. Scatter the scallops, haddock and mushrooms into a large gratin dish, brush with melted butter, season and grill for 2 minutes.

5 Add the prawns, mussels and crab meat to the dish and then spoon over the sauce. Sprinkle with the cheese, dust with a little paprika and cayenne pepper and grill for another 1–2 minutes, until golden and bubbling.

ALTERNATIVE FISH

A selection of cooked lobster, monkfish, cod and queen scallops.

hot shellfish with garlic and lemon juice

SERVES 4

8 cooked Dublin Bay prawns or Mediterranean prawns
    (crevettes)

4 whelks

32 winkles

24 mussels, cleaned (see page 88)

50 ml (2 fl oz) dry white wine

20 cockles, washed

16 small clams such as carpetshell, cleaned
    (see page 89)

8 Pacific oysters

85 ml (3 fl oz) extra virgin olive oil

2 garlic cloves, finely chopped

1 handful of flat-leaf parsley leaves, chopped

1 medium-hot red Dutch chilli, seeded and chopped

Juice of ½ lemon

1 Prepare a steamer as described on pages 46–7. Reheat the Dublin Bay prawns, and the winkles and whelks if they are already cooked, for 2–3 minutes.

2 If the winkles and whelks are raw, drop them into separate pans of boiling salted water and cook the winkles for 1 minute and the whelks for 4 minutes. Drain and keep warm.

3 Put the mussels into a pan with the white wine. Cover and cook over a high heat for 3–4 minutes until they have opened. Lift out with a slotted spoon, cover and keep warm. Repeat with the cockles, small clams and oysters using the same cooking liquor. The oysters will not open fully, so finish opening them with a short, thick-bladed knife (see page 91).

4 Strain all but the last tablespoon of the cooking liquor into a pan and add the olive oil, garlic, parsley, chilli and lemon juice.

5 Arrange the warmed shellfish on a large, warmed serving platter. Bring the dressing to the boil, pour over the shellfish and serve with plenty of French bread.

linguine ai frutti di mare (linguine with mixed seafood)

SERVES 4

1 kg (2¼ lb) prepared mixed shellfish, such as carpetshell clams, smooth venus clams, mussels, uncooked langoustines and small unpeeled raw prawns

50 ml (2 fl oz) dry white wine

450 g (1 lb) cherry tomatoes or small vine-ripened tomatoes

450 g (1 lb) linguine

120 ml (4 fl oz) olive oil

5 garlic cloves, thinly sliced

A pinch of dried chilli flakes

3 tablespoons chopped flat-leaf parsley

Salt and freshly ground black pepper

1 Put the clams and mussels in a large pan with the wine, cover and cook over a high heat for 3–4 minutes, until they have opened (discard any that remain closed). Tip into a colander placed over a bowl and set aside.

2 Squeeze the tomatoes to remove most of the seeds and juice, then coarsely chop them.

LINGUINE AI FRUTTI DI MARE

3 Bring a large pan of well-salted water (i.e. 1 teaspoon per 600 ml/1 pint) to the boil. Add the linguine, bring back to the boil and cook for about 8 minutes or until *al dente*.

4 Meanwhile, put the olive oil and garlic into a large pan and heat slowly until the garlic begins to sizzle. Add the chilli flakes and tomatoes and simmer for 5 minutes. Add all but the last tablespoon or two of the cooking liquor from the clams and mussels. Bring back to the boil and simmer until the mixture has reduced to a sauce-like consistency.

5 Stir the langoustines into the sauce and turn them over until they go pink. Add the prawns and simmer for 2–3 minutes, until they are both cooked. Stir in the cooked clams and mussels with the parsley and turn them over a few times until heated through. Season if necessary with a little salt and some pepper.

6 Drain the pasta well and tip it into a large warmed serving dish. Pour over the seafood sauce and toss together well.

ALTERNATIVE FISH
Any mixture of shellfish plus maybe some prepared and sliced scallops or squid.

seafood paella

SERVES 6

1 x 450 g (1 lb) cooked lobster
1.2 litres (2 pints) Chicken Stock (see page 222)
2 bay leaves
1 large leek, cleaned and sliced
12 mussels, cleaned (see page 88)
85 ml (3 fl oz) extra virgin olive oil
450 g (1 lb) monkfish fillet, cut into 1 cm (½ inch) thick
    slices (see page 62, steps 1–5)
175 g (6 oz) chicken breast fillet, cut into thin strips
100 g (4 oz) small prepared squid (see page 92)
1 medium onion, finely chopped
8 cloves garlic, 4 finely chopped and 4 cut into quarters
1 red pepper, seeded and thinly sliced
450 g (1 lb) Arborio or Valencia rice
½ teaspoon saffron strands
6 cooked Mediterranean prawns (crevettes)

1 Pull the claws and legs off the lobster and then detach the head from the tail (see page 77). Cut the tail through the shell into pieces at each section and the claws into 3 and set aside.

2 Put the lobster head and legs into a pan with the chicken stock, bay leaves, and the green part of the leek. Bring to the boil, then leave to

simmer for about 20 minutes. Strain through a sieve into a clean pan. You will need 900 ml (1½ pints), so either boil to reduce or make up with water to the required amount. Set aside.

3 Put the mussels into a pan with a splash of the stock. Cover and cook over a high heat for 3–4 minutes until they have all opened. Tip into a colander set over a bowl to collect the liquor. Pour all but the last tablespoon of the liquor back into the stock. Cover the mussels and set aside.

4 Heat the oil in a large, deep, 30 cm (12 inch) frying pan. Add the monkfish and fry for 3 minutes, turning it over after 2 minutes. Transfer to a plate and set aside. Add the chicken (and a little more oil if necessary) and fry for 2–3 minutes until lightly browned. Set aside with the monkfish. Add the squid and stir-fry for 2–3 minutes, until lightly browned. Set aside with the monkfish and chicken.

5 Add the onion, all the garlic, the rest of the leek and the red pepper to the pan and fry for 4–5 minutes, until soft and lightly browned.

6 Add the rice to the pan and stir until all the grains are well coated with the oil. Add the saffron and stock and bring to the boil. Lower the heat, cover and simmer gently for 15 minutes.

7 Uncover the rice and lay the pieces of lobster, monkfish, chicken, squid, mussels and prawns on top. Cover and cook gently for a further 5 minutes. Remove from the heat and leave for 5 minutes. Then uncover and gently fork the seafood and the rice together before serving.

rice-shaped pasta with seafood, rocket and roasted vegetables

SERVES 4

350 g (12 oz) rice-shaped pasta, such as orzo or
  puntalette
1 small aubergine, cut into 2.5 cm (1 inch) cubes
1 red onion, cut into thin wedges
1 red pepper, seeded and cut into 2.5 cm (1 inch) pieces
1 plum tomato, cut into thin wedges
2 garlic cloves, finely chopped
75 ml (3 fl oz) extra virgin olive oil
½ teaspoon coarse sea salt
450 g (1 lb) mussels, cleaned (see page 88)
100 g (4 oz) prepared squid (see page 92), cut across
  into rings
100 g (4 oz) peeled cooked North Atlantic prawns
3 sun-dried tomatoes in oil, drained and thinly sliced
1 medium-hot red Dutch chilli, seeded and finely chopped
25 g (1 oz) Parmesan cheese, finely grated
1 tablespoon white wine vinegar
5 tablespoons chopped flat-leaf parsley
50 g (2 oz) rocket
Salt and freshly ground black pepper

1 Pre-heat the oven to 220°C/425°F/Gas Mark 7. Bring a large pan of well-salted water (i.e. 1 teaspoon per 600 ml/l pint) to the boil in a large pan. Add the pasta and cook for 8 minutes, or until *al dente*, then drain and leave to cool.

2 Meanwhile, put the aubergine, onion, red pepper and tomato into a bowl with the garlic, 2 tablespoons of the oil and the sea salt and mix together well. Spread out in a small roasting tin, transfer to the oven and cook for about 30 minutes or until well coloured around the edges. Remove from the oven and leave to cool.

3 Put the mussels into a large pan with a splash of water, cover and cook over a high heat for 3–4 minutes until they have opened. Tip into a colander and leave to cool slightly. Then remove the meats from the shells and set aside.

4 Heat 1 tablespoon of the remaining oil in a frying pan. Add the squid and fry over a high heat for 2½ minutes, until lightly browned. Season with salt and pepper and leave to cool.

5 When the pasta, roasted vegetables, mussels and squid are all cold, put them into a large bowl with the remaining olive oil, prawns, sun-dried tomatoes, chilli, Parmesan cheese, vinegar, 4 tablespoons of the parsley, 1 teaspoon of salt and 10 turns of the black pepper mill. Toss together lightly, then fold in the rocket. Spoon the salad on to a large serving platter and sprinkle with the remaining chopped parsley.

le plateau de fruits de mer

SERVES 2

1 x 450 g (1 lb) cooked lobster
1 x 750 g (1½ lb) cooked brown crab
2 native oysters
2 Pacific oysters
12 mussels, cleaned (see page 88)
12 carpetshell clams, washed
6 cooked Dublin Bay Prawns (langoustines)
4 Mediterranean prawns (crevettes)
12 winkles, cooked (see page 111)
2 whelks, cooked (see page 111)
TO SERVE:
50 ml (2 fl oz) red wine
50 ml (2 fl oz) red wine vinegar
1 shallot, finely chopped
½ quantity Mayonnaise (see page 224), made with olive
  oil
Plenty of crushed ice
1.5 kg (3 lb) bladderack seaweed, washed
1 lemon, cut in half

1 Cut the lobster lengthways in half (see page 76). Cut the crab in half right through the back shell, down between the eyes. Open the oysters as described on page 91 and open the raw mussels and clams as described on pages 88 and 89.

2 Mix together the red wine, red wine vinegar and shallot and pour into one small bowl. Spoon the mayonnaise into another bowl.

3 To assemble the dish, cover the base of a large serving platter with a thick layer of crushed ice and cover with the seaweed. Arrange the shellfish on top and garnish with the halved lemon. Serve with the shallot vinegar and mayonnaise.

ALTERNATIVE FISH
Raw cleaned scallops, prepared sea urchins, raw cockles (prepared as for clams), cooked pink shrimp, cooked shore crabs, etc.

LE PLATEAU DE FRUITS DE MER

recipes

chapter 6

large meaty fish, skate and eels

poached bonito with warm thyme-and-tomato potatoes

SERVES 4

4 x 175 g (6 oz) pieces of thick bonito fillet
4 tablespoons Mayonnaise (see pages 224),
     made with olive oil
6 black olives, such as Kalamata, pitted and thinly sliced
Salt and freshly ground black pepper
4 parsley sprigs, to garnish

FOR THE WARM THYME-AND-TOMATO POTATOES:

450 g (1 lb) firm potatoes, such as Désirée or Wilja,
     peeled and cut into 2 cm (¾ inch) pieces
25 g (1 oz) unsalted butter
1 large shallot, finely chopped
Leaves from 1 sprig thyme
1 plum tomato, skinned, seeded and diced
1 tablespoon chopped parsley

1 Cook the potatoes in boiling salted water for about 8 minutes or until just tender, then drain. Melt the butter in a medium-sized pan, add the shallot and the thyme leaves and cook for about 4 minutes, until the shallot is soft but not browned. Add the potatoes and cook for 2 minutes, turning them over very gently every now and then so as not to break them up too much. Take the pan off the heat and stir in the tomato, parsley and some seasoning.

2 While the potatoes are cooking, bring 600 ml (1 pint) water and 1 tablespoon of salt to the boil in a large frying pan. Reduce to a simmer, add the bonito fillets and poach for 3 minutes, turning them over after 1½ minutes. Lift them out with a slotted spoon on to one side of a large warmed serving plate, cover and keep warm.

3 Stir 40 ml (1½ fl oz) of the poaching liquor into the mayonnaise with the black olives and pour into a small warmed serving bowl. Garnish the fish with the parsley sprigs, spoon the thyme-and-tomato potatoes alongside and serve the sauce separately.

ALTERNATIVE FISH

This dish can be made equally well with those beautiful, plump, big mackerel you get in the winter in Britain. You'll need ones weighing about 350–400 g (12–14 oz). It would also work well with sea trout, skipjack tuna and salmon.

tuna carpaccio with rocket and parmesan cheese (see technique 39, page 63)

SERVES 4

225 g (8 oz) piece of tuna loin fillet
4 tablespoons extra virgin olive oil
15 g (½ oz) Parmesan shavings
50 g (2 oz) rocket
Maldon sea-salt flakes
Coarsely ground black pepper

1 Wrap the piece of tuna tightly in some cling film so that it takes on a nice cylindrical shape. Place it in the freezer for about 3 hours until it is firm but not completely frozen.

2 Remove the tuna from the freezer, unwrap and place on a chopping board. Cut across into very thin slices using a very sharp, long-bladed knife. They should be as thin as, if not thinner than, smoked salmon.

3 Arrange about 4 slices of tuna over the base of 4 cold plates in a single layer, pressing them out slightly so that they butt up together. Drizzle over the oil and then sprinkle with a little black pepper and a few sea-salt flakes.

4 Scatter the Parmesan shavings over the tuna and pile the rocket leaves into the centre of each plate. Serve with a little crusty fresh bread.

VARIATION

carpaccio of monkfish with lemon olive oil

Replace the tuna with prepared monkfish fillets (see page 62). Wrap and freeze for just 1 hour. Serve drizzled with Lemon Olive Oil (see page 227) or extra virgin olive oil.

TUNA CARPACCIO WITH ROCKET AND PARMESAN CHEESE

TUNA

grilled tuna salad with guacamole

SERVES 4

450 g (1 lb) piece of tuna loin fillet

Oil, for brushing

Sea salt and freshly ground black pepper

4 sprigs coriander, to garnish

FOR THE GUACAMOLE:

1 large avocado

1 jalapeño chilli, seeded

Juice of 1 lime

2 spring onions, chopped

1 tablespoon chopped coriander

3 tablespoons sunflower oil

½ teaspoon salt

FOR THE SOY DRESSING:

50 ml (2 fl oz) water

1 tablespoon dark soy sauce

1 spring onion, finely chopped

¼ jalapeño or green Dutch chilli, seeded and chopped

Juice and zest of ½ lime

½ lemongrass stalk, outer leaves removed and core finely sliced

1 teaspoon finely chopped fresh ginger

1 Heat a ridged cast-iron griddle until it is very hot. Brush the piece of tuna with oil and sprinkle liberally with salt and freshly ground black pepper. Cook the tuna for 1–1½ minutes on each face, until coloured all over. Remember the centre of the tuna should remain raw. Remove from the pan and season again. Leave to cool completely.

2 Blend all the guacamole ingredients in a food processor until smooth, then mix all the soy dressing ingredients together.

3 Slice the tuna into 5 mm (¼ inch) slices and arrange on 4 cold plates. The slices should slightly overlap and be to the side of the plates. Put a spoonful of the guacamole on each plate, again slightly to the side (offsetting food on plates makes it look more natural). Add a generous pool of dressing and decorate the guacamole with a sprig of coriander.

tonno con fagioli (tuna and cannellini beans)

SERVES 4

225 g (8 oz) dried cannellini beans

1 bay leaf

1 shallot, thinly sliced

2 sprigs thyme

1 garlic clove, peeled but left whole, plus 1 small garlic clove, crushed

85 ml (3 fl oz) extra virgin olive oil, plus a little extra to serve

3 tablespoons lemon juice

1 small red onion, thinly sliced

3 tablespoons chopped flat-leaf parsley, plus extra to garnish

Salt and freshly ground black pepper

FOR THE TUNA CONFIT:

275 g (10 oz) thick tuna loin steak

About 300 ml (10 fl oz) inexpensive olive oil

1 onion, thinly sliced

2 garlic cloves, sliced

2 fresh or dried bay leaves

¼ small lemon, sliced

1 large sprig thyme

1 Cover the beans with plenty of cold water and leave to soak overnight.

2 Make the tuna confit (if possible, do this the day before as well, so you can leave it for 24 hours to allow all the flavours to permeate the fish): sprinkle a thin layer of salt in a shallow dish, lay the tuna on top and cover it with another layer of salt. Set aside for 10 minutes. Now brush most of the salt off the fish and rinse it under cold water. Dry on kitchen paper, then cut it, if necessary, into pieces that will fit neatly in a single layer in a small saucepan.

3 Heat 3 tablespoons of the oil in the pan, add the onion and garlic and fry gently for 5 minutes, until soft but not coloured. Add the bay leaves, lemon slices and thyme, put the tuna on top and then pour over the rest of the oil. If the oil does not cover the fish, add a little more. Place the pan over a low heat and slowly bring the temperature of the oil up to 100°C (212°F). Remove the pan from the heat and leave the tuna to cool.

4 Drain the beans, tip them into a large pan and add enough fresh water to cover them by about 2.5 cm (1 inch). Bring to the boil and add the bay leaf, shallot, thyme sprigs and the whole clove of garlic. Simmer for about 45 minutes or until tender, topping them up with boiling water if necessary to make sure that they stay just covered.

5 Just as the beans are ready, return the tuna to a low heat and bring back up to 100°C (212°F). Drain the beans, discard the bay leaf, thyme and garlic and tip the beans into a bowl. Toss with the extra virgin olive oil, crushed garlic, lemon juice, some salt and plenty of freshly ground black pepper. Leave to cool slightly.

6 As soon as the tuna is back up to temperature, lift it out of the pan and allow the excess oil to drain away. Break the fish into chunky pieces and season them with ½ teaspoon of salt and pepper.

7 Toss the red onion and parsley into the beans and then carefully stir in the tuna so that you don't break up the flakes too much. Spoon into a large serving bowl, drizzle over a little extra olive oil and sprinkle with chopped parsley. Serve with plenty of crusty fresh bread.

seared tuna with rice noodle and coriander salad

SERVES 4
4 x 200 g (7 oz) tuna loin steaks
6 tablespoons dark soy sauce
4 tablespoons balsamic vinegar
FOR THE RICE NOODLE AND CORIANDER SALAD:
1 tablespoon sesame seeds
50 g (2 oz) coriander
6 spring onions, trimmed
Coarsely grated zest and juice of 1 lime
2 tablespoons Thai fish sauce (nam pla)
75 ml (3 fl oz) water
2 teaspoons roasted sesame oil
2 tablespoons sunflower oil
85 g (3 oz) rice vermicelli noodles
3 medium-hot green Dutch chillies, seeded
   and finely chopped
2 tablespoons Japanese pickled ginger, cut into shreds
1 small bunch garlic chives, chopped (optional)
1 bunch watercress, larger stalks removed and
   broken into sprigs

1 For the salad, pre-heat the grill to high. Spread the sesame seeds on to a baking ray and toast, shaking the pan now and then, until golden. Pick the leaves off the coriander and discard the stalks – if they are quite large, very roughly chop them. You will need about 6 tablespoons in all. Very thinly slice the spring onions on the diagonal. Mix together the lime juice, fish sauce, water, sesame oil and sunflower oil.

2 Bring a pan of water to the boil, drop in the noodles and take it off the heat. Leave to soak for 2 minutes, then drain well and tip the noodles back into the pan. Cover and keep warm. Heat a heavy-based frying pan until very hot. Brush with a little oil, add the tuna steaks and cook for 2 minutes on each side. Add the soy sauce and balsamic vinegar to the pan and boil vigorously, turning the steaks once, until they become coated in a rich brown glaze. Remove from the heat and keep warm while you finish the salad.

3 Add the sesame seeds, coriander, spring onions, lime zest, green chillies, pickled ginger, the garlic chives, if using, and the watercress to the noodles. Add the dressing and toss everything together.

4 Pile some of the salad into the centre of 4 warmed plates, slice each tuna steak into 3 on the angle and rest on top of the salad. Serve the rest of the salad separately.

char-grilled white tuna on a warm salad of green beans, garlic and tomatoes

SERVES 4
4 x 175–225 g (6–8 oz) pieces of white tuna loin (Albacore)
A little olive oil
Salt and freshly ground black pepper
FOR THE WARM SALAD OF GREEN BEANS:
350 g (12 oz) fine beans, trimmed
2 tablespoons extra virgin olive oil
3 tomatoes, seeded and cut into small dice
1 large garlic clove, finely chopped
½ teaspoon picked thyme leaves

1 For the salad, bring a pan of salted water to the boil. Drop in the beans and cook for 3 minutes or until al dente. Drain, refresh briefly under cold water and drain once more.

2 Heat a ridged cast-iron griddle until it is really hot. Brush the tuna generously on both sides with olive oil and season well with salt and pepper. Put on the griddle and cook for just 2 minutes on each side.

3 Meanwhile, return the beans to the pan and add the extra virgin olive oil, tomatoes, garlic, thyme leaves and some salt and pepper to taste. Gently turn over until heated through.

4 To serve, spoon the beans into the centre of 4 warmed plates and put the tuna on top. Drizzle a little virgin olive oil around the outside of the plate and sprinkle with some coarsely crushed black pepper.

shark vindaloo

SERVES 4

900 g (2 lb) small skinned shark steaks
3–4 tablespoons groundnut or sunflower oil
1 onion, chopped
2 tomatoes, roughly chopped
4 tablespoons Vindaloo Curry Paste (see pages 226)
300 ml (10 fl oz) water
8 small green chillies
Coconut vinegar or white wine vinegar, to taste
Salt

1 Season the shark steaks with salt and set aside. Heat the oil in a large deep frying pan, add the onion and fry until richly browned.

2 Add the tomatoes and cook until they form a deep golden paste.

3 Now stir in the vindaloo paste and fry gently for 5 minutes, stirring, until it has slightly caramelized. Pour in the water and leave the sauce to simmer for 10 minutes, giving it a stir every now and then.

4 Meanwhile, slit the green chillies open along their length and scrape out the seeds but leave them whole.

5 Add the shark steaks and chillies to the sauce and simmer for 10 minutes, carefully turning over the steaks half-way through.

6 Add vinegar and salt to taste and serve with some pilau rice (see the recipe for Herring Recheado on page 160).

VARIATION

monkfish vindaloo

Replace the shark steaks with one 900 g (2 lb) skinned monkfish tail (see page 62), sliced across into 2.5 cm (1 inch) steaks. Add to the sauce and simmer for 10 minutes. Then lift the steaks out onto a plate and boil the sauce rapidly until reduced to a good consistency (monkfish releases a lot more liquid during cooking than shark). Return the steaks to the sauce to reheat and continue as for the main recipe.

ALTERNATIVE FISH
Swordfish, kingfish.

SHARK VINDALOO

char-grilled swordfish kebabs with oregano, olive oil and lemon juice

550 g (1¼ lb) swordfish steaks, cut about
    2.5 cm (1 inch) thick
50 ml (2 fl oz) olive oil
1 teaspoon chopped oregano
Juice of ½ lemon
1 teaspoon Maldon sea-salt flakes
½ teaspoon cracked black peppercorns

1 Cut the swordfish steaks into 2.5 cm (1 inch) square pieces. Mix all the other ingredients together in a bowl. Add the swordfish pieces, mix together well and set aside to marinate at room temperature for 20 minutes. Submerge 8 bamboo skewers in water and leave them to soak too.

2 Thread the pieces of swordfish on to the bamboo skewers and char-grill for 2–3 minutes, turning them as they brown. Serve perhaps with some char-grilled chips (see page 146), or some chips deep-fried in olive oil, and a mixed salad.

kingfish curry

SERVES 4

4 x 175–225 g (6–8 oz) pieces of thick kingfish fillet,
    skinned
3 tablespoons groundnut oil
½ teaspoon black mustard seed
½ teaspoon cumin seed
½ teaspoon fennel seed
¼ teaspoon fenugreek seed
1 onion, thinly sliced
1 quantity Goan Masala Paste (see page 226)
1 teaspoon turmeric powder
6 curry leaves
2 medium-hot red Dutch chillies, seeded and sliced
    across diagonally
12 small okra, topped and tailed
3 tomatoes, skinned and quartered
400 ml (14 fl oz) coconut milk
4 tablespoons Tamarind Water (see page 227)
150 ml (5 fl oz) water
Salt

1 Lightly salt the pieces of fish. Heat the oil in a pan that is just large enough to take the fish in one layer. Add the whole spices and fry them for about 30 seconds, then add the sliced onion and fry until golden.

2 Add the Goan masala paste and turmeric and fry for 3–4 minutes. Add the curry leaves, chillies, okra, tomatoes, coconut milk, tamarind water, water and salt to taste and simmer for 5 minutes.

3 Add the pieces of fish and simmer for another 5 minutes. Serve with steamed basmati rice.

ALTERNATIVE FISH
This also works well with other big fish like shark, tuna, bonito, or some of the really big game fish like marlin or sail fish. But you could make it with pieces of the humble cod too if you wish.

SKATE, EEL

gratin of skate cheeks with cheddar cheese and breadcrumbs

SERVES 4

600 ml (1 pint) milk
1 small onion, peeled and halved
6 cloves
4 bay leaves
4 gratings of fresh nutmeg
2 small sprigs thyme
1 teaspoon black peppercorns
75 g (3 oz) unsalted butter
40 g (1½ oz) plain flour
120 ml (4 fl oz) double cream
550 g (1¼ lb) prepared skate cheeks (see page 35)
75 g (3 oz) mature Cheddar cheese, coarsely grated
25 g (1 oz) coarse white breadcrumbs,
    made from day-old bread
¼ teaspoon cayenne pepper
10 turns of the black pepper mill
Salt and freshly ground white pepper

1 Put the milk into a pan with the onion, cloves, bay leaves, nutmeg, thyme and black peppercorns. Bring to the boil and simmer for 5 minutes. Remove from the heat and set aside for 1 hour to allow the flavours to infuse.

2 Bring the milk back to the boil, then strain through a sieve into a clean pan. Melt 50 g (2 oz) of the butter in a pan, add the flour and cook gently for 2–3 minutes without letting it colour. Gradually stir in the hot milk, then bring to the boil and simmer gently over a very low heat for 10 minutes, giving it an occasional stir, until slightly reduced and thickened. Stir in the cream and season with some salt and freshly ground white pepper to taste.

3 Heat the remaining butter in a large frying pan until foaming. Season the skate cheeks with salt and white pepper, add to the pan and fry briskly for 4 minutes, turning them now and then, until lightly browned and just cooked through.

4 Divide the cheeks between 4 individual gratin dishes and pour over the sauce.

5 Pre-heat the grill to high. Mix the grated cheese with the breadcrumbs, cayenne pepper and black pepper and sprinkle them over each dish. Grill for 2–3 minutes, until crisp and golden. Serve with hot brown toast.

ALTERNATIVE FISH
Large chunks of skinned white fish such as cod, haddock or monkfish.

skate with black butter

SERVES 4

4 x 225 g (8 oz) skinned skate wings (see page 34)
15 g (½ oz) capers in brine, drained and rinsed
FOR THE COURT-BOUILLON:
300 ml (10 fl oz) dry white wine
1.2 litres (2 pints) water
85 ml (3 fl oz) white wine vinegar
2 bay leaves
12 black peppercorns
1 onion, roughly chopped
2 carrots, roughly chopped
2 celery sticks, roughly chopped
1 teaspoon salt
FOR THE BLACK BUTTER:
175 g (6 oz) butter
50 ml (2 fl oz) red wine vinegar
1 tablespoon chopped parsley

1 For the court-bouillon, put all the ingredients into a large pan, bring to the boil and simmer for 20 minutes. Set aside to cool, to allow the flavour to improve before using.

2 Put the skate wings into a large pan. Pour over the court-bouillon, bring to the boil and simmer very gently for 15 minutes, until they are cooked through.

3 Carefully lift the skate wings out of the pan, allow the excess liquid to drain off and then place them on to 4 warmed plates. Sprinkle with the capers and keep warm.

4 For the black butter, melt the butter in a frying pan. As soon as it starts to foam, turn quite brown and smell very nutty, add the vinegar, then the parsley. Let it boil down for a minute or so, until slightly reduced. Pour the butter over the skate and serve straight away.

6

ROASTED SKATE WINGS WITH CHILLI BEANS

roasted skate wings with chilli beans (see technique 17, page 34)

SERVES 4

4 x 225 g (8 oz) prepared skate wings (see page 34)
1 teaspoon paprika
1 teaspoon coarsely crushed black pepper
50 g (2 oz) butter
3 tablespoons sherry vinegar
Salt and freshly ground black pepper

FOR THE CHILLI BEANS:

350 g (12 oz) dried cannellini beans, soaked in cold
    water overnight
2 tablespoons extra virgin olive oil
1 garlic clove, finely chopped
2 medium-hot red Dutch chillies, seeded and finely
    chopped
1 small onion, finely chopped
350 ml (12 fl oz) Chicken Stock (see page 222)
2 beef tomatoes, skinned, seeded and diced
1 teaspoon chopped tarragon

1 Drain the cannellini beans and put them into a pan with plenty of fresh water to cover. Bring to the boil, skimming off any scum as it rises to the surface. Cover and leave to simmer for 1 hour or until just tender. Drain and set aside.

2 Pre-heat the oven to 200°C/400°F/Gas Mark 6. Dry the skate wings with kitchen paper and then sprinkle on both sides with some paprika and coarsely crushed black pepper.

3 For the chilli beans, put the extra virgin olive oil, garlic and red chillies into a pan. As soon as the garlic and chillies start to sizzle, add the onion and cook for 5 minutes until soft. Add the beans and 300 ml (10 fl oz) of the stock and leave them to simmer for 10 minutes.

4 To cook the skate wings, melt the butter in a roasting tin on top of the stove. Add the wings and lightly brown them for 1 minute on either side. Sprinkle with a little salt, transfer to the oven and roast for 10 minutes.

5 Meanwhile, stir the tomatoes into the beans and simmer for a further 10 minutes. Stir in the chopped tarragon and season to taste with some salt and pepper.

6 To serve, spoon some of the beans on to the centre of 4 warmed plates and put one of the roasted skate wings on top. Place the roasting tin over a moderate heat, add the sherry vinegar and the rest of the chicken stock and leave it to boil for a minute or two, scraping up all the crusty bits from the bottom of the tin. Strain the sauce through a fine sieve into a small pan, season to taste and then spoon over the top of the skate.

a poêle of conger eel

SERVES 4

6 garlic cloves
1 x 1.25 kg (2½ lb) piece of skinned conger eel, cut
    from just behind the gut cavity
100 g (4 oz) caul fat or 4 rashers rindless streaky bacon
100 g (4 oz) carrots
100 g (4 oz) celery sticks
50 g (2 oz) butter
100 g (4 oz) button onions, peeled
Salt and freshly ground black pepper

1 Pre-heat the oven to 230°C/450°F/Gas Mark 8. Thinly slice 2 of the garlic cloves. Make small deep incisions all over the piece of conger eel and insert a slice of garlic into each. Then wrap it in the caul fat or bacon and tie in place with some fine string.

2 Cut the carrots and celery into 4 cm (1½ inch) pieces, then cut each piece lengthways into 1 cm (½ inch) batons.

3 Melt the butter in a flameproof casserole dish large enough to take the piece of eel. Add the carrots, celery, onions and the remaining whole garlic cloves, cover and cook gently for 5 minutes.

4 Add the eel and turn it once or twice until it is well coated in butter. Season with some salt and pepper. Cover once more, transfer to the oven and cook for 20 minutes, basting twice with the butter while it cooks.

5 Uncover the casserole, baste once more with the butter and cook for a further 10 minutes.

6 Lift the eel on to a warmed serving plate and spoon the vegetables and juices around it. Carve lengthways into long slices to serve.

anguilles au vert

SERVES 4

300 ml (10 fl oz) Fish Stock (see page 222)

15 g (½ oz) butter

2 large shallots, very finely chopped

½ garlic clove, crushed

1 small sprig thyme

1 small bay leaf

50 ml (2 fl oz) dry vermouth, such as Noilly Prat

25 g (1 oz) spinach leaves, shredded

25 g (1 oz) watercress leaves (stalks removed)

1 tablespoon each chopped tarragon, parsley, chervil and
   chives, plus extra to garnish

25 g (1 oz) sorrel leaves, shredded

¼ loaf of French bread

50 ml (2 fl oz) Clarified Butter (see page 226)

350 g (12 oz) skinned eel fillets (see page 36), cut into
   pieces about 10 cm (4 inches) long

175 ml (6 fl oz) double cream

3 egg yolks

Lemon juice

Salt and freshly ground black pepper

1 For the sauce, boil the fish stock rapidly until reduced to about
4 tablespoons. Melt the butter in another pan, add the shallots, garlic,
thyme and bay leaf and cook gently until soft but not coloured. Add the
reduced fish stock and the vermouth and boil until reduced by about
three-quarters. Discard the thyme and bay leaf. Add the spinach,
watercress and chopped herbs and cook for 2 minutes. Add the sorrel
and just allow it to wilt into the sauce, then tip into a liquidizer and
whizz until smooth. Return the sauce to the pan and set aside.

2 Cut the bread on the diagonal into four long slices, no more than
1 cm (½ inch) thick. Fry the bread pieces in half the clarified butter for a
couple of minutes on each side, until crisp and lightly golden. Keep
warm in a low oven.

3 Pre-heat the grill to high. Brush the pieces of eel with the rest of the
clarified butter and season. Lay on a greased baking tray and grill for
1–1½ minutes. Keep warm.

4 Mix the cream and egg yolks together until smooth, then stir them
into the sauce. Cook over a low heat, stirring, until lightly thickened, but
take care not to get it too hot or it will scramble. Season with a little
lemon juice, salt and pepper to taste and whisk to make it slightly frothy.

5 To serve, put the slices of fried bread on to 4 warmed plates and put
some of the eel pieces on top. Spoon over the sauce and garnish each
plate with a very small bunch of tarragon, parsley, chervil and chives.

ALTERNATIVE FISH

This is a classic eel dish, so eel it's got to be ... or has it? I have a feeling
it would work well with thin fillets of any white fish like plaice, lemon
sole or whiting.

jellied eels

SERVES 4–6

900 g (2 lb) skinned eels (see page 36)

Pared zest and juice of 1 lemon

3 bay leaves

4 cloves

8 black peppercorns

4 teaspoons salt

1 small bunch curly parsley, chopped

Good malt vinegar

Freshly ground white pepper

Brown bread and butter, to serve

1 Cut the spines out from the top and bottom edges of the eels, then
cut them across into 4 cm (1½ inch) pieces.

2 Put the pieces of eel into a large saucepan with the lemon zest, juice,
bay leaves, cloves, peppercorns and salt. Add enough cold water just to
cover, then bring to the boil and simmer for 20 minutes.

3 Transfer the eels and their cooking liquor to a bowl and leave to cool.

4 Stir in the chopped parsley and divide the mixture between 4–6
small pots. Cover and chill until the jelly has set, then serve with the
vinegar, pepper, and bread and butter.

stir-fried eel with black bean sauce (see technique 18, page 36)

SERVES 2

225–275 g (8–10 oz) skinned eel fillet (see page 36)
1½ teaspoons cornflour
1½ tablespoons Chinese fermented salted black beans
½ teaspoon caster sugar
2 tablespoons sesame oil
2 garlic cloves, cut into fine shreds
2.5 cm (1 inch) peeled fresh root ginger, cut into very
   thin shreds
1 medium-hot red Dutch chilli, thinly sliced
3 tablespoons Chinese rice wine or dry sherry
1 teaspoon dark soy sauce
4 spring onions, cut on the diagonal into long thin slices
Salt

1 Cut the eel fillet diagonally into pieces 2.5 cm (1 inch) wide. Toss with a little salt and then the cornflour.

2 Put the black beans, sugar and 2 tablespoons of cold water into a small bowl and crush to a coarse paste.

3 Heat a wok over a high heat until it smoking hot. Add the sesame oil and garlic, quickly followed by the ginger, red chilli and black bean paste. Stir-fry for a few seconds, then add the eel pieces and stir-fry for 1 minute.

4 Add the rice wine or sherry, soy sauce and 3–4 tablespoons of water and cook for 2 minutes, until the eel is cooked through.

5 Add the spring onions to the wok and stir-fry for about a minute. Serve immediately with some steamed rice.

STIR-FRIED EEL WITH BLACK BEAN SAUCE

recipes
chapter 7

large
round fish

cod with
red wine sauce (see technique 4, page 20)

SERVES 4

75 g (3 oz) unsalted butter

4 x 175 g (6 oz) pieces of thick unskinned cod fillet
(see page 20)

50 g (2 oz) carrot, finely chopped

50 g (2 oz) celery, finely chopped

50 g (2 oz) onion, finely chopped

A small pinch of ground allspice

A small pinch of ground cloves

A small pinch of grated nutmeg

A large pinch of curry powder

600 ml (1 pint) red wine

600 ml (1 pint) Chicken Stock (see page 222)

1 teaspoon sugar

1 tablespoon plain flour

Coarse sea salt and freshly ground black pepper

FOR THE LENTILS:

50 g (2 oz) dried Puy lentils

300 ml (10 fl oz) Fish Stock (see page 222)

1 clove and 1 bay leaf

2 slices peeled onion

1/2 teaspoon salt

1 Put all the ingredients for the lentils into a pan and simmer until tender. Drain, remove the clove and bay leaf, then cover and keep warm.

2 Melt 50 g (2 oz) of the butter in a medium-sized pan and brush a little over the cod. Season the fish on both sides with sea salt and a little black pepper and put, skin-side up, on a greased baking tray.

3 For the sauce, add the carrot, celery, onion and spices to the melted butter in the pan and fry over a high heat for about 10 minutes until the vegetables are well browned. Add the red wine, stock, sugar and 1/4 teaspoon of salt, bring to the boil and boil until the sauce is reduced to 175 ml (6 fl oz) and well concentrated in flavour. Strain the reduced sauce into a clean pan and keep warm.

4 Pre-heat the grill to high. Grill the cod for 8 minutes, until the skin is well browned. Meanwhile, mix the remaining 25 g (1 oz) butter with the flour to make a smooth paste (beurre manié). Bring the sauce to the boil and then whisk in the paste, a little at a time. Simmer for 2 minutes until the sauce is smooth and thickened. Adjust the seasoning if necessary.

5 To serve, spoon the lentils on to 4 warmed plates and place the cod on top. Spoon the sauce around the edge of the plate.

fish cakes

SERVES 4

900 g (2 lb) floury potatoes such as Maris Piper or King
    Edward, peeled and cut into chunks
900 g (2 lb) skinned cod fillet
25 g (1 oz) butter, melted
15 g ($\frac{1}{2}$ oz) chopped parsley
Sunflower oil, for deep-frying
50 g (2 oz) seasoned flour
2 eggs, beaten
150 g (5 oz) fresh white breadcrumbs
1 quantity of Tartare Sauce (see page 224)
Salt and freshly ground black pepper

1 Cook the potatoes in boiling salted water for 20 minutes until tender. Drain well, tip back into the pan and mash until smooth. Leave to cool slightly.

2 Bring some water to the boil in a large deep frying pan. Add the fish, bring back to the boil and simmer for 8 minutes. Lift the fish out on to a plate and, when it is cool enough to handle, break it into large flakes, discarding the skin and any bones.

3 Put the fish into a bowl with the mashed potatoes, melted butter, parsley and some salt and pepper and mix together well. Shape the mixture into 8 rounds, about 2.5 cm (1 inch) thick, cover with cling film and chill for 20 minutes.

4 Heat some oil for deep-frying to 180°C (350°F). Put the seasoned flour, beaten eggs and breadcrumbs in 3 separate shallow bowls. Dip the fish cakes into the flour, then into the egg and finally in the breadcrumbs, pressing them on well to give an even coating. Deep-fry in batches for about 4 minutes until crisp and golden. Lift out with a slotted spoon and drain briefly on kitchen paper, then keep warm in a low oven while you cook the rest. Serve with the tartare sauce.

VARIATIONS

salmon fish cakes

Replace the white fish fillet with salmon fillet and replace 1 tablespoon of the chopped parsley with chopped dill.

mackerel fish cakes

Replace the white fish fillet with 900 g (2 lb) whole mackerel. Slash the fish 2–3 times on both sides and grill for 5 minutes on each side. Leave to cool and then flake the flesh, discarding the skin and bones. Replace the parsley with 2 tablespoons of chopped fennel herb and beat in with 1 tablespoon of Pernod or Ricard.

coley and smoked salmon fish cakes

Replace the white fish fillet with 750 g (1½ lb) coley fillet and 150 g (5 oz) finely chopped smoked salmon. Replace the chopped parsley with 2 tablespoons of chopped fresh dill. Poach the coley as for the main recipe and mix into the mashed potatoes with the smoked salmon and dill.

fish and chips with tartare sauce

SERVES 4

240 g (8½ oz) plain flour
3½ teaspoons baking powder
270 ml (9 fl oz) ice-cold water
900 g (2 lb) floury potatoes, such as Maris Piper
Sunflower oil, for deep-frying
4 x 175 g (6 oz) pieces of thick cod fillet, cut from the
    head end, not the tail
1 quantity Tartare Sauce (see page 224)
Salt and freshly ground black pepper

1 To make the batter, mix the flour, 1 teaspoon of salt and the baking powder with the water. Keep cold and use within 20 minutes of making.

2 Pre-heat the oven to 150°C/300°F/Gas Mark 2. Line a baking tray with plenty of kitchen paper and set aside.

3 Peel the potatoes and cut them lengthways into chips 1 cm (½ inch) thick. Pour some sunflower oil into a large deep pan until it is about a third full and heat it to 130°C (260°F). Drop half the chips into a frying basket and cook them for about 5 minutes, until tender when pierced with the tip of a knife but not coloured. Lift them out and drain off the excess oil. Repeat with the rest of the chips and set aside.

4 To fry the fish, heat the oil to 160°C (325°F). Season the cod fillets with salt and pepper and then dip into the batter. Fry, 2 pieces at a time, for 7–8 minutes, until crisp and golden brown. Lift out and drain on the paper-lined tray. Keep hot in the oven while you cook the other 2 pieces.

5 Raise the temperature of the oil to 190°C (375°F) and cook the chips in small batches for about 2 minutes, until they are crisp and golden. Lift them out of the pan and give them a shake to remove the excess oil, then drain on kitchen paper and keep them hot while you cook the rest. Sprinkle with salt and serve them with the deep-fried cod and tartare sauce.

large round fish

grilled cod on spring onion mash with a soy butter sauce

SERVES 4

4 x 175–225 g (6–8 oz) pieces of unskinned thick cod fillet

Maldon sea-salt flakes and freshly ground black pepper

A little melted butter, for brushing

FOR THE SPRING ONION MASH:

1.25 kg (2$^1\!/_2$ lb) Maris Piper potatoes, peeled and cut into chunks

50 g (2 oz) butter

1 bunch spring onions, trimmed and thinly sliced

A little milk

Salt and freshly ground white pepper

FOR THE SOY BUTTER SAUCE:

600 ml (1 pint) Chicken Stock (see page 222)

2 tablespoons dark soy sauce

75 g (3 oz) unsalted butter

1 tomato, skinned, seeded and diced

1 heaped teaspoon chopped coriander

1 Put the fish, skin-side down, in a shallow dish and sprinkle with 1 teaspoon of salt. Set aside for 30 minutes.

2 Rinse the salt off the fish and dry well on kitchen paper. Brush each piece with melted butter and put them skin-side up on a greased baking tray or the rack of the grill pan. Sprinkle the skin with a few sea-salt flakes and some coarsely crushed black pepper.

3 For the spring onion mash, cook the potatoes in boiling unsalted water for 20 minutes until tender.

4 Meanwhile for the sauce, put the chicken stock and soy sauce into another pan and boil it rapidly until it has reduced by half.

5 Pre-heat the grill to high. Grill the cod for 8 minutes on one side only.

6 Just before the fish is ready, add the butter to the sauce and whisk until it has blended in. Remove from the heat and add the tomato and chopped coriander.

7 Drain the potatoes and, when the steam has died down, return them to the pan and mash until smooth. Heat the butter in another pan, add the spring onions and turn them over in the butter for a few seconds. Beat them into the potato with a little milk and some salt and ground white pepper to taste.

8 To serve, spoon the spring onion mash into the centre of 4 warmed plates. Rest the cod on top and spoon the sauce around the outside of the plate.

grilled cod with lettuce hearts and a rich chicken and tarragon dressing

SERVES 4

550 g (1$^1\!/_4$ lb) piece of skinned thick cod fillet

1.2 litres (2 pints) Chicken Stock (see page 222)

A few tarragon stalks

2 garlic cloves, peeled but left whole

2 tablespoons extra virgin olive oil

100 g (4 oz) asparagus tips

4 soft round lettuces

12 very thin slices of pancetta

1 teaspoon chopped chives

1 teaspoon chopped tarragon

1$^1\!/_2$ teaspoons white wine vinegar

Salt and freshly ground black pepper

1 Put the cod into a shallow dish and sprinkle liberally with salt. Set aside for 20 minutes. Meanwhile, put the chicken stock, tarragon stalks and garlic cloves into a large pan and boil until reduced to about 85 ml (3 fl oz) and nicely concentrated in flavour. Strain into a small clean pan and keep warm.

GRILLED COD WITH LETTUCE HEARTS AND A RICH CHICKEN AND TARRAGON DRESSING

2 Rinse the salt off the fish and dry well on kitchen paper. Brush with a little of the olive oil, season with some pepper and place on a lightly oiled baking tray.

3 Cook the asparagus tips in boiling salted water until just tender. Drain, refresh and keep warm. Remove the outside leaves from each lettuce until you get down to the pale green hearts. Cut each one into quarters.

4 Pre-heat the grill to high, then grill the cod for about 10–12 minutes. Put the slices of pancetta over the fish and grill for 1–2 minutes, until it is crisp and lightly golden.

5 Put the quartered lettuce hearts in the centre of 4 warmed plates. Break the pancetta into small pieces and the cod into chunky flakes. Arrange the cod around the lettuce with the pancetta and asparagus. Sprinkle over the chopped chives and tarragon. Spoon the warm chicken stock over the lettuce and a little over the rest of the plate. Whisk the remaining olive oil, the vinegar and some seasoning together, drizzle over the plate and serve straight away.

ALTERNATIVE FISH
I particularly like thick fillets of flaky fish for this. Haddock would be a good alternative, of course, but salmon would work well, too.

FISH PIE

fish pie

SERVES 4

1 small onion, thickly sliced
2 cloves
1 bay leaf
600 ml (1 pint) milk
300 ml (10 fl oz) double cream
450 g (1 lb) unskinned cod fillet
225 g (8 oz) undyed smoked cod or haddock fillet
4 eggs
100 g (4 oz) butter
45 g (1¾ oz) plain flour
5 tablespoons chopped flat-leaf parsley
Freshly grated nutmeg
1.25 kg (2½ lb) peeled floury potatoes such as Maris Piper or King Edward
1 egg yolk
Salt and freshly ground white pepper

1 Stud a couple of the onion slices with the cloves. Put the onion slices in a large pan with the bay leaf, 450 ml (15 fl oz) of the milk, the cream, cod and smoked fish. Bring just to the boil and simmer for 8 minutes.

Lift the fish out on to a plate and strain the cooking liquor into a jug. When the fish is cool enough to handle, break it into large flakes, discarding the skin and any bones. Sprinkle it over the base of a shallow 1.75 litre (3 pint) ovenproof dish.

2 Hard-boil the eggs for 8 minutes, then drain and leave to cool. Peel them, cut into chunky slices and arrange on top of the fish.

3 Melt 50 g (2 oz) of the butter in a pan, add the flour and cook for 1 minute. Take the pan off the heat and gradually stir in the reserved cooking liquor. Return it to the heat and bring slowly to the boil, stirring all the time. Leave it to simmer gently for 10 minutes to cook out the flour. Remove from the heat once more, stir in the parsley and season with nutmeg, salt and white pepper. Pour the sauce over the fish and leave to cool. Chill in the fridge for 1 hour.

4 Boil the potatoes for 15–20 minutes. Drain, mash and add the rest of the butter and the egg yolk. Season with salt and freshly ground white pepper. Beat in enough of the remaining milk to form a soft spreadable mash.

5 Pre-heat the oven to 200°C/400°F/Gas Mark 6. Spoon the potato over the filling and mark the surface with a fork. Bake for 35–40 minutes, until piping hot and golden brown.

ALTERNATIVE FISH
Try making this with haddock and smoked haddock or, if you live in Australia, substitute flat-head for the unsmoked fish.

COD,
HADDOCK

taramasalata (see technique 45, page 69)

SERVES 4

100 g (4 oz) stale white bread
175 g (6 oz) prepared smoked cod's roe (see page 69)
1 garlic clove, crushed
1 thin slice onion
2 tablespoons lemon juice
6 tablespoons olive oil
Black olives and lemon wedges, to garnish
Lightly toasted pitta bread or crusty bread, to serve

1 Remove the crusts from the white bread and leave it to soak in cold water for 10 minutes.

2 Lift the bread out of the water and squeeze out the excess. Put it into a food processor with the smoked cod's roe, garlic, onion and lemon juice and blend for 2 minutes until smooth.

3 With the motor still running, gradually add the olive oil as you would for mayonnaise. Transfer the mixture to a shallow serving dish, cover and chill for 1 hour. Serve garnished with the olives and lemon wedges, with some lightly toasted pitta bread or chunks of crusty bread.

brandade de morue (see technique 42, page 67)

SERVES 4–6

12 thin slices French bread
150 ml (5 fl oz) olive oil
450 g (1 lb) Fresh Salted Cod (see pages 67 and 227), soaked
3 garlic cloves, crushed
175 ml (6 fl oz) double cream
Lemon juice and freshly ground black pepper, to taste
Black olives and chopped flat-leaf parsley, to garnish

1 Fry the slices of French bread in 2 tablespoons of the olive oil for a minute or two on either side until golden brown. Drain briefly on kitchen paper and keep warm in a low oven.

2 Drain the soaked salted cod and remove the skin and any bones. Put it into a pan with enough fresh water to cover, bring to the boil and simmer for 5 minutes. Lift out with a slotted spoon, drain away the excess water and then put into a food processor.

3 Put the garlic, remaining olive oil and cream into a small pan and bring to the boil. Add to the fish and blend together until just smooth. Season to taste with lemon juice and plenty of black pepper, but only add salt if necessary.

4 Spoon the mixture into a warmed serving dish and arrange the fried bread slices around the outside of the dish. Garnish with the black olives and parsley and serve warm.

tortilla of salt cod with sweet onions and potatoes

SERVES 6

350 g (12 oz) Fresh Salted Cod (see pages 67 and 227), soaked
85 ml (3 fl oz) extra virgin olive oil
1 large onion, thinly sliced
450 g (1 lb) potatoes, peeled and cut into chunky matchsticks
8 eggs
3 tablespoons chopped flat-leaf parsley
Salt and freshly ground black pepper

TORTILLA OF SALT COD WITH SWEET ONIONS AND POTATOES

1 Drop the salted cod into a pan of boiling water and simmer for about 6–8 minutes or until just cooked. Lift out and, when cool enough to handle, break it into large flakes, discarding the skin and any bones.

2 Heat the oil in a deep 23 cm (9 inch) well-seasoned or non-stick frying pan. Add the onion and cook over a medium heat for 3–4 minutes. Add the potatoes and cook, stirring now and then, for 15 minutes or until just tender. Add the flaked fish and a little seasoning and turn everything over once or twice to distribute the ingredients evenly. Beat the eggs with the parsley and a little salt and pepper. Pour them into the pan and cook over a very low heat for about 15 minutes, until almost set.

3 Pre-heat the grill to high. Put the pan under the grill for 2–3 minutes, until the tortilla is lightly browned on top. Cut it into wedges and serve warm.

ALTERNATIVE FISH

All fish from the cod family, such as haddock, hake, pollack or coley, are pleasant to eat when salted. I think the cheaper the fish, the more appropriate it is for salting. Pollack, for example, is much better salted than as a fresh fish.

mild potato curry topped with smoked haddock and a poached egg

SERVES 4

4 x 100 g (4 oz) pieces of undyed smoked haddock fillet
2 teaspoons white wine vinegar
4 eggs
Sprigs of coriander, to garnish

FOR THE POTATO CURRY:

350 g (12 oz) waxy main-crop potatoes such as Wilja, peeled and cut into 1 cm (1/2 inch) dice
2 tablespoons sunflower oil
1/2 teaspoon yellow mustard seeds
1/4 teaspoon turmeric powder
100 g (4 oz) onions, finely chopped
2 tomatoes, peeled and chopped
1 teaspoon roughly chopped coriander
Salt and freshly ground black pepper

1 For the potato curry, cook the potatoes in boiling salted water for 6–7 minutes until tender, then drain. Meanwhile, heat the oil in a pan, add the mustard seeds and, when they begin to pop, add the turmeric and onions. Fry for 5 minutes or until the onions are soft and lightly browned. Add the potatoes and some salt and pepper and fry for 1–2 minutes. Add the tomatoes and cook for 1 minute. Stir in the chopped coriander, set aside and keep warm.

2 Bring about 5 cm (2 inches) of water to the boil in a shallow pan. Add the pieces of smoked haddock, bring back to a simmer and poach for 4 minutes. Lift out with a slotted spoon, cover and keep warm.

3 Discard the fish poaching liquor, pour another 5 cm (2 inches) of water into the pan and bring to a very gentle simmer; the water should be just trembling and there should be a few bubbles rising up from the bottom of the pan. Add the vinegar, break in the eggs and poach for 3 minutes. Lift out with a slotted spoon and drain briefly on kitchen paper.

4 To serve, spoon the potato curry into the centre of 4 warmed plates. Remove the skin from each piece of haddock and put it on top of the potatoes. Put a poached egg on top of the fish and garnish with the sprigs of coriander.

smoked haddock kedgeree

SERVES 4

25 g (1 oz) butter
1 small onion, chopped
2 green cardamom pods, split open
¹/₄ teaspoon turmeric powder
2.5 cm (1 inch) piece of cinnamon stick
1 bay leaf, very finely shredded
350 g (12 oz) basmati rice
600 ml (1 pint) Chicken Stock (see page 222)
2 eggs
450 g (1 lb) undyed smoked haddock fillet
2 tablespoons chopped flat-leaf parsley, plus a few
  sprigs to garnish
Salt and freshly ground black pepper

1 Melt the butter in a large pan, add the onion and cook over a medium heat for 5 minutes, until soft but not browned. Add the cardamom pods, turmeric, cinnamon stick and shredded bay leaf and cook, stirring, for 1 minute.

2 Add the rice and stir for about 1 minute, until it is well coated in the spicy butter. Add the stock and ½ teaspoon of salt and bring to the boil. Cover the pan with a close-fitting lid, lower the heat and leave it to cook very gently for 15 minutes.

3 Meanwhile, hard-boil the eggs for 8 minutes. Bring some water to the boil in a large shallow pan, add the smoked haddock and simmer for 4 minutes, until the fish is just cooked. Lift the fish out on to a plate and leave until cool enough to handle, then break it into flakes, discarding the skin and any bones (see page 39). Drain the eggs, cool slightly, then peel and cut into small pieces.

4 Uncover the rice and gently fork in the fish and the chopped eggs. Cover again and return to the heat for 5 minutes or until the fish has heated through. Then gently stir in the chopped parsley and season with a little more salt and black pepper to taste. Serve garnished with sprigs of parsley.

braised haddock with mussels, spinach and chervil

SERVES 4

150 g (5 oz) butter
1 shallot, finely chopped
600 ml (1 pint) mussels, cleaned (see page 88)
4 x 175 g (6 oz) pieces of unskinned haddock fillet
900 g (2 lb) fresh spinach, washed, large stalks removed
1 tablespoon malt whisky
1 teaspoon lemon juice
1 teaspoon chopped chervil
Salt and freshly ground black pepper

1 Heat 25 g (1 oz) of the butter in a medium pan, add the shallot and cook gently for 3 minutes, until soft. Add the mussels and 150 ml (5 fl oz) of water, then cover and cook over a high heat for 3-4 minutes, until the mussels have opened. Tip them into a colander set over a bowl to collect the cooking liquor. When they are cool enough to handle, remove the mussels from all but 8 of the nicest shells. Cover and set aside.

2 Pour all the mussel liquor except the last tablespoon or two (which might be gritty) into a 30 cm (12 inch) sauté pan, bring to a simmer and then add the haddock, skin-side up. Cover and simmer gently for 3 minutes. Remove from the heat (leaving the lid in place) and set aside for about 4 minutes to continue cooking.

3 Meanwhile, melt another 25 g (1 oz) of the butter in a large pan. Add the spinach and stir over a high heat until it has wilted. Cook, stirring briskly, until all the excess liquid has evaporated, then season to taste with some salt and pepper.

4 Divide the spinach between 4 warmed plates and put the haddock on top. Keep warm. Return the sauté pan to the heat, add the remaining butter and boil rapidly for 3-4 minutes, until the liquor has reduced and emulsified into a sauce. Stir in the whisky and lemon juice and boil for 30 seconds. Add the chervil and mussels and stir for a few seconds, until they have heated through.

5 Spoon the mussels around the spinach and haddock, dividing the unshelled mussels equally between the plates, then pour over the sauce and serve.

HADDOCK

EGGS BENEDICT WITH SMOKED HADDOCCK

OMELETTE ARNOLD BENNETT

eggs benedict with smoked haddock

SERVES 4

¹/₂ quantity of Hollandaise Sauce (see page 223)

300 ml (10 fl oz) milk

3 bay leaves

2 slices onion

6 black peppercorns

4 x 100 g (4 oz) pieces of thick undyed smoked
   haddock fillet

1 tablespoon white wine vinegar

4 eggs

2 English muffins

Coarsely crushed black peppercorns and a few chopped
   chives, to garnish

1 Make the hollandaise sauce and keep it warm, off the heat, over a pan of warm water. Bring the milk and 300 ml (10 fl oz) of water to the boil in a shallow pan. Add the bay leaves, onion, peppercorns and smoked haddock pieces, bring back to a simmer and poach for 4 minutes (see page 38). Lift the haddock out on to a plate, peel off the skin and keep warm.

2 Bring about 5 cm (2 inches) of water to the boil in a medium-sized pan, add the vinegar and reduce it to a gentle simmer. Break the eggs into the pan one at a time and poach for 3 minutes. Meanwhile, slice the muffins in half and toast them until lightly browned. Lift the poached eggs out with a slotted spoon and drain briefly on kitchen paper.

3 To serve, place the muffin halves on to 4 warmed plates and top with the haddock and poached eggs. Spoon over the hollandaise sauce and garnish with a sprinkling of crushed black pepper and chopped chives.

omelette arnold bennett

SERVES 2

300 ml (10 fl oz) milk

3 bay leaves

2 slices onion

6 black peppercorns

275 g (10 oz) undyed smoked haddock fillet

6 eggs

20 g (³/₄ oz) unsalted butter

2–3 tablespoons double cream

2 tablespoons freshly grated Parmesan cheese

Salt and freshly ground black pepper

1 Mix the milk with 300 ml (10 fl oz) of water, pour it into a large shallow pan and bring to the boil. Add the bay leaves, onion slices and peppercorns and bring to the boil. Add the smoked haddock, bring back to a gentle simmer and poach for about 3–4 minutes, until the fish is just cooked. Lift the fish out on to a plate and leave until cool enough to handle, then break it into flakes, discarding any skin and bones (see page 38).

2 Pre-heat the grill to high. Whisk the eggs together with some seasoning. Heat a 23–25 cm (9–10 inch) non-stick frying pan over a medium heat, then add the butter and swirl it around to coat the base and sides of the pan. Pour in the eggs and, as they start to set, drag the back of a fork over the base of the pan, lifting up little folds of egg to allow the uncooked egg to run underneath.

3 When the omelette is set underneath but still very moist on top, sprinkle over the flaked smoked haddock. Pour the cream on top, sprinkle with the Parmesan cheese and put the omelette under the hot grill until lightly golden brown. Slide it on to a warmed plate and serve with a crisp green salad, if you wish.

grilled hake with spring onion mash and morel mushroom sauce

SERVES 4

4 x 175–225 g (6–8 oz) pieces of thick unskinned hake fillet

A little melted butter, for brushing

Maldon sea-salt flakes and coarsely crushed black pepper

FOR THE SPRING ONION MASH:

1.25 kg (2¹/₂ lb) Maris Piper potatoes, peeled and cut into chunks

50 g (2 oz) butter

1 bunch spring onions, trimmed and thinly sliced

A little milk

Salt and freshly ground white pepper

FOR THE MOREL MUSHROOM SAUCE:

75 g (3 oz) unsalted butter

50 g (2 oz) each finely chopped onion, carrot, celery and leek

1 tablespoon Laphroaig whisky

1 tablespoon balsamic vinegar

1.2 litres (2 pints) Fish Stock (see page 222)

15 g (¹/₂ oz) dried porcini mushrooms

7 g (¹/₄ oz) dried morel mushrooms

1 teaspoon chopped celery herb or celery tops

1 For the sauce, melt 40 g (1½ oz) of the unsalted butter in a shallow pan. Add the onion, carrot, celery and leek and cook over a high heat, stirring until nicely coloured. Take the pan off the heat, add the whisky and balsamic vinegar and let them boil away to almost nothing. Add 1 litre (1¾ pints) of the fish stock and the dried porcini mushrooms, bring to the boil and leave to simmer for 30 minutes.

2 Meanwhile, put the dried morel mushrooms and the remaining fish stock into a small pan. Bring to the boil, take off the heat and leave them to soak for 20 minutes, or until soft. Strain, reserving the soaking liquor, and slice the mushrooms into rounds.

3 Strain the stock through a fine sieve into a clean pan and add the reserved mushroom-soaking liquor. Bring to the boil and boil rapidly until reduced to about 175 ml (6 fl oz) and well concentrated in flavour. Keep warm. Meanwhile, for the spring onion mash, cook the potatoes in boiling salted water for 20 minutes until tender.

4 Brush each piece of hake with melted butter and put them skin-side up on the rack of the grill pan. Sprinkle the skin with a few sea-salt flakes and some coarsely crushed black pepper. Pre-heat the grill to high.

5 Grill the hake for 8 minutes. Drain the potatoes and, when the steam has died down, return them to the pan and mash until smooth. Heat the butter in another pan, add the spring onions and turn them over in the butter for a few seconds. Beat them into the potato with a little milk and some salt and white pepper to taste. Keep warm.

6 Whisk the remaining butter, the chopped celery herb or celery tops and some seasoning to taste into the sauce, then stir in the sliced morel mushrooms.

7 Spoon the spring onion mash into the centre of 4 warmed plates and put the hake on top. Spoon the sauce around the outside of the plate and serve.

HAKE

hake en papillote with oven-roasted tomatoes and tapenade (see technique 32, page 53)

SERVES 4

Olive oil, for brushing

2 tablespoons finely shredded basil leaves

4 x 175–225 g (6–8 oz) pieces of thick unskinned hake fillet

4 tablespoons Tapenade (see page 226)

Salt and freshly ground black pepper

FOR THE OVEN-ROASTED TOMATOES:

750 g (1½ lb) ripe plum tomatoes

½ teaspoon Maldon sea-salt flakes

1 teaspoon thyme leaves

1 For the oven-roasted tomatoes, pre-heat the oven to 240°C/475°F/Gas Mark 9. Cut the tomatoes in half and place them cut-side up in a lightly oiled shallow roasting tin. Sprinkle over the sea-salt flakes, thyme leaves and some pepper and roast for 15 minutes. Lower the oven temperature to 150°C/300°F/Gas Mark 2 and roast them for a further 1½ hours until shrivelled to about half their original size and concentrated in flavour. Remove and leave to cool. These can be done in advance if you wish.

2 Raise the oven temperature to 240°C/475°F/Gas Mark 9 again. Prepare the paper and foil squares as described on page 53. Put 3 pieces of tomato slightly off-centre on each square and sprinkle over the basil. Season the pieces of hake on both sides with salt and pepper and put them on top of the tomatoes. Seal the parcels (see page 53), place them on a baking sheet and bake for 15 minutes.

3 Serve the papillotes on a large plate and slit them open at the table so that everyone can enjoy the aroma. Place the contents on to 4 warmed plates and spoon around some of the tapenade.

ALTERNATIVE FISH

Any thick fillets of good-sized fish such as cod, haddock, salmon and even large sea bass or other grouper-type fish would work well cooked in this way.

simon hopkinson's warm hake with thinned mayonnaise and capers

SERVES 4

1 quantity Basic Court-bouillon (see page 223)

1.75 kg (4 lb) piece of hake on the bone

1 small garlic clove, finely chopped

450 g (1 lb) tinned flageolet beans, drained and rinsed

2 large tomatoes, skinned, seeded and finely diced

2 teaspoons tarragon vinegar

2 tablespoons olive oil

1 tablespoon small capers, rinsed

A few tarragon leaves, to garnish

A pinch of cayenne pepper

Salt and freshly ground black pepper

FOR THE MAYONNAISE:

2 egg yolks

1 teaspoon Dijon mustard

A few dashes of Tabasco sauce

2 teaspoons dry white wine vinegar

150 ml (5 fl oz) sunflower oil

150 ml (5 fl oz) olive oil

Leaves from 4 sprigs tarragon, finely chopped

1 Make the mayonnaise as described on page 224. Stir in the tarragon and set aside.

2 Bring the court-bouillon to the boil in a large pan. Add the hake, bring back to the boil, cover and turn off the heat. Leave to poach for 20–30 minutes.

3 Put the garlic, flageolet beans, tomatoes, vinegar, olive oil and some seasoning together in a pan and warm through gently until hot, but do not let the mixture boil.

4 To serve, pour the beans into a warmed, large, oval serving dish. Lift the hake on to a board or large plate and remove the skin. Carefully lift off the fillets and lay them on top of the beans. Stir 1–2 tablespoons of the warm court-bouillon into the mayonnaise to give it a good coating consistency. Spoon it over the fish, then sprinkle over the capers and the tarragon leaves. Dust with a little cayenne pepper and serve.

ALTERNATIVE FISH

Sea bass, cod.

braised ling with lettuce, peas and crisp smoked pancetta

SERVES 4

4 x 175–225 g (6–8 oz) pieces of thick ling fillet, skinned
100 ml (3½ fl oz) Chicken Stock (see page 222)
100 g (4 oz) butter
12 large salad onions, trimmed and cut into
    2.5 cm (1 inch) pieces
4 Little Gem lettuce hearts, cut into quarters
350 g (12 oz) fresh peas or frozen petits pois
8 very thin slices smoked pancetta or rindless smoked
    streaky bacon
1 tablespoon chopped chervil or parsley
Salt and freshly ground white pepper

1 Season the pieces of ling with some salt. Bring the chicken stock to the boil in a small pan and keep hot.

2 Melt half the butter in a wide shallow casserole dish, add the onions and cook gently for 2–3 minutes, until tender but not browned. Add the quartered lettuce hearts and turn them over once or twice in the butter. Add the peas, hot chicken stock and some salt and pepper and simmer rapidly for 3–4 minutes, turning the lettuce hearts now and then, until the vegetables have started to soften and about three-quarters of the liquid has evaporated. Put the pieces of ling on top of the vegetables, then cover and simmer for 7–8 minutes, until the fish is cooked through.

3 Shortly before the fish is cooked, heat a ridged cast-iron griddle over a high heat and grill the pancetta or bacon for about 1 minute on each side, until crisp and golden. Keep warm.

4 Uncover the casserole dish, dot the remaining butter around the pan and sprinkle the chopped chervil or parsley over the vegetables. Shake the pan over the heat until the butter has melted and amalgamated with the cooking juices to make a sauce. Garnish the fish with the grilled pancetta, take the dish to the table and serve with some small new potatoes.

LING, COLEY

BRAISED LING WITH LETTUCE, PEAS AND CRISP SMOKED PANCETTA

salt ling, tomato and potato pasties

MAKES 9

550 g (1¼ lb) commercially prepared salt ling, salt cod or 750 g (1½ lb) Fresh Salted Cod (see pages 67 and 227), soaked

1.5 kg (3 lb) chilled fresh puff pastry

225 g (8 oz) plum tomatoes, roughly chopped

275 g (10 oz) peeled potatoes, cut into small pieces

1 medium onion, cut into quarters and thinly sliced

100 g (4 oz) chorizo sausage, finely diced

2 garlic cloves, finely chopped

15 g (½ oz) chopped fresh parsley

Salt and freshly ground black pepper

2 tablespoons olive oil or 25 g (1 oz) butter, melted

1 egg, beaten

1 Rinse the excess salt off the commercial salt ling or salted cod and place it in a large mixing bowl. Cover with plenty of cold water and leave to soak for 24–48 hours, changing the water now and then.

2 The next day, divide the pastry into 9 pieces and roll each piece out on a lightly floured surface. Cut out 19 cm (7½ inch) circles, using a small plate as a template, and keep cool while you prepare the filling.

3 Drain the soaked fish and remove the skin and any bones. Cut the flesh into 2.5 cm (1 inch) pieces and mix in a bowl with the tomatoes, potatoes, onion, chorizo, garlic, parsley, a little salt and plenty of black pepper. Gently stir in the olive oil or melted butter.

4 Divide the fish mixture between the pastry circles, distributing the pieces of fish as evenly as you can. Brush one half of the pastry edge with a little beaten egg, bring the sides together over the top of the filling and pinch together really well to seal. Crimp the edge of each pasty decoratively between your fingers, transfer them to a lightly greased baking sheet and chill for 20 minutes.

5 Pre-heat the oven to 200°C/400°F/Gas Mark 6. Brush the pasties with some of the remaining beaten egg and bake for approximately 50 minutes or until crisp and richly golden.

VARIATIONS:

crab pasties with leek and saffron

MAKES 6

Soak ¼ teaspoon saffron strands in 2 teaspoons hot water for 5 minutes. Mix in a bowl with 550 g (1 lb 2 oz) white crab meat, 100 g (4 oz) brown crab meat, 350 g (12 oz) thinly sliced leek, 75 g (3 oz) fresh white breadcrumbs, 1½ teaspoons salt, 15 turns of the white pepper mill and 40 g (1½ oz) melted butter. Fill and bake as above.

thai fish cakes with green beans (*tod man pla*)

SERVES 4

450 g (1 lb) coley fillets, skinned and cut into chunks

1 tablespoon Thai fish sauce (*nam pla*)

1 tablespoon Thai Red Curry Paste (see page 226)

1 kaffir lime leaf or 1 strip of lime zest, very finely shredded

1 tablespoon chopped coriander

1 egg

1 teaspoon palm sugar or muscovado sugar

½ teaspoon salt

40 g (1½ oz) French beans, thinly sliced into rounds

150 ml (5 fl oz) groundnut or sunflower oil

FOR THE SWEET-AND-SOUR CUCUMBER SAUCE:

50 ml (2 fl oz) white wine vinegar

100 g (4 oz) caster sugar

1½ tablespoons water

2 teaspoons Thai fish sauce (*nam pla*)

50 g (2 oz) cucumber, very finely diced

25 g (1 oz) carrot, very finely diced

25 g (1 oz) onion, very finely chopped

2 red birdseye chillies, thinly sliced

1 For the sauce, gently heat the vinegar, sugar and water in a small pan until the sugar has dissolved. Bring to the boil and boil for 1 minute, then remove from the heat and leave to cool. Stir in the fish sauce, cucumber, carrot, onion and chillies. Pour into 4 small dipping saucers or ramekins and set aside.

2 For the fish cakes, put the fish in a food processor with the fish sauce, curry paste, kaffir lime leaf or lime zest, chopped coriander, egg, sugar and salt. Process until smooth, then stir in the sliced green beans.

3 Divide the mixture into 16 pieces. Roll each one into a ball and then flatten into a 6 cm (2½ inch) disc. Heat the oil in a large frying pan and fry the fish cakes in batches for 1 minute on each side, until golden brown. Lift out and drain on kitchen paper, then serve with the sweet-and-sour cucumber sauce.

large round fish

a feast of mahi mahi, tortillas and salsa de tomate verde

SERVES 4

1 Romaine lettuce heart, thinly sliced across
2 avocados, halved, skinned and sliced
3 tomatoes, cut into small dice
1 red onion, halved and very thinly sliced
8 fresh corn tortillas
750 g (1 1/2 lb) mahi mahi, sea bass or John Dory fillets, skinned
A little sunflower oil
Salt and freshly ground black pepper

FOR THE SALSA DE TOMATE VERDE:

2 tomatillos or green tomatoes
2 jalapeño or green Dutch chillies
1 garlic clove, roughly chopped
1 small onion, roughly chopped
1 tablespoon chopped coriander
A little freshly squeezed lime juice (if you are using green tomatoes)

1 For the salsa, peel the papery husks off the tomatillos, if using. Drop them or the green tomatoes and the chillies into a pan of boiling water. Simmer for 10 minutes, then strain and cool slightly. Tip them into a food processor and add the rest of the salsa ingredients and a little lime juice if you have used green tomatoes instead of tomatillos. Pulse the mixture for a few seconds until you have a fairly smooth sauce with a little bit of texture. Season with salt and spoon into a serving bowl.

2 Put the shredded lettuce, avocados, tomatoes and onion into 5 other small serving bowls.

3 To reheat the tortillas, stack them on a plate, cover with a tea towel and cook in the microwave on high for about 30 seconds. Alternatively, heat a dry frying pan over a medium heat. Add a tortilla, leave it for a seconds, then turn it over, adding a second tortilla on top of it. After a few seconds, turn them over together and add a third one to the pan. Continue like this until all your tortillas are in the pan, then remove them and wrap them in a napkin. Keep them warm in a low oven while you cook the fish.

4 Pre-heat the grill to high. Cut the mahi mahi fillets into short, chunky strips. Toss them with a little oil and plenty of seasoning, spread them out on a baking tray and cook them for about 2 minutes on one side only until just cooked through.

5 Transfer the fish strips to a warmed serving plate and take it to the table with all the other bits and pieces. Leave everyone to fill their own tortillas with whatever they fancy.

steamed wolf fish with mild greens, soy and sesame oil

SERVES 4

4 x 175 g (6 oz) pieces of thick wolf fish or cod fillet, skinned
2 thin slices peeled fresh root ginger, cut into fine julienne
8 small heads of pak choi
4 teaspoons roasted sesame oil
6–8 teaspoons dark soy sauce
2 spring onions, halved and very finely shredded
Salt

1 Season the fish on both sides with a little salt, then place the pieces side by side in a steamer over about 1 cm (1/2 inch) of water (see page 46) and sprinkle the ginger on top.

2 Cut the heads of pak choi lengthways into quarters and put them in a second steamer. Cover and steam the fish for 2–3 minutes or until just cooked through, and the pak choi for 3–4 minutes until tender.

3 Put the pak choi on 4 warmed plates and sprinkle over the sesame oil and soy sauce. Put the fish on top, spoon a tablespoon of the fish-steaming liquor over each piece of fish and garnish with the shredded spring onions.

deep-fried flathead with chopped mushrooms and walnuts

SERVES 4

750 g (1½ lb) skinned flathead, cod, halibut or monkfish fillet

4 tablespoons Mayonnaise (see page 224), made with olive oil

4 tablespoons warm water

6 good-quality green olives, stones removed and thinly sliced

Sunflower oil, for deep-frying

150 g (5 oz) chestnut or button mushrooms, wiped clean and very finely chopped

100 g (4 oz) lightly toasted walnut pieces, very finely chopped

50 g (2 oz) plain flour

2 eggs, beaten

1 tablespoon chopped flat-leaf parsley

Salt and freshly ground black pepper

Sprigs of flat-leaf parsley, to garnish

1 Cut the fish fillets across into 1 cm (½ inch) thick slices. Season with a little salt and pepper. Put the mayonnaise, warm water and sliced green olives into a small pan and set aside.

2 Heat some oil for deep-frying to 180°C (350°F). Mix the finely chopped mushrooms and toasted walnuts together on a large plate. Season the flour, put it on another plate and whisk the eggs together in a shallow bowl.

3 Pat the pieces of flathead dry on kitchen paper. Dip 4–6 pieces at a time in the flour, then beaten egg and finally the mushroom and walnut mixture, pressing it on well to give a thick even coating. Lower them into the hot oil and cook for 3 minutes until crisp and golden. Lift on to a baking tray lined with kitchen paper and keep hot in a low oven while you cook the rest.

4 Very gently heat the mayonnaise mixture in the pan until it feels warm to your little finger, but not hot. Do not let it boil or it will curdle. Stir in the parsley and season to taste with some salt and pepper.

5 Arrange the pieces of flathead in the centre of 4 warmed plates. Spoon some of the sauce around the edge of the plate and garnish with a sprig of fresh parsley.

braised red emperor fillet with olive oil, tomatoes, capers and olives

SERVES 4

4 x 175 g (6 oz) pieces thick red emperor fillet, skinned

10 good-quality black olives in olive oil

4 tablespoons olive oil

150 ml (5 fl oz) water

Juice of ½ lemon

3 medium-sized vine tomatoes, seeded and roughly chopped

1 teaspoon small capers, drained and rinsed

2 tablespoons chopped flat-leaf parsley

Salt and freshly ground black pepper

1 Season the pieces of red emperor on each side with a little salt and pepper. Cut 4 slices from each black olive and discard the stones.

2 Heat the oil in a large deep frying pan. Add the red emperor and sear for 2 minutes on each side until lightly coloured. Lower the heat, add the water, lemon juice and ½ teaspoon of salt and bring up to a simmer.

3 Cover and cook over a gentle heat for 2 minutes until the fish is just cooked through.

4 Lift the pieces of fish out on to a plate, cover and keep warm. Bring the juices in the pan up to a vigorous boil. Throw in the olives, chopped tomatoes, capers and chopped parsley and boil for 30 seconds more.

5 Put the pieces of fish on to 4 warmed plates, spoon over the sauce and serve.

ALTERNATIVE FISH

Red emperor, one of Australia's best-flavoured fish, could successfully be substituted with sea bass, John Dory or even turbot.

whole salmon baked in foil with tarragon (see technique 31, page 52)

SERVES 4

50 g (2 oz) butter, melted
1 x 1.5 kg (3 lb) salmon, cleaned and
    trimmed (see page 14)
1 small bunch tarragon, roughly chopped
120 ml (4 fl oz) dry white wine
Juice of ½ lemon
Salt and freshly ground black pepper
1 quantity Beurre Blanc (see pages 223–4), to serve

1 Pre-heat the oven to 220°C/425°F/Gas Mark 7. Brush the centre of a large sheet of foil with some of the melted butter. Place the salmon in the centre and bring the edges of the foil up around the fish slightly. Put the open parcel on to a large baking sheet.

2 Mix the tarragon with the rest of the melted butter, plus the wine, lemon juice, salt and pepper. Spoon the mixture into the cavity of the fish and over the top. Bring the sides of the foil up over the fish and pinch together, folding over the edges a few times to make a loose airtight parcel. Bake for 30 minutes.

3 Remove the fish from the oven and open up the parcel. If you wish, remove the skin as follows: cut through the skin just behind the head and above the tail and lift it off. Carefully turn the fish over and repeat on the other side (see page 38).

4 Lift the salmon on to a warmed serving dish and serve with the beurre blanc and some boiled new potatoes.

ALTERNATIVE FISH
Large sea bass, snapper,
sea trout or the Atlantic
trout from Australia.

salmon en croûte with currants and ginger (see technique 29, page 50)

SERVES 6

2 x 550 g (1¼ lb) pieces of skinned salmon fillet, taken
    from behind the gut cavity of a 3–4 kg
    (7–9 lb) fish (see page 28, steps 1 and 2)
100 g (4 oz) unsalted butter, softened
4 pieces of stem ginger in syrup, well drained and finely
    diced
25 g (1 oz) currants
½ teaspoon ground mace
750 g (1½ lb) chilled puff pastry
1 egg, beaten, to glaze
Salt and freshly ground black pepper

1 Season the salmon fillets well on both sides with salt. Mix the softened butter with the stem ginger, currants, mace, ½ teaspoon of salt and some black pepper. Spread the inner face of 1 salmon fillet evenly with the butter mixture and then lay the second fillet on top.

2 Cut the pastry in half and, on a lightly floured surface, roll out 1 piece into a rectangle about 4 cm (1½ inches) bigger than the salmon all the way around – approximately 18 × 33 cm (7 × 13 inches). Roll out the second piece into a rectangle 5 cm (2 inches) larger than the first one all the way round.

3 Lay the smaller rectangle of pastry on a well-floured baking sheet and place the salmon in the centre. Brush a wide band of beaten egg around the salmon and lay the second piece of pastry on top, taking care not to stretch it. Press the pastry tightly around the outside of the salmon,

SALMON EN CROÛTE WITH
CURRANTS AND GINGER

SALMON

trying to ensure that you have not trapped in too much air, and then press the edges together well.

4 Trim the edges of the pastry neatly to leave a 2.5 cm (1 inch) band all the way around. Brush this once more with egg. Mark the edge with a fork and decorate the top with a fish scale effect by pressing an upturned teaspoon gently into the pastry, working in rows down the length of the parcel. Chill for at least an hour.

5 Pre-heat the oven to 200°C/400°F/Gas Mark 6 and put in a large baking sheet to heat up. Remove the salmon en croûte from the fridge and brush it all over with beaten egg.

6 Take the hot baking sheet out of the oven and carefully transfer the salmon parcel on to it. Return it to the oven and bake for 35–40 minutes.

7 Remove the salmon from the oven and leave it to rest for 5 minutes. Transfer it to a warmed serving plate and take it to the table whole. Cut it across into slices to serve.

escalopes of salmon with sorrel sauce (see technique 11, page 28)

SERVES 4

750 g (1¹/₂ lb) salmon fillet, taken from a good-sized salmon
2 tablespoons sunflower oil
Salt
FOR THE SORREL SAUCE:
600 ml (1 pint) Fish Stock (see page 222)
175 ml (6 fl oz) double cream
50 ml (2 fl oz) dry vermouth, such as Noilly Prat
25 g (1 oz) sorrel leaves, washed and dried
75 g (3 oz) unsalted butter
2 teaspoons lemon juice

1 Cut the salmon fillet into 12 escalopes (see page 28). Brush each one with oil, season with a little salt and lay on a lightly oiled baking tray.

2 For the sauce, put the fish stock, 85 ml (3 fl oz) of the cream and the vermouth into a large saucepan and boil vigorously until reduced to 175 ml (6 fl oz). Meanwhile, remove the stalks from the sorrel leaves and slice the leaves very thinly. When the sauce has reduced to the required amount, add the remaining cream, the butter and lemon juice and simmer until it has thickened slightly and reached a good sauce consistency. Meanwhile, pre-heat the grill to high.

ESCALOPES OF SALMON WITH SORREL SAUCE

3 Stir all but a pinch of the sorrel into the sauce, season to taste and keep warm. Grill the salmon escalopes for about 30 seconds to 1 minute until only just firm.

4 To serve, spoon some of the sauce into the centre of 4 warmed plates. Slightly overlap 3 escalopes on top of the sauce and serve sprinkled with the remaining shredded sorrel.

VARIATION

champagne and chive sauce

Melt 7 g (¼ oz) of unsalted butter in a medium-sized saucepan. Add 1 finely chopped shallot and cook gently, without colouring, until soft. Add 100 ml (4 fl oz) champagne and boil for 2 minutes. Add 600 ml (1 pint) fish stock and ½ teaspoon of caster sugar and boil rapidly until reduced by three-quarters to about 175 ml (6 fl oz). Add 50 ml (2 fl oz) double cream, bring back to the boil and simmer until it has reached a good sauce consistency. Keep warm. Whisk together another 50 ml (2 fl oz) double cream with 1 tablespoon of champagne and 2 teaspoons of chopped chives until it forms soft peaks. When you are ready to serve, bring the sauce back to the boil, whisk in 20 g (¾ oz) unsalted butter, then the whipped cream mixture. Overlap the escalopes in the centre of each warmed plate and pour the sauce around. Sprinkle with a few chopped chives and serve immediately, while the sauce is still foaming.

salmon steaks with muscadet, watercress and dill potatoes

SERVES 4

750 g (1½ lb) large new potatoes, scrubbed
1 small bunch dill
4 x 200 g (7 oz) salmon steaks
25 g (1 oz) Clarified Butter (see page 226)
50 ml (2 fl oz) Muscadet or another dry white wine
120 ml (4 fl oz) Fish Stock or Chicken Stock (see page 222)
50 g (2 oz) unsalted butter
1 tablespoon chopped parsley
75 g (3 oz) watercress, large stalks removed
2 tablespoons extra virgin olive oil
1 teaspoon white wine vinegar
Salt and freshly ground black pepper

1 Cut each potato lengthways into 4 or 6 pieces. Cook in some boiling salted water with 2 sprigs of the dill for 10 minutes or until tender.

2 Meanwhile, pre-heat the oven to 200°C/400°F/Gas Mark 6. Season the salmon steaks on both sides with some salt and pepper. Heat the clarified butter in an oven-proof frying pan. Add the salmon and cook for 1–2 minutes on each side until lightly browned.

3 Remove the pan from the heat and leave to cool for 30 seconds. Then pour over the wine, transfer the pan to the oven and cook for 5 minutes.

4 Remove the salmon from the oven and lift the steaks on to a plate. Keep warm. For the sauce, pour the fish or chicken stock into the frying pan, bring to the boil and add the unsalted butter. Boil rapidly until the liquid has reduced by half. Add the parsley and adjust the seasoning if necessary.

5 To serve, arrange the salmon steaks, watercress and potatoes on 4 warmed plates. Mix together the olive oil, vinegar and ½ teaspoon of salt. Pour the dressing over the watercress, pour the sauce over the salmon and serve.

pavés of salmon with roasted tomatoes and fennel (see technique 12, page 29)

SERVES 4

4 x 175 g (6 oz) prepared pavés of salmon (see page 29)
Olive oil, for brushing
A splash of white wine
FOR THE ROASTED TOMATOES AND FENNEL:
450 g (1 lb) small vine-ripened tomatoes
Olive oil, for brushing
Maldon sea-salt flakes
Cracked black peppercorns
3 large fennel bulbs, trimmed
FOR THE SAUCE VIERGE:
120 ml (4 fl oz) Cabernet Sauvignon vinegar
½ teaspoon fennel seeds, lightly crushed
½ teaspoon black peppercorns, coarsely crushed
150 ml (5 fl oz) extra virgin olive oil
A good pinch of Maldon sea-salt flakes

1 For the roasted tomatoes and fennel, pre-heat the oven to 220°C/425°F/Gas Mark 7. Cut the tomatoes in half horizontally and lay them, cut-side up, in a lightly oiled, shallow roasting tin. Sprinkle over some salt and pepper and roast them for 10 minutes. Lower the oven temperature to 150°C/300°F/Gas Mark 2 and roast for a further hour or until they have shrivelled to about half their original size and are well concentrated in flavour. Cut the fennel down through the root into thin slices. Lay in a single layer in a lightly oiled roasting tin and roast at 180°C/350°F/Gas Mark 4 for 35–40 minutes until softened and with a good colour. Remove both from the oven and keep warm.

2 For the sauce vierge, put the vinegar, fennel seeds and black pepper into a small pan and boil until reduced to 2 tablespoons. Add the olive oil, season to taste with some Maldon salt and set aside.

3 Brush the pieces of salmon on both sides with olive oil and season with salt and pepper. Heat a ridged cast-iron griddle until smoking-hot. Add the salmon, skinned-side down, and sear until it has taken on a good golden colour. Sprinkle over some wine, leave to sizzle for a few seconds and then turn. Cook for 30 seconds, then remove from the heat and leave them to continue cooking in the residual heat of the pan for another 30 seconds or so.

4 To serve, arrange some of the fennel slices attractively in the centre of each plate. Rest the salmon on top and then arrange a few tomatoes around the fish. Spoon some of the dressing (make sure you take up some of the vinegar reduction with the oil) around the edge of the plate and serve.

gravlax (dill-cured salmon) (see technique 41, page 66)

SERVES 6

2 x 750 g (1½ lb) unskinned salmon fillets

1 large bunch dill, roughly chopped

100 g (4 oz) coarse sea salt

75 g (3 oz) white sugar

2 tablespoons crushed white peppercorns

FOR THE HORSERADISH AND MUSTARD SAUCE:

**2 teaspoons finely grated horseradish
(fresh or from a jar)**

2 teaspoons finely grated onion

1 teaspoon Dijon mustard

1 teaspoon caster sugar

2 tablespoons white wine vinegar

A good pinch of salt

175 ml (6 fl oz) double cream

1 Put one of the salmon fillets, skin-side down, on to a large sheet of cling film. Mix the dill with the salt, sugar and crushed peppercorns and spread it over the cut face of the salmon. Place the other fillet on top, skin-side up.

2 Tightly wrap the fish in 2 or 3 layers of cling film and lift it on to a large, shallow tray. Rest a slightly smaller tray or chopping board on top of the fish and weigh it down. Refrigerate for 2 days, turning the fish every 12 hours so that the briny mixture, which has developed inside the parcel, bastes the outside of the fish.

3 For the horseradish and mustard sauce, stir together all the ingredients except for the cream. Whip the cream into soft peaks, stir in the horseradish mixture, cover and chill.

4 To serve, remove the fish from the briny mixture and slice it as you would smoked salmon (see page 66). Arrange a few slices of the gravlax on each plate and serve with some of the sauce.

GRAVLAX

tetsuya wakuda's confit of salmon (see technique 28, page 49)

SERVES 4

**350 g (12 oz) skinned salmon fillet,
taken from a large fish (see page 28,
steps 1 and 2)**
100 ml (3½ fl oz) grapeseed oil
80 ml (2½ fl oz) olive oil
½ tablespoon freshly ground coriander seed
½ teaspoon freshly ground white pepper
10 whole basil leaves
3 sprigs thyme
½ teaspoon finely chopped garlic
25 g (1 oz) each finely chopped carrot and celery
3 tablespoons chopped chives
4 tablespoons finely chopped dried kombu (Japanese kelp)
2 tablespoons keta (salmon roe)
Salt

FOR THE FENNEL SALAD:

½ bulb of fennel
1 teaspoon lemon juice
½ teaspoon Lemon Olive Oil (see page 227)
Salt and freshly ground black pepper

FOR THE PARSLEY OIL:

A large handful of flat-leaf parsley leaves
100 ml (3½ fl oz) olive oil
½ teaspoon small salted capers, rinsed and drained

1 Cut the salmon fillet across into 65–90 g (2½–3½ oz) pieces (each piece should not weigh more than 100 g/4 oz). Put the grapeseed oil, olive oil, coriander, pepper, basil leaves, thyme and garlic into a small, shallow dish. Immerse the pieces of salmon in the mixture, cover and leave to marinade in the fridge for a few hours.

2 To cook the fish, pre-heat the oven to 110°C/225°F/Gas Mark ¼. Take the fish out of the marinade and allow it to come back to room temperature. Spread the chopped vegetables on to a small baking tray and put the pieces of salmon on top, ensuring that they don't come into contact with the tray.

3 Cook the salmon in the oven for 8–10 minutes, brushing it occasionally with the flavoured oil. The flesh should not change colour at all, but remain a brilliant orange-red. It should be lukewarm to the touch, and when you press the end part, your finger should just go through the flesh.

4 Remove the fish from the oven and allow it to cool down to room temperature. Meanwhile, for the parsley oil, put the parsley leaves into a liquidizer and blend together. Add the capers and blend once more.

5 For the fennel salad, finely slice the fennel on a mandolin. Toss with the lemon juice, lemon oil and some seasoning to taste.

6 To serve, sprinkle the top of the salmon with the chives, dried kombu and a little salt. Put some of the the fennel salad into the centre of each plate and put the salmon on top. Drizzle a little parsley oil around the plate and then dot the keta at regular intervals around the salmon.

poached salmon with mayonnaise, new potatoes and cucumber salad (see technique 19, page 38)

SERVES 4

1 quantity Basic Court-bouillon (see page 223)
**1 x 1.5–1.75 kg (3–4 lb) salmon or coral trout, cleaned
and trimmed (see page 14)**
750 g (1½ lb) new potatoes, scraped
3 sprigs mint
1 cucumber
1 tablespoon white wine vinegar
**1 quantity Mayonnaise (see pages 224), made with
olive oil**
Salt

1 Put the ingredients for the court-bouillon into a fish kettle, bring to the boil and simmer for 20 minutes. Then carefully lower the salmon into the court-bouillon, bring back to a gentle simmer and poach gently for 16–18 minutes.

2 Meanwhile, boil the potatoes in salted water with one of the mint sprigs until tender, then drain and keep warm.

3 Peel the cucumber and slice it as thinly as possible, preferably on a mandolin. Chop the leaves from the remaining mint sprigs and mix with the cucumber, the white wine vinegar and a pinch of salt.

4 Lift the salmon, still sitting on the trivet, out of the fish kettle and allow any excess water to drain away. Carefully lift it off the trivet with 2 fish slices and put it on a serving plate.

5 Remove the skin by making a shallow cut through the skin along the backbone and around the back of the head and carefully peeling it back. Carefully turn the fish over and repeat on the other side.

6 To serve, run a knife down the length of the fish between the 2 fillets and gently ease them apart and away from the bones. Lift portion-sized pieces of the salmon on to each plate, then turn the fish over and repeat. Serve with the new potatoes, mayonnaise and cucumber salad.

grilled fillet of hapuku with roasted wild mushrooms and a cider vinegar butter sauce

SERVES 4

4 x 175–225 g (6–8 oz) pieces of unskinned hapuku, sea bass or grey mullet fillet

15 g (1/2 oz) butter, melted

FOR THE ROASTED WILD MUSHROOMS:

5 slices dried porcini mushroom

3 tablespoons warm water

350 g (12 oz) mixed wild mushrooms

Leaves from 1 sprig thyme

3 tablespoons olive oil

Salt and freshly ground black pepper

FOR THE CIDER VINEGAR BUTTER SAUCE:

50 ml (2 fl oz) good-quality cider vinegar

175 g (6 oz) chilled unsalted butter, cut into small pieces

1 For the roasted mushrooms, pre-heat the oven to 200°C/400°F/Gas Mark 6. Put the dried porcini mushroom slices into a small bowl, cover with the warm water and leave to soak for 10 minutes. Meanwhile, brush any dirt off the wild mushrooms with a pastry brush and trim away the base of the stems. Thickly slice the mushrooms and put them in a small roasting tin. Lift the porcini mushrooms out of their soaking liquor and thinly slice them. Add them to the wild mushrooms with the thyme leaves, olive oil, salt and pepper and 3 tablespoons of the soaking liquor. Toss together well, spread out over the base of the tin and roast in the oven for 15 minutes. Meanwhile, pre-heat the grill to high.

2 Brush the pieces of hapuku with melted butter and season on both sides with some salt and pepper. Put, skin-side up, on a lightly buttered baking tray or the rack of the grill pan.

3 After the mushrooms have been cooking for 7 minutes, grill the hapuku for 6–7 minutes. Meanwhile, for the sauce, bring the vinegar to the boil in a small pan. Whisk in the butter, a few pieces at a time, until you have a smooth, emulsified sauce. Season to taste with salt and pepper.

4 Spoon the roasted wild mushrooms into the centre of 4 warmed plates and put the hapuku on top. Spoon a little of the sauce over the fish and the rest around the outside edge of the plate. Serve with some boiled new potatoes.

grilled mulloway with asparagus and a cream and caviar sauce (see technique 43, page 68)

SERVES 4

4 x 175 g (6 oz) pieces of thick unskinned mulloway or hake fillet

15 g (1/2 oz) butter, melted

225–350 g (8–12 oz) fresh asparagus

Salt and freshly ground black pepper

FOR THE CREAM AND CAVIAR SAUCE:

600 ml (1 pint) Fish Stock (see page 222)

50 ml (2 fl oz) dry vermouth, such as Noilly Prat

85 ml (3 fl oz) double cream

1 teaspoon lemon juice

1 heaped teaspoon caviar

1 For the sauce, put the stock, vermouth and cream into a wide-based pan. Boil rapidly until it has reduced by three-quarters to about 175 ml (6 fl oz). Keep warm.

2 Pre-heat the grill to high. Brush the mulloway fillets on both sides with melted butter and season with some salt and pepper. Put, skin-side up, on a lightly greased baking tray or the rack of the grill pan.

3 Bring about 2.5 cm (1 inch) of water to the boil in a large deep frying pan. Trim off and discard the woody ends of the asparagus and put on a petal steamer.

4 Grill the fish for 7–8 minutes or until just cooked through. Just before the fish is ready, put the petal steamer into the shallow pan, cover and steam the asparagus for 3–4 minutes until just tender.

5 To serve, put the asparagus in the centre of 4 warmed plates and put the fish on top. Whisk the lemon juice, caviar and some seasoning to taste into the sauce, spoon a little around the edge of each plate and serve.

char-grilled king snapper with lemon, thyme and charmoula

SERVES 4

4 x 175 g (6 oz) pieces of king snapper, red snapper or
   large John Dory fillet
2 tablespoons extra virgin olive oil
Pared zest of 1 lemon, finely chopped
3 bay leaves, finely shredded
Leaves from 3 sprigs thyme
1 teaspoon dried chilli flakes
1/2 teaspoon Maldon sea-salt flakes

FOR THE CHARMOULA:

2 tablespoons roughly chopped coriander
3 garlic cloves, chopped
1 1/2 teaspoons ground cumin
1/2 medium-hot red Dutch chilli, seeded and chopped
1/2 teaspoon saffron strands
4 tablespoons extra virgin olive oil
Juice of 1 lemon
1 1/2 teaspoons paprika
1 teaspoon salt

FOR THE CHAR-GRILLED CHIPS:

900 g (2 lb) floury main-crop potatoes, such as
   Maris Piper
2 tablespoons olive oil, plus extra for cooking
2 large garlic cloves, finely chopped
Leaves from 2 sprigs thyme
Salt and freshly ground black pepper

1 For the char-grilled chips, cut the potatoes lengthways into chunky wedges. Drop them into a pan of boiling salted water, bring back to the boil and drain. Leave to cool slightly and then toss in a bowl with the olive oil, garlic, thyme leaves and some seasoning.

2 For the snapper, mix the olive oil, lemon zest, bay leaves, thyme leaves, chilli flakes and Maldon salt together in a shallow dish. Add the pieces of snapper and turn them over once or twice to coat them well with the mixture.

3 Meanwhile, put all the ingredients for the charmoula into a food processor and blend until smooth. Transfer to a bowl and stir in some seasoning to taste.

4 Heat a ridged cast-iron griddle over a high heat until smoking hot. Drizzle with a little oil, lay the chips diagonally across the griddle, lower the heat and cook in batches for 4–5 minutes on each side until crisp and golden brown. Transfer to a serving dish and keep hot in a low oven.

5 Lift the pieces of snapper out of the marinade and place skin-side down on to the griddle. Cook for 3–4 minutes, then turn over and cook for another 1–2 minutes or until cooked through.

6 Lift the snapper on to warmed serving plates and spoon over some of the charmoula. Pile some of the chips alongside and serve.

char-grilled snapper with a mango, prawn and chilli salsa

SERVES 4

4 x 175 g (6 oz) pieces of unskinned snapper fillet
Extra virgin olive oil
Salt and freshly ground black pepper
Coriander sprigs, to garnish

FOR THE SALSA:

2 large medium-hot red Dutch chillies
100 g (4 oz) peeled cooked tiger prawns, thickly sliced
4 spring onions, thinly sliced
1 small garlic clove, finely chopped
1 ripe but firm avocado, peeled and cut into small dice
1/2 ripe but firm mango, peeled and cut into small dice
Juice of 1 lime
A pinch of salt

1 If you are using a barbecue, light it 30–40 minutes before you want to cook the fish.

2 For the salsa, cut the chillies in half lengthways and scrape out the seeds with the tip of a small knife but leave the ribs behind to give the salsa a little more heat. Cut them across into thin slices. Then simply mix all the ingredients together.

3 If you are not cooking the fish on a barbecue, put a ridged cast-iron griddle over a high heat or pre-heat the grill to high. Brush the snapper fillets on both sides with olive oil and season well with salt and pepper. Cut each one into 3, slightly on the diagonal.

4 Cook the pieces of snapper either skin-side down on the griddle or barbecue, or skin-side up under the grill, for 3–4 minutes.

5 To serve, spoon the salsa on to 4 plates and arrange the grilled strips of fish on top. Drizzle a little oil around the edge of the plate and garnish with coriander sprigs.

ALTERNATIVE FISH
Red mullet, sea bass, bream, John Dory or grey mullet.

CHAR-GRILLED SNAPPER WITH A MANGO, PRAWN AND CHILLI SALSA

baked sea bass with roasted red peppers, tomatoes, anchovies and potatoes

(see technique 27, page 48)

(see technique 27, page 48)

SERVES 4

A good pinch of saffron strands
900 g (2 lb) potatoes, peeled and cut into 1 cm
    (1/2 inch) slices
4 plum tomatoes, skinned and cut lengthways into
    quarters
50 g (2 oz) anchovy fillets in oil, drained
150 ml (5 fl oz) Chicken Stock (see page 222)
4 red peppers, each one seeded and cut into 8 chunks
8 garlic cloves, each sliced into 3
8 small sprigs oregano
85 ml (3 fl oz) olive oil
1 x 1.5–1.75 g (3–4 lb) sea bass, striped bass or kingfish,
    cleaned and trimmed (see page 14)
Salt and freshly ground black pepper

SEA BASS
SEA TROUT

1 Pre-heat the oven to 200°C/400°F/Gas Mark 6. Place the saffron in a tea cup, pour over 2 tablespoons of hot water and leave to soak.

2 Put the potatoes in a pan of boiling salted water and par-boil for 7 minutes. Drain well and arrange them in a narrow strip over the base of a roasting dish large enough to hold the sea bass either lengthways or diagonally. The potatoes should form a bed for the fish, leaving plenty of room on either side for the red peppers.

3 Scatter the tomatoes and anchovy fillets over the potatoes, then pour over the saffron water and stock. Scatter the pieces of red pepper down either side of the potatoes and sprinkle over the garlic, oregano sprigs and olive oil. Season everything well with salt and pepper and bake in the oven for 30 minutes.

4 Slash the fish 5–6 times down each side and then slash it in the opposite direction on just one side to give an attractive criss-cross pattern. Rub it generously with some olive oil, season well with salt and pepper and then rest it on top of the potatoes.

5 Return the dish to the oven and bake for a further 35 minutes, until the fish is cooked through. Serve with the roasted vegetables.

BAKED SEA BASS WITH ROASTED RED PEPPERS,
TOMATOES, ANCHOVIES AND POTATOES

braised sea trout fillets with white wine and basil (see technique 24, page 44)

(see technique 24, page 44)

SERVES 4

75 g (3 oz) butter
75 g (3 oz) carrots, very thinly sliced
75 g (3 oz) celery, very thinly sliced
75 g (3 oz) leeks, very thinly sliced
85 ml (3 fl oz) dry white wine
600 ml (1 pint) Chicken Stock (see page 222)
4 x 150 g (5 oz) pieces of skinned sea trout fillet
A handful of very finely shredded basil leaves, plus sprigs
    of basil to garnish
1 teaspoon lemon juice
Salt and freshly ground black pepper

1 Melt 50 g (2 oz) of the butter in a shallow pan large enough to hold the fish in one layer. Stir in the carrots, celery and leeks, cover and cook gently over a medium heat for about 3 minutes.

2 Add the wine and stock to the pan and simmer, uncovered, until almost all the liquid has evaporated but the vegetables are still moist.

3 Lay the sea trout fillets on top, season with some salt and pepper and sprinkle over half the basil. Cover and simmer very gently for 8–10 minutes, or until the fish is just cooked through.

4 Put the fish on to 4 warmed plates and keep warm. If there is a little too much liquid left in the pan, boil rapidly until the juices have reduced and the sauce is glistening. Stir in the rest of the butter, the lemon juice and the rest of the basil and adjust the seasoning if necessary. Spoon the sauce over the fish and garnish with basil sprigs.

ALTERNATIVE FISH
Salmon or king trout fillets.

marinated sea trout with lime and pink peppercorns

SERVES 4

1 x 225 g (8 oz) piece of unskinned sea trout fillet
120 ml (4 fl oz) sunflower oil
7 g (¼ oz) fresh root ginger, very finely chopped
1 teaspoon pink peppercorns in brine, drained and rinsed
Finely grated zest and juice of 1 lime
½ teaspoon salt

1 Put the sea trout fillet, skin-side down, on to a chopping board and slice it as you would gravlax or smoked salmon (see page 66).

2 Flatten the slices slightly and arrange them over the base of 4 dinner plates, overlapping them very slightly.

3 Mix together the rest of the ingredients. Five minutes before serving, drizzle the dressing over the fish and spread it out with the back of a teaspoon. Serve immediately.

large round fish

sea bass baked in a salt crust with lemon sauce and a potato, tomato and basil confit (see technique 30, page 51)

SERVES 4

2 x 750g (1½ lb) sea bass, gutted but not scaled or
   trimmmed (see page 14)

1.75 g (4 lb) cooking salt

2 egg whites

FOR THE LEMON SAUCE:

600 ml (1 pint) Fish Stock (see page 222)

1 tablespoon fennel seeds

1 small lemon, sliced

120 ml (4 fl oz) dry white wine

1 egg

1 egg yolk

300 ml (10 fl oz) olive oil

Salt and freshly ground black pepper

FOR THE POTATO, TOMATO AND BASIL CONFIT:

50 ml (2 fl oz) olive oil

1 small onion, finely chopped

1 garlic clove, finely chopped

450 g (1 lb) waxy new potatoes, peeled and cut into
   quarters

1 beefsteak tomato or 2 large plum tomatoes, skinned
   and chopped

2 tablespoons finely shredded basil

1 Pre-heat the oven to 200°C/400°F/Gas Mark 6. For the sauce, put the fish stock, fennel seeds, sliced lemon and white wine into a pan and boil rapidly until the liquid has reduced to about 4 tablespoons. Strain into a small bowl and leave to cool. Put the whole egg, egg yolk, reduced stock mixture and some salt and pepper into a liquidizer. With the motor running, gradually pour in the oil to make a thick, mayonnaise-like mixture. Transfer to a bowl and season to taste.

SEA BASS BAKED IN A SALT CRUST WITH LEMON SAUCE AND A
POTATO, TOMATO AND BASIL CONFIT

2 For the potato confit, heat the olive oil in a pan, add the onion and garlic and cook for 5 minutes until soft and lightly browned. Add the potatoes, tomato and basil and cook gently for 25 minutes or until the potatoes are tender.

3 While the potatoes are cooking, mix the salt with the egg whites. Spread a thick layer of the mixture in the bottom of a large, ovenproof frying pan or small roasting tin. Put the sea bass on top and then cover completely with the remaining salt mixture, making sure that there are no gaps (but don't worry if the tail is still exposed). Bake in the oven for 20 minutes.

4 Remove the fish from the oven and crack the top of the salt crust with the back of a large knife. Lift the crust away from the top of the fish and then carefully transfer the fish to a serving plate, leaving behind the rest of the salt crust.

5 Pull the skin away from the top of the fish and gently lift the fillets off the bones (see pages 38–9) on to 4 warmed serving plates. Season the potato, tomato and basil confit with some salt and pepper and spoon alongside the fish together with some of the lemon sauce.

3 Lift the char fillet out of the brine and dry it on kitchen paper. Rest a sushi mat (or something else that is flat and permeable and will let the smoke through) on top of the chopsticks and lay the fish on top. Cover the wok or pan with a lid and smoke the fish for 3–4 minutes.

4 Remove the mat of fish from the pan and, with a palette knife, carefully lift the fish off the mat on to a board. Cut into 4 even-sized pieces.

5 For the chive dressing, set aside 4 of the chives for a garnish and finely chop the remainder. Mix them with the shallot, olive oil, vinegar and salt.

6 Heat a ridged cast-iron griddle until smoking-hot. Brush the pieces of smoked char with a little oil, place diagonally on to the griddle and cook for 30 seconds on each side until it is lightly marked by the ridges and the centre of the fish is just warm.

7 Spoon some of the dressing into the centre of 4 plates and put the pieces of arctic char on top. Garnish with the reserved chives and serve immediately.

char-grilled lightly smoked arctic char with chive dressing (see technique 40, page 64)

SERVES 4

1 x 350–450 g (12 oz–1 lb) arctic char or sea trout
   fillet, skinned
1 small bunch chives
1 small shallot, finely chopped
85 ml (3 fl oz) extra virgin olive oil
1 tablespoon white wine vinegar
1/2 teaspoon salt
Hardwood sawdust, for smoking

FOR THE LIGHT BRINE:

50 g (2 oz) salt
600 ml (1 pint) water

1 Make the brine by dissolving the salt in the water. Pour it into a shallow dish, add the arctic char fillet, cover and leave for 20 minutes.

2 To smoke the arctic char, put a 2.5 cm (1 inch) layer of hardwood sawdust into the bottom of a wok or chef's pan. Rest 6 wooden chopsticks over the top of the sawdust, to act as a platform. Place the pan over a high heat until the sawdust starts to smoke, then reduce the heat to low.

roast stuffed monkfish with saffron, lemon, tomato and capers

SERVES 6

1 x 1.5 kg (3 lb) monkfish tail, skinned and boned (see page 62)
1 tablespoon black peppercorns, coarsely crushed
1 tablespoon roughly chopped thyme
1 tablespoon Maldon sea-salt flakes
Salt and freshly ground black pepper

FOR THE STUFFING:

A good pinch of saffron strands
50 g (2 oz) can anchovy fillets in oil, drained
1/2 Preserved Lemon (see page 227), cut into thin slices
1 Roasted Red Pepper (see page 227), seeded and torn into wide strips
4–5 sun-dried tomatoes in oil, drained and thinly sliced
2 tablespoons olive oil

FOR THE SAUCE:

175 ml (6 fl oz) Fish Stock (see page 222)
2 tablespoons extra virgin olive oil
15 g (1/2 oz) butter
1 tablespoon lemon juice
1 tablespoon chopped flat-leaf parsley
1 tablespoon capers in brine, drained and rinsed

1 Pre-heat the oven to 220°C/400°F/Gas Mark 6. Mix the saffron for the stuffing with 2 teaspoons of warm water and set to one side.

2 To remove the bone from the monkfish tail, but still keeping the fillets attached, put the fish on to a board with the side with the bone sticking out more facing upwards. Carefully cut along either side of the bone, keeping the fillets attached where you can on the underside. Trim away the membrane from the outside of the fillets as described on page 62.

3 Season the cavity of the fish from which the bone was removed with a little salt and pepper. Lay the anchovy fillets at regular intervals along the cut face of each fillet, followed by the slices of preserved lemon, pieces of roasted red pepper and finally the sun-dried tomatoes. Sprinkle over the saffron water and a little of the olive oil and then bring the sides up together so that you trap all the stuffing in place. Tie the fish at 2.5 cm (1 inch) intervals along its length with fine string.

4 Sprinkle the crushed black peppercorns, thyme and sea salt over the base of a small roasting tin. Add the monkfish and turn it over in the mixture so that it takes on an even coating. Now turn it right-side up again and sprinkle over the rest of the olive oil.

5 Roast the monkfish for 25 minutes, then remove from the oven and transfer to a serving plate. Slice it across, between the pieces of string, into slices 2.5 cm (1 inch) thick. Keep warm while you make the sauce.

6 Place the roasting tin over a medium heat and add the fish stock. Bring to the boil, scraping up all the bits and pieces from the bottom of the tin as you do so. Strain the juices into a small pan and add any juices from the serving plate, plus the extra virgin olive oil, butter and lemon juice. Bring to the boil and leave it to boil vigorously for about 4 minutes, until it has reduced slightly and emulsified. Remove from the heat and stir in the parsley, capers and 1/2 teaspoon of salt. Spoon the sauce around the fish and serve.

ALTERNATIVE FISH

Substitute 2 thick loin fillets from a large cod, stuff them in the same way and then tie them together gently with plenty of fine string, as you would a rolled joint of meat. It will not be as firm as the monkfish but will taste just as good. You will probably be able to break it apart with a fork to serve.

roast monkfish with crushed potatoes, olive oil and watercress

SERVES 4

2 x 350 g (12 oz) pieces of prepared thick monkfish fillet (see page 62)
750 g (1 1/2 lb) new potatoes, scraped clean
2 tablespoons olive oil
85 ml (3 fl oz) extra virgin olive oil, plus extra to serve
50 g (2 oz) watercress sprigs, very roughly chopped
Balsamic vinegar, Maldon sea-salt flakes and coarsely crushed black pepper, to serve

1 Pre-heat the oven to 200°C/400°F/Gas Mark 6. Season the monkfish with some salt and set it aside for 15 minutes.

2 Cook the potatoes in well-salted boiling water until tender. While the potatoes are cooking, heat the 2 tablespoons of olive oil in a large ovenproof frying pan. Pat the monkfish dry on kitchen paper, add to the pan and sear for 3–4 minutes, turning it 3 or 4 times, until nicely browned

ROAST MONKFISH WITH CRUSHED POTATOES, OLIVE OIL AND WATERCRESS

on all sides. Transfer the pan to the oven and roast for 10–12 minutes, until the fish is cooked through but still moist and juicy in the centre. Remove from the oven, cover with foil and set aside for 5 minutes.

3 When the potatoes are done, drain them well and return them to the pan with the extra virgin olive oil. Gently crush each potato against the side of the pan with the back of a fork until it just bursts open.

4 Season the potatoes and add any juices from the fish. Add the watercress and turn over gently until the watercress is well mixed in.

5 To serve, cut the monkfish across into thick slices. Spoon the crushed potatoes on to 4 warmed plates and put the monkfish on top. Put your thumb over the top of the bottle of extra virgin olive oil and drizzle a little of it around the outside edge of each plate. Do the same with the balsamic vinegar and then sprinkle around a few sea-salt flakes and coarsely crushed black pepper.

MONKFISH

pan-fried fillet of monkfish with the new season's garlic and fennel

SERVES 4

100 g (4 oz) semolina

16 large new season's garlic cloves

15 g ($^1/_2$ oz) sprigs of fennel herb

100 g (4 oz) unsalted butter

450 g (1 lb) fennel bulb, thinly sliced

600 ml (1 pint) Fish Stock (see page 222)

4 x 225 g (8 oz) pieces prepared monkfish fillet (see page 62)

4 tablespoons sunflower oil

2 teaspoons lemon juice

A splash of Pernod or Ricard

Salt and freshly ground black pepper

1 Put the semolina, 2 sliced cloves of garlic and all but 1 sprig of fennel into a food processor and blend until you have an aromatic pale-green powder.

2 Cut the rest of the garlic cloves lengthways into long thin pieces. Melt half the butter in a pan, add the garlic and sliced fennel and fry over a medium heat until lightly browned. Add the fish stock and some seasoning and simmer for 15 minutes until the fennel is tender.

3 Pre-heat the oven to 200°C/400°F/Gas Mark 6. Coat the pieces of monkfish in the semolina mixture. Heat the oil in an ovenproof frying pan, add a small knob of butter and the monkfish pieces and fry over a moderate heat, turning now and then, until they are golden brown all over. Transfer the pan to the oven and cook the monkfish for a further 10 minutes.

4 Remove the pan from the oven and lift the fillets on to a chopping board. Slice diagonally into thick slices, keeping each piece in shape. Transfer to a plate and keep warm.

5 Add the sautéed fennel mixture, lemon juice, Pernod and remaining fennel herb, finely chopped, to the pan in which the monkfish was cooked. Simmer rapidly until slightly reduced, then add the remaining butter and simmer until it has blended in to make a rich sauce. Adjust the seasoning if necessary. Lift the fish on to 4 warmed plates and spoon some of the sauce around each piece.

barbecued monkfish with saffron and roasted red pepper dressing

SERVES 4

2 tablespoons olive oil

1 tablespoon chopped thyme

$^1/_2$ teaspoon salt

Freshly ground black pepper

4 x 200 g (7 oz) pieces of prepared monkfish fillet (see page 62)

FOR THE ROASTED RED PEPPER DRESSING:

600 ml (1 pint) Fish Stock (see page 222)

85 ml (3 fl oz) dry vermouth, such as Noilly Prat

A large pinch of saffron strands

2 Roasted Red Peppers (see page 227)

85 ml (3 fl oz) extra virgin olive oil

1 tablespoon balsamic vinegar or sherry vinegar

1 teaspoon unsalted butter

FOR THE SALAD:

50 g (2 oz) bag mixed salad leaves

1 tablespoon Lemon Olive Oil (see page 227)

A good pinch of Maldon sea-salt flakes

Salt and freshly ground black pepper

1 For the roasted red pepper dressing, put the fish stock, vermouth and saffron into a small pan and simmer until reduced to 175 ml (6 fl oz). Meanwhile, break the roasted red peppers in half and remove the stalks, seeds and skin. Finely chop the flesh. Mix together the extra virgin olive oil, vinegar and some salt and pepper to taste.

2 Pre-heat the barbecue for 30–40 minutes, or pre-heat a ridged cast-iron griddle. Mix together the olive oil, thyme, salt and some black pepper. Brush the fillets of monkfish with the mixture, place them on the barbecue or griddle and cook for 10 minutes, turning them every now and then.

3 While the monkfish fillets are cooking, return the pan of reduced fish stock to the heat and add the red peppers and olive oil dressing. Bring to a brisk boil and check the seasoning. Whisk in the butter and remove from the heat.

4 Mix the salad leaves with the lemon oil and Maldon salt. Pile them into the centre of 4 plates. Lift the monkfish fillets on to a board and cut each diagonally into 4 slices. Lift each piece on top of the salad and pour some of the dressing around the edge of the plate. Serve immediately.

ceviche of monkfish
with avocado (see technique 38, page 62)

SERVES 6

500 g (1 lb 2 oz) prepared monkfish fillets (see page 62)
Juice of 3 limes
1 medium-hot red Dutch chilli, halved and seeded
1 small red onion
6 vine-ripened tomatoes, skinned
3 tablespoons extra virgin olive oil
2 tablespoons chopped coriander
Salt
1 large ripe but firm avocado

1 Cut the monkfish fillets across into thin slices and put them into a shallow dish. Pour over the lime juice, making sure that all the slices of fish are completely covered in juice. Cover with cling film and refrigerate for 40 minutes, during which time the fish will turn white and opaque.

2 Meanwhile, slice across each chilli half so that you get very thin, slightly curled slices. Cut the onion into quarters and then each wedge lengthways into thin, arc-shaped slices. Cut each tomato into quarters and remove the seeds. Cut each piece of flesh lengthways into thin, arc-shaped slices.

3 Just before you are ready to serve, lift the monkfish out of the lime juice with a slotted spoon and put into a large bowl with the chilli, onion, tomato, olive oil, most of the coriander and a little salt to taste. Toss together lightly.

4 Halve the avocado, remove the stone and peel. Slice each half lengthways into thin slices.

5 Arrange 3–4 slices of the avocado on one side of each plate. Pile the ceviche on to the other side and sprinkle with the rest of the coriander. Serve at once.

CEVICHE OF MONKFISH WITH AVOCADO

recipes

chapter 8

small
round fish

salt pilchard bruschetta

SERVES 4

4 salt pilchards, scales removed (see page 16)
1 loaf of ciabatta or other rustic white bread, cut into
    slices 1 cm (1/2 inch) thick
3 garlic cloves, peeled
85 ml (3 fl oz) extra virgin olive oil
6 vine-ripened tomatoes, thinly sliced
1 small red onion, halved and very thinly sliced
3 tablespoons coarsely chopped flat-leaf parsley or basil
Freshly ground black pepper

1 Pre-heat the grill to high. Grill the pilchards for about 3 minutes on each side, until cooked through. Leave to cool, then break the fish into small flakes, discarding the skin and bones.

2 Toast the bread on both sides until golden brown. Rub one side of each piece with the peeled garlic cloves, then drizzle over some of the olive oil. Put the flaked pilchards, tomatoes, onion and parsley on top of the bread, then drizzle with the remaining oil and season well with black pepper. Serve straight away, before the bread has time to go soft.

devilled mackerel with mint and tomato salad

SERVES 4

4 x 350 g (12 oz) mackerel, cleaned and trimmed
    (see page 14)
40 g (1 1/2 oz) butter
1 teaspoon caster sugar
1 teaspoon English mustard powder
1 teaspoon cayenne pepper
1 teaspoon paprika
1 teaspoon ground coriander
2 tablespoons red wine vinegar
1 teaspoon freshly ground black pepper
2 teaspoons salt

DEVILLED MACKEREL WITH MINT AND TOMATO SALAD

hot potato salad with smoked mackerel and dandelions

SERVES 4

300 g (10 oz) new potatoes, scrubbed
25 g (1 oz) dandelion leaves
75 g (3 oz) smoked mackerel fillet
2 tablespoons red wine vinegar
150 ml (5 fl oz) sunflower oil
15 g ($^{1}/_{2}$ oz) finely chopped onion
$^{1}/_{2}$ teaspoon salt
Freshly ground black pepper

1 Cook the potatoes in boiling salted water for 15 minutes or until tender.

2 Meanwhile, wash the dandelions and discard the stems. Blanch them in boiling water for a few seconds, then drain and refresh under cold running water.

3 Remove the skin and bones from the smoked mackerel, cut it across into thin 2.5 cm (1 inch) slices. Whisk together the vinegar, oil, salt and some pepper.

4 Drain the potatoes and thinly slice. Put them into a large pan with the dandelion leaves, mackerel, onion and dressing and turn together over a low heat until warmed through. Divide the mixture between the plates, grind over a little more black pepper and serve.

FOR THE MINT AND TOMATO SALAD:

225 g (8 oz) small vine-ripened tomatoes, sliced
1 small onion, halved and very thinly sliced
1 tablespoon chopped mint
1 tablespoon lemon juice

1 Pre-heat the grill to high. Slash the skin of the mackerel at 1 cm ($^{1}/_{2}$ inch) intervals on both sides from the head all the way down to the tail, taking care not to cut too deeply into the flesh.

2 Melt the butter in a small roasting tin. Remove from the heat, stir in the sugar, mustard, spices, vinegar, pepper and salt and mix together well. Add the mackerel to the butter and turn them over once or twice until well coated in the mixture, spreading some into the cavity of each fish as well. Transfer them to a lightly oiled baking sheet or the rack of the grill pan and grill for 4 minutes on each side, until cooked through.

3 Meanwhile, for the salad, layer the sliced tomatoes, onion and mint on 4 serving plates, sprinkling the layers with the lemon juice and some seasoning. Put the cooked mackerel alongside and serve, with some fried sliced potatoes if you wish.

poached mackerel fillets with a warm mint, sherry vinegar and butter sauce (see technique 5, page 22)

SERVES 4

8 x 75 g (3 oz) mackerel fillets (see page 22)
Mint sprigs, to garnish

FOR THE SAUCE:

2 tablespoons sherry vinegar
1 shallot, very finely chopped
2 tablespoons cold water
2 egg yolks
225 g (8 oz) Clarified Butter (see page 226)
1 teaspoon lemon juice
A good pinch of cayenne pepper
1 tablespoon chopped mint
Salt and freshly ground black pepper

1 First make the sauce. Put the sherry vinegar and shallot in a small pan and bring to the boil. Boil until reduced to about 1 teaspoon. Half-fill a pan with water and bring to the boil, then reduce to a simmer and rest a glass or stainless-steel bowl on top. Put the water, egg yolks and sherry vinegar reduction into the bowl and whisk vigorously until voluminous and fluffy.

2 Remove the bowl from the heat and gradually whisk in the clarified butter, building up an emulsion as if making mayonnaise. Add the lemon juice, cayenne pepper, chopped mint, ½ teaspoon of salt and some black pepper. Set aside and keep warm in a bowl of warm water.

3 Bring 1.2 litres (2 pints) of water and 2 tablespoons of salt to the boil in a large clean frying pan. Reduce to a simmer, add the mackerel fillets and poach for 3 minutes, turning them over halfway through cooking. Lift out, drain away the excess water and put 2 mackerel fillets on to each warmed plate. Spoon a little of the sauce over and the rest around the fish and garnish with sprigs of fresh mint.

POACHED MACKEREL FILLETS WITH A WARM MINT, SHERRY VINEGAR AND BUTTER SAUCE

split herrings with a caper and fresh tomato salsa (see technique 2, page 16)

SERVES 4

4 x 225 g (8 oz) herrings, fins trimmed (see page 14, step 2)
225 g (8 oz) vine-ripened tomatoes, roughly diced
1 garlic clove, very finely chopped
25 g (1 oz) capers in brine, drained and rinsed
1 tablespoon coarsely chopped flat-leaf parsley
Salt and freshly ground black pepper

1 Pre-heat the grill to high. Remove the bones from the herrings as described on page 16.

2 Sprinkle them with a little salt and pepper on both sides, then lift them off the board and push them gently back into shape. Place them on a lightly oiled baking tray and grill for 2 minutes on each side.

3 For the salsa, mix together the diced tomatoes, chopped garlic, capers, parsley and some seasoning. Serve the herrings with the salsa.

herrings in oatmeal with bacon

SERVES 4

4 x 225 g (8 oz) herrings, cleaned and filleted (see page 22, steps 1–3)
100 g (4 oz) medium oatmeal (called pinhead oatmeal)
2 tablespoons sunflower oil
4 rashers of rindless streaky bacon, cut into lardons (short strips)
Salt and freshly ground black pepper
1 lemon, cut into wedges, to serve

1 Season the herring fillets on both sides with salt and pepper. Spread the oatmeal over a plate and coat the herring fillets in it, pressing it well on to both sides.

2 Heat the oil in a large frying pan. Add the streaky bacon strips and fry until crisp and golden. Remove from the pan with a slotted spoon and keep warm.

3 Add the herring fillets to the pan, flesh-side down, and fry for 1 minute. Turn over and fry for another 1–2 minutes, until the skin is golden brown. Put the fillets on 4 warmed plates and sprinkle over the bacon. Serve with the lemon wedges, and some boiled floury potatoes that have been tossed with a little chopped parsley.

marinated herring and potato salad

SERVES 4 AS A STARTER

15 g (½ oz) salt
1½ teaspoons caster sugar
¾ teaspoon crushed white peppercorns
225 g (8 oz) prepared herring fillets (see page 22)
Sunflower oil, to cover
450 g (1 lb) new potatoes, scraped
3 tablespoons chopped chives
Freshly ground black pepper

1 At least 2 days before you want to serve this, mix together the salt, sugar and crushed white pepper to make a dry cure. Layer the herring fillets in a shallow dish, sprinkling each layer generously with the dry cure mix. Cover with cling film and leave in the fridge for 24 hours, turning them once after 12 hours.

2 The next day, cut the herring fillets slightly on the diagonal into long thin strips. Pack them into a large airtight glass container (a kilner jar is ideal) and pour in enough sunflower oil to cover. Refrigerate for at least another 24 hours before serving.

3 To serve, cook the potatoes in well-salted boiling water (i.e. 1 teaspoon of salt to every 600 ml/1 pint of water) until tender – about 15 minutes. Drain and cut lengthways into quarters.

4 Put the warm potatoes into a bowl with the herring strips, chives and another 3 tablespoons of sunflower oil. Toss together.

5 Pile the salad into the centre of 4 large plates and grind over a little black pepper. Serve while the potatoes are still warm.

pan-fried herring milt on toasted brioche with beurre noisette and capers (see technique 44, page 69)

SERVES 4

2 tablespoons extra virgin olive oil
½ teaspoon white wine vinegar
50 g (2 oz) mixed baby salad leaves
1 small bunch chervil sprigs, large stalks removed
4 x 1 cm (½ inch) thick slices of brioche or white bread
75 g (3 oz) unsalted butter
350 g (12 oz) soft herring roes
25 g (1 oz) seasoned flour
Juice of ½ lemon
1 tablespoon chopped parsley
1 tablespoon capers in brine, drained and rinsed
Salt

1 Whisk together the olive oil, vinegar and a pinch of salt. Toss with the salad leaves and then divide them between 4 slightly warmed plates. Scatter over the chervil. Toast the brioche and put beside the salad.

2 Melt 25 g (1 oz) of the butter in a frying pan. Dust the roes in the seasoned flour and fry for 2 minutes, turning once, until lightly browned. Put them on top of the brioche.

3 Wipe the pan clean, add the rest of the butter and cook over a medium heat until it foams and starts to smell nutty. Add the lemon juice, parsley and a pinch of salt, spoon over the roes and then scatter over the capers. Serve immediately.

herring recheado
with katchumber salad
and pilau rice (see technique 6, page 23)

SERVES 4 AS A STARTER

4 x 225 g (8 oz) herrings
1 quantity Goan Masala Paste (see page 226)

FOR THE RICE:

Sunflower oil, for frying
6 large shallots, peeled and thinly sliced
3 whole cloves
3 green cardamom pods
5 cm (2 inch) piece of cinnamon stick
1 bay leaf
275 g (10 oz) basmati rice
1/2 teaspoon salt
600 ml (1 pint) boiling water

FOR THE KATCHUMBER SALAD:

450 g (1 lb) vine-ripened tomatoes, thinly sliced
1 medium red onion, quartered and thinly sliced
2 tablespoons roughly chopped coriander
1/4 teaspoon ground cumin
Pinch of cayenne pepper
1 tablespoon white wine vinegar
1/4 teaspoon salt

1 If you are cooking the herrings on the barbecue, light it 40 minutes before you are ready to cook.

2 Prepare the herrings as described on page 23. Spread the cut face of one fillet with a teaspoon of the masala paste. Put the fish back into shape and tie in two places with string.

3 For the rice, heat 1 cm (½ inch) of oil in a large frying pan. Add the sliced shallots and fry them, stirring now and then, until they are crisp and golden. Lift out with a slotted spoon on to plenty of kitchen paper and leave to drain.

4 Heat 2 tablespoons of oil in a large pan, add the whole spices and the bay leaf and cook for a few seconds until they start to smell aromatic. Stir in the rice, salt and water, bring to the boil, then cover and cook over a low heat for 10 minutes. If you are cooking the herrings under the grill, pre-heat it to high.

5 For the katchumber salad, layer all the ingredients together in a shallow dish.

6 Remove the rice from the heat and leave for another 5 minutes. Meanwhile, barbecue or grill the herrings for 3 minutes on each side until crisp and lightly golden. Lift them on to 4 warmed plates. Toss the fried shallots with a little salt and then stir them into the cooked rice. Serve with the herrings and some of the katchumber salad.

VARIATION:

mackerel recheado

Replace the herrings with four 225 g (8 oz) mackerel and spread each one with 1 tablespoon of masala pasta. Cook for 3–4 minutes on each side.

grilled smelts with
coarsely chopped green
herbs (see technique 35, page 57)

SERVES 4

2 strips of pared lemon zest
1/2 tablespoon finely chopped rosemary
1 tablespoon finely chopped parsley
1 garlic clove, very finely chopped
1/2 tablespoon finely chopped pitted green olives
1/2 tablespoon chopped capers
1/2 teaspoon Maldon sea-salt flakes
1/4 teaspoon freshly ground black pepper
16–20 smelts, cleaned and trimmed (see page 14)
Extra virgin olive oil, for brushing and serving
Lemon wedges and crusty fresh bread, to serve

1 Soak 4 bamboo skewers in cold water for 30 minutes. Cut the strips of lemon zest across into very thin shreds and then chop them up finely. Mix with the rosemary, parsley, garlic, olives, capers, salt and pepper. Set to one side.

2 Pre-heat the grill to high. Thread the smelts on to the skewers by piercing them through the head. Lay them on a lightly oiled baking tray and sprinkle them with some extra virgin olive oil, salt and pepper. Grill for 2 minutes on one side only.

3 To serve, lift the skewered smelts into the centre of 4 warmed plates and scatter over some of the herb mixture. Pour a little more oil around the edge of the plate and serve with the lemon wedges and plenty of crusty bread.

8

jansson's temptation

SERVES 4

1 x 50 g (2 oz) can of good-quality
    anchovies in olive oil (e.g. Ortiz)
2 medium onions, thinly sliced
175 ml (6 fl oz) milk
900 g (2 lb) peeled potatoes, such as King Edwards
175 ml (6 fl oz) double cream
Butter, for greasing
Salt and freshly ground black pepper

1 Pre-heat the oven to 190°C/375°F/Gas Mark 5. Tip the anchovies and their oil into a frying pan. Add the onions and fry over a medium-high heat for 5 minutes, until soft and lightly browned.

2 Meanwhile cut the potatoes into 5 mm (¼ inch) thick slices. Stack the slices up a few at a time and cut them lengthways into 5 mm (¼ inch) matchsticks.

3 Add the milk and cream to the onions and bring to the boil. Season to taste with salt (depending on the saltiness of the anchovies) and pepper and then stir in the potatoes and mix well so that the ingredients are evenly distributed.

4 Pour the mixture into a lightly buttered, shallow, ovenproof dish and bake in the oven for 45 minutes, until the potatoes are tender and the top is lightly browned. Serve with a crisp green salad.

marinated anchovies (see technique, page 57)

SERVES 4

450 g (1 lb) fresh anchovies
Juice of 1 lemon
1 teaspoon finely chopped medium-hot, red, Dutch chilli
1 garlic clove, finely chopped
1 tablespoon chopped flat-leaf parsley
50 ml (2 fl oz) extra virgin olive oil
Salt and freshly ground black pepper

1 To prepare the anchovies, pinch off the heads and pull them away: the guts should come out with them. Then pinch along the top edge of each fish and pull out the spine – it should come away quite easily because the fish is soft. You will then be left with lots of little double fillets.

2 Lay them skin-side down in a large shallow dish and pour over the lemon juice. Leave for 20 minutes, during which time the flesh will go slightly opaque and firm.

3 Drain off the excess lemon juice and then sprinkle over the chilli, garlic, parsley and some salt and pepper. Pour over the oil, cover and leave for 24 hours in the fridge to allow all the flavours to permeate the fish.

ALTERNATIVE FISH
Sprats, sardines or small mackerel.

linguine with tomato and anchovy sauce and flaked fresh sardines

SERVES 4

8 fresh sardines, cleaned (see page 14)
4 tablespoons extra virgin olive oil
3 garlic cloves, finely chopped
4 sage leaves, finely shredded
1 medium-hot red Dutch chilli, seeded and
 finely chopped
450 g (1 lb) vine-ripened tomatoes, skinned
 and chopped
50 g (2 oz) capers, drained
100 g (4 oz) well-flavoured black olives, pitted
 and chopped
100 g (4 oz) anchovy fillets in oil, drained and
 finely chopped
1 tablespoon chopped oregano
450 g (1 lb) dried linguine or spaghetti
3 tablespoons chopped flat-leaf parsley
Salt and freshly ground black pepper

1 Brush the sardines on both sides with olive oil, season with plenty of salt and pepper and put them on to a lightly oiled baking tray or the rack of the grill pan.

2 Heat the extra virgin olive oil in a pan, add the garlic and sage and cook until the garlic begins to take on a little colour. Add the red chilli and fry for a few seconds. Add the tomatoes, capers, olives, anchovies, oregano and some freshly ground black pepper and leave to simmer for 10 minutes.

3 Cook the pasta in well-salted boiling water for about 8 minutes or until al dente. Meanwhile, pre-heat the grill to high. Grill the sardines for 2 minutes on each side. Allow to cool slightly and then flake the fish away from the bones in largish pieces.

4 Drain the pasta and tip it into a large serving bowl. Stir the chopped parsley into the sauce, pour it over the pasta and toss together well. Add the flaked sardines and turn over gently to mix.

ALTERNATIVE FISH
Fresh mackerel, pilchards or herrings.

sardine and potato curry puffs

MAKES 12

100 g (4 oz) potato, peeled and cut into
 1 cm (½ inch) cubes
1 tablespoon groundnut or sunflower oil, plus extra for
 deep-frying
2 garlic cloves, crushed
1 cm (½ inch) fresh root ginger, finely grated
½ onion, thinly sliced
1 tablespoon Goan Masala Paste (see page 226) or
 good-quality garam masala paste
225 g (8 oz) sardines, cleaned, filleted (see page 22) and
 cut across into strips 2.5 cm (1 inch) wide
1 medium-hot red Dutch chilli, seeded and finely
 chopped
1 tablespoon lemon juice
¼ teaspoon salt
2–3 spring onions, sliced
2 tablespoons chopped coriander
450 g (1 lb) fresh puff pastry
Lemon wedges and coriander sprigs, to garnish

1 Boil the potato in salted water until just tender, then drain. Heat the oil in a large frying pan and fry the garlic, ginger and onion for 1 minute. Add the masala paste and fry for 1 minute, then add the pieces of sardine and fry for another minute. Finally add the potato, chilli, lemon juice and salt and cook for 1 minute. Take the pan off the heat, stir in the spring onions and coriander and leave to cool.

2 Roll out the pastry on a lightly floured surface and cut out twelve 10 cm (4 inch) circles. Spoon a heaped teaspoon of the filling mixture on to each circle. Brush half of the pastry edge with a little water, then fold it over the filling and press together well to seal the edge. Mark along the edge with a fork to make an even tighter seal.

3 Heat some oil for deep frying to 190°C (375°F). Deep-fry the puffs 3 or 4 at a time for 7–8 minutes, turning them over every now and then, until they are golden brown. Drain on kitchen paper. Keep warm in a low oven while you cook the rest. Pile them on a plate and serve warm, garnished with some lemon wedges and coriander.

ALTERNATIVE FISH
Mackerel, pilchards, sprats, herrings or any other oily fish with lots of flavour.

escabèche of sardines

SERVES 4

12 sardines, cleaned (see page 16)
50 g (2 oz) seasoned plain flour
150 ml (5 fl oz) olive oil
85 ml (3 fl oz) red wine vinegar
1 medium onion, thinly sliced
5 cm (2 inch) strip of pared orange zest
1 sprig thyme
1 sprig rosemary
1 bay leaf
4 garlic cloves, crushed
2 dried red chillies
1 small bunch flat-leaf parsley, roughly chopped
Salt and freshly ground black pepper

1 Remove the heads from the sardines (see page 16), then dust them in the seasoned flour. Fry them in half the olive oil for 1 minute on each side, then transfer to a shallow dish.

2 Add the vinegar, onion, orange zest, thyme, rosemary, bay leaf, garlic, chillies and 1 teaspoon salt to the pan, bring to the boil and simmer for about 15 minutes.

3 Add the rest of the olive oil and the parsley, pour the hot marinade over the sardines and leave until cold.

fillets of bass with vanilla butter vinaigrette

SERVES 4

4 x 100 g (4 oz) skinned sea bass fillets
100 g (4 oz) Clarified Butter (see page 226)

FOR THE VANILLA BUTTER VINAIGRETTE:

½ vanilla pod
50 ml (2 fl oz) dry vermouth, such as Noilly Prat
2 teaspoons white wine vinegar
1 shallot, peeled and halved
150 ml (5 fl oz) Fish Stock (see page 222)
25 g (1 oz) peeled, seeded and finely diced tomato
1 tablespoon coarsely chopped chervil
Salt and freshly ground black pepper

1 Brush both sides of each sea bass fillet with a little of the clarified butter and season with salt and pepper.

2 For the vanilla butter vinaigrette, split the vanilla pod open lengthways, scrape out the seeds with a small teaspoon and then chop the pod very finely. Put the seeds and pod into a small pan with the vermouth, vinegar and shallot. Bring to the boil and boil for a few minutes until reduced to about 1 tablespoon. Add the fish stock and boil once more until reduced to about 3 tablespoons. Remove the shallot halves and add the remaining clarified butter, the diced tomato, chervil, ¼ teaspoon of salt and 6 turns of the black pepper mill. Keep warm over a very low heat.

3 Heat a ridged cast-iron griddle until very hot. Add the sea bass fillets, skin-side down, and cook for 1 minute, pressing down on top of each fillet in turn with the back of a fish slice to help mark them with the lines from the griddle. Turn over and cook for 30 seconds on the other side.

4 To serve, put the fish fillets on to 4 warmed plates and spoon some of the vanilla butter vinaigrette to one side.

barbecued whole sea bass with pernod and fennel

(see technique 1, page 14)

SERVES 4

4 x 450–550 g (1–1¼ lb) sea bass, cleaned and
trimmed (see page 14)
2 tablespoons olive oil
1 large bunch fennel herb
3 tablespoons Pernod
1 quantity Fennel Mayonnaise (see page 224)
Salt and freshly ground black pepper

1 Light the barbecue 40 minutes before you are ready to cook.

2 Slash each fish 4 or 5 times down each side. Rub them with the oil and season well with salt and pepper on the outside and inside the gut cavities. Push some of the fennel herb into the gut cavity of each fish.

3 If you wish to cook the fish under the grill, pre-heat it to medium-high.

4 Barbecue or grill the fish for 6–8 minutes. Sprinkle each one with about 1 teaspoon of Pernod, carefully turn over the wire clamp (or the fish, if grilling them) and cook for another 6–8 minutes until they are cooked right through to the backbone. Sprinkle with the rest of the Pernod.

5 Lift the fish on to a warmed serving plate and serve with the fennel mayonnaise and some boiled new potatoes.

deep-fried sea bass with chilli sauce

SERVES 4

4 × 350 g (12 oz) sea bass or black bream, cleaned and
trimmed (see page 14)
50 g (2 oz) plain flour, seasoned with salt and pepper
Sunflower oil, for deep-frying

FOR THE CHILLI SAUCE:

2 tablespoons finely chopped garlic
2 medium-hot red Dutch chillies, finely chopped
2 tablespoons sunflower oil
2 tablespoons palm sugar or light muscovado sugar
3 tablespoons Thai fish sauce (*nam pla*)
1 tablespoon Tamarind Water (see page 227)

FOR THE GARNISHES:

4 shallots, thinly sliced
2 garlic cloves, thinly sliced
50 g (2 oz) cashew nuts, halved
2 kaffir lime leaves, finely shredded (optional)
25 g (1 oz) basil leaves

1 For the sauce, pound together the garlic and chillies in a mortar until they form a coarse paste. Heat the oil in a small saucepan, add the garlic and chilli paste and fry for 1 minute. Stir in the sugar, fish sauce and tamarind water, bring to a simmer and keep warm.

2 Next prepare the garnishes. Fill a pan large enough to accommodate the fish about one-third full with sunflower oil. Heat to 190°C (375°F). Add the sliced shallots, garlic and cashew nuts and fry for 2 minutes. Lift out with a slotted spoon and drain on kitchen paper. Add the shredded lime leaves, if using, and the basil leaves and fry for about 30 seconds. Drain and set aside.

3 Rinse the fish and pat dry. Coat in the seasoned flour and deep-fry, one at a time, for 5–6 minutes, until crisp and golden. Lift out, drain briefly on kitchen paper and keep warm while you cook the remaining fish.

4 Put the fish on 4 warmed plates and spoon over the sauce. Scatter with the garnishes and serve.

black bream steamed over seaweed with a fennel butter sauce (see technique 26, page 47)

SERVES 4

4 x 225 g (8 oz) black bream, cleaned and trimmed
(see page 14)
750 g (1½ lb) fresh bladderack
seaweed
Salt and freshly ground black pepper

FOR THE FENNEL BUTTER SAUCE:

200 g (7 oz) unsalted butter
½ fennel bulb, trimmed and thinly sliced
40 g (1½ oz) onion, thinly sliced
½ small garlic clove, chopped
150 ml (5 fl oz) Fish Stock or Chicken Stock
(see page 222)
1 tablespoon white wine
2 tablespoons Pernod
2 teaspoons lemon juice
2 egg yolks
3 tablespoons chopped fennel herb

1 Season the fish inside and out with a little salt and pepper. Wash the seaweed and spread it over the base of a sauté pan large enough to hold the fish in a single layer (if you don't have a pan large enough, use two). Add 300 ml (10 fl oz) of water, put the fish on top and cover with a tight-fitting lid. Set to one side.

BLACK BREAM STEAMED OVER SEAWEED WITH
A FENNEL BUTTER SAUCE

164

2 For the fennel butter sauce, melt 25 g (1 oz) of the butter in a pan. Add the fennel, onion and garlic and fry for 5 minutes until soft but not browned. Add the stock, white wine and some salt and pepper and simmer for 15 minutes until the vegetables are very soft and most of the liquid has evaporated.

3 Spoon the mixture into a liquidizer and leave to cool slightly. Then add the Pernod, lemon juice and egg yolks. Melt the rest of the butter in a clean pan. As soon as it begins to bubble, turn on the machine and blend the contents for 1 minute. Then slowly pour in the hot melted butter to make a hollandaise-like mixture. Pour the sauce into a bowl and stir in chopped fennel herb and some seasoning to taste. Keep warm.

4 Place the pan of fish and seaweed over a high heat and, as soon as some steam starts to leak from underneath the lid, turn the heat down and steam for 5 minutes until the fish are cooked through. Without lifting the lid, take the pan of fish to the table, together with the fennel butter sauce. Remove the lid so your guests can appreciate the aroma and serve with some plain boiled potatoes.

baked red bream with fennel, orange and provençal herbs

SERVES 4

1 orange
3 fennel bulbs
1 teaspoon dried herbes de Provence or 1 tablespoon
      chopped mixed thyme, rosemary and oregano
1^1/$_2$ teaspoons chopped fennel herb
2 tablespoons of Pernod
1 large onion, chopped
2 bay leaves, finely shredded
3 garlic cloves, thinly sliced
2 tablespoons white wine vinegar
85 ml (3 fl oz) olive oil
1 teaspoon caster sugar
4 x 550 g (1^1/$_4$ lb) red sea bream, trimmed and scaled
      (see page 14)
Salt and freshly ground black pepper

1 Pare the zest from half the orange with a potato peeler, then finely cut each strip across into fine shreds like pine needles. Squeeze the juice from the whole orange. Remove the outer leaves from the fennel bulbs and chop the remainder.

2 Put the herbs, orange zest and juice, chopped fennel, fennel herb, Pernod, onion, bay leaves, garlic, white wine vinegar, olive oil and sugar into a heavy-based saucepan. Cover and cook for 15 minutes until the fennel is soft.

3 Pre-heat the oven to 200°C/400°F/Gas Mark 6. Spoon half of the fennel mixture into the bottom of a shallow ovenproof dish. Put the fish on top, then spoon over the rest of the fennel mixture. Cover with foil and bake for 20 minutes.

4 Remove the foil and bake for a further 5 minutes. Drizzle with a little extra oil before serving.

patricia wells' grilled porgy with red peppers, capers and cumin

SERVES 4

5–6 tablespoons extra virgin olive oil
2 large red peppers, halved, seeded and diced
2 tablespoons capers in brine, drained and rinsed
2 teaspoons cumin seeds
4 x 300 g (10 oz) Porgy, red bream or black bream,
      cleaned and trimmed (see page 14)
Salt and freshly ground black pepper

1 Heat 1 tablespoon of the oil in a medium-sized frying pan. Add the red peppers and fry for 4–5 minutes until tender. Remove the pan from the heat and stir in the capers and cumin seeds. Set aside.

2 Season the cavities of each fish with some salt and pepper, then generously brush with oil. Heat another 2 tablespoons of the oil in a frying pan, add 2 of the fish and cook for 4–5 minutes on each side. Keep warm while you cook the other fish.

3 Re-heat the sauce. Lift the fish on to warmed plates and spoon some of the red peppers alongside. Drizzle a little more oil around the outside of the plate and serve.

DEEP-FRIED WHITEBAIT WITH LEMON AND PERSILLADE

deep-fried whitebait with lemon and persillade (see technique 34, page 56)

SERVES 4

550 g (1¼ lb) whitebait
Sunflower oil, for deep-frying
75 g (3 oz) plain flour
½ teaspoon cayenne pepper
1 teaspoon salt
1 lemon, cut into wedges, to serve

FOR THE PERSILLADE:

2 garlic cloves
1 small bunch parsley, large stalks removed

1 Wash the whitebait in plenty of cold water, then drain and shake vigorously in a colander.

2 Heat some oil for deep-frying to 190°C (375°F). For the persillade, finely chop the garlic on a chopping board. Then add the parsley and continue to chop them together until you have a very fine mixture.

3 Put the flour, cayenne pepper and salt into a large bowl and mix together well. Add the whitebait, toss together until they are all well coated, then lift them out and shake off the excess flour.

4 Deep-fry the fish in batches for about 3 minutes, until crisp. Drain briefly on kitchen paper, then tip into a large serving bowl and sprinkle with the persillade. Serve with the lemon wedges.

merlan frit en colère (deep-fried whiting) (see technique 16, page 32)

SERVES 4

4 x 350 g (12 oz) whiting, cleaned and trimmed
(see page 14)
Sunflower oil, for deep-frying
75 g (3 oz) plain flour
2 eggs, beaten
175 g (6 oz) fresh white breadcrumbs,
made from day-old bread
Salt and freshly ground black pepper

FOR THE TOMATO TARTARE SAUCE:

3 tablespoons white wine vinegar
6 black peppercorns, coarsely crushed
½ shallot, finely chopped
A few tarragon stalks, broken into small pieces
2 plum tomatoes, skinned, seeded and finely chopped
15 g (½ oz) each finely chopped green olives, gherkins
and capers
2 teaspoons each chopped tarragon, parsley and chives
100 g (4 oz) Mustard Mayonnaise (see page 224)

1 For the tomato tartare sauce, put the vinegar, peppercorns, shallot, and tarragon stalks into a small pan and boil until the vinegar is reduced to 1 teaspoon. Cool slightly and then strain into a bowl. Mix in the rest of the ingredients and some salt and pepper to taste.

2 Prepare the whiting for cooking as described on page 32. Heat some oil for deep-frying to 160°C (325°F). Season the flour with ½ teaspoon of salt and some pepper. Season each fish with a little salt, then coat them one at a time in the flour, followed by the beaten egg and then the breadcrumbs.

3 Deep-fry the fish for 5 minutes or until crisp and golden and cooked through. Transfer to a baking tray lined with kitchen paper and keep warm in a low oven while you coat and cook the rest of the fish in the same way. Serve with the tomato tartare sauce and some chunky chips.

ALTERNATIVE FISH

Small hake (pin hake) or codling.

8

salad of griddled garfish fillets with sun-dried tomatoes and fennel seeds (see technique 14, page 31)

SERVES 4

3 tablespoons olive oil

2 teaspoons lemon juice

1 teaspoon chopped thyme

1 teaspoon fennel seeds, lightly crushed

A pinch of dried chilli flakes

4 x 275–350 g (10–12 oz) garfish, mackerel or gurnard, filleted (see page 31)

25 g (1 oz) rocket

25 g (1 oz) prepared curly endive

15 g (½ oz) flat-leaf parsley leaves

15 g (½ oz) chervil sprigs

4–6 sun-dried tomatoes in oil, drained and thinly sliced

1 tablespoon sherry vinegar

Salt and freshly ground black pepper

1 Mix together the olive oil, lemon juice, thyme, fennel seeds, chilli flakes, ½ teaspoon of salt and a few twists of freshly ground black pepper. Brush a little of this mixture over both sides of the garfish fillets and set aside for 5 minutes.

2 Toss the rocket, curly endive, parsley and chervil together and divide between 4 plates.

3 Heat a flat or ridged cast-iron griddle over a high heat until smoking-hot. Add the garfish fillets, skin-side down, and cook for 1–1½ minutes, turning them over half-way through. Transfer them to a plate to stop them cooking further. Break them into 7.5 cm (3 inch) pieces.

4 Arrange the pieces of fish and the strips of sun-dried tomato in amongst the salad leaves, taking care not to flatten the leaves too much.

5 Add the remaining marinade and the sherry vinegar to the pan and swirl it around briefly. Spoon a little over the salad and the rest around the outside of the plate and serve straight away.

SALAD OF GRIDDLED GARFISH FILLETS WITH
SUN-DRIED TOMATOES AND FENNEL SEEDS

POMPANO,
JOHN DORY

grilled pompano fillet with a noilly prat and thyme butter sauce

SERVES 4

4 x 175 g (6 oz) pompano fillets or pieces of salmon
    fillet, skinned
25 g (1 oz) butter, melted
Salt and freshly ground black pepper

FOR THE NOILLY PRAT AND THYME BUTTER SAUCE:

600 ml (1 pint) Fish Stock (see page 222)
50 ml (2 fl oz) double cream
50 ml (2 fl oz) dry vermouth, such as Noilly Prat
75 g (3 oz) chilled unsalted butter, cut into small pieces
1 teaspoon thyme leaves

1 For the sauce, put the fish stock, double cream and Noilly Prat into a medium-sized pan and boil rapidly until reduced by three-quarters to about 175 ml (6 fl oz). Keep warm.

2 Pre-heat the grill to high. Brush the pompano fillets on both sides with melted butter and season. Place on a lightly buttered baking tray and grill for 8 minutes until just cooked through.

3 Bring the sauce reduction back to a simmer, then whisk in the chilled butter a piece at a time. Stir in the thyme leaves and season to taste.

4 Lift the pieces of pompano into the centre of 4 warmed plates and spoon some of the sauce over the fish and the rest around the outside edge of the plate.

fillets of john dory with warm potatoes, olives, capers and rosemary

SERVES 4

450 g (1 lb) unskinned John Dory fillets
4 tablespoons extra virgin olive oil, plus extra for
    brushing
4 small waxy new potatoes, such as Wilja
2 anchovy fillets in olive oil, drained
2 vine-ripened tomatoes, skinned and seeded
3 sun-dried tomatoes in oil, drained and cut into thin
    strips
4 black olives, stones removed and sliced
12 small capers in brine, drained and rinsed
10 'needles' of rosemary
A small handful of roughly chopped flat-leaf parsley
Salt and freshly ground black pepper

1 Cut small John Dory fillets in half lengthways, and larger ones lengthways into 3. Brush them with the oil and put them on to a lightly oiled baking tray, skin-side up. Season with salt and pepper.

2 Cut each potato lengthways into quarters and cook in boiling salted water for about 10 minutes or until tender. Drain and keep warm.

3 Cut the anchovy fillets lengthways into long thin slivers. Cut each wedge-shaped piece of tomato flesh into thin arc-shaped pieces.

4 Pre-heat the grill to high. Grill the John Dory for 2–3 minutes until just cooked through. Meanwhile, put the rest of the extra virgin olive oil into a shallow pan with the potatoes, anchovies, tomato pieces, sun-dried tomato strips, olives, capers and rosemary. Warm through over a gentle heat. Add the parsley and season to taste.

5 Arrange the pieces of fish and the warmed vegetables attractively on 4 warmed plates. Serve immediately.

john dory with griddled leeks, soft-boiled eggs and mustard vinaigrette (see technique 13, page 30)

(see technique 13, page 30)

SERVES 4

16–20 baby leeks, trimmed and cleaned

2 eggs

A thick piece of Parmesan cheese

2 x 350–450 g (12 oz–1 lb) John Dory, filleted
   (see page 30)

25 g (1 oz) butter, melted

Maldon sea-salt flakes and freshly ground black pepper

Coarsely crushed black pepper, to serve

FOR THE MUSTARD VINAIGRETTE:

1½ teaspoons Dijon mustard

1½ teaspoons white wine vinegar

8 teaspoons extra virgin olive oil

1 Pre-heat the grill to high. Cook the leeks in boiling salted water for 2–3 minutes, until just tender but still *al dente*. Drain and refresh under cold water, then dry out on kitchen paper.

2 Cook the eggs in boiling water for just 7 minutes so that the yolks remain slightly soft. Cool, peel and cut in half. Shave some thin slices off the piece of Parmesan cheese with a sharp potato peeler and set aside.

3 For the mustard vinaigrette, mix the mustard and vinegar together in a small bowl and then gradually whisk in the olive oil. Season to taste with some salt and pepper.

4 Heat a ridged cast-iron griddle over a high heat. Brush with a little oil, then place the leeks diagonally across it and grill them for slightly less than 1 minute on each side, so that they get nicely marked with diagonal lines. Remove the leeks from the griddle and arrange in the centre of 4 large warmed plates.

5 Cut each John Dory fillet diagonally across into two similar-sized pieces. Brush on both sides with the melted butter and season well with salt and pepper. Lay the fillets, skin-side up, on a lightly greased baking sheet or the rack of the grill pan and grill for 4 minutes. Remove and place on top of the leeks. Put one egg half on to each plate. Stir 1½ teaspoons of warm water into the mustard vinaigrette and drizzle over the leeks. Scatter over the Parmesan shavings, sprinkle over a little coarsely crushed black pepper and some sea-salt flakes and serve.

JOHN DORY WITH GRIDDLED LEEKS, SOFT-BOILED EGGS
AND MUSTARD VINAIGRETTE

hard-fried fish in red curry

SERVES 4

2 tablespoons groundnut or sunflower oil, plus extra for deep-frying
3 tablespoons Thai Red Curry Paste (see page 226)
200 ml (7 fl oz) coconut milk
1 tablespoon Thai fish sauce (*nam pla*)
1 teaspoon palm sugar or light muscovado sugar
4 x 225 g (8 oz) John Dory steaks
Juice of ¹/₂ lime
Salt and freshly ground black pepper

1 Heat the 2 tablespoons of oil in a large deep frying pan. Add the red curry paste and fry for about 2 minutes, until the paste starts to separate from the oil. Add the coconut milk, fish sauce and sugar and simmer very gently for 10 minutes, until thickened.

2 Meanwhile, heat some oil for deep-frying to 190°C (375°F). Deep-fry the John Dory steaks, 2 at a time, for 2 minutes until crisp, golden and cooked through. Lift on to a tray lined with kitchen paper and keep warm in a low oven while you cook the rest.

3 Once the excess oil has drained off the fish, place the steaks on to 4 warmed serving plates. Stir the lime juice into the sauce with some seasoning to taste, spoon it over the fish and serve with some steamed rice.

ALTERNATIVE FISH

Steaks of haddock, hake or salmon or even steaks of monkfish, skinned and cut across the bone, would be a great idea. You could also try shark and swordfish steaks.

JOHN DORY,
RED MULLET,
GREY MULLET

HARD-FRIED FISH IN RED CURRY

8

moroccan fish tagine

SERVES 4 AS A STARTER

2 tablespoons olive oil, plus extra for brushing

2 celery sticks, chopped

1 carrot, chopped

1 small onion, chopped

1/4 Preserved Lemon (see page 227), finely chopped

1 quantity Charmoula (see page 146)

4 plum tomatoes, sliced

600 ml (1 pint) Fish Stock (see page 222)

8 small new potatoes, cut lengthways into quarters

2 x 450 g (1 lb) red mullet, filleted (see page 22)

8 black olives, halved

1 teaspoon chopped coriander

1 teaspoon chopped mint

Salt and freshly ground black pepper

1 Heat the oil in a large pan. Add the celery, carrot and onion and fry gently for 5 minutes, until softened but not browned. Add half the chopped preserved lemon, 2 tablespoons of the charmoula, the tomatoes and the stock. Bring to the boil and simmer for 30 minutes. Add the potatoes and simmer for 6–8 minutes until tender.

2 Pre-heat the grill to high. Brush the red mullet fillets with olive oil, season with salt and pepper and then cut each one diagonally in half. Put skin-side up on to an oiled baking tray on the rack of the grill pan and grill for 6 minutes or until cooked through.

3 Stir the olives, the rest of the charmoula and the remaining preserved lemon into the sauce and check the seasoning. Put the fish in 4 warmed soup bowls, spoon over the sauce and sprinkle with the chopped coriander and mint.

ALTERNATIVE FISH

Grey mullet, ocean perch.

steamed grey mullet with garlic, ginger and spring onions (see technique 25, page 46)

SERVES 2

2 x 450 g (1 lb) grey mullet, cleaned and trimmed (see page 14, steps 1–4)

2.5 cm (1 inch) fresh root ginger, cut into fine julienne

4 spring onions, trimmed and thinly sliced

2 tablespoons dark soy sauce

2 tablespoons sesame oil

4 garlic cloves, finely chopped

1 Put the fish into a steamer (see page 46) and sprinkle over the ginger. Cover and steam for 10–12 minutes until cooked through. Lift the fish on to 2 warmed serving plates, scatter over the spring onions and keep warm.

2 Pour 4 tablespoons of the cooking juices into a small pan and add the soy sauce. Bring up to the boil and pour over the fish.

3 Heat the sesame oil in a small pan. Add the garlic, fry for a few seconds, then pour over the fish and serve.

red mullet en papillote with thyme

SERVES 4

4 x 225–275 g (8–10 oz) red mullet, cleaned and trimmed (see page 14)

1 small bunch thyme

120 ml (4 fl oz) extra virgin olive oil

50 ml (2 fl oz) dry white wine

Juice of 1 lemon (about 8 teaspoons)

Sea salt and freshly ground black pepper

FOR THE TOMATO, BLACK OLIVE AND CHILLI SALAD:

450 g (1 lb) small vine-ripened tomatoes, cut into wedges

1/2 medium-hot red Dutch chilli, seeded and finely chopped

1 garlic clove, finely chopped

50 g (2 oz) good-quality black olives, pitted

4 tablespoons extra virgin olive oil

1 tablespoon chopped flat-leaf parsley

1 Pre-heat the oven to 220°/425°F/Gas Mark 7. Season the fish inside and out with salt and pepper and put 2 sprigs of thyme in the cavity of each one.

2 Brush four 30 cm (12 inch) squares of foil with a little of the olive oil and put a fish diagonally across the centre of each piece. Bring the sides of the foil up around the fish and crimp it together tightly at each end, leaving the top open.

3 Mix the wine with 50 ml (2 fl oz) of water. Pour 2 tablespoons of the wine and water mixture, 2 tablespoons of olive oil and 2 teaspoons of lemon juice into each parcel, add the remaining sprigs of thyme and season with a little more salt and pepper. Seal the parcels well and place on a large baking sheet. Bake the fish for 10 minutes.

4 Meanwhile, for the salad, scatter the tomato wedges, red chilli, garlic and olives on 4 small plates and drizzle with the olive oil. Season with some salt and pepper and sprinkle with the chopped parsley.

5 To serve, put the unopened parcels of fish on 4 warmed plates and take them to the table with a bowl of chips cooked in olive oil and the plates of tomato salad. Allow each person to open up their own parcel.

RED MULLET

RED MULLET EN PAPILLOTE WITH THYME

grilled red mullet with sauce vierge and toasted fennel seeds

SERVES 4

4 x 175 g (6 oz) red mullet, cleaned and trimmed
(see page 14)
A little melted butter, for brushing
Salt and freshly ground black pepper
4 small dried heads of fennel seeds or a small
pinch of ordinary fennel seeds

FOR THE SAUCE VIERGE:

4 tablespoons extra virgin olive oil
1 teaspoon lemon juice
$^1/_4$ teaspoon Pernod
$^1/_4$ teaspoon dark soy sauce
1 small garlic clove, finely chopped
4 vine-ripened cherry tomatoes, skinned, seeded and cut
into small dice
Maldon sea-salt flakes
Coarsely crushed black pepper
10 whole tarragon leaves

1 Brush the red mullet on both sides with melted butter and season inside and out with salt and pepper.

2 For the sauce, put the extra virgin olive oil, lemon juice, Pernod, soy sauce, garlic and tomatoes in a small pan with some Maldon salt to taste and a pinch of pepper. Set aside.

3 Pre-heat the grill to high. If you have some fennel seed heads, put them, seed-side up, on a baking tray and grill for a few seconds until they are starting to smoke and have darkened slightly in colour. Remove and add about 10 seeds to the pan of sauce. Set aside the rest for garnishing. Alternatively, lightly toast the pinch of dried fennel seeds in a hot dry frying pan for a few seconds until they start to smell aromatic then add these to the pan of sauce.

4 Brush another baking tray really well with ordinary olive oil and put under the grill to get hot. Remove, add the red mullet and grill them on one side only for about 5 minutes until cooked through. Just before the fish is cooked, warm through the sauce over a very low heat and then add the whole tarragon leaves.

5 Lift the red mullet on to 4 warmed plates and garnish with toasted fennel seed heads, if using. Spoon a tablespoon of the sauce alongside the fish and serve with some chips cooked in olive oil.

sautéed red mullet with parsley, garlic and spaghettini

SERVES 4

4 x 150 g (5 oz) red mullet, filleted (see page 22)
450 g (1 lb) dried spaghettini
4 tablespoons olive oil
2 garlic cloves, finely chopped
1 medium-hot red Dutch chilli, seeded and finely
chopped
4 plum tomatoes, skinned, seeded and chopped
20 g ($^3/_4$ oz) flat-leaf parsley, finely chopped
Salt and freshly ground black pepper
Extra virgin olive oil, to serve

1 Cut the red mullet fillets across into strips 2 cm ($^3/_4$ inch) wide.

2 Bring 3.4 litres (6 pints) of water to the boil in a large pan with 2 tablespoons of salt. Add the spaghettini, bring back to the boil and cook for 5 minutes or until *al dente*.

3 Meanwhile, heat the olive oil in a large frying pan. Fry the strips of red mullet, skin-side down, for 3 minutes. Turn them over, fry for 1 minute and then season with some salt and pepper.

4 Drain the pasta well and tip it into a large warmed serving bowl.

5 Add the garlic and red chilli to the frying pan with the red mullet and fry for 30 seconds. Add the tomatoes and fry for a further 30 seconds.

6 Tip everything into the bowl with the pasta, scraping up all the little bits that may have stuck to the bottom of the pan, add 3 tablespoons of the parsley and gently toss everything together so that the fish just begins to break up. Serve immediately, drizzled with extra virgin olive oil and sprinkled with the remaining parsley.

gurnard fillets with a potato, garlic and saffron broth

SERVES 4

4 tablespoons extra virgin olive oil

4–6 sprigs oregano, plus 1¹/₂ teaspoons chopped
 oregano

1 small head of garlic, broken into cloves

50 ml (2 fl oz) dry white wine

1 leek, cleaned and sliced

550 g (1¹/₄ lb) potatoes, peeled and thickly sliced

600 ml (1 pint) Fish Stock or Chicken Stock
 (see page 222)

A pinch of saffron strands

4 x 450 g (1 lb) gurnard, cleaned and filleted (see
 pages 14 and 22)

2 tablespoons Rouille (see pages 224–5)

1 teaspoon capers in brine, drained and rinsed

Salt and freshly ground black pepper

1 Heat 2 tablespoons of the oil in a medium saucepan. Add the oregano sprigs and unpeeled garlic cloves and cook for 2 minutes, until the garlic is lightly browned. Remove the pan from the heat, cool a little, then add the wine. Return to the heat and boil rapidly until it has almost completely evaporated. Add the leek to the pan and cook, stirring, for 1 minute. Add the sliced potatoes with the stock, saffron and some seasoning, then cover and leave to simmer for 15–20 minutes until the potatoes are tender.

2 Shortly before the potatoes are ready, heat the rest of the olive oil in a large frying pan. Add the gurnard fillets, skin-side down, and fry for 2 minutes, until lightly browned. Turn over and fry for another minute or until they have cooked through and are lightly browned on both sides.

3 Put the rouille into a small bowl and whisk in 50 ml (2 fl oz) of slightly cooled cooking liquor from the pan of potatoes. Stir this back into the pan and cook over a gentle heat for about 1 minute, being careful not to let it boil or it will curdle. Divide the potatoes and their liquor between 4 warmed soup plates and place the gurnard fillets on top. Sprinkle with the capers and chopped oregano and serve.

poached quenelles of gurnard with prawn sauce (see technique 36, page 58)

SERVES 4

25 g (1 oz) butter

150 ml (5 fl oz) milk

50 g (2 oz) fresh white breadcrumbs

350 g (12 oz) gurnard fillets, skinned and boned
 (see page 32)

Pinch of freshly grated nutmeg

2 teaspoons lemon juice

1 egg

120 ml (4 fl oz) double cream

Salt and freshly ground white pepper

FOR THE PRAWN SAUCE:

1 quantity Shellfish Reduction (see page 222), made
 with prawns

85 ml (3 fl oz) double cream

1 teaspoon Beurre Manié (see page 227)

1 egg yolk

1 To make the quenelles, melt the butter and mix with the milk and breadcrumbs to form a coarse paste. Cover and chill for 30 minutes. Make sure all the other ingredients are cold too.

2 Cut the gurnard fillets into small pieces and put into a food processor with the breadcrumb paste, nutmeg, lemon juice, egg and seasoning. Blend for at least 1 minute to a very smooth paste.

3 Transfer the mixture to a large bowl sitting inside a bowl of iced water. Add the cream a little at a time, beating between each addition, so that the mixture becomes light and thickens. Cover and chill for 30 minutes.

4 For the sauce, heat the shellfish reduction in a small pan. Add half of the cream and the beurre manié and whisk over a medium heat for a few minutes until smooth and thickened. Keep warm.

5 Bring a wide, shallow pan of lightly salted water to the boil, then reduce the heat to a slow simmer. Mould the fish mixture into quenelles (see page 59) and drop them into the simmering water. Poach for 3–4 minutes, turning them over half-way through, then remove with a slotted spoon on to a clean tea towel and leave to drain briefly.

6 Divide the quenelles between 4 individual dishes or 1 large gratin dish. Pre-heat the grill to high.

7 Whisk together the egg yolk and remaining cream and stir it into the sauce. Stir over a low heat until thickened, but not boiling. Pour the sauce over the quenelles and grill for about a minute until lightly browned. Serve.

GURNARD

pan-fried gurnard with sage and garlic butter (see technique 15, page 32)

SERVES 4

4 x 350–450 g (12 oz–1 lb) gurnard
4 teaspoons sunflower oil
75 g (3 oz) unsalted butter
2 garlic cloves, finely chopped
2 tablespoons small sage leaves
2 tablespoons lemon juice
Salt and freshly ground black pepper

1 Skin the whole gurnard as described on page 32, then season them on both sides with some salt and pepper.

2 Heat the oil in a large frying pan. Add the fish and 15 g (½ oz) of the butter to the pan and fry over a medium-high heat for about 4 minutes on each side until golden brown. Lift into the centre of 4 warmed serving plates and keep warm.

3 Pour away any remaining oil from the pan and wipe it out with kitchen paper. Add the rest of the butter to the pan and, as it starts to melt, add the garlic and whole sage leaves. Return the pan to the heat and leave the butter to cook gently for about 30 seconds. Quickly add the lemon juice and some seasoning, then immediately spoon it over the fish, trying to divide the bits of garlic and sage leaves equally between each plate. Serve straight away.

PAN-FRIED GURNARD WITH SAGE AND GARLIC BUTTER

recipes

chapter 9

flat fish

steamed fillet of brill with poached oysters

SERVES 4

300 ml (10 fl oz) Fish Stock (see page 222)
50 g (2 oz) butter
1 shallot, finely chopped
50 ml (2 fl oz) dry white wine
16 oysters
4 x 225 g (8 oz) brill fillets (see page 25)
2 tablespoons double cream
1 tablespoon chopped chives
Salt and freshly ground black pepper

1 Put the fish stock into a small pan and boil it rapidly until reduced to about 120 ml (4 fl oz).

2 Melt a knob of the butter in a medium-sized pan. Cut the rest into small pieces. Add the shallot to the pan and cook gently for 5 minutes, until soft. Add the wine and simmer until reduced to about 2 tablespoons. Add the reduced fish stock and keep warm.

3 Open the oysters as described on page 91. Remove the meats and clean 4 of the deeper shells for serving.

4 Season the fish fillets on both sides with a little salt and lay them on a heatproof plate. Place a trivet or an upturned plate in a large pan and pour in about 25 cm (1 in) of water. Bring to a vigorous simmer, then put the plate on the trivet, cover the pan and steam for 4 minutes. Lift the fish out of the steamer and pour the juices from the plate into the sauce. Cover the fish and keep it warm.

5 Bring the sauce to a gentle simmer, add the oyster meats and their juice and poach for 2 minutes. Lift them out with a slotted spoon and keep them warm with the brill.

6 Add the cream to the sauce and simmer vigorously for 3 minutes. Then whisk in the remaining butter, a few pieces at a time, to form an emulsified sauce. Stir in the chives and season with black pepper and a little salt if necessary.

7 To serve, place the fish fillets skin-side down on 4 warmed plates. Rest one of the oyster shells alongside the fish. Put a poached oyster in each shell and arrange the rest over and around the fish. Pour the sauce over and serve.

ALTERNATIVE FISH

This is a dish where only a few fish will do – turbot, lemon sole, American flounder or John Dory.

a casserole of brill with shallots and wild mushrooms

SERVES 4

15 g (^{1}/$_2$ oz) dried porcini mushrooms
90 g (3^1/$_2$ oz) unsalted butter
12 small shallots
^{1}/$_2$ teaspoon sugar
8 garlic cloves
900 ml (1^1/$_2$ pints) Chicken Stock (see page 222)
1 thick slice of cooked ham, cut into small dice
1 carrot, chopped
1 leek, cleaned and chopped
1 celery stick, chopped
^{1}/$_2$ medium onion, chopped
2 teaspoons balsamic vinegar
2 sprigs thyme
50 ml (2 fl oz) red wine
4 x 175 g (6 oz) unskinned brill fillets
100 g (4 oz) wild mushrooms, cleaned and sliced
Salt and freshly ground black pepper

1 Soak the dried porcini in 150 ml (5 fl oz) warm water for 30 minutes.

2 Melt 25 g (1 oz) of the butter in a shallow pan large enough to take the fillets of brill side by side. Add the shallots, sugar and garlic and cook until lightly browned. Barely cover with some of the chicken stock, add the ham, ¼ teaspoon salt and some pepper, and simmer gently until both the shallots and garlic are tender. Then turn up the heat and boil rapidly until the stock has reduced to a thick sticky glaze, shaking the pan now and then so that the onions and garlic become well coated. Remove them from the pan to a plate and keep warm. Set the pan to one side, unwashed.

3 Melt another 25 g (1 oz) of the butter in a medium-sized saucepan. Add the carrot, leek, celery and onion and fry until nicely coloured. Add the remaining chicken stock, balsamic vinegar, 1 thyme sprig, the red wine and the soaking liquor from the dried mushrooms and simmer for 20–30 minutes. Then strain through a fine sieve and discard all the vegetables.

4 Heat a small knob of butter in a frying pan. Add the brill fillets, skin-side down, and cook for about 1 minute until lightly browned. Season with salt and pepper and put side-by-side in the pan used for glazing the shallots. Pour over the stock, add the second thyme sprig, cover and simmer for 5 minutes until the brill is cooked.

5 Meanwhile, melt another 15 g (½ oz) of the butter in the frying pan, add the soaked porcini and wild mushrooms and fry briskly for 2–3 minutes. Season with a little salt and pepper.

6 Remove the brill from the pan and keep warm. Boil the remaining liquid until reduced and well-flavoured, then whisk in the remaining butter. Stir in the mushrooms.

7 Put the brill on to 4 warmed plates. Add the glazed shallots and garlic, spoon over the sauce and serve.

PLAICE,
FLOUNDER

grilled scored plaice with roasted red pepper, garlic and oregano (see technique 7, page 24)

SERVES 4

4 x 450 g (1 lb) plaice
1 Roasted Red Pepper (see page 227)
1/2 medium-hot red Dutch chilli,
    deseeded and finely chopped
50 ml (2 fl oz) extra virgin olive oil
1 large garlic clove, finely chopped
1 teaspoon chopped oregano
2 teaspoons lemon juice
Salt and freshly ground black pepper

1 Trim the fins from the plaice and then cut away the frills as described on page 24. Put the fish dark-side up on a board. Make a deep cut down the centre of each fish from head to tail. Then make a series of smaller cuts out from the first one towards the sides so that they look like the veins of a leaf. Turn the fish over and repeat on the other side.

2 Remove the skin and seeds from the roasted red pepper and very finely chop the flesh. Mix with the chilli, oil, garlic, oregano, lemon juice, 1 teaspoon of salt and some pepper to make the marinade.

3 One hour before cooking, put the fish into a shallow dish and pour over the marinade, making sure it goes right into the slashes. Set aside.

4 Pre-heat the grill to high. Transfer the fish to baking trays, dark-side up. Depending on the size of your grill, cook them 1 or 2 at a time for 7–8 minutes or until the flesh is firm and white at the thickest part, just behind the head. Spoon over the remaining marinade 4 minutes before the end of cooking. Keep warm while you cook the rest. Serve with some chips and a salad of soft green leaves.

plaice with leeks, mint and beaujolais

SERVES 4 AS A STARTER

1 x 100 g (4 oz) leek, cleaned
100 g (4 oz) butter
1 rasher of smoked back bacon, cut into thin strips
1 teaspoon chopped mint
175 ml (6 fl oz) Beaujolais
50 ml (2 fl oz) port
300 ml (10 fl oz) Fish Stock (see page 222)
1/4 teaspoon caster sugar
4 x 75 g (3 oz) skinned plaice fillets
Sprigs of mint, to garnish
Salt and freshly ground white pepper

1 Cut the leek in half lengthways and once more into quarters if it is quite large. Cut across these strips into 1 cm (1/2 in) pieces. Bring a small pan of salted water to the boil, add the leek and simmer for a few minutes until tender but still al dente. Drain well.

2 Melt 15 g (1/2 oz) of the butter in a small pan, add the bacon and leeks and cook gently until all the excess water has evaporated. Stir in the mint and season with some salt and pepper. Set aside and keep warm.

3 Pre-heat the grill to high. Put the Beaujolais, port, fish stock and sugar into a large pan and boil rapidly until reduced by three-quarters.

4 Melt another 15 g (1/2 oz) of the butter and brush over both sides of each plaice fillet. Season with salt and pepper and lay them on the lightly oiled rack of the grill pan. Grill for 2 minutes.

5 Dice the remaining butter. Bring the reduced wine and stock back up to the boil and then whisk in the butter, a few small pieces at a time. Adjust the seasoning if necessary.

6 To serve, spoon the leeks on to 4 warmed plates. Put the plaice fillets on top and pour the sauce around. Garnish with sprigs of mint.

9

deep-fried flounder with spring onion and chilli seasoning

SERVES 4

750 g (1½ lb) skinned thick flounder fillets
  (see page 25)

Sunflower oil, for deep-frying

Salt

1 small bunch coriander sprigs, to garnish

Lime wedges, to serve

FOR THE SPRING ONION AND CHILLI SEASONING:

Sunflower oil, for frying

1 small onion, finely chopped

2 garlic cloves, finely chopped

1 medium-hot red Dutch chilli, thinly sliced

2 spring onions, thinly sliced

1 teaspoon Maldon sea-salt flakes

½ teaspoon Sichuan peppercorns, crushed

FOR THE BATTER:

50 g (2 oz) plain flour

50 g (2 oz) cornflour

A pinch of salt

175 ml (6 fl oz) ice-cold soda water from a new bottle

1 For the spring onion and chilli seasoning, pour about 1 cm (½ inch) of sunflower oil into a frying pan and leave it to get hot. Add the chopped onion and fry for about 3–4 minutes, until it is beginning to brown. Then add the garlic and cook for 1 minute. Add the chilli and fry until the onion and garlic are crisp and golden brown.

2 Lift the mixture out with a slotted spoon on to lots of kitchen paper and leave to go cold. Then transfer it to a bowl and mix in the spring onions, salt and Sichuan pepper.

3 Heat some oil for deep-frying to 190°C (375°F). Meanwhile, season the flounder fillets with salt on both sides and cut them into strips about 25 cm (1 inch) wide.

4 For the batter, sift the flour, cornflour and salt into a bowl and stir in the ice-cold soda water until only just mixed; it should be a bit lumpy.

5 Dip the strips of flounder into the batter a few pieces at a time, then drop them into the hot oil and fry for 2 minutes, until golden. Drain briefly on kitchen paper and keep hot while you cook the rest.

6 Pile the fried flounder on to a serving platter and sprinkle over the spring onion and chilli seasoning. Scatter over the fresh coriander sprigs and serve straight away, with the lime wedges.

spiced fillets of flounder in warm tortillas with a fresh coriander and tomato salsa

SERVES 4

450 g (1 lb) skinned flounder fillets (see page 25)

8 flour tortillas

8 tablespoons Mayonnaise (see page 224)

FOR THE MARINADE:

1 teaspoon ground cumin

1 teaspoon hot paprika

2 garlic cloves, crushed

Juice of 1 lemon (about 3 tablespoons)

Maldon sea salt flakes and freshly ground black pepper

FOR THE FRESH CORIANDER AND TOMATO SALSA:

4 vine-ripened tomatoes, seeded and diced

1 small red onion, finely chopped

2 tablespoons chopped coriander

2 medium-hot red Dutch chillies, deseeded and finely
  chopped

1 For the marinade, mix the ground cumin, paprika, garlic, 2 tablespoons of the lemon juice and some salt and pepper together in a shallow dish. Add the flounder fillets, turn them over once or twice and leave them to marinate at room temperature for 20 minutes.

2 Pre-heat the grill to high. Lift the flounder fillets out of the marinade and put them on to a lightly oiled baking tray or the rack of the grill pan. Mix all the ingredients for the salsa together in a small bowl with the rest of the lemon juice and ½ teaspoon salt. Spoon the mayonnaise into another bowl.

3 Grill the flounder fillets for 3–4 minutes on one side only. Meanwhile, lightly toast the tortillas, one at a time, in a dry hot frying pan for about 15 seconds on each side. Wrap in a napkin and keep warm.

4 When the fish is cooked, break it into large flakes and pile it into a warmed serving bowl. Take the grilled fish, salsa, tortillas and mayonnaise to the table and leave everyone to fill their own tortillas.

goujons of lemon sole with parmesan breadcrumbs (see technique 8, page 25)

SERVES 4

450 g (1 lb) skinned lemon sole fillets (see page 25)
100 g (4 oz) fresh white breadcrumbs
25 g (1 oz) Parmesan cheese, finely grated
1/2 teaspoon cayenne pepper
Sunflower oil, for deep-frying
50 g (2 oz) plain flour
3 eggs, beaten
Salt
Lemon wedges, to serve

1 Cut each lemon sole fillet diagonally across into strips about the thickness of your little finger. Mix the breadcrumbs with the grated Parmesan and cayenne pepper and set aside.

2 Heat some oil for deep-frying to 190°C (375°F) and line a baking tray with plenty of kitchen paper.

3 Coat the goujons a few at a time in the flour, then in beaten egg and finally in the breadcrumb mixture, making sure that they all take on an even coating and remain separate.

4 Drop a handful of goujons into the oil and deep-fry for about 1 minute until crisp and golden. Lift out with a slotted spoon on to the paper-lined tray to drain and repeat with the remainder, making sure the oil has come back to temperature first.

5 Pile the goujons on to 4 warmed plates and garnish with the lemon wedges. Serve if you wish with a mixed whole leaf or herb salad, dressed with a little extra virgin olive oil and some seasoning.

deep-fried fillets of lemon sole with salsa verde mayonnaise

SERVES 4

Sunflower oil, for deep-frying
1 loaf of black olive ciabatta
12 x 65 g (2½ oz) skinned lemon sole fillets (see page 25)
50 g (2 oz) plain flour
2 large eggs, beaten
Salt and freshly ground black pepper
Lemon wedges, to serve

FOR THE SALSA VERDE MAYONNAISE:

3 heaped tablespoons parsley leaves
1 heaped tablespoon mint leaves
3 tablespoons capers, drained and rinsed
6 anchovy fillets in oil, drained
1 garlic clove
6 tablespoons Mayonnaise (see page 224), made with olive oil
1 teaspoon Dijon mustard
1 tablespoon lemon juice
1/2 teaspoon salt

1 For the salsa verde mayonnaise, coarsely chop the parsley, mint, capers, anchovy fillets and garlic all together and mix with the mayonnaise, mustard, lemon juice and salt.

2 Heat some oil for deep-frying to 190°C (375°F). Process the ciabatta in a food processor into fine breadcrumbs. Season the fish fillets with a little salt and pepper, then coat each one with flour, then beaten egg, then breadcrumbs.

3 Deep-fry the fish, 2 pieces at a time, for about 2 minutes, until crisp and golden. Drain on kitchen paper and keep warm while you fry the rest. Serve straight away with the salsa verde mayonnaise and some lemon wedges.

ALTERNATIVE FISH
Plaice, cod, haddock or Australian flathead fillets.

9

sole veronique

SERVES 4

8 x 75 g (3 oz) skinned Dover sole fillets (see page 25)
A little butter, for greasing
600 ml (1 pint) Fish Stock (see page 222)
75 ml (3 fl oz) dry vermouth, such as Noilly Prat
300 ml (10 fl oz) double cream
25–30 seedless green grapes, halved
Lemon juice, salt and freshly ground white pepper

1 Pre-heat the oven to 180°C/350°F/Gas Mark 4. Season the sole fillets lightly on both sides. Fold them in half, skinned-side innermost, and lay side-by-side in a buttered shallow ovenproof dish. Pour over the fish stock, cover with foil and bake for 20 minutes.

2 Remove the fish from the dish and put on a warmed serving plate. Cover once again with the foil and keep warm. Pour the cooking liquor into a saucepan, add the vermouth, bring to the boil and boil vigorously until reduced to about 6 tablespoons. Add the cream and a squeeze of lemon juice and simmer until it has thickened to a good sauce consistency.

3 Add the grapes to the sauce and warm through gently. Season the sauce to taste, pour over the fish and serve immediately.

dover sole à la meunière (see technique 3, page 18)

SERVES 2

25 g (1 oz) plain flour
2 x 400–450 g (14 oz–1 lb) Dover soles, trimmed and
    skinned (see page 18)
2 tablespoons sunflower oil
50 g (2 oz) unsalted butter
2 teaspoons lemon juice
1 tablespoon chopped parsley
Salt and freshly ground white pepper
1 lemon, cut into 6 wedges, to serve

1 Season the flour with ½ teaspoon of salt and 10 turns of the pepper mill. Coat the Dover soles on both sides with the flour and then knock off the excess.

DOVER SOLE À LA MEUNIÈRE

2 Heat half of the oil in a large well-seasoned or non-stick frying pan. Add one of the soles, lower the heat slightly and add 7 g (¼ oz) of the butter. Fry over a moderate heat for 4–5 minutes, without moving, until richly golden.

3 Carefully turn the fish over and cook for another 4–5 minutes until golden brown and cooked through. Lift on to a serving plate and keep warm. Repeat with the second fish. Prepare the fish for serving as described on page 19 if you wish.

4 Discard the frying oil and wipe the pan clean. Add the remaining butter and allow it to melt over a moderate heat. When the butter starts to smell nutty and turn light brown, add the lemon juice, parsley and some seasoning. Pour some of this beurre noisette over each fish and serve straight away.

TURBOT,
HALIBUT

roasted tronçons of turbot with a sauce vierge (see technique 9, page 26)

SERVES 4

85 ml (3 fl oz) extra virgin olive oil,
 plus extra for brushing
1 teaspoon chopped rosemary
1 teaspoon chopped thyme
1 bay leaf, very finely chopped
1/2 teaspoon crushed fennel seeds
1 teaspoon coarsely crushed black peppercorns
Maldon sea-salt flakes
4 x 175–225 g (6–8 oz) tronçons of turbot (see page 26)

FOR THE SAUCE VIERGE:

85 ml (3 fl oz) extra virgin olive oil
2 tablespoons lemon juice
1 plum tomato, seeded and cut into small dice
8 black olives, pitted and cut into fine strips
2 small anchovy fillets in oil, drained and diced
1 garlic clove, finely chopped
1 heaped teaspoon coarsely chopped parsley
Salt and coarsely ground black pepper

1 Pre-heat the oven to 230°C/450°F/Gas Mark 8. Mix together the olive oil, chopped herbs, fennel seeds, crushed peppercorns and 1 teaspoon of sea salt in a small roasting tin. Add the pieces of turbot and turn them over in the mixture so that they are well coated.

2 For the sauce, put everything except the chopped parsley and seasoning into a small pan, ready to warm through just before serving.

3 Heat a heavy-based ovenproof frying pan over a high heat until smoking-hot. Add the tronçons of turbot, dark-side down, to the pan and sear for about 1 minute until the skin has taken on a good colour. Turn them over, transfer the pan to the oven and roast for 8–10 minutes. Just as the fish is ready, place the sauce over a very low heat to warm through.

4 To serve, lift the pieces of fish onto the centre of 4 warmed plates. Stir the parsley and seasoning into the sauce and spoon it around the fish. Brush the top of each piece of fish with a little more oil and sprinkle with a few sea-salt flakes.

ALTERNATIVE FISH
Thick fillets of brill, John Dory or sea bass, or fillets of flaky fish such as cod, haddock or hake.

myrtle's turbot (see technique 23, page 42)

SERVES 4

1 x 1.5 kg (3 lb) turbot
1 small bunch thyme
1 small bunch parsley
1 small bunch chives
75 g (3 oz) butter
Maldon sea-salt flakes and freshly ground black pepper

1 Pre-heat the oven to 200°C/400°F/Gas Mark 6. With a sharp knife, cut through the skin on the top (dark) side only, all the way around the fish close to the frill-like fins.

2 Sprinkle some salt over the base of a roasting tin large enough to hold the turbot. Put the fish into the tin and sprinkle the top with some more salt and some pepper. Pour about 600ml (1 pint) of water around the fish so that it is just covered and bake for 30 minutes. Meanwhile, finely chop half the herbs. Gently melt the butter in a small pan, stir in the chopped herbs and set aside.

3 Remove the fish from the oven and carefully peel away the top skin. Transfer it to a warmed serving dish.

4 Pour the sauce over the white flesh of the turbot. Shape the rest of the herbs into a bouquet and lay them near the head as a garnish. Serve, as described on page 43, with plenty of boiled new potatoes.

ROASTED TRONÇONS OF TURBOT WITH A SAUCE VIERGE

9

braised fillet of turbot with slivers of potato, mushrooms and truffle oil

SERVES 4

600 ml (1 pint) Chicken Stock (see page 222)
175 g (6 oz) waxy main-crop potatoes, such as Wilja
100 g (4 oz) unsalted butter
1 thin slice of cooked ham, weighing about 25 g (1 oz),
    cut into very fine dice
25 g (1 oz) shallots, finely chopped
85 ml (3 fl oz) dry vermouth, such as Noilly Prat
100 g (4 oz) button mushrooms, thinly sliced
2 teaspoons lemon juice
1 tablespoon truffle oil
750 g (1½ lb) piece of unskinned turbot fillet, cut into
    8 pieces
1 tablespoon chopped parsley
Salt and freshly ground black pepper

1 Put the chicken stock into a wide-based pan and boil rapidly until reduced by half.

2 Peel the potatoes and slice as thinly as you can, then cut them across into thin matchsticks.

3 Melt half the butter in a frying pan that is large enough to hold all the pieces of fish in one layer. Add the potatoes, ham and shallots and cook gently for 4–5 minutes.

4 Add the vermouth and chicken stock and simmer for about 8 minutes, until the potatoes are almost, but not quite, cooked. You can prepare the dish to this stage some time in advance if you wish.

5 Stir the mushrooms, lemon juice, truffle oil and some salt and pepper into the pan and then rest the pieces of turbot on top, skin-side up. Cover and simmer for about 6 minutes or until the fish is cooked through.

6 Lift the fish on to a plate and keep warm. Add the remaining butter to the pan and boil rapidly for 10 minutes or until the sauce has thickened and the potatoes are just beginning to break up.

7 To serve, peel the skin off the turbot and place the fish on 4 warmed plates. Stir the parsley into the sauce and spoon it on top of the fish.

HALIBUT POACHED IN OLIVE OIL WITH CUCUMBER AND DILL

halibut poached in olive oil with cucumber and dill (see technique 22, page 41)

SERVES 4

600 ml (1 pint) inexpensive olive oil
4 x 175 g (6 oz) pieces of thick halibut fillet, skinned
1 tablespoon extra virgin olive oil
1 large cucumber, peeled and thinly sliced
1 tablespoon chopped dill, plus a few sprigs to garnish
2 teaspoons white wine vinegar
Sea salt

1 Pour a thin layer of the olive oil into a pan just large enough to hold the pieces of halibut side by side. Season the fish on both sides with a little salt, put it in the pan and pour over the rest of the oil – it should just cover the fish. Very slowly heat the oil to 55–60°C (130–140°F), agitating it with a fish slice now and then so that it heats evenly. If you don't have a thermometer, the oil should just feel unpleasantly hot to your little finger.

2 Now take the pan off the heat and leave it somewhere warm on top of the stove for 15 minutes to poach gently in the oil. The temperature should remain at 55–60°C (130–140°F); if necessary, keep taking the pan on and off a low heat to maintain this temperature.

3 Shortly before the fish is ready, heat the extra virgin olive oil in a large frying pan. Add the cucumber slices and toss over a medium heat for 1 minute. Add the dill, vinegar and a little salt.

4 To serve, divide the cucumber between 4 serving plates. Carefully lift the fish out of the oil, allowing the excess to drain off, and put it on top of the cucumber. Pour the oil off into a jug, leaving behind the juices from the fish, which will have settled at the bottom of the pan. Spoon these juices around the edge of each plate, sprinkle the fish with a few sea-salt flakes and garnish with a sprig of fresh dill. Serve with some boiled new potatoes.

recipes
chapter 10

crustaceans

steamed crab with lemongrass dressing (see technique 56, page 84)

SERVES 4

8–12 Asian swimming crabs or 2 x 900 g (2 lb) brown
   crabs, live or cooked

FOR THE LEMONGRASS DRESSING:

1 lemongrass stalk, outer leaves removed and the core
   finely chopped
Finely grated zest and juice of 1 lime
2 tablespoons Thai fish sauce (*nam pla*)
150 ml (5 fl oz) water
1 green Dutch chilli, seeded and finely chopped
1/2 teaspoon caster sugar
1 tablespoon roughly chopped coriander

1 Prepare the crabs as described on pages 80 and 84. Mix all the
ingredients for the lemongrass dressing together and set aside.

2 Bring about 2.5 cm (1 inch) of water to the boil in a wide shallow
pan. Either put some sort of trivet in the bottom on which you can rest
a plate – a couple of pastry cutters or another upturned plate will do –
or use a petal steamer. Pour in some water so that it doesn't quite cover
the trivet and bring to the boil.

3 Pile the pieces of crab on to the petal steamer or a heatproof plate
and lower it into the pan. Cover and steam for 8 minutes, by which time
the crab should be cooked. If you are using cooked crabs, just give them
3–4 minutes to heat through.

4 Arrange the pieces of crab on a large warmed serving plate. Spoon
over the lemongrass dressing and serve straight away.

ALTERNATIVE FISH

Lobster, steamed and served with this dressing, is a bit of a work of art.
If you throw all the dressing ingredients in a large pot of mussels and
steam them open, you'll be amazed too.

singapore chilli crab

SERVES 4

2 x 900 g (2 lb) live or cooked crabs
4 tablespoons groundnut or sunflower oil
4 fat garlic cloves, finely chopped
2.5 cm (1 inch) fresh root ginger, finely chopped
4 tablespoons tomato ketchup
3 medium-hot, red, Dutch chillies, finely chopped
2 tablespoons dark soy sauce
150 ml (5 fl oz) water
A few turns of the black pepper mill
2 spring onions, cut into 5 cm (2 inch) pieces and finely
  shredded lengthways

1 If using live crabs, kill them as described on page 80 and prepare them for stir-frying (see page 84).

SINGAPORE CHILLI CRAB

2 Heat the oil in a large wok. Add the crab pieces and stir-fry for 3 minutes, adding the garlic and the ginger after 1 minute.

3 Add the juices from the back shell, the tomato ketchup, red chillies, soy sauce, water and black pepper. Cover and simmer over a medium heat for 5 minutes if the crab is fresh or 2–3 minutes if using cooked crab.

4 Spoon the crab on to 1 large plate or 4 soup plates, sprinkle over the shredded spring onions and serve straight away.

ALTERNATIVE FISH
Large raw prawns or uncooked lobster.

crab and gruyère tartlets

SERVES 4

1 quantity Shortcrust Pastry (see page 227)
1 egg white
225 g (8 oz) fresh white crab meat
50 g (2 oz) fresh brown crab meat
2 egg yolks
85 ml (3 fl oz) double cream
A pinch of cayenne pepper
50 g (2 oz) Gruyère cheese, finely grated
Salt and freshly ground black pepper

1 Pre-heat the oven to 220°C/425°F/Gas Mark 7. Briefly knead the pastry on a lightly floured surface until smooth. Roll out and use to line 4 shallow 11 cm (4½ inch) loose-based tartlet tins. Chill for 20 minutes.

2 Line the pastry cases with crumpled greaseproof paper, cover the base with a generous layer of baking beans and bake blind for 15 minutes. Remove the paper and beans, brush the inside of each pastry case with a little unbeaten egg white and return to the oven for 2 minutes. Remove from the oven and lower the temperature to 200°C/400°F/Gas Mark 6.

3 Mix the crab meat with the egg yolks, cream, cayenne and some salt and pepper. Spoon the mixture into the tartlet cases and sprinkle with the grated Gruyère cheese. Bake at the top of the oven for 15–20 minutes, until lightly golden. Serve warm.

ravioli of fresh crab with warm parsley and lemon butter

SERVES 4

175 g (6 oz) fresh white crab meat
1 tablespoon melted butter
A pinch of cayenne pepper
Salt and freshly ground black pepper
1 quantity Fresh Egg Pasta (see page 227)

FOR THE PARSLEY AND LEMON BUTTER:

100 g (4 oz) butter
2 tablespoons chopped flat-leaf parsley
1/2 teaspoon finely grated lemon zest
2 teaspoons of lemon juice
2 garlic cloves, very finely chopped

1 For the filling, mix the crab meat with the melted butter, cayenne pepper and a little salt to taste.

2 Cut the pasta dough in half and set one piece aside, wrapped in cling film, so that it doesn't dry out. Roll the other piece out on a floured work surface into a 38 cm (15 inch) square, making sure it doesn't stick.

3 With your fingertips, make small marks at 7.5 cm (3 inch) intervals in 3 evenly spaced rows (i.e. 3 rows of 5 indentations) over one half of the square.

4 Place a teaspoon of the crab mixture on each mark, then brush lines of water between the piles of mixture.

5 Fold over the other half of the square so that the edges meet, then working from the centre of the folded edge moving outwards and towards you, press firmly around each pile of mixture with your fingers to press out any trapped air and seal in the filling.

6 Trim off the edges of the dough and cut between the rows with a sharp knife. Lift the ravioli on to a lightly floured tray. Repeat with the second piece of pasta dough to make 30 ravioli in all.

7 Bring 3.5 litres (6 pints) of water to the boil in a large pan with 2 tablespoons of salt. Drop the ravioli into the pan of boiling water and cook for 4 minutes.

8 For the parsley and lemon butter, gently melt the butter with the parsley, lemon zest, lemon juice and garlic. Season to taste with a little salt and pepper.

9 Drain the ravioli well and divide them between 4 warmed pasta plates. Spoon over the warm parsley and lemon butter and serve.

NOTE

If you want to make the ravioli in advance, drop them into the pan of boiling water and cook for just 20 seconds. Drain well, place in a single layer on a plastic tray and cover with clingfilm. Chill until required.

betsy apple's crab salad with basil, parsley and chives in a lemon vinaigrette

SERVES 4

450 g (1 lb) fresh white crab meat
2 tablespoons finely shredded basil
2 tablespoons each finely chopped flat-leaf parsley and chives
A few whole chives, with blossoms attached if possible

FOR THE LEMON VINAIGRETTE:

1 1/2 tablespoons lemon juice
1 teaspoon Dijon mustard
4–5 tablespoons extra virgin olive oil
Salt and freshly ground black pepper

BETSY APPLE'S CRAB SALAD WITH BASIL, PARSLEY AND CHIVES IN A LEMON VINAIGRETTE

1 Pick over the crab meat for any tiny pieces of shell, then put it into a serving bowl.

2 For the vinaigrette, mix together the lemon juice and mustard and then gradually whisk in the oil, ½ teaspoon of salt and plenty of freshly ground black pepper.

3 Stir the vinaigrette into the crab with the chopped herbs just before serving. Check it for seasoning and garnish with a few whole chives. Serve with plenty of crusty French bread and chilled white wine.

maryland crab cakes with a tarragon and butter sauce (see technique 54, page 82)

SERVES 4

40 g (1½ oz) cream crackers or Saltines
450 g (1 lb) fresh white crab meat
1 egg, beaten
2 tablespoons Mayonnaise (see pages 224), made with sunflower oil
1 tablespoon English mustard powder
1 tablespoon lemon juice
A dash of Worcestershire sauce
2 tablespoons chopped parsley
4 tablespoons Clarified Butter (see page 226)
Salt and freshly ground white pepper

FOR THE TARRAGON AND BUTTER SAUCE:

50 ml (2 fl oz) white wine vinegar
4 tablespoons Clarified Butter (see page 226)
1 plum tomato, skinned, seeded and diced
1 teaspoon chopped tarragon

1 Put the cream crackers into a plastic bag and crush into fine crumbs with a rolling pin. Put the crab meat into a bowl and add just enough of the cracker crumbs to absorb any moisture from the crab. You may not need to add them all.

2 Break the egg into a small bowl and whisk in the mayonnaise, mustard, lemon juice, Worcestershire sauce and some seasoning. Fold this mixture

MARYLAND CRAB CAKES WITH A
TARRAGON AND BUTTER SAUCE

into the crab meat but try not to break up the lumps of crab too much. Stir in the parsley. Shape the mixture into eight 7.5 cm (3 inch) patties, put them on a plate, cover with cling film and chill for at least 1 hour.

3 Heat the clarified butter in a large frying pan. Add the crab cakes (in 2 batches if necessary) and cook over a medium heat for 2–3 minutes on each side until crisp and richly golden. Keep the first lot warm if you need to, while you cook the second batch.

4 Meanwhile, for the sauce, boil the vinegar in a small pan until reduced to about 2 tablespoons. Add the clarified butter, diced tomato, chopped tarragon and some salt and pepper to taste and gently warm through. Serve with the crab cakes.

CRAB

sautéed soft-shell crabs with garlic butter (see technique 55, page 83)

SERVES 4

8–12 American soft-shell crabs

100 g (4 oz) plain flour

1 tablespoon shrimp boil seasoning (see the recipe below) or 'Old Bay' seasoning mix

3 tablespoons Clarified Butter (see page 226)

100 g (4 oz) butter, at room temperature

3 garlic cloves, crushed

1 tablespoon lemon juice

2 tablespoons chopped parsley

Salt and freshly ground black pepper

FOR THE SHRIMP BOIL SEASONING:

2 tablespoons yellow mustard seeds

1 tablespoon black peppercorns

1 tablespoon dried chilli flakes

3 dried bay leaves

$\frac{1}{2}$ tablespoon celery seeds

$\frac{1}{2}$ tablespoon coriander seeds

$\frac{1}{2}$ tablespoon ground ginger

2 pieces of blade mace

4 tablespoons salt

1 To make the shrimp boil seasoning, put everything except for the salt into a spice grinder and grind to a fine powder. Add the salt and blend for 2–3 seconds.

2 Prepare the crabs as described on page 83. Sift the flour, shrimp boil seasoning, 1 teaspoon of salt and some pepper on to a plate. Dredge the crabs well in the flour, then pat off the excess.

3 Heat the clarified butter in a large frying pan. Fry the crabs in batches over a moderate heat for 2 minutes on each side, until lightly browned. Shake off any excess butter as you remove them from the pan on to warmed plates. Keep warm while you fry the rest.

4 Add the rest of the butter and the crushed garlic to the pan and allow it to sizzle for a few seconds. Add the lemon juice, then throw in the parsley and some seasoning. Spoon the butter over the crabs and serve immediately.

BAKED CROMER CRABS WITH BERKSWELL CHEESE

baked cromer crabs with berkswell cheese

SERVES 4

4 dressed Cromer crabs

25 g (1 oz) butter

Juice of $\frac{1}{2}$ lemon

1 teaspoon made English mustard

4 gratings of fresh nutmeg

A good pinch of cayenne pepper

Lemon wedges, to serve

FOR THE TOPPING:

15 g ($\frac{1}{2}$ oz) fresh white breadcrumbs

1 tablespoon melted butter

25 g (1 oz) Berkswell cheese, finely grated

1 Pre-heat the oven to 200°C/400°F/Gas Mark 6. Remove the crab meat from the shells and put it in a large bowl. Melt the butter and then mix in the lemon juice, mustard, nutmeg and cayenne pepper. Gently fold this mixture through the crab meat, taking great care not to break up the large chunks.

2 Spoon the crab mixture back into the shells and lightly level the tops.

3 For the topping, mix the breadcrumbs with the melted butter, then stir in the grated cheese and sprinkle the mixture evenly over the crab.

4 Place the crabs on a baking tray and bake for 10–12 minutes, until they are golden brown and the filling has heated through. Serve hot, with the lemon wedges.

ALTERNATIVE FISH
Other small dressed crabs.

spider crab with pasta, parsley and chilli

SERVES 4

450 g (1 lb) dried linguine or spaghetti
3 medium vine-ripened tomatoes, skinned, seeded and
 chopped
275 g (10 oz) fresh white spider crab meat
1 tablespoon chopped parsley
1¹/₂ tablespoons lemon juice
50 ml (2 fl oz) extra virgin olive oil
A pinch of dried chilli flakes
1 garlic clove, finely chopped

1 Cook the pasta in a large pan of boiling well-salted water (i.e. 1 teaspoon per 600 ml/1 pint) for 8 minutes or until *al dente*.

2 Meanwhile, put the tomatoes, crab meat, parsley, lemon juice, olive oil, chilli and garlic into another pan and warm through over a gentle heat.

3 Drain the pasta, return to the pan with the sauce and briefly toss together. Divide between 4 warmed plates and serve immediately.

warm salad of samphire, asparagus and crab

SERVES 4 AS A STARTER

1 x 1.25–1.5 kg (2¹/₂–3 lb) cooked brown crab
 (see page 80)
350 g (12 oz) thin asparagus
225 g (8 oz) samphire, picked over and washed
¹/₄ garlic clove, finely chopped
2 tablespoons extra virgin olive oil, plus extra to serve
2 teaspoons lemon juice
1 tablespoon chopped flat-leaf parsley
Salt and freshly ground black pepper
Maldon sea-salt flakes
A few Parmesan shavings, to garnish

1 Remove the meat from the crab (see page 80).

2 Snap off the woody ends from the asparagus where they break naturally and discard them. Cut the asparagus stalks in half. Break off and discard the woody ends of the samphire and break the rest into 2.5 cm (1 in) pieces.

3 Bring a pan of water to the boil. Add the samphire and asparagus and cook for 1 minute. Drain and refresh under cold water to stop them cooking and help set the colour. Drain well once more and then tip into a bowl. Add the garlic, olive oil and lemon juice, toss together lightly and season to taste if necessary.

4 Divide the asparagus and samphire between 4 plates and arrange pieces of the white crab meat and a little of the brown meat over the top. Sprinkle with the chopped parsley, drizzle over a little more olive oil and season with a few sea-salt flakes. Scatter over the Parmesan shavings and serve.

shangurro
(basque-style stuffed crab)

SERVES 4

2 large cooked brown crabs, or approximately 450 g
    (1 lb) fresh white crab meat and 100 g (4 oz) fresh
    brown crab meat
3 tablespoons olive oil
2 onions, finely chopped
9 small garlic cloves, finely chopped
225 g (8 oz) plum tomatoes, skinned, seeded and
    chopped
50 ml (2 fl oz) dry white wine
1 teaspoon caster sugar
1/4 teaspoon dried chilli flakes
3 tablespoons chopped parsley
50 g (2 oz) fresh white breadcrumbs
15 g (1/2 oz) butter, melted
Salt and freshly ground black pepper

1 Pre-heat the oven to 200°C/400°F/Gas Mark 6. If using cooked crabs, remove the meat from the shell (see page 80). Wash out the back shells and then break away the edge along the visible natural line to give a flat open shell. Set aside.

2 Heat the oil in a heavy-based frying pan, then add the onions and all except 1 chopped garlic clove. Fry over a gentle heat for 2 minutes, until softened.

3 Increase the heat, add the tomatoes, wine, sugar, chilli flakes and some salt and pepper and simmer for about 4 minutes, until the mixture has reduced to a thick sauce.

4 Stir in 2 tablespoons of the parsley and the flaked crab meat and spoon the mixture into the crab shells, if using, or individual gratin dishes. If using crab shells, rest them in a shallow ovenproof dish.

5 Mix the breadcrumbs with the melted butter and the rest of the parsley and garlic, sprinkle this mixture over the crab and bake in the oven for 10 minutes or until the topping is crisp and golden.

grilled dublin bay prawns
with a pernod and olive oil
dressing (see technique 49, page 74)

SERVES 4

16 large or 24 smaller cooked Dublin Bay prawns
    (langoustines) (see page 74)
2 small shallots, finely chopped
1/2 tablespoon roughly chopped tarragon
1/2 tablespoon roughly chopped flat-leaf parsley
1 teaspoon Dijon mustard
1 teaspoon dark soy sauce
85 ml (3 fl oz) extra virgin olive oil
1 1/2 tablespoons lemon juice
1 teaspoon Pernod
50 g (2 oz) butter, melted
Salt and freshly ground black pepper

1 Pre-heat the grill to high. Cut the Dublin Bay prawns open lengthways and scoop out the creamy contents of the heads and any red roe with a teaspoon. Put this into a small bowl and stir in the shallots, tarragon, parsley, mustard, soy sauce, oil, lemon juice, Pernod and a little salt and pepper to taste.

2 Place the halved prawns cut-side up on a baking tray or the rack of the grill pan and brush with the melted butter. Season lightly and grill for 1–2 minutes, until the shells as well as the meat are heated through.

3 Put the prawns on 4 serving plates and spoon over a little of the dressing. Divide the rest of the dressing between 4 dipping saucers or small ramekins and serve.

ALTERNATIVE FISH
Two 450 g (1 lb) cooked lobsters, halved.

goan lobster with cucumber and lime salad

SERVES 4

2 x 750–900 g (1½–2 lb) cooked lobsters

2 tablespoons groundnut oil

1 onion, chopped

3 garlic cloves, crushed

2.5 cm (1 inch) fresh root ginger, finely grated

2 green chillies, seeded and chopped

3 tablespoons Goan Masala Paste (see page 226) or a
good-quality bought curry paste

FOR THE CUCUMBER AND LIME SALAD:

1 cucumber

2 limes

Salt

1 Pre-heat the oven to 150°C/300°F/Gas Mark 2. Remove the meat from the cooked lobsters as described on page 76. Place the shells on a baking tray and warm them through in the oven.

2 For the salad, peel the cucumber and cut it into thick slices. Overlap the cucumber slices on a plate and sprinkle with the juice of one of the limes and some salt. Slice the other lime into wedges to serve with the lobster.

3 Heat the oil in a large deep frying pan. Add the onion, garlic, ginger and chillies and fry for about 5 minutes, until soft. Add the masala paste and fry for 2–3 minutes. Fold in the lobster meat and cook gently until it has heated through.

4 Spoon the mixture back into the lobster shells and serve with the cucumber and lime salad, the lime wedges and maybe some warm naan bread.

ALTERNATIVE FISH

Any spiny lobster is ideal for this dish, i.e. the native lobsters of Australia, New Zealand, South Africa, the west coast of America and, for that matter, India.

GOAN LOBSTER WITH CUCUMBER AND LIME SALAD

LOBSTER

lobster tourte

SERVES 6

1 x 1.75 kg (4 lb) cooked lobster
450 g (1 lb) chilled puff pastry
1 egg, beaten
Salt and freshly ground black pepper

FOR THE MOUSSELINE:

175 g (6 oz) skinned whiting or coley fillets
1 egg
1 small shallot, finely chopped
120 ml (4 fl oz) double cream

FOR THE SAUCE:

65 ml (2½ fl oz) Shellfish Reduction (see page 222),
    made with the lobster shell
150 ml (5 fl oz) double cream
75 g (3 oz) chilled unsalted butter, cut into small pieces
2 teaspoons lemon juice

1 Remove the meat from the lobster (see page 76). Make the shellfish reduction with the shell as described on page 222. Leave to cool.

2 For the mousseline, cut the fish fillets into small pieces and put them into a food processor with 40 ml (1½ fl oz) of the shellfish reduction, the egg, shallot and ¾ of a teaspoon of salt. Process until smooth, then, with the motor still running, add the cream in a steady stream, taking care not to process for more than 10 seconds or the mixture may curdle. Scrape into a bowl, cover and chill for 1 hour.

3 Pre-heat the oven to 220°C/425°F/Gas Mark 7. Cut the pastry in half and roll out one piece into a 25 cm (10 inch) disc. Roll out the second piece into a 28 cm (11 inch) disc.

4 Put the smaller disc of pastry on to a lightly greased baking tray and spread half the mousseline over it to within 4 cm (1½ inches) of the edge. Arrange the lobster meat over the mousseline, season with salt and pepper and then carefully spread the remaining mousseline over the top.

5 Brush the edge of the pastry with a little water, cover with the larger disc of pastry and press the edges together to seal. Crimp the edges decoratively, then brush the top with the beaten egg. Using the tip of a small sharp knife, score either a diamond pattern over the top, or mark with curves radiating from the centre. Make a hole in the centre and bake for 25 minutes.

6 Shortly before the tourte is ready, make the sauce. Put the rest of the shellfish reduction and the cream into a pan, bring to the boil and simmer for 5 minutes. Whisk in the butter, a piece at a time, followed by the lemon juice.

7 Take the tourte out of the oven and pour about 2 tablespoons of the sauce into it through the hole in the top. Return it to the oven for 5 minutes. Then remove once more and transfer to a warmed serving plate. Serve the rest of the sauce separately.

VARIATION

Replace the lobster meat with 20 cooked mussels, 6 prepared scallops, sliced in half horizontally, and 100 g (4 oz) fresh white crab meat.

ALTERNATIVE FISH

Spiny lobster.

grilled lobster with *fines herbes* (see technique 52, page 79)

SERVES 4

2 x 750–800 g (1½–1¾ lb) live lobsters
15 g (½ oz) butter, melted
175 ml (6 fl oz) Fish Stock (see page 222)
½ teaspoon Thai fish sauce (*nam pla*)
2 teaspoons lemon juice
50 g (2 oz) unsalted butter, cut into small pieces
1 teaspoon each chopped parsley, chervil,
    chives and tarragon
Salt and freshly ground black pepper

1 Pre-heat the grill to medium-high. Prepare the lobster for grilling as described on page 79.

2 Put the lobster halves onto a baking tray or the rack of the grill pan. Brush the meat with melted butter and season with a little salt and pepper. Grill for 8–10 minutes until cooked through.

3 Just before the lobster is ready, bring the fish stock, fish sauce and lemon juice to the boil in a small pan and boil for 1 minute. Whisk in the butter a piece at a time to build up an emulsified sauce. Stir in the chopped herbs and adjust the seasoning if necessary.

4 Lift the lobster halves on to 4 warmed plates and spoon over the sauce.

10

lobster with ginger, spring onions and soft egg noodles (see technique 51, page 78)

SERVES 2-3

1 x 750 g (1½ lb) live lobster or spiny lobster
Sunflower oil, for deep-frying, plus 1 tablespoon
1 teaspoon salt
½ teaspoon sugar
1 tablespoon dark soy sauce
1 tablespoon oyster sauce
A pinch of freshly ground white pepper
1 teaspoon roasted sesame oil
2 tablespoons Chinese rice wine or dry sherry
2 tablespoons cornflour
2 garlic cloves, crushed
120 g (4½ oz) fresh root ginger, peeled and thinly sliced
    on a mandolin
90 g (3½ oz) spring onions, cut into 2.5 cm
    (1 inch) pieces
250 ml (8 fl oz) Chicken Stock (see page 222)
175 g (6 oz) fresh egg thread noodles

1 Prepare the lobster for stir-frying as described on page 78.

2 Heat some oil for deep-frying to 190°C (375°F). Mix the salt, sugar, dark soy sauce, oyster sauce, white pepper, sesame oil and Chinese rice wine or sherry together in a small bowl and set aside. Bring a large pan of water to the boil for the noodles.

3 Sprinkle the lobster pieces with 1½ tablespoons of the cornflour and deep-fry, in 2 or 3 batches if necessary, for 2 minutes. The larger claw might take longer – about 3 minutes. Lift out and drain on kitchen paper.

4 Heat the tablespoon of sunflower oil in a wok. Add the garlic, ginger and spring onions and stir-fry for a few seconds. Add the lobster to the wok with the soy sauce mixture and stir-fry for 1 minute. Add the chicken stock, then cover and cook over a medium heat for 2 minutes.

5 Meanwhile, drop the noodles into the pan of boiling water, cover and remove from the heat. Leave them to soak for 2 minutes, loosening them now and then with some chopsticks or a fork.

6 Mix the rest of the cornflour with 2 tablespoons of cold water, add to the wok and stir for 1 minute, until the sauce thickens.

7 Drain the noodles and put them on a large oval serving plate. Spoon the lobster mixture on top and serve straight away.

LOBSTER WITH GINGER, SPRING ONIONS AND
SOFT EGG NOODLES

open ravioli of lobster with tomato and basil sauce

SERVES 4 AS A STARTER

½ quantity of Fresh Egg Pasta (see page 227)

175 g (6 oz) cooked lobster tail meat, thinly sliced (see page 77)

Sprigs of basil, to garnish

FOR THE TOMATO AND BASIL SAUCE:

2 vine-ripened tomatoes, skinned, seeded and diced

6 basil leaves, finely sliced

50 ml (2 fl oz) extra virgin olive oil

Salt and freshly ground black pepper

FOR THE CREAM SAUCE:

150 ml (5 fl oz) Fish Stock (see page 222)

2 tablespoons double cream

2 tablespoons white wine

4 tablespoons Mayonnaise (see pages 224), made with olive oil

1 Bring a large pan of well-salted water to the boil. Roll out the pasta dough on a lightly floured surface into a 15 × 30 cm (6 × 12 inch) rectangle. Cut into eight 7.5 cm (3 inch) squares.

2 For the tomato and basil sauce, put all the ingredients into a small pan and place over a very low heat to warm through.

3 For the cream sauce, bring the fish stock, double cream and white wine to the boil and boil until reduced by half to about 75 ml (3 fl oz). Put the mayonnaise into a bowl and gradually whisk in the reduced fish stock. Season to taste with salt. Keep warm, but take care not to get it too hot or it will curdle.

4 Put the slices of lobster meat on to a plate and warm through in a steamer for 2–3 minutes. Meanwhile, drop the pasta squares into the boiling water and cook for 3–4 minutes or until *al dente*, then drain and lay out on a sheet of cling film.

5 To serve, put a square of pasta in the centre of each of 4 warmed plates. Spoon a little of the cream sauce on to each one, divide the lobster meat between them and then spoon over half the tomato and basil sauce. Cover with the remaining pasta squares and pour the remaining cream sauce over and around each ravioli. Spoon on the rest of the tomato and basil sauce and serve immediately, garnished with the sprigs of basil.

lobster thermidor (see technique 50, page 76)

SERVES 2

1 x 750 g (1½ lb) cooked lobster

25 g (1 oz) butter

2 large shallots, finely chopped

600 ml (1 pt) Fish Stock (see page 222)

50 ml (2 fl oz) Noilly Prat

75 ml (3 fl oz) double cream

½ teaspoon English mustard

1 teaspoon chopped *fines herbes* (chervil, tarragon, parsley and chives)

1 teaspoon lemon juice

15 g (½ oz) finely grated Parmesan cheese

Salt and freshly ground black pepper

1 Remove the meat and any roe from the lobster as described on page 76. Scoop out the head matter and set it aside for the sauce. Cut the meat into small chunky pieces and return it to the cleaned half-shells with any roe. Cover and set aside.

2 For the sauce, melt the butter in a small pan. Add the shallots and cook gently for 3–4 minutes until soft but not browned. Add the fish stock, Noilly Prat and half the double cream and boil until reduced by three-quarters to about 175 ml (6 fl oz). Add the rest of the cream and simmer until it has reduced to a good coating-sauce consistency. Whisk in the reserved head matter, the mustard, *fines herbes* and lemon juice. Season to taste with salt and pepper.

3 Pre-heat the grill to high. Carefully spoon the sauce over the lobster meat and sprinkle lightly with Parmesan cheese. Grill for 2–3 minutes until lightly golden and bubbling.

spiny lobster salad with a tomato, tarragon and chervil dressing

SERVES 4

1 x 1.75–2.3 kg (4–5 lb) spiny lobster

2 tablespoons Lemon Olive Oil (see page 227)

1/2 teaspoon white wine vinegar

50 g (2 oz) prepared salad leaves, such as curly endive, watercress, escarole and chicory

Salt and freshly ground black pepper

FOR THE DRESSING:

300 ml (10 fl oz) Fish Stock (see page 222)

4 tablespoons olive oil

1 tablespoon Clarified Butter (see page 226)

1 plum tomato, skinned, seeded and diced

1 small garlic clove, very finely chopped

1 teaspoon each chopped tarragon and chervil

1/4 small medium-hot red Dutch chilli, seeded and very finely chopped

1 tablespoon white wine vinegar

A small pinch of saffron strands

1/2 teaspoon finely chopped anchovy fillets

1 Cook the spiny lobster as described on page 76. Meanwhile, for the dressing, put the fish stock into a pan and boil rapidly until it has reduced to about 2 tablespoons. Remove from the heat.

2 Remove the spiny lobster from the water and leave it until it is cool enough to handle. Then remove the meat from the tail as described on page 77. Cut it across into slices, put on to a plate and keep warm while you remove the rest of the meat from the claws and legs (see page 76).

3 Add all the other dressing ingredients to the pan containing the reduced fish stock and leave to warm through over a low heat – but don't let it come anywhere near boiling.

4 Whisk together the lemon olive oil, vinegar, salt and pepper to make a light salad dressing. Toss with the salad leaves and divide between 4 plates. Arrange the lobster meat to the side of the leaves, spoon over the warm dressing and serve immediately.

potted squat lobsters with ginger and basil

SERVES 4 AS A STARTER

60 cooked squat lobsters, about 2 kg (4½ lb), or 175–225 g (6–8 oz) cooked squat lobster meats

100 g (4 oz) unsalted butter

1/2 teaspoon finely grated fresh root ginger

1/2 teaspoon salt

1/2 teaspoon finely grated lemon zest

1 tablespoon finely shredded basil

1 If using whole squat lobsters, remove the meats from the shells as you would for raw prawns (see page 72), but take care because the shells are quite sharp. There should be about 175 g (6 oz) of meat.

2 Melt the butter in a pan, add the ginger, salt and lemon zest, then the squat lobster meats, and stir together over a low heat for a couple of minutes until the lobster meats have heated through.

3 Take the pan off the heat and stir in the basil. Divide the lobster meats between four 6 cm (2½ inch) ramekins; try to arrange them neatly in the ramekins so that they will look attractive when you turn them out. Pour any remaining butter into the ramekins and leave them somewhere cool to set for at least 2 hours – if you can avoid doing this in the fridge, they will have a softer, smoother texture.

4 To serve, dip the ramekins briefly into hot water, unmould them on to 4 plates and accompany with plenty of warm brown toast.

NOTE

An alternative way to serve this is to divide 50 g (2 oz) mixed baby salad leaves between the plates. Spoon over the warmed mixture, sprinkle with a little extra salt and serve while the squats are still warm.

ALTERNATIVE FISH

Cooked peeled prawns, or diced cooked lobster meat.

moreton bay bug and fennel risotto with lemon oil

SERVES 4

10 x raw Moreton Bay bug tails or 2 x 450 g (1 lb)
    raw lobsters
1.2–1.25 litres (2–2¼ pints) Chicken Stock
    (see page 222)
1 teaspoon fennel seeds
2 tablespoons olive oil
½ fennel bulb, thinly sliced
¼ teaspoon dried chilli flakes
2 shallots, very finely chopped
1 garlic clove, crushed
350 g (12 oz) risotto rice, such as arborio
50 g (2 oz) Parmesan cheese, finely grated
15 g (½ oz) butter
1 tablespoon lemon juice
2 tablespoons chopped fennel herb (or the frondy tops
    from the fennel bulb)
Salt and freshly ground black pepper

TO GARNISH:

Sprigs of fennel herb
Parmesan shavings
Lemon Olive Oil (see page 227)

1 If you are using Moreton Bay bugs, break open the shell along the underside of each one and lift out the meats. Cut the bug meats across into slices 2 cm (¾ in) thick. If you are using lobsters, kill them (see page 76) and then drop them into a large pan of rapidly boiling water. Bring back to the boil and simmer for 5 minutes. They will still be partly raw but this will enable you to get the meat out of the shell. Lift out of the pan and, when cool enough to handle, crack open the shells and remove the meat as described on page 76. Cut the meat into chunks.

2 Bring the chicken stock to the boil in a pan and leave over a low heat. Heat a dry heavy-based frying pan over a high heat, add the fennel seeds and toss them around for a few seconds until they start to darken slightly and smell nicely aromatic. Tip into a mortar or spice grinder and grind to a fine powder.

3 Heat the olive oil in a pan, add the fennel, ground fennel seeds, chilli flakes, shallots and garlic and cook until the shallots are soft and translucent – about 7 minutes. Season with a little salt and pepper. Add the rice and stir until it is well coated in the oil. Increase the heat, add a ladleful of the hot chicken stock and bring to the boil. Reduce the heat

to very low and leave it to simmer, adding another ladleful of stock as each one is absorbed and stirring frequently, until the rice is almost cooked – approximately 20–25 minutes.

4 Add the sliced bug tails or lobster meat and simmer for 2–3 minutes or until just cooked through.

5 Fold in the Parmesan, butter, lemon juice and some seasoning to taste. Stir in the fennel herb and make sure the mixture is not too wet – increase the heat and cook to allow the excess liquid to evaporate if it is.

6 Spoon the risotto into warmed bowls, garnish with the fennel sprigs, Parmesan shavings, a little black pepper and a drizzle of lemon oil.

ALTERNATIVE FISH

Bugs are from the same family as lobster, spiny lobster and crayfish and all would be suitable for this dish. Large peeled raw prawns would also work very well, but leave them whole – don't cut them up. You'll need to use about 12–16. You could also use cooked lobster meat, folded in at the end of cooking just to heat through.

pad thai noodles with prawns

SERVES 2

175 g (6 oz) flat rice noodles
50 ml (2 fl oz) groundnut oil
2 garlic cloves, finely chopped
½ teaspoon dried chilli flakes
10 peeled large raw prawns (see page 72)
2 eggs, beaten
2–3 tablespoons Thai fish sauce (*nam pla*)
2–3 tablespoons Tamarind Water (see page 227)
1 tablespoon palm sugar or light muscovado sugar
1 tablespoon dried shrimps, coarsely chopped
4 heaped tablespoons roasted peanuts, coarsely chopped
4 spring onions, cut into 5 cm (2 inch) pieces and finely
    shredded lengthways
50 g (2 oz) fresh beansprouts
2 tablespoons roughly chopped coriander

1 Soak the noodles in cold water for 1 hour, then drain and set to one side.

2 Heat the oil in a wok over a high heat. Add the garlic, chilli flakes and prawns and stir-fry for 2–3 minutes, until the prawns are just cooked.

3 Pour in the beaten eggs and stir-fry for a few seconds, until they just start to look scrambled. Lower the heat, add the noodles, fish sauce, tamarind water and sugar and toss together for a minute or two until the noodles are tender.

4 Add the dried shrimps, half the peanuts, half the spring onions, half the beansprouts and all the coriander and toss for another minute. Serve sprinkled with the rest of the peanuts, spring onions and beansprouts.

ALTERNATIVE FISH
Thinly sliced squid, sliced scallops or mussels.

PRAWN CALDINE

prawn caldine (see technique 48, page 72)

SERVES 4

550 g (1¼ lb) unpeeled headless raw prawns
2 tablespoons coconut vinegar or white wine vinegar
1 teaspoon turmeric powder
1 teaspoon black peppercorns
1 tablespoon coriander seeds
1 teaspoon cumin seeds
2 tablespoons white poppy seeds or ground almonds
4 tablespoons groundnut oil
1 onion, thinly sliced
3 garlic cloves, cut into slivers
2.5 cm (1 inch) fresh root ginger, finely chopped
400 ml (14 fl oz) coconut milk
4 tablespoons Tamarind Water (see page 227)
150 ml (5 fl oz) water
5 mild green chillies, halved, seeded and cut into long thin shreds
2 tablespoons chopped coriander
Salt

1 Peel the prawns, leaving the last tail segment in place (see page 72). Mix the prawns with the vinegar and ½ teaspoon of salt. Set aside for 5 minutes.

2 Meanwhile, put the turmeric powder, peppercorns, coriander seeds, cumin seeds and white poppy seeds, if using, into a spice grinder and grind to a fine powder.

3 Heat the oil in a medium-sized pan. Add the onion, garlic and ginger and fry gently for 5 minutes. Stir in the ground spices and fry for 2 minutes. Add the ground almonds if you aren't using poppy seeds, plus the coconut milk, tamarind water, water, three-quarters of the sliced chillies and ½ teaspoon of salt. Bring to a simmer and cook for 5 minutes.

4 Add the prawns and simmer for just 3–4 minutes so they don't overcook. Stir in the rest of the sliced chillies and the coriander and serve with some steamed rice.

ALTERNATIVE FISH
Any type of raw prawns and goujons of fish such as brill or John Dory.

large cooked prawns in marie rose sauce with avocado and romaine lettuce salad

SERVES 4

350 g (12 oz) peeled large cooked prawns

FOR THE MARIE ROSE SAUCE:

**1 quantity Mayonnaise (see page 224), made with
225 ml (8 fl oz) sunflower oil**

5 tablespoons tomato ketchup

4 tablespoons Greek-style natural yogurt

Salt and freshly ground white pepper

FOR THE ROMAINE LETTUCE SALAD:

1 romaine lettuce heart

2 ripe but firm avocados

1 For the Marie Rose sauce, put the mayonnaise into a bowl and stir in the tomato ketchup and yogurt. Season to taste with a little white pepper.

2 Dry the prawns on kitchen paper and then stir them into the sauce. Spoon this into a serving bowl and set to one side.

3 For the salad, cut the lettuce across into 2.5 cm (1 inch) wide strips, toss with a little salt and pepper and divide between 4 serving plates.

4 Cut each avocado in half and remove the stone. Peel off the skin and then cut it across into semi-circular slices. Arrange these in amongst the lettuce leaves.

5 To serve, take the plates of salad and the bowl of prawns to the table separately and allow everyone to help themselves to the prawns.

ALTERNATIVE FISH

This salad would also taste great made with large cooked and peeled North Atlantic prawns.

gremolata prawns

SERVES 4

1 large lemon

2 tablespoons olive oil

20 unpeeled large raw prawns

Cayenne pepper (optional)

3 garlic cloves, very finely chopped

4 tablespoons chopped flat-leaf parsley

Coarse sea salt and freshly ground black pepper

1 Peel the zest off the lemon with a potato peeler. Pile the pieces up a few at a time and then cut them across into short thin strips.

2 Heat the oil in a large frying pan. Add the prawns and toss them over a high heat for 4–5 minutes, seasoning them with some cayenne pepper or black pepper and sea salt as you do so.

3 Cut the lemon in half and squeeze the juice from one half over the prawns. Continue to cook until the juice has almost evaporated –

GREMOLATA PRAWNS

the prawns should be quite dry. Take the pan off the heat and leave for about 1 minute to cool very slightly.

4 Then sprinkle over the lemon zest, chopped garlic, parsley and ¼ teaspoon of salt and toss together well. Pile the prawns into a large serving dish and serve with some finger bowls and plenty of napkins.

ALTERNATIVE FISH
Any raw prawns in the shell.

po' boys

MAKES 6

2 French baguettes
Sunflower oil, for deep-frying
350 g (12 oz) peeled large raw prawns (see page 72)
175 g (6 oz) Mayonnaise (see pages 224), made with
    sunflower oil, plus extra Mayonnaise to serve
2½ tablespoons milk
25 g (1 oz) plain flour
175 g (6 oz) fresh white breadcrumbs
1 small crisp green lettuce
Salt and cayenne pepper

1 Pre-heat the grill to high. Cut each baguette into 3 and then cut each piece in half lengthways. Pull out a little of the soft white crumb to make a very shallow dip in each half. Lay them on a baking tray, cut-side up, and toast very lightly under the grill. Remove and set aside.

2 Heat some oil for deep-frying to 190°C (375°F). Season the prawns well with salt and cayenne pepper. Whisk the mayonnaise and milk together in a bowl, put the flour into a second bowl and spread the breadcrumbs over a large plate.

3 Dip the prawns into the flour, mayonnaise and then the breadcrumbs so that they take on an even coating. Treat them gently once they are done because the coating is quite delicate. Pick them up by their tails, drop them into the hot oil about 6 at a time and fry for 1 minute, until crisp and golden. Transfer to a tray lined with kitchen paper and keep warm in a low oven while you cook the rest.

4 To serve, spread the bottom half of each piece of bread with a little mayonnaise, then put some lettuce leaves on top. Pile on a few of the fried prawns, cover with the tops and eat straight away.

ALTERNATIVE FISH
Oysters, small goujons of fish such as lemon sole and plaice, or soft-shell clams from the east coast of America.

PO' BOYS

199

crustaceans

tandoori prawns <small>(see technique 47, page 70)</small>

SERVES 4

32 large raw prawns

175 g (6 oz) Greek-style natural yogurt

FOR THE LEMON CHILLI MARINADE:

1 teaspoon cayenne pepper

1 teaspoon salt

Juice of 1 lemon

FOR THE TANDOORI MASALA PASTE:

15 g (½ oz) fennel seeds

1 tablespoon coriander seeds

1 tablespoon cumin seeds

25 g (1 oz) fresh root ginger, roughly chopped

6 garlic cloves, chopped

4 medium-hot red Dutch chillies, seeded and roughly chopped

2 teaspoons paprika

1 teaspoon turmeric powder

Juice of 1 lemon

1–2 tablespoons cold water

FOR THE KATCHUMBER SALAD:

3 tomatoes, halved and thinly sliced

1 medium onion, halved and thinly sliced

2 tablespoons roughly chopped coriander

¼ teaspoon ground cumin

A large pinch of cayenne pepper

1 tablespoon white wine vinegar

½ teaspoon salt

1 If you are cooking the prawns on the barbecue, light it now. Mix together the ingredients for the lemon chilli marinade. Make 3 small slits in either side of each prawn, between the shell segments, to allow the marinade to penetrate (see page 70). Put the prawns and marinade into a bowl, toss together well and set aside for 20 minutes.

2 For the tandoori masala paste, put the fennel seeds, coriander seeds and cumin seeds together in a spice grinder or mortar and grind to a fine powder. Tip the spices into a food processor, add the rest of the masala paste ingredients and blend until smooth. Stir the paste into the yogurt and then stir this into the prawns. Leave for another 20 minutes.

3 If you are cooking the prawns under the grill, pre-heat the grill to high. Thread the prawns on to metal or soaked bamboo skewers, piercing them just behind the head and through the tail (see page 71). Cook them on the barbecue or under a very hot grill for 2 minutes on each side.

4 While the prawns are cooking, layer the ingredients for the salad in a shallow dish. Serve the prawns with the salad and maybe some warm naan bread.

TANDOORI PRAWNS

deep-fried prawn wontons with chilli jam

SERVES 4

20 unpeeled raw headless prawns

20 Chinese wonton wrappers

Sunflower oil, for deep-frying

FOR THE CHILLI JAM:

50 ml (2 fl oz) sunflower oil

15 g (1/2 oz) garlic cloves, finely chopped

15 g (1/2 oz) fresh root ginger, finely chopped

225 g (8 oz) onions, finely chopped

5 medium-hot red Dutch chillies, seeded and finely
   chopped

120 ml (4 fl oz) red wine vinegar

2 tablespoons dark soy sauce

1/2 teaspoon ground star anise

15 g (1/2 oz) palm sugar or light muscovado sugar

Salt

1 Peel the prawns, leaving the last tail segment in place (see page 72), and reserve the shells.

2 For the chilli jam, heat the sunflower oil in a medium-sized pan. Add the prawn shells and fry over a high heat for 1–2 minutes, until they are quite crisp. Tip into a sieve resting over a small pan and press really well to remove all the oil which will now be pleasantly flavoured with prawn.

3 Re-heat the oil, add the garlic and ginger and fry quickly until they are lightly browned. Add the onions and chillies and fry for 3–4 minutes. Stir in the vinegar, soy sauce, star anise, sugar and some salt to taste. Bring to the boil and simmer gently for 20–30 minutes, until the onions are very soft and the jam is well reduced and thick. Leave to cool, then spoon into 4 small dipping bowls or small ramekins.

4 Wrap each prawn in one of the wonton wrappers, leaving the tail end uncovered, and seal with a little water.

5 Heat some oil for deep-frying to 190°C (375°F). Fry the prawns in batches for 1–1½ minutes, until crisp and golden. Lift out and drain briefly on kitchen paper. Serve hot with the chilli jam.

prawn jambalaya

SERVES 6

4 tablespoons sunflower oil

100 g (4 oz) chorizo or spicy smoked sausage, sliced

2 teaspoons paprika

8 garlic cloves, chopped

1 medium onion, chopped

2 green peppers, seeded and chopped

4 celery sticks, sliced

2 medium-hot red Dutch chillies, seeded and
   finely chopped

450 g (1 lb) skinned boneless chicken, cut into
   2.5 cm (1 inch) pieces

450 g (1 lb) peeled raw headless prawns (see page 72)

2 bay leaves

Leaves from 1 sprig thyme

1 teaspoon chopped oregano

450 g (1 lb) long-grain rice

1.2 litres (2 pints) Chicken Stock (see page 222)

3 spring onions, trimmed and thinly sliced

Salt and cayenne pepper

1 Heat the oil in a large deep frying pan. Add the sliced sausage and fry until lightly browned. Add the paprika and stir to colour the oil.

2 Add the garlic, cook for 30 seconds, and then add the onion, green peppers, celery and red chillies. Cook over a medium heat until lightly browned.

3 Add the chicken, prawns, bay leaves, thyme and oregano and fry over a medium heat for 5 minutes.

4 Add the rice and stir for 2 minutes. Add the chicken stock and 1 teaspoon of salt, bring to the boil, cover and simmer for about 15 minutes, until the rice has absorbed all the liquid and is tender.

5 Stir in the spring onions and some cayenne pepper to taste. Serve with a green salad.

potted shrimps

SERVES 6

100 g (4 oz) butter
2 pieces of blade mace
A good pinch of cayenne pepper
Freshly grated nutmeg
600 ml (1 pint) peeled cooked brown shrimps
6 tablespoons Clarified Butter (see page 226)

1 Put the butter, mace, cayenne pepper and a little grated nutmeg into a pan and leave to melt very slowly over a gentle heat, so that the butter becomes infused by the spices.

2 Add the peeled shrimps and stir for a couple of minutes until they have heated through, but don't let the mixture boil.

3 Remove the mace and divide the shrimps and butter between 6 small ramekins. Level the tops and then leave them to set in the fridge.

4 Spoon over a thin layer of clarified butter and leave to set once more. Serve with plenty of brown toast or crusty brown bread.

cream of shrimp soup

SERVES 4

100 g (4 oz) butter
1 carrot, finely diced
1 onion, finely chopped
750 g (1½ lb) unpeeled raw or cooked shrimps
900 ml (1½ pints) Fish Stock (see page 222)
1 bay leaf
150 ml (5 fl oz) dry white wine
25 g (1 oz) plain flour
300 ml (10 fl oz) milk
150 ml (5 fl oz) double cream
A pinch of cayenne pepper
Salt and freshly ground black pepper

1 Melt 25 g (1 oz) of the butter in a medium-sized pan. Add the carrot and onion and cook over a medium heat for 3–4 minutes. If you are using raw shrimps, add them to the pan and turn them over for 5 minutes, until they are just cooked and have all turned pink.

2 Remove a third of the shrimps from the pan and, when they are cool enough to handle, shell them and return the shells to the pan. If you are using cooked shrimps, just shell a third of them and put the shells and the rest of the shrimps into the pan. Add the fish stock, bay leaf and white wine, bring to the boil and simmer for 20 minutes.

3 Liquidize the soup, in batches if necessary, for a few seconds until coarsely blended but not completely smooth. Pour into a conical sieve set over a clean pan and press out all the liquid with the back of a ladle (see page 86).

4 Melt 40 g (1½ oz) of the remaining butter in another pan, stir in the flour and cook for 30 seconds. Gradually stir in the milk and then the strained soup and simmer over a low heat for 15 minutes, stirring occasionally. Whisk in the rest of the butter, plus the cream and cayenne pepper and season with a little more black pepper and some salt.

5 Pour the soup into a warmed tureen and serve with a bowl of the peeled shrimps. Place a few of the shrimps into each bowl before ladling over the soup.

ALTERNATIVE FISH
Unpeeled cooked North Atlantic prawns.

SHRIMPS

10

shrimp and samphire risotto

SERVES 4

750 g (1½ lb) unpeeled cooked pink shrimps or
    North Atlantic prawns
100 g (4 oz) samphire, picked over and washed
75 g (3 oz) unsalted butter
½ onion, chopped
1.2 litres (2 pints) Fish Stock (see page 222)
1 piece of blade mace
2 shallots, finely chopped
1 garlic clove, finely chopped
350 g (12 oz) risotto rice
120 ml (4 fl oz) dry white wine
25 g (1 oz) Parmesan cheese, grated
Salt and freshly ground black pepper

1 Peel the shrimps and set them aside, reserving the shells. Break off and discard the woody ends of the samphire and break the rest into 2.5 cm (1 inch) pieces.

2 Melt 25 g (1 oz) of the butter in a large saucepan, add the onion and fry for 5 minutes, until soft and lightly browned. Add the shrimp shells and fry for 3–4 minutes, then add the stock and mace and bring to the boil. Cover and simmer for 20 minutes. Pass the stock through a conical sieve into a clean pan, pressing out as much liquid as you can with the back of a ladle. Bring back to a simmer and keep hot over a low heat.

3 Melt the rest of the butter in a large saucepan. Add the shallots and garlic and cook gently for a couple of minutes. Add the rice and turn it over until all the grains are coated in the butter. Pour in the wine and simmer, stirring constantly, until it has been absorbed. Then add a ladleful of the hot stock and stir until it has all been taken up before adding another. Continue like this for about 20 minutes, stirring constantly, until all the stock has been used and the rice is tender but still a little *al dente*.

4 Shortly before the risotto is ready, drop the samphire into a pan of boiling water and cook for 1 minute, then drain well. Stir the shrimps, Parmesan cheese and some seasoning into the risotto. Heat for 1 minute, then stir in all but a handful of the samphire. Divide the risotto between 4 warmed bowls and serve, garnished with the rest of the samphire.

SHRIMP AND SAMPHIRE RISOTTO

recipes

chapter 11

molluscs and other seafood

new england clam chowder (see technique 60, page 89)

SERVES 4

16 medium-sized clams, such as quahogs,
or 600 ml (1 pint) small clams, such as carpetshell, washed
25 g (1 oz) butter
50 g (2 oz) thickly sliced green streaky bacon, cut into small dice
1 small onion, finely chopped
300 ml (10 fl oz) milk
100 ml (4 fl oz) double cream
225 g (8 oz) peeled potatoes, cut into small dice
1 bay leaf, very finely shredded
1 tablespoon chopped parsley
Salt and freshly ground white pepper

1 Remove the part-cooked meats from the larger clams (see page 89) and cut them into smaller pieces. Put the smaller clams into a pan with 50 ml (2 fl oz) water. Cover and cook over a high heat for about 4 minutes or until they have opened. Tip them into a colander set over a bowl to collect the liquor, leave to cool slightly and then remove the meats from the shells.

2 Melt the butter in the pan, add the bacon and fry over a medium heat until golden. Add the onion and cook gently until softened.

3 Add the milk, cream, potatoes, bay leaf and reserved clam liquor, bring to the boil, then simmer for 5 minutes or until the potatoes are tender.

4 Return the clam meats to the pan with the chopped parsley and season to taste with some salt and pepper. Reheat gently and serve.

clams with sauce mignonette (see technique 61, page 89)

SERVES 4

600 ml (1 pint) carpetshell clams, washed
A little bladderrack seaweed, to serve

FOR THE SAUCE MIGNONETTE:

3 tablespoons good-quality white or red wine vinegar
1 teaspoon sunflower oil
1/4 teaspoon coarsely crushed black peppercorns
1 tablespoon thinly sliced spring onion tops

1 Prepare the clams as described on page 89.

2 Mix together the ingredients for the sauce just before serving. Arrange the clams on a plate with a little seaweed, spoon a little of the sauce into each one and serve.

linguine alle vongole (clams with linguine, garlic, parsley and white wine)

SERVES 4

350 g (12 oz) dried linguine
50 ml (2 fl oz) extra virgin olive oil
4 garlic cloves, thinly sliced
1/2 medium-hot red Dutch chilli, seeded and finely
   chopped
3 tablespoons chopped flat-leaf parsley
900 g (2 lb) small clams, such as carpetshell, washed
2 tablespoons dry white wine

1 Cook the linguine pasta in a large pan of well-salted boiling water (i.e. 1 teaspoon per 600 ml/1 pint) for just 5 minutes.

2 Meanwhile, put the olive oil, garlic and chilli into a small pan and heat until the garlic begins to sizzle. Lower the heat and cook gently for 1–2 minutes until the garlic is soft. Add the parsley and remove from the heat.

3 Drain the pasta. Return the empty pan to a high heat and add the clams, the white wine and the par-cooked linguine. Cover and cook over a high heat, shaking the pan now and then, for 3–4 minutes until all the clams have opened.

4 Uncover the pan and add the olive oil mixture. Simmer for a further 2 minutes or until the linguine is tender, then serve.

RAZOR CLAMS A LA PLANCHA

razor clams a la plancha

SERVES 4

24 razor clams, washed
Good olive oil
Lemon wedges, to serve (optional)

1 Heat your largest heavy-based frying pan or a flat griddle over a high heat until very hot. Add a little olive oil and a single layer of the clams, hinge-side down.

2 As soon as they have opened right up, turn them over so that the meats come into contact with the base of the pan and cook for about 1 minute, until lightly browned.

3 Turn the clams back over, drizzle over a little more olive oil and put them on a warmed serving plate. Serve with a lemon wedge or two, if you wish, and any juices from the pan. Repeat the process with any remaining clams.

ALTERNATIVE FISH
Large carpetshell clams.

stir-fried clams with garlic and ginger

SERVES 4

12 large hard-shelled clams, such as quahogs, or
36 small clams, such as carpetshell, washed
3 tablespoons sunflower oil
3 garlic cloves, finely chopped
5 cm (2 inch) piece of peeled fresh root ginger,
very finely shredded
100 g (4 oz) shiitake mushrooms, sliced
1 head of pak choi, sliced into 2.5 cm (1 inch) strips
A good pinch of dried chilli flakes
1 tablespoon dark soy sauce
1 tablespoon oyster sauce
Freshly ground Sichuan pepper or black pepper
4–6 spring onions, sliced on the diagonal

1 Place the hard-shelled clams in a single layer in a large shallow pan with a little water. Cover and cook over a high heat for 2–3 minutes, until only just opened – this is so that you can remove the clam meats from the shells, but not cook them completely (see page 89).

2 Slide a small knife into each shell and cut through the two muscles that hold the shells together. Break off the top shells, remove the clams from the bottom shells and slice them thinly (see page 89).

3 If using small clams, put them into a pan with 50 ml (2 fl oz) water. Cover and cook over a high heat for 2–3 minutes until just opened. Strain through a colander and, when cool enough to handle, remove the meats from the shells and leave whole.

4 Heat a wok over a high heat. Add the oil, followed by the garlic and ginger, and stir-fry for 30 seconds. Add the clams and stir-fry for another 30 seconds to 1 minute, then add the mushrooms and stir-fry for 30 seconds. Add the pak choi and chilli flakes, stir-fry for 30 seconds, then add the soy sauce, oyster sauce, Sichuan or black pepper and finally the spring onions. Toss together briefly and serve.

steamed pipis with toasted almonds, garlic and parsley

SERVES 4

100 g (4 oz) unsalted butter
2 fat garlic cloves, finely chopped
2.75 kg (6 lb) Australian pipis or carpetshell clams,
washed 50 ml (2 fl oz) dry white wine
Juice of ½ lemon
25 g (1 oz) lightly toasted almonds, finely chopped
3–4 tablespoons chopped flat-leaf parsley

1 Melt the butter in a very large saucepan. Add the garlic and cook very gently for 3–4 minutes. Add the pipis or clams, white wine, lemon juice and chopped almonds. Cover and cook over a high heat, giving the pan a good shake every now and then, until they have all opened. Add half the chopped parsley and stir well.

2 Using a large slotted spoon, divide the pipis between 4 large warmed bowls, discarding any that have remained closed, then spoon over the cooking juices, leaving behind the last tablespoon or two because it might be a bit gritty. Sprinkle over the remaining parsley and serve with plenty of crusty sourdough bread.

salad of ormers with noodles, shiitake mushrooms, ginger and truffle oil

SERVES 4

4 x 50 g (2 oz) prepared ormers or abalone, or a 100 g
   (4 oz) piece of cleaned cuttlefish
120 ml (4 fl oz) olive oil
5 cm (2 inch) piece of cinnamon stick
2 star anise
25 g (1 oz) dried rice vermicelli noodles
100 g (4 oz) mixed enoki and shiitake mushrooms
4 thin slices of peeled fresh root ginger, cut into fine
   julienne
2 spring onions, halved and very finely shredded
2 teaspoons dark soy sauce
4 teaspoons truffle oil

1 Pre-heat the oven to 110°C/225°F/Gas Mark ¼. Put the ormers, abalone or cuttlefish into a small casserole with the olive oil, cinnamon and star anise. Cover and bake for 4–5 hours if using ormers or abalone, or just 1 hour for the cuttlefish, until tender.

2 Remove the casserole from the oven, lift the fish out of the oil and leave to cool. Then cut it into the thinnest possible slices and set to one side.

3 Drop the noodles into a pan of boiling water, then remove from the heat and leave to soak for 2 minutes. Drain and refresh under cold water. Drain well again.

4 Slice the enoki mushrooms away from their matted base and break into separate stems, leaving them as long as possible. Trim the stalks of the shiitake mushrooms and cut the caps into thin slices.

5 Build up the salad in layers on 4 plates, using the noodles, mushrooms, ginger, spring onions and sliced ormers, abalone or cuttlefish, shaping them into small mounds about the size of a cricket ball. Drizzle with the soy sauce and truffle oil and serve.

cockle and laverbread vol-au-vents with hollandaise sauce

MAKES 12

350 g (12 oz) chilled puff pastry
1 egg, beaten, to glaze
100 g (4 oz) Clarified Butter (see page 226)
900 g (2 lb) cockles, washed
1 egg yolk
1 teaspoon fresh lemon juice
4 teaspoons prepared laverbread
Salt

1 Pre-heat the oven to 200°C/400°F/Gas Mark 6. Roll out the pastry on a lightly floured surface until it is 5 mm (¼ inch) thick. Cut out twelve 6.5 cm (2½ inch) discs using a plain pastry cutter, then press a 5 cm (2 inch) plain cutter into the centre of each one, only half-way down into the pastry. Take care not to cut all the way through.

2 Put the vol-au-vents on a lightly buttered baking sheet and brush the tops with a little beaten egg. Bake for about 10–12 minutes, until crisp and richly golden, then remove from the oven. While they are still warm, carefully remove the centres with a teaspoon, making sure you scoop out all the partly cooked pastry from inside. Cover and keep warm in a low oven.

3 Pour the clarified butter into a small pan and leave it over a low heat. Put the cockles into a large pan with 120 ml (4 fl oz) of water. Cover and cook over a high heat for 4–5 minutes, shaking the pan well every now and then, until they have all opened. Tip them into a colander and, when they are cool enough to handle, remove them from their shells. Transfer to a bowl and keep warm.

4 Put the egg yolk, lemon juice and 1 tablespoon of water into a liquidizer. Heat the clarified butter until it begins to bubble. Turn on the liquidizer and slowly pour in the butter through the hole in the lid to make a smooth, creamy hollandaise sauce.

5 Scrape the mixture into a bowl and stir in the laverbread and a little salt to taste. Fold in the cooked cockles, leaving behind any liquid that might have collected at the bottom of the bowl. Spoon the mixture into the warm vol-au-vents and serve immediately.

cockle cream with bacon, tomatoes and potatoes

SERVES 4

2.4 litres (4 pints) cockles, washed
900 ml (1½ pints) water
25 g (1 oz) butter
50 g (2 oz) lean rindless bacon, cut into small dice
1 leek, cleaned and thinly sliced
1 celery stick, thinly chopped
2 plum tomatoes, skinned and thinly sliced
2 potatoes (about 350 g/12 oz), peeled and diced
Juice of 1 small lemon
2 eggs
2 tablespoons chopped parsley
Salt and freshly ground black pepper

1 Put the cockles into a large pan with 150 ml (5 fl oz) of the water. Cover and cook over a high heat for 4–5 minutes, occasionally shaking the pan, until they have all opened. Tip them into a colander set over a bowl to collect the liquid and leave them to cool a little.

2 Melt the butter in a large pan, add the bacon and cook until it is just beginning to brown. Add the leek, celery and tomatoes and cook until the mixture begins to 'flop'. Meanwhile, remove the cockle meats from the shells.

3 Pour all but the last tablespoon or two of the cockle liquor into the pan, add the rest of the water and the potatoes and leave the soup to simmer until the potatoes are soft – about 10 minutes.

4 Add the shelled cockles to the soup and season to taste with some salt and pepper. Whisk the lemon juice with the eggs in a bowl. Pour on a ladle full of the hot soup, whisk together and then stir the liaison into the soup. Stir it over a low heat to thicken slightly but don't let the soup boil. Stir in the parsley and serve.

grilled mussels with romesco sauce

MAKES APPROX. 60

900 g (2 lb) mussels, cleaned (see page 88)
50 ml (2 fl oz) dry white wine
FOR THE ROMESCO SAUCE:
1 dried choricero pepper
225 g (8 oz) vine-ripened tomatoes
4 garlic cloves, peeled
15 g (½ oz) blanched hazelnuts
15 g (½ oz) slice of day-old white bread, crusts removed
120 ml (4 fl oz) olive oil
A pinch of dried chilli flakes
1 tablespoon sherry vinegar
2 tablespoons chopped oregano
Salt and freshly ground black pepper

1 For the romesco sauce, pull out the stalk of the dried pepper, cover with warm water and leave it to soak overnight. The next day, drain it, slit it open and remove the seeds. Chop up roughly.

2 Pre-heat the oven to 200°C/400°F/Gas Mark 6. Put the tomatoes and 3 garlic cloves into a small roasting tin and roast for 10 minutes. Sprinkle over the hazelnuts and roast for a further 15 minutes until they are golden. Remove the tin from the oven and leave to cool.

3 Rub the slice of bread with the remaining garlic clove. Heat a little of the olive oil in a frying pan, add the bread and fry until richly golden on both sides. Leave to cool, then break it into pieces and put it into a liquidizer with the contents of the roasting tin, the soaked red pepper, chilli flakes, sherry vinegar, ½ teaspoon of salt and some freshly ground black pepper. Blend until smooth, then, with the motor still running, very gradually add the rest of the olive oil to make a thick mayonnaise-like sauce. Scrape into a bowl and set aside.

4 Put the mussels into a large pan with the wine. Cover and cook over a high heat, shaking the pan now and then, for 3–4 minutes until they have opened. Tip into a colander set over a bowl and leave until cool enough to handle. Meanwhile, return all but the last 2 tablespoons of the mussel liquor to a sauté pan and boil vigorously until reduced to about 1 tablespoon. Leave to cool, then stir into the romesco sauce.

5 Break the empty half-shell off each mussel, loosen the meats from the outer shell and lay them on a baking tray. Dot each mussel meat with about 1 teaspoon of the romesco sauce and sprinkle with a little of the chopped oregano. Put under a hot grill and cook for about 1 minute until bubbling and hot. Serve straight away.

cozze con fagioli (mussels with cannellini beans)

SERVES 4

225 g (8 oz) dried cannellini beans, soaked overnight
1 bay leaf
1 sprig thyme
4 garlic cloves, peeled
1 kg (2½ lb) mussels, cleaned (see page 88)
50 ml (2 fl oz) dry white wine
120 ml (4 fl oz) extra virgin olive oil
2 large plum tomatoes, roughly chopped
2 tablespoons chopped flat-leaf parsley
Salt and freshly ground black pepper

1 Drain the beans and tip them into a pan. Pour in enough fresh water to cover them by about 5 cm (2 inches), then add the bay leaf, thyme and 2 of the peeled garlic cloves. Bring to the boil, skimming any scum from the surface as it appears, then lower the heat and simmer for about 1 hour or until the beans are very soft.

2 Now increase the heat and boil rapidly until most of the liquid has disappeared. Discard the thyme and bay leaf.

3 Put the mussels into a pan with the wine. Cover and cook over a high heat for 3–4 minutes, until they have opened. Strain them through a colander set over a bowl to catch the cooking liquor. When they are cool enough to handle, remove about three-quarters of the mussels from their shells.

4 Slice the rest of the garlic into a large pan and add the olive oil. Slowly heat the oil, then, as soon as the garlic begins to sizzle, add the tomatoes and simmer for 2–3 minutes. Add the cooked beans and 150 ml (5 fl oz) of the mussel cooking liquor. Simmer for 5 minutes, until the liquid has reduced to a rich creamy sauce. Season with pepper and a little salt if necessary (you probably won't need any because mussels are quite salty).

5 Add the mussels and simmer for 1–2 minutes, until they have heated through. Stir in the chopped parsley and spoon into 4 warmed soup plates to serve.

la mouclade

SERVES 4

A good pinch of saffron strands
1.75 kg (4 lb) mussels, cleaned (see page 88)
120 ml (4 fl oz) dry white wine
25 g (1 oz) butter
1 small onion, finely chopped
2 garlic cloves, finely chopped
½ teaspoon good-quality medium curry powder
2 tablespoons cognac
2 teaspoons plain flour
200 ml (7 fl oz) crème fraîche
3 tablespoons chopped parsley
Salt and freshly ground black pepper

1 Put the saffron into a small bowl and moisten it with 1 tablespoon of warm water.

2 Place the mussels and wine in a large pan, cover and cook over a high heat for 3–4 minutes, shaking the pan now and then, until the mussels have opened. Tip them into a colander set over a bowl to catch all the cooking liquor. Transfer the mussels to a large serving bowl and keep warm.

3 Melt the butter in a pan, add the onion, garlic and curry powder and cook gently without browning for 2–3 minutes.

4 Add the cognac and cook until it has almost all evaporated, then stir in the flour and cook for 1 minute. Gradually stir in the saffron liquid and all except the last tablespoon or two of the mussel cooking liquor (which might contain some grit).

5 Bring the sauce to a simmer and cook for 2–3 minutes. Add the crème fraîche and simmer for a further 3 minutes, until slightly reduced. Season to taste, stir in the parsley and then pour the sauce over the mussels. Stir them together gently and serve with plenty of French bread.

mussels en croustade with leeks and white wine

SERVES 4

4 large round crusty bread rolls

175 g (6 oz) butter

900 g (2 lb) mussels, cleaned (see page 88)

50 ml (2 fl oz) dry white wine

2 large or 4 small leeks, cleaned and finely chopped

2 tablespoons double cream

1 teaspoon Beurre Manié (see page 227)

1 tablespoon chopped chives

Salt and freshly ground white pepper

1 Pre-heat the oven to 200°C/400°F/Gas Mark 6. Cut a thin slice off the top of each bread roll and set aside. With a teaspoon, scoop out all the soft bread from inside each roll, leaving a wall about 5 mm (¼ inch) thick. Melt 50 g (2 oz) of the butter and use to brush the inside of each roll and the lids. Place them on a baking sheet and bake for 5–7 minutes, until crisp and golden. Keep warm.

2 Put the mussels into a large pan with the wine, then cover and cook over a high heat for about 3 minutes, shaking the pan now and then, until they have just opened. Tip them into a colander set over a bowl to collect all the cooking liquor. Remove the mussels from their shells, cover and set aside.

3 Melt another 25 g (1 oz) of the butter in a pan. Add the leeks, cover and cook for 4–5 minutes, until soft. Add all the mussel cooking liquor except the last tablespoon or two (which might contain some grit), then bring to the boil and simmer until reduced by half. Stir in the remaining butter, the double cream and the beurre manié. Simmer for 1 minute until slightly thickened.

4 Stir the mussels, chives and some seasoning into the sauce. Spoon the mixture into the warm rolls, partly cover with the lids and serve.

MUSSELS

MUSSELS EN CROUSTADE WITH LEEKS AND WHITE WINE

tarte aux moules

1 quantity Shortcrust Pastry (see page 227)
1 egg white
900 g (2 lb) mussels, cleaned (see page 88)
50 ml (2 fl oz) dry white wine
3 tablespoons chopped parsley (keep the stalks)
25 g (1 oz) butter
5–6 shallots, finely chopped
5 garlic cloves, finely chopped
3 eggs, beaten
300 ml (10 fl oz) double cream
Salt and freshly ground black pepper

1 Pre-heat the oven to 200°C/400°F/Gas Mark 6. Briefly knead the pastry on a lightly floured work surface until smooth. Roll out and use to line a 25 cm (10 inch) loose-bottomed flan tin, 4 cm (1½ inches) deep. Prick the base here and there with a fork and chill for 20 minutes.

2 Line the pastry case with a sheet of crumpled greaseproof paper, fill with baking beans and bake blind for 15 minutes. Remove the paper and beans and return the pastry to the oven for 5 minutes.

3 Remove the pastry case once more and brush the base with the unbeaten egg white. Return to the oven for 1 minute. Remove and lower the oven temperature to 190°C/375°F/Gas Mark 5.

4 Put the mussels into a large pan with the wine and parsley stalks. Cover and cook over a high heat for 3–4 minutes, shaking the pan every now and then, until the mussels have opened. Tip them into a colander set over a bowl to collect all the cooking liquor. Leave to cool slightly and then remove the mussels from their shells.

5 Melt the butter in a pan, add the shallots and garlic and cook gently for about 7 minutes until very soft. Add all but the last tablespoon or two of the mussel cooking liquor and simmer rapidly until it has evaporated. Scrape the mixture into a bowl and leave it to cool. Then stir in the eggs, cream and chopped parsley and season to taste with pepper and a little salt if necessary.

6 Scatter the mussels over the base of the pastry case and pour in the egg mixture. Bake for 25–30 minutes until just set and lightly browned. Remove and leave to cool slightly before serving.

mussel, leek and saffron soup

1.5 kg (3 lb) mussels, cleaned (see page 88)
50 ml (2 fl oz) dry white wine
450 g (1 lb) leeks, cleaned
75 g (3 oz) unsalted butter
1 small onion, finely chopped
20 g (¾ oz) plain flour
450 ml (15 fl oz) Fish Stock (see page 222)
A good pinch of saffron strands
50 ml (2 fl oz) double cream
Salt and freshly ground black pepper

1 Put the mussels and 2 tablespoons of the wine into a large pan. Cover and cook over a high heat, shaking the pan every now and then, until they have opened. Tip them into a colander set over a bowl to collect the liquid and leave to cool slightly. Then remove the meats from all but 12 of the nicest-looking shells.

2 Cut one 5 cm (2 in) piece of leek into matchsticks. Finely chop the rest. Melt the butter in a pan, add the chopped leeks and the onion and cook gently for 3–4 minutes until soft but not browned.

3 Stir in the flour and cook gently for 1 minute. Gradually stir in the mussel liquor, the remaining wine and the fish stock and bring to the boil, stirring. Add the saffron and leave to simmer for 25 minutes.

4 Meanwhile, drop the leek matchsticks into a pan of boiling salted water, bring back to the boil, then drain and refresh under running cold water.

5 Liquidize the soup, in batches if necessary, until smooth. Return to a clean pan and stir in the cream. Bring back up to a simmer, then stir in the mussels and leek matchsticks. Adjust the seasoning if necessary and serve.

molluscs and other seafood

moules farcies (stuffed grilled mussels)

SERVES 4 AS A STARTER

48 large mussels, cleaned (see page 88)
50 ml (2 fl oz) water
1 large garlic clove, halved
1 large shallot, halved
A handful of parsley leaves
Pared zest of ¼ lemon
100 g (4 oz) unsalted butter, softened
75 g (3 oz) fresh white breadcrumbs
Salt and freshly ground black pepper

1 Put the mussels and water into a large pan, cover and place over a high heat for 3–4 minutes, shaking the pan now and then, until the mussels have just opened.

2 Drain the mussels through a colander, then break off and discard the empty half-shells, leaving the mussels in the other shell.

3 Pre-heat the grill to high. Very finely chop the garlic, shallot, parsley and lemon zest together – if you have one of those mini food processors it will do the job beautifully. Mix with the softened butter in a bowl and season to taste.

4 Dot each mussel with some of the garlic and parsley butter, then sprinkle with some of the breadcrumbs. Lay them on a baking tray and grill for 2–3 minutes, or until they are crisp and golden brown. Serve immediately.

grilled mussels with pesto

SERVES 4 AS A STARTER

60 large mussels, cleaned (see page 88)
A splash of dry white wine or water
2 slices white bread, made into breadcrumbs

FOR THE PESTO:

15 g (½ oz) basil leaves
2 large garlic cloves
175 ml (6 fl oz) olive oil
15 g (½ oz) Parmesan cheese, finely grated
15 g (½ oz) pine kernels

1 Put the mussels and wine into a large pan, cover and place over a high heat for 3–4 minutes, shaking the pan now and then, until the mussels have just opened. Remove from the heat straight away and discard one side of the shell.

2 Tip the mussels into a colander set over a bowl to collect the cooking liquor.

3 Pour all but the last tablespoon or two of the cooking liquor into a small pan and boil rapidly until reduced to about 1 tablespoon.

4 Put the pesto ingredients and the reduced mussel cooking liquor into a food processor and blend to a coarse paste.

5 Pre-heat the grill to high. Arrange the mussels on a grilling tray and spoon a little pesto on to each one. Sprinkle over the breadcrumbs and grill for 2–3 minutes until the breadcrumbs are beginning to brown.

11

MOULES MARINIÈRE

warm oysters with black beans, ginger and coriander (see technique 63, page 91)

SERVES 4

20 Pacific oysters
2.5 cm (1 inch) fresh root ginger,
   very finely chopped
7.5 cm (3 inches) cucumber
1 tablespoon chopped coriander
1 teaspoon chopped chives
1 tablespoon Chinese fermented salted black beans
1 garlic clove, very finely chopped
1 tablespoon dark soy sauce
2 tablespoons dry sherry
4 tablespoons sesame oil
Salt

1 Pre-heat the grill to high. Open the oysters as described on page 91 and pour away half the liquor surrounding the meats. Nestle the oysters on a heatproof platter covered in a thick layer of salt or in the grill pan so that they can't roll over during cooking. Sprinkle each one with the chopped ginger and set aside.

2 Cut the cucumber into 2.5 cm (1 inch) pieces, then thinly slice each piece and cut lengthways into matchsticks. Mix with the coriander and chives and set aside.

3 Rinse the black beans and then chop them up a little. Put them into a small pan with the garlic, soy sauce, sherry and sesame oil. Leave over a very low heat to warm through.

4 Grill the oysters for 3 minutes. Sprinkle a little of the cucumber mixture over each one. Spoon over a little of the sauce and serve immediately.

moules marinière (see technique 59, page 88)

SERVES 4

1.75 kg (4 lb) mussels, cleaned (see page 88)
50 g (2 oz) unsalted butter
1 medium onion, finely chopped
50 ml (2 fl oz) dry white wine
1 tablespoon coarsely chopped parsley

1 Put the mussels, butter, onion and white wine into a very large pan. Cover and cook over a high heat for 3–4 minutes, shaking the pan every now and then, until the mussels have opened.

2 Spoon the mussels into 1 large or 4 individual warmed bowls. Add the parsley to the remaining juices, then pour all but the last tablespoon or two, which might contain some grit, back over the mussels. Serve with plenty of crusty white bread.

oysters charentais

SERVES 4

20 Pacific oysters

FOR THE SAUSAGES:

350 g (12 oz) belly pork, roughly chopped

1/2 teaspoon salt

1/2 teaspoon paprika

1/2 teaspoon freshly ground black pepper

1/2 teaspoon thyme leaves

1/2 teaspoon cayenne pepper

75 g (3 oz) chorizo sausage, chopped

100 g (4 oz) caul fat

1 Put all the sausage ingredients (except for the caul fat) into a food processor and process into a coarse paste. Scrape the mixture into a bowl. Cut the caul into 10 cm (4 inch) squares.

2 Divide the sausage mixture into 12 pieces about the size of a golf ball and shape them into small sausages. Wrap each one in a piece of the caul fat.

3 Twenty minutes before serving, carefully open the oysters (see page 91), taking care not to lose too much of the liquor. Divide them between 4 plates.

4 Pre-heat the grill to high. Grill the sausages, turning them now and then, until lightly browned and cooked through. Put 3 of the sausages on to each plate and serve immediately.

grilled oysters with parmesan cheese

SERVES 4

24 Pacific oysters

175 ml (6 fl oz) double cream

25 g (1 oz) Parmesan cheese, finely grated

50 g (2 oz) butter, melted

Freshly ground black pepper

1 Pre-heat the grill to high. Open the oysters (see page 91), release them from the deeper bottom shells and then pour off most of the liquor. Put them on a baking tray or the rack of the grill pan.

OYSTERS IN TEMPURA BATTER WITH SESAME SEEDS AND LIME

2 Spoon about 1 1/2 teaspoons of the cream over each oyster and season with a little black pepper. Sprinkle over the Parmesan cheese and then drizzle with the melted butter.

3 Grill the oysters for 1 minute, until the cheese is golden brown. Serve straight away.

oysters in tempura batter with sesame seeds and lime

SERVES 4

20 Pacific oysters
Sunflower oil, for deep-frying
Lime wedges, to serve

FOR THE TEMPURA BATTER:

50 g (2 oz) plain flour
50 g (2 oz) cornflour
A small pinch of salt
4 teaspoons toasted sesame seeds
175 ml (6 fl oz) ice-cold soda water from a new bottle

FOR THE DIPPING SAUCE:

4 tablespoons dark soy sauce
4 tablespoons water
Juice of 1 lime

1 Open the oysters (see page 91) and pour off all the liquor. Carefully release the meats from the deeper bottom shells. Keep these deeper shells for serving.

2 Mix together the ingredients for the dipping sauce and pour into 4 small dipping saucers or bowls.

3 Heat some oil for deep-frying to 190°C (375°F). Make the batter by sifting the flour, cornflour and salt into a bowl. Stir in the sesame seeds, then stir in the ice-cold soda water (it must be very, very cold and from a new bottle for this batter to be successful) until only just mixed in; the batter should still be a little lumpy. If it seems a bit thick, add a drop more water. You want the batter to be very thin and almost transparent.

4 Dip the oysters, one at a time, into the batter, then drop them into the hot oil and fry for 1 minute, until crisp and golden. Lift out and drain very briefly on kitchen paper.

5 Put the oysters back in their shells and arrange on 4 plates. Serve with the lime wedges and dipping sauce.

SEARED SCALLOPS WITH IBÉRICO HAM

seared scallops with ibérico ham (see technique 61, page 90)

SERVES 4

8 thin slices of ibérico ham or a similar cured ham
Leaves from 1 frisée lettuce heart and a handful of other bitter salad leaves
50 g (2 oz) chilled unsalted butter
12 prepared scallops (see page 90)
3 tablespoons sherry vinegar
1 tablespoon chopped parsley
Salt and freshly ground black pepper

1 Arrange the ham and a pile of the salad leaves on 4 plates. Generously rub the base of a large non-stick frying pan with the block of butter and cut the remainder into small pieces.

2 Set the pan over a high heat and, as soon as the butter starts to smoke, add the scallops and sear for 2 minutes on each side, seasoning them with a little salt and pepper as they cook. Arrange the scallops on top of the ham.

3 For the dressing, remove the pan from the heat, add the sherry vinegar and stir to scrape up any residue from the bottom of the pan. Return the pan to the heat and whisk in the butter, a few pieces at a time, then add the parsley and season with a little salt and pepper. Spoon the dressing over the leaves and serve at once.

steamed scallops in the shell with ginger, soy, sesame oil and spring onions

SERVES 4

16 prepared scallops in the shell (see page 90)
1 teaspoon finely chopped fresh root ginger
1 tablespoon sesame oil
2 tablespoons dark soy sauce
1 tablespoon roughly chopped coriander
3 spring onions, thinly sliced

1 Pour 2.5 cm (1 inch) of water into the base of a wide shallow pan and bring it up to the boil. Loosen the scallops from their shells but leave them in place. Sprinkle each one with some of the ginger.

2 Arrange the scallops, in batches if necessary, on a petal steamer. Lower them into the pan, reduce the heat to medium, cover and cook for about 4 minutes until just set. Remove and keep warm while you cook the rest.

3 Meanwhile, put the sesame oil and soy sauce into a small pan and warm through.

4 Lift the scallops on to 4 warmed plates and pour over some of the warm soy sauce and sesame oil. Sprinkle over the coriander and spring onions and serve immediately.

GRILLED SCALLOPS IN THE SHELL WITH
TOASTED HAZELNUT AND CORIANDER BUTTER

grilled scallops in the shell with toasted hazelnut and coriander butter

SERVES 4

16 prepared scallops in the shell (see page 90)
25 g (1 oz) unsalted butter, melted
Salt and freshly ground black pepper
FOR THE TOASTED HAZELNUT
AND CORIANDER BUTTER:
20 g (³/₄ oz) unblanched hazelnuts
75 g (3 oz) unsalted butter, softened
7 g (¹/₄ oz) coriander leaves
2 tablespoons flat-leaf parsley leaves
7g (¹/₄ oz) shallot, roughly chopped
1 teaspoon lemon juice

1 Pre-heat the grill to high. For the toasted hazelnut and coriander butter, spread the hazelnuts over a baking tray and toast under the grill for 4–5 minutes, shaking the tray now and then, until they are golden brown. Tip them into a clean tea towel and rub off the skins. Leave to cool, then chop them roughly and tip them into a food processor. Add the softened butter with the coriander, parsley, shallot, lemon juice, a good pinch of salt and some pepper and blend together until well mixed.

2 Put the scallops on to a large baking tray (or do them in batches if necessary) and brush the meats with the melted butter. Season with a little salt and pepper, then grill for 1¹/₂ minutes.

3 Drop a generous teaspoonful of the hazelnut and coriander butter on to each scallop and return to the grill for 1¹/₂ minutes, until they are cooked through. Serve immediately.

11

scallops with duck livers and spaghettini

SERVES 4

12 large prepared scallops (see page 90)
100 g (4 oz) duck livers
300 ml (10 fl oz) Fish Stock (see page 222)
120 ml (4 fl oz) double cream
120 ml (4 fl oz) Muscat de Beaumes de Venise or a
**   similar sweet white wine**
175 g (6 oz) dried spaghettini
25 g (1 oz) unsalted butter
Salt and freshly ground black pepper
Sprigs of flat-leaf parsley, to garnish

1 Bring a large pan of well salted water (i.e. 1 teaspoon per 600 ml/ 1 pint) to the boil. Meanwhile, slice the scallops horizontally in half and cut the duck livers into similar-sized pieces, being sure to remove any traces of the greeny-yellow gall bladder.

2 Put the fish stock, 85 ml (3 fl oz) of the cream and the wine into a wide-based pan and boil rapidly until reduced to 150 ml (5 fl oz).

3 Add the pasta to the pan of boiling water and cook for 4 minutes or until *al dente*. Drain, then cover and keep warm.

4 Melt a small knob of the butter in a frying pan over a high heat. Add the scallop slices and fry them for 30 seconds on each side. Transfer them to a plate and keep warm.

5 Add the rest of the butter to the pan with the duck livers and fry for just 1 minute, turning them over as they colour. Set aside with the scallops.

6 Add the reduced stock and wine mixture to the pan and bring to the boil, scraping up all the bits from the bottom of the pan. Strain through a sieve into a small pan, stir in the rest of the cream, check the seasoning and heat through.

7 To serve, pile the pasta on to 4 warmed plates and arrange the scallops and duck livers on top. Pour the sauce around the pasta and serve garnished with the flat-leaf parsley.

OCTOPUS, PEA AND RED WINE STEW FROM LA VELA IN NAPLES

octopus, pea and red wine stew from la vela in naples (see technique 64, page 94)

SERVES 4

1 x 750 g (1½ lb) octopus, cleaned (see pages 94–5)
120 ml (4 fl oz) extra virgin olive oil
2 garlic cloves, thinly sliced
4 shallots, sliced
600 ml (1 pint) Italian red wine
1 teaspoon caster sugar
2 plum tomatoes, halved
100 g (4 oz) fresh peas or frozen petits pois
1 tablespoon finely chopped flat-leaf parsley
Salt and freshly ground black pepper

1 Pre-heat the oven to 150°C/300°F/Gas Mark 2. Put the octopus into a small casserole dish with 85 ml (3 fl oz) of the olive oil. Cover and cook in the oven for 2 hours, until very tender.

2 Heat the rest of the olive oil in a large shallow pan with the garlic until it begins to sizzle. Add the shallots and cook gently until they are

soft and lightly coloured. Add the red wine, sugar and tomatoes, bring to the boil and then leave to simmer until almost all the wine has evaporated. Lift out the tomato skins and discard them.

3 Lift the octopus out of its cooking juices and cut it across into smaller pieces. Add to the red wine reduction with the cooking juices and 120 ml (4 fl oz) of water. Bring to a simmer and cook for 15–20 minutes, until the liquid has reduced by about three-quarters.

4 Add the peas and simmer for 5 minutes. Season to taste, stir in the parsley and serve hot or cold in large soup plates, with plenty of crusty Italian bread.

pulpo a la feria (fairground octopus)

SERVES 4
1 octopus, weighing about 750 g (1½ lb)
1 onion, peeled
4 bay leaves
½ teaspoon paprika
A good pinch of cayenne pepper
50 ml (2 fl oz) good olive oil
½–1 teaspoon Maldon sea-salt flakes

1 You will need to start the preparation for this dish well in advance. Seal the octopus in a plastic bag and leave it in the freezer for 2 weeks (this helps to tenderize it). Then transfer it to the fridge the day before you want to cook it to allow it to thaw gently for 24 hours.

2 The next day, clean the octopus as described on page 94. Bring a large pan of water to the boil with the onion and bay leaves.

3 Add the octopus and simmer for at least 1 hour. Test after 30 minutes and cook for a further 30 minutes if it is still a bit tough, but don't cook any longer than that as it loses its fresh taste with long cooking.

4 Lift the octopus out of the pan and drain away all the excess water. Put it on a board, cut off the tentacles and slice each one on the diagonal into pieces about 5 mm (¼ inch) thick. Cut the body into similar-sized pieces.

5 Divide the octopus between 4 small pine boards or one large warmed serving plate and sprinkle with the paprika and the cayenne. Heat the olive oil in a small pan until it is sizzling. Drizzle it over the octopus and then finally sprinkle with the sea salt. Serve with plenty of crusty fresh bread.

pasta with sea urchin roe, lemon and parsley (see technique 67, page 97)

SERVES 4
450 g (1 lb) dried spaghetti
4 tablespoons extra virgin olive oil
1 garlic clove, finely chopped
A very small pinch of dried chilli flakes
50 g (2 oz) fresh sea urchin roe (see page 97)
2 tablespoons chopped, flat-leaf parsley
2 teaspoons lemon juice
Salt and freshly ground black pepper

1 Cook the spaghetti in boiling well-salted water (i.e. 1 teaspoon of salt for every 600 ml/1 pint of water) for 8 minutes or until *al dente*.

2 Just before you drain the pasta, put the olive oil, garlic and chilli flakes into another large pan and set it over a medium heat until it just begins to sizzle. Cook gently for 1 minute without letting the garlic colour.

3 Drain the spaghetti, add to the oil with the sea urchin roe and parsley and turn together over a low heat for 1 minute. You simply want the residual heat in the pasta to lightly cook the roe. Season with the lemon juice, a pinch of salt and a little pepper and serve.

risotto nero

SERVES 4

450 g (1 lb) uncleaned small cuttlefish

1.2 litres (2 pints) Fish Stock (see page 222)

25 g (1 oz) butter

3 tablespoons olive oil

2 large shallots, finely chopped

3 garlic cloves, finely chopped

350 g (12 oz) risotto rice, such as Carnaroli or Arborio

150 ml (5 fl oz) dry white wine

3 tablespoons chopped flat-leaf parsley

1 tablespoon finely grated Parmesan cheese

Salt and freshly ground black pepper

1 Prepare the cuttlefish as described on page 96, carefully removing the little pearly-white ink sacs without bursting them. Squeeze out the ink into the fish stock, then slit open the sacs and rinse them out in the stock to remove as much of the ink as you can. Bring the stock to the boil in a pan and keep it hot over a low heat. Cut the cuttlefish bodies into very thin strips and slice the tentacles into 4 cm (1½ inch) pieces.

2 Heat the butter and 1 tablespoon of the oil in a heavy-based saucepan. Add the shallots and garlic and cook gently until soft but not browned.

3 Stir in the rice so that all the grains get well coated in the oil and butter. Add the wine and simmer over a low heat for a few minutes until it has almost disappeared.

4 Add a ladleful of stock and simmer, stirring frequently, until it has all been absorbed. Continue to add the stock a ladleful at a time, stirring, until it has all been used and the rice is creamy and tender but still with a little bit of a bite – *al dente*. This should take about 20–25 minutes.

5 Heat the rest of the oil in a large frying pan. Add the cuttlefish and fry it over a high heat for 1½ minutes. Remove from the heat, stir in the chopped parsley and season with some salt and pepper. Stir the Parmesan cheese into the risotto. Season with salt and pepper.

6 Spoon the risotto into 4 warmed bowls and pile some of the cuttlefish into the centre. Serve straight away.

ALTERNATIVE FISH

Squid would be a good substitute but there's not enough ink in squid to make this satisfactorily. However, you can buy little sachets of ink from your fishmonger. You'll need about 4 sachets for this dish.

a salad of raw cuttlefish with vine tomatoes and rocket (see technique 66, page 96)

SERVES 4

1 small uncleaned cuttlefish

6 medium-sized vine-ripened tomatoes

Juice of ¼ lemon

extra virgin olive oil

40 g (1½ oz) wild rocket leaves

Maldon sea-salt flakes and coarsely ground black pepper

1 Clean the cuttlefish as described on page 96 and reserve the tentacles for another dish. Cut the cleaned body in half lengthways and then cut each piece across, slightly on the diagonal, into very thin slices.

2 Slice each of the tomatoes across into very thin slices.

3 To serve, arrange 6 tomato slices in one layer over the base of each plate. Arrange 25 g (1 oz) of the cuttlefish slices loosely over the top of the tomatoes. Squeeze over a few drops of lemon juice, sprinkle with some sea-salt flakes and a little coarsely ground black pepper and then drizzle over a little oil. Scatter over a few rocket leaves and serve straight away.

deep-fried squid and aïoli

SERVES 4

350 g (12 oz) cleaned squid (see page 92)

1 quantity Aïoli (see page 224)

50 g (2 oz) seasoned flour

Sunflower oil, for deep-frying

Thin lemon wedges, to serve

FOR THE TOMATO AND DILL SALAD:

2 vine-ripened tomatoes, thinly sliced

1 sprig dill, broken into small pieces

Maldon sea-salt flakes and coarsely ground black pepper

1 Cut the squid pouches across into rings.

2 Season the squid with a little salt, toss in the seasoned flour and deep-fry in batches at 190°C (375°F) for 1 minute until crisp and golden. Drain briefly on kitchen paper.

3 For the salad, layer 3–4 thin slices of tomato on each plate with the dill and some seasoning. Put the squid and 1 heaped tablespoon of the aïoli alongside. Garnish with the lemon wedges and serve.

SQUID

steamed stuffed squid with sweet chilli sauce

SERVES 4

4 small squid with pouches no longer than 15 cm
(6 inches), cleaned (see page 92)

25 g (1 oz) peeled raw prawns

100 g (4 oz) minced pork

1 cm (½ inch) fresh root ginger, finely grated

2 garlic cloves, crushed

1 tablespoon light soy sauce

1 tablespoon chopped coriander

¼ teaspoon caster sugar

1½ teaspoons sesame oil

½ teaspoon salt

Freshly ground Sichuan pepper

2 spring onions, chopped, plus 1 spring onion,
finely shredded, to garnish

FOR THE SWEET CHILLI SAUCE:

2 tablespoons dark soy sauce

2 tablespoons sweet chilli sauce

2 teaspoons rice vinegar or white wine vinegar

1 teaspoon sesame oil

1 Rinse out the squid pouches. Roughly chop the tentacles and fins and put them in a food processor with the prawns and minced pork. Blend to a coarse mixture. Scrape the mixture into a bowl, add the rest of the ingredients (except for the shredded spring onion and the sauce ingredients) and mix together well.

2 Spoon the pork mixture into the squid pouches and secure the open ends with cocktail sticks.

3 Pour about 2.5 cm (1 inch) of water into a shallow wide-based pan and bring to the boil. Arrange the squid on a petal steamer, lower it into the pan, cover and steam for 20–25 minutes, until they are cooked through.

4 Meanwhile, put the ingredients for the sauce into a small pan. Just before the squid are ready, warm the sauce through. Lift the squid on to a board and cut each one across into about 6 thin slices. Arrange them on 4 warmed plates, spoon over some of the sauce and garnish with the spring onion shreds.

squid, mint and coriander salad with roasted rice

SERVES 4

225 g (8 oz) prepared small squid (see page 92)

2 tablespoons groundnut oil

A good pinch of cayenne pepper

2 teaspoons long-grain rice

1 Romaine lettuce heart, cut across into wide strips

4 spring onions, trimmed, halved and finely shredded

A handful of mint leaves

A handful of coriander sprigs

Salt and freshly ground black pepper

FOR THE DRESSING:

1 medium-hot red Dutch chilli, thinly sliced into rings

50 ml (2 fl oz) white wine vinegar

Juice of 1 lime

2 tablespoons Thai fish sauce (*nam pla*)

2 tablespoons water

½ teaspoon caster sugar

1 lemongrass stalk, outer leaves removed and core very
finely chopped.

1 Cut along one side of each squid pouch and open it out flat. Score the inner side into a diamond pattern with the tip of a small sharp knife and then cut into 5 cm (2 inch) squares. Separate the tentacles if large (see page 93). Season with a little salt and pepper.

2 For the dressing, cover the chilli slices with vinegar and leave to steep for half an hour.

3 Heat the oil in a wok. Add the squid and stir-fry for 2 minutes. Transfer to a plate, sprinkle with the cayenne and leave to cool, but don't refrigerate.

4 Meanwhile, heat a small heavy-based frying pan over a high heat. Add the rice and toss for a few minutes until it is richly browned and smells nutty. Tip into a mortar or mug and pound it with a pestle or the end of a rolling pin to break it up, but don't grind it into fine powder.

5 To serve, toss together the lettuce, spring onions, mint and coriander and spread on a large oval platter. Scatter over the squid and any oil left in the pan. Lift the chilli slices out of the vinegar and mix with the rest of the dressing ingredients. Spoon over the squid and sprinkle with the roasted rice. Serve straight away.

11

STIR-FRIED SALT-AND-PEPPER SQUID WITH RED CHILLI AND SPRING ONION

stir-fried salt-and-pepper squid with red chilli and spring onion (see technique 64, page 92)

SERVES 4 AS A STARTER

750 g (1½ lb) squid
½ teaspoon black peppercorns
½ teaspoon Sichuan peppercorns
1 teaspoon Maldon sea-salt flakes
1–2 tablespoons sunflower oil
1 medium-hot red Dutch chilli, thinly sliced (seeds removed, if you prefer)
3 spring onions, sliced

FOR THE SALAD:

¼ cucumber, peeled, halved and seeded
50 g (2 oz) beansprouts
25 g (1 oz) watercress, large stalks removed
2 teaspoons dark soy sauce
2 teaspoons roasted sesame oil
¼ teaspoon caster sugar
A pinch of salt

1 Prepare the squid as described on pages 92–3.

2 For the salad, cut the cucumber lengthways into short strips. Toss with the beansprouts and watercress and set aside in the fridge until needed. Whisk together the soy sauce, sesame oil, sugar and salt.

3 Heat a small heavy-based frying pan over a high heat. Add the black peppercorns and Sichuan peppercorns and dry-roast them for a few seconds, shaking the pan now and then, until they darken slightly and become aromatic. Tip into a mortar and crush coarsely with the pestle, then stir in the sea-salt flakes.

4 Heat a wok over a high heat until smoking. Add half the oil and half the squid and stir-fry it for 2 minutes, until lightly coloured. Tip on to a plate, then cook the remaining squid in the same way.

5 Return the first batch of squid to the wok and add 1 teaspoon of the salt-and-pepper mixture (the rest can be used in other stir-fries). Toss together for about 10 seconds, then add the red chilli and spring onions and toss together very briefly.

6 Divide the squid between 4 serving plates. Toss the salad with the dressing and pile alongside the squid. Serve immediately.

recipes
chapter 12

12

stocks, sauces and basic recipes

fish stock

MAKES 1.2 LITRES (2 PINTS)

**1 kg (2¹/₄ lb) fish bones, such as lemon
   sole, brill and plaice**
2.4 litres (4 pints) water
1 onion, chopped
1 fennel bulb, chopped
100 g (4 oz) celery, sliced
100 g (4 oz) carrot, chopped
25 g (1 oz) button mushrooms, sliced
1 sprig thyme

1 Put the fish bones and water into a large pan, bring just to the boil and simmer very gently for 20 minutes.

2 Strain through a fine sieve into a clean pan, add the vegetables and the thyme and bring back to the boil. Simmer for 35 minutes or until reduced to about 1.2 litres (2 pints).

3 Strain once more and use or store as required.

shellfish stock and shellfish reduction

MAKES 900 ML (1¹/₂ PINTS) OF STOCK
OR 150 ML (5 FL OZ) OF REDUCTION

15 g (¹/₂ oz) unsalted butter
50 g (2 oz) carrot, chopped
50 g (2 oz) onion, chopped
50 g (2 oz) celery, chopped
**350 g (12 oz) unshelled North Atlantic
   prawns, small crabs or shrimps**
1 tablespoon cognac
2 tablespoons white wine
1 teaspoon chopped fresh tarragon
75 g (3 oz) tomato, roughly chopped
**1.2 litres (2 pints) Fish Stock
   (see above)**
A pinch of cayenne pepper

TO MAKE THE STOCK:

1 Melt the butter in a large saucepan. Add the carrot, onion and celery and fry over a medium-high heat for 3–4 minutes.

2 Add the prawns, crabs or shrimps and the cognac and fry for a further 2 minutes.

3 Add the remaining ingredients, lower the heat, cover and leave to simmer for 40 minutes.

4 Strain the stock through a fine sieve, pressing out as much liquid as you can with the back of a ladle. It is now ready to use.

TO MAKE THE REDUCTION:

1 Liquidize the stock, in batches if necessary, before straining. Press the pulpy mixture through a muslin-lined sieve into a clean pan, pressing out as much liquid as you can.

2 Bring the stock to the boil, and boil rapidly until it has reduced to about 150 ml (5 fl oz). It is now ready to use.

chicken stock

MAKES 1.7 LITRES (3 PINTS)

**Bones from a 1.5 kg (3 lb) uncooked
   chicken or 450 g (1 lb) chicken wings**
1 large carrot, chopped
2 celery sticks, sliced
2 leeks, sliced
2 fresh or dried bay leaves
2 sprigs thyme
2.4 litres (4 pints) water

1 Put all the ingredients into a large pan and bring just to the boil, skimming off any scum from the surface as it appears. Leave to simmer very gently for 2 hours – it is important not to let it boil as this will force the fat from even the leanest chicken and make the stock cloudy.

2 Strain the stock through a fine sieve and use as required. If not using immediately, leave to cool, then chill and refrigerate or freeze for later use.

basic court-bouillon

6 fresh bay leaves
1 teaspoon black peppercorns
1 carrot, sliced
1 small onion, sliced
2 tablespoons salt
4 tablespoons white wine vinegar
3.4 litres (6 pints) water

Put all the ingredients into a saucepan or fish kettle, bring to the boil and simmer for 20 minutes. You can set the court-bouillon aside or chill at this stage until needed. Bring back to the boil before using.

shellfish bouillon

MAKES 2.4 LITRES (4 PINTS)
1 fennel bulb
1 large onion
4 celery sticks
A handful of button mushrooms
1/2 teaspoon salt
1 teaspoon black peppercorns
2 bay leaves
3 sprigs thyme
1/2 teaspoon fennel seeds
300 ml (10 fl oz) dry white wine

1 Roughly chop all the vegetables and put them into a large pan with the salt, peppercorns, herbs, fennel seeds and enough water to cover.

2 Bring to the boil and simmer for 20 minutes. Take the pan off the heat and add the wine. Cover and leave to cool for 2 hours.

3 Strain the stock into another pan and use or store as required.

hollandaise sauce

SERVES 4
2 tablespoons water
2 egg yolks
225 g (8 oz) Clarified Butter
    (see page 226), warmed
Juice of 1/2 lemon

A good pinch of cayenne pepper
3/4 teaspoon salt

1 Put the water and egg yolks into a stainless-steel or glass bowl set over a pan of simmering water, making sure that the base of the bowl is not touching the water. Whisk until voluminous and creamy.

2 Remove the bowl from the pan and gradually whisk in the clarified butter until thick. Then whisk in the lemon juice, cayenne pepper and salt.

NOTE
This sauce is best used as soon as it is made but will hold for up to 2 hours if kept covered in a warm place, such as over a pan of warm water.

VARIATIONS

béarnaise sauce

Put 1 tablespoon chopped tarragon, 2 finely chopped shallots, 20 turns of black pepper and 50 ml (2 fl oz) white wine vinegar into a small pan. Boil rapidly until reduced to 1 tablespoon. Stir into 1 quantity of Hollandaise Sauce.

maltaise sauce

Stir the finely grated zest of 1 blood orange and the juice of 2 blood oranges into 1 quantity of Hollandaise Sauce.

vanilla hollandaise

Slit open 1 vanilla pod and scrape out the seeds. Put 300 ml (10 fl oz) Fish Stock (see page 222), 2 tablespoons Noilly Prat, the vanilla pod and the seeds into a small pan and boil rapidly until reduced to 1½–2 tablespoons. Strain and stir into 1 quantity of Hollandaise Sauce.

mussel sauce

Put 450 g (1 lb) small mussels, 2 tablespoons white wine, 1 finely chopped shallot and 1 teaspoon chopped parsley into a pan. Cover and cook over a high heat for 3–4 minutes until the mussels have opened. Tip into a colander set over a bowl to collect the cooking liquor. When they are cool enough to handle, remove the meats from the shells and put to one side. Then, boil the cooking liquor until reduced to 1–2 tablespoons. Stir the reduced liquor and meats into 1 quantity of Hollandaise Sauce.

seafood sauce

Stir 1 quantity of Shellfish Reduction (see page 222) into 1 quantity of Hollandaise Sauce.

sauce messine

Bring 1 teaspoon French mustard, 2 finely chopped shallots and 50 ml (2 fl oz) double cream to the boil in a small pan. Stir into 1 quantity of Hollandaise Sauce with 1 teaspoon each of chopped chervil, tarragon and chives.

quick hollandaise sauce

Using the same quantities as for Hollandaise Sauce, (see left, below) put the egg yolks, lemon juice and water into a liquidizer. Turn on the machine and then slowly pour in the warm butter through the lid. Season with cayenne pepper and salt.

beurre blanc

SERVES 4
50 g (2 oz) shallots, or onion, very finely
    chopped
2 tablespoons white wine vinegar

stocks, sauces and basic recipes

4 tablespoons dry white wine
6 tablespoons water or Fish Stock
(see page 222)
2 tablespoons double cream
175 g (6 oz) unsalted butter, cut into
small pieces
Salt and freshly ground white pepper

1 Put the shallots, vinegar, wine and water into a small pan and simmer until nearly all the liquid has evaporated.

2 Add the cream and boil until reduced a little more.

3 Lower the heat and gradually whisk in the butter, a few pieces at a time, until the sauce has amalgamated. Season to taste with salt and white pepper.

mayonnaise

This recipe includes instructions for making mayonnaise in the liquidizer or by hand. It is lighter when made mechanically because the process uses a whole egg and is very quick. You can use either sunflower oil, olive oil or a mixture of the two if you prefer. It will keep in the fridge for up to 1 week.

MAKES 300 ML (10 FL OZ)
1 egg or 2 egg yolks
2 teaspoons white wine vinegar
1/2 teaspoon salt
300 ml (10 fl oz) sunflower oil or olive oil

TO MAKE THE MAYONNAISE BY HAND:

1 Make sure all the ingredients are at room temperature before you start. Put the egg yolks, vinegar and salt into a mixing bowl and then rest the bowl on a cloth to stop it slipping. Lightly whisk to break the yolks.

2 Using a wire whisk, beat the oil into the egg mixture a few drops at a time until you have incorporated it all. (Once you have added the same volume of oil as the original mixture of egg yolks and vinegar, you can add the oil a little more quickly.)

TO MAKE THE MAYONNAISE IN A
MACHINE:

Put the whole egg, vinegar and salt into a liquidizer or food processor. Turn on the machine and then slowly add the oil through the hole in the lid until you have a thick emulsion.

VARIATIONS

fennel mayonnaise

Stir 3 teaspoons Pernod, 1 teaspoon chopped chives and 1 tablespoon finely chopped fennel bulb into 1 quantity of Mayonnaise made with olive oil.

sauce verte

Blanch 25 g (1 oz) each of spinach and rocket leaves in boiling water for 1 minute. Drain and refresh under cold water. Squeeze dry and then put into a food processor with 25 g (1 oz) of mixed parsley, chervil, tarragon and chives and 1 quantity of Mayonnaise made with olive oil. Blend until smooth.

marie rose sauce

Stir 5 tablespoons tomato ketchup, 4 tablespoons Greek-style natural yogurt and some salt and freshly ground white pepper into 1 quantity of Mayonnaise made with sunflower oil.

lemon mayonnaise

Make the mayonnaise in a machine, using 1 tablespoon lemon juice in place of the vinegar, adding the finely grated zest of 1 small lemon

and using a mixture of half sunflower oil and half olive oil.

mustard mayonnaise

Make the mayonnaise in a liquidizer using a whole egg, 1 tablespoon white wine vinegar, 1 tablespoon English mustard, 3/4 teaspoon salt, a little white pepper and sunflower oil.

tartare sauce

Stir 1 teaspoon each of finely chopped green olives, gherkins and capers and 2 teaspoons each of chopped chives and chopped parsley into a 1/2 quantity of Mustard Mayonnaise (see above).

aïoli

MAKES 175 ML (6 FL OZ)
4 garlic cloves, peeled
1/2 teaspoon salt
1 medium egg yolk
2 teaspoons lemon juice
175 ml (6 fl oz) extra virgin olive oil

1 Put the garlic cloves on to a chopping board and crush them under the blade of a large knife. Sprinkle them with the salt and then work them with the knife blade into a smooth paste.

2 Scrape the garlic paste into a bowl and add the egg yolk and the lemon juice. Using an electric hand mixer, whisk everything together and then very gradually whisk in the olive oil to make a thick mayonnaise-like mixture.

rouille

MAKES 300 ML (10 FL OZ)
25 g (1 oz) slice day-old crustless white
bread
A little Fish Stock (see page 222) or water
3 fat garlic cloves, peeled
1 egg yolk
250 ml (8 fl oz) olive oil
FOR THE HARISSA:
1 quantity Roasted Red Peppers
(see page 227)

12

1 teaspoon tomato purée
1 teaspoon ground coriander
A pinch of saffron strands
2 medium-hot red Dutch chillies, stalks
    removed and roughly chopped
1/4 teaspoon cayenne pepper
1/2 teaspoon salt

1 For the harissa, put the roasted red pepper flesh, tomato purée, ground coriander, saffron, chillies, cayenne pepper and 1/4 teaspoon of the salt into a food processor and blend until smooth.

2 Cover the slice of bread with the fish stock or water and leave to soften. Squeeze out the excess liquid and put the bread into the food processor with 2 tablespoons of the harissa paste, the garlic, egg yolk and the remaining salt. Blend until smooth.

3 With the machine still running, gradually add the oil until you have a smooth, thick, mayonnaise-like mixture. This will store in the fridge for up to 1 week.

italian salsa verde

SERVES 6-8

20 g (3/4 oz) flat-leaf parsley leaves, very
    roughly chopped
7 g (1/4 oz) mint leaves, very roughly
    chopped
3 tablespoons capers in brine, drained
    and rinsed
6 anchovy fillets in olive oil, drained
1 garlic clove
1 teaspoon Dijon mustard
11/2 tablespoons lemon juice
120 ml (4 fl oz) extra virgin olive oil
1/2 teaspoon salt

1 Pile the parsley, mint, capers, anchovies and garlic on to a chopping board and chop together into a coarse paste.

2 Transfer the mixture into a bowl and stir in the mustard, lemon juice, olive oil and salt.

parsley butter

1 small bunch of parsley, large stalks
    removed
5 anchovy fillets in olive oil, drained
100 g (4 oz) unsalted butter, softened
2 teaspoons lemon juice
5 turns of the black pepper mill
1/2 teaspoon salt

1 Chop the parsley and anchovy fillets together on a board into a coarse paste.

2 Mix into the butter with the lemon juice, pepper and salt.

3 Spoon into the centre of a large sheet of cling film and shape into a 4 cm (1½ inch) thick roll. Wrap and chill in the fridge or freezer until firm.

garlic butter

2 large garlic cloves
100 g (4 oz) unsalted butter, softened
1 teaspoon lemon juice
1 teaspoon brandy
25 g (1 oz) chopped parsley
Salt and freshly ground black pepper

1 Crush the garlic cloves on a board with the blade of a large knife. Add a large pinch of salt and work into a smooth paste.

2 Beat into the butter with the lemon juice, brandy, parsley and some freshly ground black pepper. Shape and chill as before.

prawn butter

75 g (3 oz) unpeeled cooked North
    Atlantic prawns or pink shrimps
100 g (4 oz) unsalted butter, softened
1 teaspoon lemon juice
1/4 teaspoon salt and a pinch of cayenne
    pepper

1 Put all the ingredients into a food processor and blend until smooth, then press through a chinois or very fine sieve with the back of a wooden spoon.

2 Adjust the salt if necessary, then shape and chill as before.

lemongrass butter

1 lemongrass stalk, outer leaves removed
    and core finely chopped
Finely grated zest of 1/2 lime
2 teaspoons lime juice
1 cm (1/2 inch) fresh root ginger, very
    finely chopped
2 tablespoons chopped parsley
100 g (4 oz) slightly salted butter, softened
1 tablespoon Thai fish sauce (nam pla)
Freshly ground black pepper

Put everything into a food processor and season well with freshly ground black pepper. Blend until smooth, then shape and chill as before.

roasted red pepper
and chilli butter

1 quantity Roasted Red Peppers
    (see page 227)
2 sun-dried tomatoes in oil, drained and
    finely chopped
1 medium-hot red Dutch chilli, seeded
    and finely chopped
2 tablespoons chopped parsley

stocks, sauces and basic recipes

100 g (4 oz) slightly salted butter, softened
½ teaspoon salt

1 Chop the flesh of the roasted red peppers very finely.

2 Mix into the butter with the rest of the ingredients, then shape and chill as before.

pesto butter

15 g (½ oz) basil leaves
2 large garlic cloves, roughly chopped
15 g (½ oz) Parmesan cheese, finely grated
15 g (½ oz) pine kernels
3 tablespoons olive oil
½ teaspoon salt
100 g (4 oz) butter, softened

1 Put the basil leaves, garlic, Parmesan cheese, pine kernels, olive oil and salt into a food processor and blend until smooth.

2 Add the butter and blend again until smooth. Shape and chill as before.

vindaloo curry paste

MAKES 16 TABLESPOONS

40 g (1½ oz) dried red Kashmir chillies
1 small onion
1 teaspoon black peppercorns
1½ teaspoons cloves
7.5 cm (3 inch) cinnamon stick
1 teaspoon cumin seeds
2.5 cm (1 inch) fresh root ginger
4 tablespoons chopped garlic
A walnut-sized piece of tamarind pulp, without seeds
1 teaspoon light soft brown sugar
2 tablespoons white wine vinegar

1 Cover the dried chillies with plenty of hot water, keep them submerged under a small plate and leave to soak overnight.

2 The next day, pre-heat the oven to 230°C/450°F/ Gas Mark 8. Place the unpeeled onion on the

middle rack of the oven and roast for 1 hour, until the centre is soft and nicely caramelized. Leave to cool and then peel off the skin.

3 Drain the chillies and squeeze out the excess water. Grind the peppercorns, cloves, cinnamon and cumin seeds to a fine powder in a spice grinder.

4 Put the chillies, roasted onion, ground spices, ginger, garlic, tamarind pulp, sugar and vinegar into a food processor and blend to a smooth paste.

goan masala paste

1 teaspoon cumin seeds
1 teaspoon coriander seeds
1 teaspoon black peppercorns
½ teaspoon fennel seeds
½ teaspoon cloves
½ teaspoon turmeric powder
50 g (2 oz) medium-hot red Dutch chillies, roughly chopped
½ teaspoon salt
3 garlic cloves, chopped
1 teaspoon light muscovado sugar
1½ teaspoons Tamarind Water (see opposite)
2.5 cm (1 inch) fresh root ginger, roughly chopped
1 tablespoon red wine vinegar

Grind the spices to a fine powder in a spice grinder. Put them into a food processor with the rest of the ingredients and blend to a smooth paste.

thai red curry paste

SERVES 4

5 large medium-hot red Dutch chillies, stalks removed, then roughly chopped
2.5 cm (1 inch) fresh root ginger, chopped
2 lemongrass stalks, outer leaves removed and core roughly chopped
6 garlic cloves
3 shallots, roughly chopped
1 teaspoon ground coriander
1 teaspoon ground cumin
¼ teaspoon blachan (Thai shrimp paste)
2 teaspoons paprika
½ teaspoon turmeric powder
1 teaspoon salt
1 tablespoon sunflower oil

Put everything into a food processor and blend to a smooth paste.

tapenade

MAKES 1 SMALL JAR

75 g (3 oz) pitted black olives, drained and rinsed
4 anchovy fillets in olive oil, drained
25 g (1 oz) capers, drained and rinsed
3 garlic cloves
75 ml (3 fl oz) olive oil
Freshly ground black pepper

1 Put the olives, anchovies, capers and garlic into a food processor and pulse 3 or 4 times. Then turn the processor on and add the oil in a thin steady stream through the lid.

2 Stir in black pepper to taste, spoon the mixture into a sterilized glass jar, seal and store in the fridge for up to 3 months. Use as required.

clarified butter

Place the butter in a small pan and leave it over a very low heat until it has melted. Then skim off any scum from the surface and pour off the clear (clarified) butter into a bowl, leaving behind the

12

milky white solids that will have settled on the bottom of the pan.

beurre manié

Blend equal quantities of softened butter and plain flour together into a smooth paste. Cover and keep in the fridge until needed. It will keep for the same period of time as butter.

tamarind water

Take a piece of tamarind pulp about the size of a tangerine and put it in a bowl with 150 ml (5 fl oz) warm water. Work the paste into the water with your fingers until it has broken down and all the seeds have been released. Strain the slightly syrupy mixture through a fine sieve into another bowl and discard the fibrous material left in the sieve. The water is now ready to use and will store in the fridge for 24 hours.

lemon olive oil

Pare the zest from 1 lemon with a potato peeler. Cut the zest into thin strips and mix with 600 ml (1 pint) of extra virgin olive oil. Leave to infuse for 24 hours before using.

preserved lemons

NOTE
The lemons must be small ones or they won't fit or fill the jar.

3–4 small lemons per 500 ml (17 fl oz) Kilner jar
75 g (3 oz) salt per jar
Fresh lemon juice

1 Cut the lemons almost into quarters, leaving them attached at the stalk end.

2 Sprinkle as much salt as you can into the cuts, push them back into shape and then push them into the jar, stalk-end down, packing them in tightly – they will fit with a little persuasion.

3 Sprinkle over the rest of the salt, seal and leave for 4–5 days, giving the jar a shake every now and then, until the lemons have produced quite a lot of juice.

4 Then top up the jar with lemon juice so that the lemons are completely covered. Seal and leave for a couple of weeks before using.

fresh egg pasta

MAKES 225 G (8 OZ)
225 g (8 oz) plain flour
1/4 teaspoon salt
1/2 teaspoon olive oil
2 medium eggs
4 medium egg yolks

1 Put all the ingredients into a food processor and blend until they come together into a dough.

2 Tip out on to a work surface and knead for about 10 minutes until smooth and elastic. Wrap in cling film and leave to rest for 10–15 minutes before using.

roasted red peppers

EITHER: Spear the stalk end of the pepper on a fork and turn the pepper in the flame of a gas burner or blowtorch until the skin has blistered and blackened.

OR: Roast the pepper in an oven pre-heated to 220°C/425°F/Gas Mark 7 for 20–25 minutes, turning once until the skin is black. Then remove the pepper from the heat and leave to cool. Break it in half and remove the stalk, skin and seeds. The flesh is now ready to use.

fresh salted cod

Sprinkle a 1 cm (½ inch) layer of salt over the base of a plastic container. Put a thick piece of unskinned cod fillet on top and then completely cover it in another thick layer of salt. Cover and refrigerate overnight. By the next day, the salt will have turned to brine. Remove the cod from the brine and rinse it under cold water. Cover with fresh water and leave to soak for 1 hour. It is now ready to use.

shortcrust pastry

225 g (8 oz) plain flour
1/2 teaspoon salt
65 g (2 1/2 oz) chilled butter, cut into pieces
65 g (2 1/2 oz) chilled lard, cut into pieces
1 1/2–2 tablespoons cold water

Sift the flour and salt into a food processor or a mixing bowl. Add the pieces of chilled butter and lard and work together until the mixture looks like fine breadcrumbs. Stir in the water with a round-bladed knife until it comes together into a ball, turn out onto a lightly floured work surface and knead briefly until smooth. Roll out on a floured surface and use as required.

chapter 13

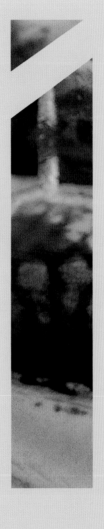

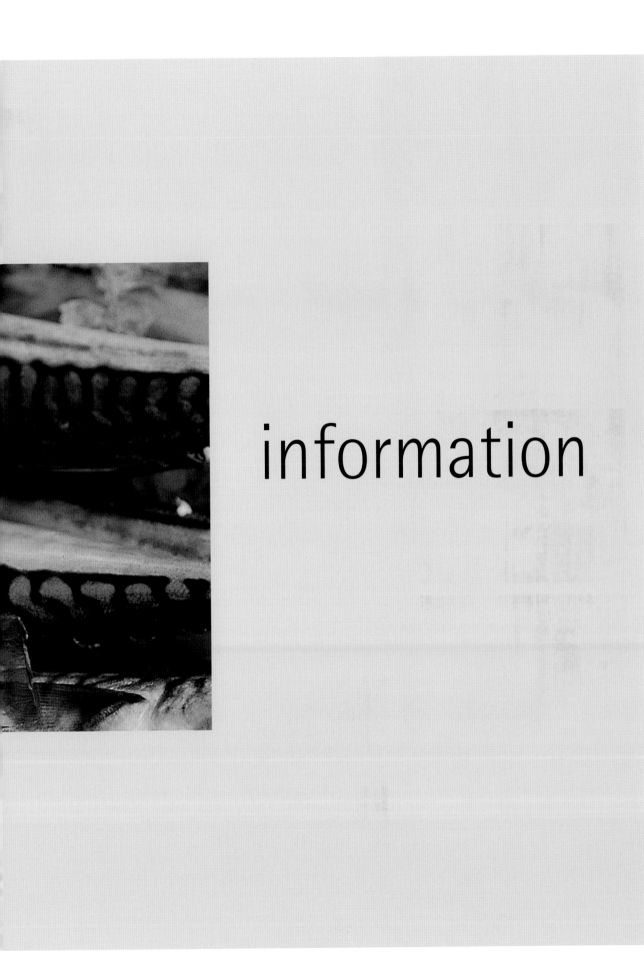

information

information
chapter 13

seafood families

introduction

In a practical book like this one it seems sensible to classify fish by 'families' for cooking purposes. First, however, you'll need to refer to Classifying Seafood on page 256 to see what family the fish you're interested in belongs to. Then go to the relevant family section of this chapter (arranged in alphabetical order of family name or category), for more information about the fish and how to cook it. The majority of species in each family are anatomically similar. Occasionally, however, I've included an odd fish, which though not related has a similar shape or similar fillet make-up and can be cooked in the same way. I've also been wildly inconsistent on occasions and grouped fish not by their biological connection but by their shape and size. It's much more significant, for example, to know that a garfish and needlefish, though not related, are so similar in looks and taste that they ought to be considered together.

The standard classification of fish throughout the world is in Latin. Paradoxically, the reason I felt resentful about learning Latin at school – namely that it's a dead language and therefore seemed impractical – is precisely why it's such a perfect language for science; it doesn't change. The problem with the colloquial naming of fish is that you end up with dozens of different names for the same fish, or dozens of different fish with the same name. Using Latin nails them down. Now I find myself trading Latin fish names with the sort of authority that I've only heard before from the lips of botanists.

It's a common misconception to think that fish on the other side of the world are different. A few are though, and I've grouped these in more detail under the headings 'Australian Catchall' and 'US Catchall'. While the Morwong, loved by spear fishermen, belongs to a family that only exists in Australia and New Zealand, most fish belong to families which can be found all over the world and broadly speaking, can all be cooked in the same way.

I've had to be selective in my choice of fish to write about in this chapter; after all, there are more than 25,000 species. For example, do you need to know about all the hagfishes, which are salt-water lampreys, or do you just need to know about lampreys in general, which though not common, are quite a colourful part of European cooking? A book which described the cooking and eating qualities of every fish would take years to write – and probably to read – so I have highlighted the most common fish in each country, in the hope that you'll find just the information you are looking for.

australian catchall

This section includes all those fish from Australia and New Zealand that don't appear anywhere else in the world. The MORWONG, known as the TERAHIKI in New Zealand is a pan-sized fish with firm, white, mildly flavoured flesh, normally caught by anglers and spear fishermen. As a testimony to the plentifulness of the morwong off the coast of New South Wales, I once went spear fishing with a couple of friends and their father near Sydney. I stayed in the boat with the old man and when one of the sons appeared with a 2 kg (4 lb 8 oz) red morwong, he was promptly told by his Dad to go and get another one as there wouldn't be enough for the barbecue that afternoon. He was soon back and quite excellent they were too.

There's another family of fish called TREVALLAS that is unique to Australasia. The most well-known are the WAREHOU, RUDDERFISH and the BLUE-EYE, often called the BLUE-EYE COD. The off-white flesh is firm, moist and delicately flavoured and they're very highly regarded in the southern states of Australia and New Zealand. There are plans to farm these fish, as they are so popular.

Also in Australia the STRIPED TRUMPETER and the TASSIE TRUMPETER (which is called the BLUE MOKI in New Zealand) are very good eating, with firm, white tasty and fatty flesh. It's suitable for cooking in any way you like, but I like to grill the fillets and serve them with a sauce of mayonnaise thinned with a little hot water, to which I add green olives, sliced into shards and a touch of garlic. This and a chopped tomato and red onion salsa, seasoned with green chilli, salt, olive oil and lime juice work a treat.

Finally, there's the Australian SAND WHITING and KING GEORGE WHITING. These fish are excellent either grilled whole or in fillets and require little addition. The best way that I've ever had a whiting was at a restaurant called the Claireville Kiosk on Pittwater in New South Wales. It was pan-fried with noisette butter and capers and a salad of warm sliced potatoes and crisp Cos lettuce. Sand whiting are a much better flavoured fish than European whiting and would make the Merlan Frit en Colère, on page 166, something quite special.

billfish

swordfish

I think Swordfish is the perfect barbecue fish. The idea of cooking fish out of doors so often proves disappointing in the execution, but you really can't go wrong with a steak of swordfish. Of course it's much better undercooked, but it seems quite forgiving in that even when the flesh is over-cooked and dry, it's quite interesting to eat. It is also the perfect flesh for marinating and is firm enough for cutting up and skewering to make kebabs. It's immensely popular in Europe and the USA, less so in Australia. I recall a visit to the Sydney fish market once when one of the traders said that he couldn't give these fish away. There is a popular misconception amongst the concerned public that all swordfish come from unsustainable sources. The same thing is happening with cod, a feeling that it's inevitable that all the cod will soon be gone. Not all swordfish fisheries are non-sustainable so don't necessarily feel guilty as you enjoy this excellent fish.

marlin and sailfish

The other main members of the billfish family, Marlin and Sailfish, have similar qualities to swordfish. However, neither quite hit the spot with me, although WHITE MARLIN is better than BLUE MARLIN and is widely used in Japan to make fish sausages. These fish should probably be reserved for some rich, game-fishing acquaintances of mine, who spend 'shed loads' of money pulling them out of the sea, only to put them back in again.

bony-cheeked fish

This is a group of fish distinguished by having a noticably hard head. It includes the Australian flathead which, when viewed from this perspective, do look similar to the gurnard, though their flatness is rather more obvious than their hard-headedness.

In the Atlantic the most common species are the REDFISH, *Sebastes marinus*, sold in the USA as OCEAN PERCH and marketed at between 1–2 kg (2 lb 4 oz–4 lb 8 oz). There is also a slightly smaller species known as NORWAY HADDOCK, *Sebastes vivipurus*. Neither fish bears any relation to the cod family, but because they have a soft, flaky texture they can be cooked in the same way. I would suggest serving the fillets grilled on some mashed potatoes with a soy, butter and coriander sauce, (see the recipe using cod on page 128). In the north Pacific, there are also a number of the same species of fish i.e. *Sebastes*, which are rather better eating than the Redfish of the Atlantic, and they are called ROCKFISH. The best tasting of these are the BOLINA and the GOLDEN EYE ROCKFISH. In the southern Pacific there is an entirely different group of redfish, which include the ALFONSINO, the BIGHT REDFISH, the IMPERADOR, the REDFISH (also known as the Red Snapper, just to be totally confusing), the SWALLOWTAIL and the YELLOWEYE REDFISH. All of these are sold at about 1 kg (2 lb 4 oz) weights and produce soft fillets of fish with a delicate flavour. They are oilier than the northern redfish and as such suit pan-frying or griddling very well. I would suggest serving them as for snapper with prawn and mango, on page 147.

flatheads

The AUSTRALIAN FLATHEAD provides thick white fillets of moderately well flavoured fish and is actually the mainstay of the fish and chip industry in Australia. It can be cooked in any of the ways that you might cook cod. Those of good eating are the DEEPWATER, DUSKY, SOUTHERN TIGER and SAND FLATHEAD, and best of all, the ROCK FLATHEAD.

gurnard and scorpion fish

Gurnard are underrated everywhere, because they're regarded as bony. But they grow quite large, up to 2½ kg (5 lb 8 oz), and a fillet cut from a large gurnard is firm and sweet. I always think of gurnard as being a Mediterranean-type of fish, it being one of the most common of three or four species such as RACASSE (SCORPION FISH) and the WEEVER FISH (see page 240) which go into a good bouillabaisse or soupe de poisson. I like to cook my gurnard in a quite robust, southern European sort of way, like the recipe on page 174. Gurnards come in two common types, RED or GREY. I've never been able to find any difference in flavour, but the red ones are much more attractive, leading perhaps to the Dutch name for them, '*engelese soldaat*' (English soldiers), presumably a reference to the red coats. In Cornwall, the very largest gurnard are known as 'tubs' and can reach as much as 2½ kg (5 lb 8 oz). This species has the most beautiful, translucent blue-green pectoral fins. A couple of oddities of this fish are, first, the name, derived from the French word 'grondin', meaning grunt, which apparently these rather porky-looking fish do underwater. Secondly, its three pectoral spines look like little legs on which the fish 'walk' along the sea bed, feeling for food. Gurnard fillets are very good lightly dusted with flour, fried in a little oil and butter and served with lightly grilled pancetta or very thin rashers of streaky bacon and some beurre noisette. The Red Gurnard also appears as the SEA ROBIN in the USA and the LATCHET in Australia and New Zealand, where they are also alternatively known as gurnards.

cephalopods

In many parts of the world, SQUID (also called INKFISH and sometimes CALAMARI in Australia), CUTTLEFISH and OCTOPUS have only recently become popular. The Southeast Asians, Japanese, Chinese and people of the Mediterranean regions, have always revered the lobster-like taste and slightly chewy texture of cephalopods. Unlike fish, each of the cephalopod groups is similar in taste and shape wherever you go in the world. However, no octopus are found on the Eastern Seaboard of America, north of the Carolinas.

seafood families

The general rule of thumb is: the smaller the species, the more tender it will be. With the exception of octopus, they need to be cooked quickly so that they remain so – no more than 1 minute in a hot pan – after which time they tend to toughen and then you should slow-cook them in the same way as octopus to render them tender again.

squid

To me the taste of squid is of pure seafood. Nothing is more exciting than the smell of fresh squid cooking quickly in hot olive oil, or in a wok with the attendant aromas of garlic and ginger, in somewhere like the Seafood Restaurant in Bangkok. Squid is popular everywhere now. It should be cooked for the briefest time, in the hottest oil or grilled, baked, or stuffed and steamed (see page 220). I don't enjoy the taste of boiled squid so, for a fish stew, I add it fried at the last minute.

There is a theory that frozen squid are as good as fresh, but I don't find this to be so. Freezing seems to make them tougher and remove most of their taste but, like all frozen seafood, the quality depends more on the length of time they have been frozen rather than any deterioration caused by the rapid drop in temperature. Cuttlefish is also becoming more popular, though it tends to be a little tougher than squid.

octopus

Actually, octopus is always tough and needs tenderizing either by slow-cooking in the oven with oil and spices, by bashing it against a rock in the Greek-style, or by freezing the cleaned bodies for two weeks before slow simmering them in salted water for 1–1½ hours. This is the treatment for the classic Spanish dish, Pulpo a la Feria, (see recipe, page 218), where it is sliced and finished with paprika, cayenne, sea salt and olive oil.

cod and cod-like fish

cod

In one of my earlier books I included a recipe for Crab Newburg by Marjorie Kinnan Rawlings, which ends 'I sit alone and weep for the misery of a world that does not have blue crabs and a Jersey cow', to which list I would add, cod.

The world cries out for a thick, white flaky fillet of fish, not assertive in flavour and not filled with bones, and cod is that fish. The fact that it is fished-out on the Grand Banks of the US Eastern Seaboard and virtually fished-out in the North Sea has, more than anything, drawn attention to the alarming reduction in fish stocks everywhere. I recall people saying that cod was bland and boring but it only takes a shortage to concentrate the mind on appreciating one of the best fish in the sea.

Anyone with even a passing interest in fish should read Mark Kurlansky's book *Cod*, published by Walker Publishing Company in 1997. In it you will discover that the cod along the Grand Banks in the US were once so plentiful that they could be gathered simply by dropping weighted baskets over the sides of the boats and lifting them, brimming with fish, back up through the shoals. As a colourful illustration of the fecundity of cod, and the appalling cack-handedness of our failure to preserve the species through greed and political expediency, I enjoy this quote by Alexander Dumas in *Le Grand Dictionaire*, 1873. 'It has been calculated that if no accident prevented the hatching of the eggs, and each egg reached maturity, it would take only three years to fill the sea, so that you could walk across the Atlantic dry shod on the backs of cod'.

There are still stocks of the smaller but similar PACIFIC COD that is marketed as TRUE COD on the west coast to distinguish it from various other unrelated fish that are sold as cod. This problem is prevalent in Australia and New Zealand too – testimony perhaps to the worldwide demand for the characteristic clean taste of this prized fish.

Fortunately, the Norwegians and Icelanders have long practised sensible conservation of cod stocks off their coasts, and much of the world's cod come from these cold waters. Though the records of enormous cod weighing 50 kg (120 lb) or more are now mere historical facts, you can still buy 5–6 kg (11–13 lb) fish, which are fantastic eating. Fish of this size are normally sold in fillets and a portion brushed with butter, sprinkled with sea salt and cracked black pepper and grilled is as good as cod gets. Wherever possible, therefore, go for thick fillets.

Small cod up to 1 kg (2 lb 4 oz), known as CODLING in Europe and SCROD in America, are nice to eat if fresh but don't have the superb falling-away flaky texture of the bigger fish. Cod when it's just caught is quite tough, and while I love this chewiness, some prefer to leave it a day or two until the flesh goes through the same enzymatic change as meat and becomes more tender.

preserved cod

Historically, far more cod was consumed salted because of lack of refrigeration, but even today the demand for SALT COD, BACALAU, and dried cod (STOCKFISH) is enormous. Properly soaked – over a couple of days – and then poached and served with some sympathetic flavours such as garlic, tomato and olive oil – it is real comfort food for the Spanish, Portuguese, Italians and French. I recently had a carpaccio of salt cod where the salt cod had been soaked for sufficiently long to remove any trace of salt and was then served raw and thinly sliced with sliced San Marzano tomatoes, rocket and extra virgin olive oil. Accompanied by a glass of Greco di Tufo, the versatility of this ancient way of curing cod was brought alive to me.

haddock

This, the next most popular member of the cod family, has also suffered from serious over-fishing. It's just as good as cod and, while it lacks the whiteness and beautiful flakes of that fish, it has a slightly sweeter flavour. Again, it is best in thick fillets, but it's not as big a fish as cod, weighing on average 2–3 kg (4 lb 8 oz–6 lb 8 oz). In Britain a great deal of rather small fish is landed, especially owing to the preference for haddock over cod in the fish-and-chip shops of the north. But I think they are rather unsuited to being battered and deep-fried because they dry out.

smoked haddock

Of all the cod family, haddock is best for smoking due to its slightly sweet flavour. All haddock-fishing countries have a range of smoked haddock specialities. In Britain, FINNAN HADDOCK is traditionally smoked over peat while ARBROATH SMOKIES are small whole haddock, hot-smoked over pits of smouldering oak. In Europe, Denmark produces some good-quality smoked haddock, as does France where it is called 'haddock' to distinguish it from the fresh fish or *eglefin*.

In the United States smoked haddock comes from Boston and Portland, Maine while the smoked haddock or cod on sale in fishmongers in Australia and New Zealand will have come from either northern Europe or North America.

hake

Of the rest of the cod family, Hake is the most far-flung species appearing not only in the North Atlantic, Mediterranean and North Pacific, but also as far south as New Zealand, as the SOUTHERN HAKE, and *Merluccius australis*. A very similar species, *Merluccius capensis*, is currently the prime target of a massive European fishery off the coast of South Africa. In Europe, the Spanish are by far and away the biggest consumers of hake in the world and, like them, I find it hard to see why it's not more popular in America and Australasia. It has a beguiling soft texture and good flavour and, I think, takes to butter or cream better than any other fish, except for turbot or brill. It is also rather good served cold with mayonnaise or sauce verte, which is an olive-oil mayonnaise with blanched spinach, rockets and herbs blitzed into it.

whiting

Whiting is extensively fished in Northern Europe. It's not the best flavoured of the cod family, but small fish cooked whole – particularly deep-fried 'en colère' (see page 166) – are a delight.

13

ling, forkbeard, white hake and pollack

I would describe all the rest of the cod family as lesser species as they don't have the same commercial appeal. All LING are firm textured with a mild, delicate flavour. I've had some success cooking fillets of our British ling on a charcoal grill. I wrote the recipe for SALT LING pasties (see page 137) after a visit to the English Market in Cork, Ireland where they specialize in dry-salting really thick fillets. It's a first-class product.

There is a species similar to ling in the Mediterranean – it's called the FORKBEARD and is usually cooked in the same way as hake – and also a couple in North America, the WHITE HAKE (also called the BOSTON LING) and the SQUIRREL HAKE.

Like hake, ling appears not just in the North Atlantic but also in the South Pacific as PINK LING and ROCK LING POLLACK, not to be confused with the North American 'POLLOCK', which is actually Coley, and is quite a good substitute for cod. Pollack doesn't grow as big as cod, its average size being 2–3 kg (4 lb 8 oz–6 lb 8 oz), but a fillet taken from a larger fish and grilled is almost as good as the real thing.

coley, cusk and pouting

Also known as SAITHE, POLLOCK or COALFISH, COLEY has quite a good flavour but is let down by its dull grey colour on the slab, some of which remains after cooking. It can be substituted for either cod or haddock in any recipe and makes very good fish cakes (see page 127). The flesh of TUSK, or CUSK, as it is more commonly known in America, is rather oilier than most *Gadidae* (members of the cod family) and is therefore best grilled or baked. POUTING or POUT is a cheap member of the cod family that doesn't keep well. Rather a dull, light brown in colour with a very fragile fillet, it is best used in fish cakes or fish pies and is most similar to whiting. It has bulbous eyes, which seem to expand when trawled up from any great depth; testimony to the fact that fish brought up from the deep suffer, as we do, from the 'bends'.

crustaceans

crabs

The meat of all crabs is fairly similar in taste all over the world, with each region asserting that theirs is the best. So I have simply organised them by size – small, medium and large.

small crabs

The very smallest of crabs are called OYSTER or PEA CRABS. Some weeks ago, I received a letter from a woman who had watched me prepare mussels on one of my television programmes. In it she warned me of the need to clean mussels on the inside, as well as the outside, because of the poisonous little crabs that live inside the shell of mussels and oysters. I've heard of this anxiety before, but actually these crabs are perfectly edible, and some oyster-shucking houses in the US used to sell them as a valuable by-product, for deep-frying or adding to soups.

The GREEN CRAB or SHORE CRAB weighs no more than 10 g (⅓ oz), but it has a ready market in Europe for such soups as the Shore Crab Bisque, on page 101. We have had success gathering them when soft-shelled, dipping them in tempura batter and serving them with a dipping sauce of chilli, lime and *nam pla* (Thai fish sauce). The SWIMMING CRAB or VELVET CRAB, called the ETRILLE by the French, is surprisingly full of sweet, fibrous meat. I once ate a plate of them in Spain and noted that there was a distinction made between the local Velvet Crabs (called NECORA) and those described as 'foreign', which presumably come from Cornwall, and fetch a lower price. I must say I couldn't tell the difference.

Of all the small crabs, the one which grabs the biggest peon of praise, is the BLUE CRAB from the Eastern Seaboard of the United States, which reaches sizes of up to 200 g (7 oz). Whether in its hard shell or in its all-edible soft-shell form, it seems to have a higher ratio of lumpy exquisite meat than any other. Would that in the UK we could buy tubs of fresh white crab meat as you can in Chesapeake Bay in America.

medium crabs

The crab most similar to the BLUE CRAB, but of medium size, is the ASIAN BLUE SWIMMER, *Portunus pelagicus*, of Australia. It is ideal for stir-frying in the shell, as it's easy to pick out the chunky, fibrous meat, and it's the best choice for Singapore Chilli Crab (see recipe, page 185). The other major crab from Australia and New Zealand is the MUD CRAB (MANGROVE CRAB), which has a much thicker shell and incredibly powerful claws. It much more resembles the European BROWN CRAB and the DUNGENESS CRAB of the northern Pacific, but is also very closely related to the excellent flavoured SAND CRAB of the Carolinas and Florida in the US. Another excellent flavoured crab, with pink-tinged meat, from America is the RED CRAB. It lives on the outer continental shelf at depths of between 369 m and 1846 m (1200 and 6000 feet).

Naturally I consider the brown crab to be second to none for flavour but possibly the European SPIDER CRAB has the most scented flavour of all crabs. The similar looking SNOW CRAB in America has rather coarser, yellowish meat.

large crabs

One of the two most spectacular large crabs is the ALASKAN KING CRAB which can weigh up to 10 kg (22 lb 8 oz). These are sold as crabmeat, rarely as whole crabs because their enormous size and the fact that they are fished for off Alaska would make bringing the whole crab to market uneconomical.

The largest crab in the world, is the KING CRAB from Southern Australia and Tasmania which can weigh up to 17 kg (38 lb), though the normal market size is about half that. These are favoured by the Chinese communities of Australian cities where they are often kept spectacularly on show in tanks at the front of the restaurant.

lobster

A trip to New England, USA last year and the pleasure of eating lobster rolls at Bob's Clam House showed that in some favoured parts of the world, Lobster need not be the frighteningly expensive luxury that it is where I come from. Lobster rolls are simply lobster meat in a slightly sweet finger bun with mayonnaise – now that's fast food I approve of!

Lobster is the world's most sought-after seafood. Its firm, sweet, white meat is satisfyingly full of flavour and the flavour of all lobsters is remarkably similar the world over. The question of which country's lobsters are the best is easily answered for me. Wherever you can get one straight from the sea and cooked on the spot, that's the place where the best one will be. Lobsters deteriorate very quickly after death, so they have to be kept alive in a re-circulation tank called a vivarium. But they can't be fed in them because this would contaminate the water and they would die. Unfortunately, the relatively small amount of water in which they live while in these tanks can affect their flavour. This explains why a lobster at the Seafood Restaurant in Padstow, straight out of the Atlantic and grilled with a little butter and chopped *fines herbes*, or cooked and served just with mayonnaise, will always taste better than one eaten in London.

The only lobsters with significant claws, the EUROPEAN and AMERICAN LOBSTERS, come from the North Atlantic. The American lobster is slightly larger than the European and is dark green when alive, whereas the European one is blue. The claws of the American lobster are more rounded and, when cooked, it has a more orange hue than the European one, but in both cases the best sizes are 500 g–1 kg (1 lb 2 oz–3 lb 5 oz).

Lobsters with claws tend to prefer cold water though they can be found as far south as the

seafood families

Mediterranean and South Carolina. SPINY LOBSTERS (CRAYFISH), on the other hand, occur both in the Southern Hemisphere and Northern Hemisphere, as far north as Norway. They grow a lot bigger than true lobsters but I still think that the best size is 500 g–2 kg (1 lb 2 oz–4 lb 8 oz). The most obvious difference between them and the true lobster is the absence of any claws, but they are cooked in the same way and make just as good eating. My current preference is for the WESTERN ROCK LOBSTER from western Australia.

Similar to spiny lobsters are various FLAT or SLIPPER LOBSTERS of Europe, called *cigales*. This is the French word for cicada, and refers to the cricket-like noises that they make underwater. With typical Australian bluntness, these slipper lobsters are known there as bugs, notably the BALMAIN BUG and MORETON BAY BUG. In the USA the similar species are known as SHOVEL-NOSED or SPANISH LOBSTERS or, echoing the French name, LOCUST LOBSTER. All these species are good eating though, due to a tendency to dryness, I find them far better if slightly undercooked. Incidentally, there is no danger in eating raw or undercooked lobster, as the splendour of thinly sliced lobster sashimi will testify. As with spiny lobsters, the meat of slipper lobsters is all in the tail.

If you find you have bought a lobster with soft, woolly flesh, it will be because it has been cooked after it has died. On death, the flesh of both lobsters and crabs goes through a rapid enzyme change, which reduces it almost to pulp within a couple of hours. The only ways to prevent this with lobster are either to remove the tail and claws from the head on death, or rapidly freeze it.

Although I have classed DUBLIN BAY PRAWNS as large prawns, they are more closely related to lobsters and in the USA are called LOBSTERETTES. They also suffer from this rapid deterioration on death, which is why cooked langoustines can so often be disappointing.

prawns and shrimps

Until it became easy in Britain to buy PRAWNS from America (called SHRIMPS there), Asia and Australia, cooked prawn dishes were relatively rare, simply because our native shrimps and prawns are small and don't suit grilling, pan-frying, barbecuing or deep-frying. We do have great dishes such as prawn cocktail or potted shrimps but generally a pile of cooked prawns and shrimps was something to peel at leisure and eat with a bowl of mayonnaise and some brown bread and butter.

There are really only three main types of prawns or shrimps native to Britain. The BROWN SHRIMP, caught off the coast of East Anglia and in Morecombe Bay in Lancashire, have a beautiful ephemeral flavour and should be eaten immediately after being boiled in seawater. I like to think of them as the seafood equivalent of violets in spring. They are also the *sine qua non* of potted shrimps, the superb delicacy that is thankfully still alive and well in Morecambe. (See recipe, page 202) The PINK SHRIMP or COMMON PRAWN is excellent but difficult to get hold of unless you live near the coast. I like to eat the larger ones just with mayonnaise but the smaller ones are great in a seafood risotto, where the shells can be used in the stock to add a good seafood flavour.

The other common prawn available on sale everywhere in Britain is the MEDITERRANEAN PRAWN or CREVETTE, which I think is best served whole with mayonnaise or aïoli, the garlic mayonnaise from Provence. I really like to squeeze the roe out of the heads of these prawns – it's delicious and a treat missed by most people.

Now though it's easy to get large prawns, so dishes like Jambalaya (page 201), Tandoori Prawns (page 200) and Prawn Caldine (page 197) are easy to make in Britain. But imported prawns are still rather unhelpfully labelled as just small, medium or large, raw or cooked. Sometimes they're called by their correct name, such as BLACK TIGER PRAWNS, but we look forward to a time when we can enjoy the subtle differences of prawns as found in Australia.

In America you'll find the luxurious ROYAL RED SHRIMP from the Gulf of Mexico, with its deep red colour even when raw, and the CARIBBEAN (GULF) WHITE SHRIMP, which is the best-eating shrimp in the country, found from North Carolina down to the Gulf of Mexico and Texas. On the Pacific coast the SIDE-STRIPE SHRIMP, the PINK SHRIMP and the COON-STRIPE SHRIMP are also, like prawns in the UK, just referred to as shrimp – small, medium and large – and not by their individual names.

In Australia, the BANANA PRAWN is known for its sweet, moist and medium-firm texture, while the KING PRAWN can reach up to 30 cm (12 inches) in length. The BAY PRAWN is only ever sold locally where it's caught and, though fetching less money than other prawns, is much sought after because of its seasonality.

dublin bay prawns, scampi or langoustine

With their rather important-sounding name of *Nephrops norvegicus*, these are the crowning glory of prawns in the UK. They can grow up to 250 g (9 oz) in weight, at which size they look like small lobsters and they are in fact a member of the lobster family. Generally I prefer to eat them as they are, served in their shell. But a very simple way to serve cooked langoustine hot is to cut them in half, brush them with melted butter and grill them briefly. Serve them with hot melted butter and lemon juice. You can add some finely chopped *fines herbes* (chives, tarragon, chervil and parsley) to the butter if you like. A similar species found on the same sort of ground off the coast of Scotland is the SQUAT LOBSTER. Species very like our langoustine are also found in the USA, Australia and New Zealand.

deep-sea fish

This is of course not a family of fish, but rather a group in which all the species have a sort of similarity, conditioned by the dark depths in which they live. For the most part this means they have enormous eyes with which to catch what little light there is and generally, possibly due to the decompression when raising them to the surface, they always look wan and flabby.

The PATAGONIAN TOOTHFISH, also known as the CHILEAN SEA BASS or ANTARCTIC SEA BASS, comes from the southern oceans of the world, around South Georgia in the Falklands and off the bottom of South America. It always comes in skinned fillets and though not related to bass at all, it can be cooked in much the same way. There is considerable concern though about the long term stability of stocks of this fish. Like all deep-water fish, there are no restrictions on the fishing of them as they are outside territorial waters.

Other prize fish from these depths are the ORANGE ROUGHY and HOKI (BLUE GRENADIER), though the Grenadier, with the other unfortunate name of RAT-TAIL, also provides firm, meaty fillets. The Orange Roughy is sometimes available fresh in Australia and New Zealand and can be extremely good, but generally it is sold as skinned and de-fatted fillets, frozen at sea, which need a lot of nurturing during cooking to make them interesting.

Other interestingly named and curiously-shaped deep-water fish are the RABBITFISH from the Atlantic, the ALFONSINO, and the RIBALDO from the Southern Pacific. Alfonsino are abundant in the Pacific Ocean and are very popular in China where they're known as POH LAP and Japan where they're called MADAI. They have thick scaly skin and white, slightly oily flesh and should be prepared like sea bream. Ribaldo also carries the name of DEEP-SEA COD. While this produces thick fillets of fish, it has soft flesh and should be eaten quickly before it deteriorates. It's just the right thing for Thai Fish Cakes (see page 137).

13

drums

DRUMS and CROAKERS in the USA and the MULLOWAY of Australia are all members of the *Sciaenidae* family. These are distinguished by having an internal muscle used to beat the swim bladder, producing a sound described as either a drumming or croaking that can sometimes even be heard from land. By far the greatest variety of species occurs in America. On the East coast the best eating varieties are the WEAKFISH and the RED DRUM. The Weakfish weighs on average between 450 g (1 lb) and 2¾ kg (6 lb). They are either sold whole or in fillets and have white, sweet and finely textured flesh. The flesh is fragile and the fish needs to be iced quickly after capture. The roes are particularly well favoured too. Weakfish and a closely related fish, the SPOTTED SEATROUT (also known as the SPOTTED SQUETEAGUE), are often just called Trout in the Southern States, which can be confusing to those used to the fish of the salmon family. Highly regarded relations to the Weakfish and Spotted Seatrout are the CORVINAS of Central America.

RED DRUM, caught along the south Atlantic and Gulf coasts, has moist, white and heavy-flaked flesh. The best Drums from the Pacific are the WHITE SEABASS from California and the SILVER PERCH, which only grows to about 1 kg (2 lb 4 oz) in size and is therefore a tasty, pan-sized fish. On the East Coast there's also the ATLANTIC CROAKER, which has lean white meat, and the TOTUAVA, the largest of the drums, which is always sold in steak form for grilling or barbecuing.

mulloway

Similar species to the drums occur in Australia with the MULLOWAY, the JEWFISH (incorrectly known in the past as the CROAKER or DRUM) and the BLACK JEWFISH (previously known as the SPOTTED CROAKER). These are large fish, common on both eastern and western coasts and usually sold in fillet form. Though not related, I find the flesh of the Mulloway similar in texture to the sea bass, and often recommend it when suggesting alternative fish. It's not a commercial fish, being regarded more as a prestige angling fish, but I've written a recipe for Mulloway with Asparagus and a Cream and Caviar Sauce on page 145.

eel and eel-like fish

It is small wonder that the FRESHWATER EEL turns up looking remarkably similar all the world over, when you consider the enormous distances they migrate from the world's seas to rivers, and back again. The EUROPEAN EEL, *Anguilla*

Anguilla, and the AMERICAN EEL, *Anguilla rostrata*, are both born in the Sargasso Sea, east of Florida and, as ELVERS, spend three years swimming to Europe or one year swimming to America. The freshwater eels of Australia and New Zealand, the LONGFIN EEL and SHORTFIN EEL, are born in the Coral Sea and take a year to swim to the rivers of Eastern Australia and New Zealand.

The eating qualities of eel fall into the three distinct eras in their lives. As elvers, they can fetch a small fortune during the short European season in early March. They are served up by the Spanish in tiny, piping-hot *cazuelas* with olive oil and garlic. The elvers that get away grow into browny-yellow adult eels and it is in this phase that most of them are caught. Then, as they start their journey back to the Sargasso Sea to spawn and die, they become more pointed. Having become very fatty they now stop eating and become sleeker and silvery, ready for the change of habitat on the long voyage home. These SILVER EELS are the best eating and favoured by eel smokers for their quality and delicious fat content. Indeed it is the fattiness of eels that makes them so special – it is of a purity and tastiness unequalled and the recipe for Stir-Fried Eel with Black Beans on page 125 reveals this. The Chinese are masters of eel cooking.

moray eel

The other two main types of eel are the Mediterranean MORAY EEL and the CONGER EEL. Moray Eel is much sought after, being firm and almost like Dover Sole in quality. There's a mosaic from Pompeii in the National Archaeological Museum in Naples, Italy, which shows a selection of the Romans' best-loved Mediterranean fish, including the yellow-speckled Moray eel. And it still looks as fresh and ready to be cooked as if it had been caught yesterday. It is a superb fish, firm-fleshed and fresh tasting and so much more interesting than the CONGER EEL.

conger eel

This appears all over the world in slightly different forms. It's a big, fierce beast and generally caught on a line. Few seem to cook it except for Europeans – notably the northern Spanish, the Bretons of France and the Cornish. It's a common ingredient in Bouillabaisse (see page 102–3) and the fish stew Cotriade from Brittany, (see pages 108–9). We use it as an essential ingredient in our fish soup (see page 100). I once created a recipe for a pot roast or Poêle of Conger (see page 123) of which I'm still very fond. I wrap the eel in a pig's caul and cook it in a heavy lidded-casserole with root vegetables.

lamprey

A brief mention must also be made of this eel-like fish that inhabits the estuarine waters of Northern Europe. It also lives in American waters but it's not esteemed, possibly because of its rather horrifying way of feeding. It attaches itself to another fish with the sucking disc, which it has instead of a mouth, bores a hole through the skin with its rasp-like teeth and sucks the blood out. Which, incidentally, doesn't always kill the fish. You sometimes catch a fish, particularly salmon, with a lamprey scar on it. The classic lamprey dish is Lamproie à la Bordelaise, where it is stewed in red wine. Lampreys have no scales and their bones are more like the cartilage in a shark.

elongated fish

There is, of course, no such scientific family as elongated fish but it seemed an apt grouping of fish that stand out in markets all over the world by virtue of their sinuousness, and which are all treated in much the same way.

barracuda

All barracuda (and there are about six types found in temperate and tropical waters around the world) are what I would call medium quality fish: firm, mild-flavoured, with a medium fat content. Because the fish are big, they are free from irritating small bones and are commonly sold in fillet form or in steaks. But beware, barracuda spoils quickly, so cook it within 24 hours of buying it. Because they're not fantastically well flavoured they are ideal in robustly flavoured dishes such as fish curries and habanero chilli-hot Caribbean dishes. Apart from their cooking qualities, they are thoroughly interesting fish. Fierce streamlined killers, they have the most amazing array of needle-like teeth, each one of which has its own hole on the opposing jaw, thus allowing the barracuda to close its mouth completely and grip its prey with no chance of escaping. The GREAT BARRACUDA is the biggest fish, reaching up to 2 metres (6½ feet) in length. Unfortunately the larger fish – anything over 2½ kg (5 lb) – can carry the toxin ciguatera, though these fish are confined to the warmer waters of the western Atlantic, from Florida down to the Caribbean. The toxins, which appear to develop in the fish from eating a type of algae called benthic alga, have a 12 per cent fatality rate in unfortunate consumers as cooking does not destroy them. Luckily the toxin doesn't appear in the most popular barracuda for eating, the PACIFIC BARRACUDA or YELLOWTAIL BARRACUDA. The similar STRIPED SEAPIKE from Southeast Asia, the Pacific and Australia can carry the toxin, but this is rare.

seafood families

silver scabbard fish

I first came upon the SILVER SCABBARD FISH in the early 80s fish market in Mapusa in Goa, India; I'd never seen anything like them before. Now they're common in specialist fish markets such as Billingsgate, in Britain. Back then though, they looked like strange creatures with their dusty, stainless-steel-like skin, long, flat sword-shaped bodies and frightening array of needle-sharp teeth. All scabbard fish are, in fact, very good eating, having firm, white meat that's coarse-textured but delicately flavoured, like eels. The tail sections are hard work to eat, being more bone than anything else, but sections of the body are good baked, grilled, pan-fried or used in soups and stews.

A similar species in the Atlantic, the BLACK SCABBARD FISH, is considered a great delicacy by the Portuguese and is caught off the island of Madeira at a depth of over 1000 metres (3280 feet). Fishing for them is a wonder of skill and tradition: the long lines have to be dyed black with a dye made from the bark of a particular Madeiran tree. The fish are fearsome-looking – shiny and black with fierce teeth and vengeful eyes – which might explain why they are of little importance elsewhere.

SOUTHERN FROSTFISH and RIBBON FISH are two other names for the same fish found in Australia and New Zealand, where they are caught as a by-catch of trawling for demersal (bottom-feeding) fish.

garfish

The other main fish in this 'elongated' family is the Garfish, *Belone belone*. Very similar species occur in northern Europe and Australia and New Zealand, though the European variety is perhaps more exotic due to its bones being of a bright green hue. These are said to make the fish less popular – I suppose people think they might be poisonous – but this is not so and their flesh is excellent, firm and fresh-tasting and slightly oily. It's not a fish that you're likely to get in fishmongers here, but in Australia it's much more common and they are sold whole or as butterfly fillets – still joined along the back.

A similar fish, which is often considered one and the same, is the NEEDLEFISH, SAURY, or SKIPPER, *scomberesox saurus*, called BALAOU or AIGUILLE DE MER in French. Though this fish is most common in the Atlantic, west from Madeira across to the Caribbean where it is eaten fried or grilled, it also swims as far north as Norway in the summer. It's popular in Denmark, fried and served with a sauce verte and boiled potatoes.

Lastly there's the BARRACOUTA, from Australia and New Zealand. With soft, light-tasting flesh it was widely used in the fish-and-chip trade there, but has largely been replaced by other fish such as flathead and flake (the common name for the GUMMY SHARK and SCHOOL SHARK).

flat fish

In the waters off Great Britain we have the greatest range of flat fish anywhere in the world and, unfortunately for the rest of the world, the two best flat fish, the DOVER SOLE and TURBOT, occur only on the eastern side of the Atlantic and the Mediterranean.

Flat fish are ideal for those who don't like bones – there are none in the fillets. Being of a largely sedentary nature, all flat fish have delicate white flesh made from muscle used to long inactivity with occasional bursts of energy. Having observed the farming of both turbot and halibut I would say that they are ideally suited for aquaculture since most of their life is spent motionless on the sea bed, almost camouflaged under the sand. They are waiting for food, which when it swims nearby, is eaten with great alacrity.

All flat fish begin life as conventional round fish but, as they grow, the eyes migrate to either the left or right side of the fish, enabling them to see in all directions when on the sea bed. The top and bottom of a flat fish are therefore the two flanks, not the back and belly. Left-sided flat fish are called sinistral and right-sided fish, dextral. Most flat fish are right-handed, the left-sided ones are TURBOT, BRILL, MEGRIM, SCALDFISH, and TOPKNOT.

Nowhere in the naming of fish are the common names more confusing than with flat fish. The name of Dover for the most exquisite of soles has nothing to do with its habitation. Historically, Dover was where the fish for the London market were landed. Also, the name DOVER SOLE, *Solea solea*, can mean either the EUROPEAN SOLE or PACIFIC FLOUNDER, *Microstomus pacificus*. In fact this last is a deep-water flat fish which can reach up to 4.5 kg (10 lb), and because it is especially slimy, is only marketed in fillet form. The alternative name of Dover sole – ENGLISH SOLE – doesn't help either, as this is also the name of a good quality flounder, *Parophrys ventulus*, found all the way from Northern Mexico to Alaska. TURBOT, *rhombus maximus*, is similarly difficult. Its name in Europe, (and it's turbot in French too), is also the name for several species of Pacific Flounder.

turbot

Turbot is possibly the best tasting fish in the world. It has the perfect combination of firm, thick fillets of moist white fish. The texture is dense and slightly gelatinous which means that it remains juicy after cooking and is never dry tasting. It is particularly suited to cooking on the bone in steak or 'tronçon' form, cut from good, large fish, weighing from 3–8 kg (6 lb 8 oz–18 lb) so that the pieces are nice and thick. This is one of the few fish I cook with confidence as the main course for a banquet.

I prefer this exquisite fish served up in a simple form, probably just grilled with hollandaise sauce and a slice of lemon. The price of turbot is now heading into the same bracket as lobster – but deservedly so. If you are lucky enough to get hold of a whole turbot, the recipe from Myrtle Allen at Ballymaloe, in Cork, Southern Ireland on page 182 is as good as it gets. I don't think, however, that turbot under 1 kg (2 lb 4 oz) in weight, and often called CHICKEN TURBOT, are particularly interesting. The smallest size worth cooking whole would be about 2 kg (4 lb 8 oz). One of the pleasures of eating whole turbot is the gelatinous, fatty flesh near to the side fins, which will have been removed if the fish is filleted.

dover sole

Filleting too, is a fate that falls to far too many DOVER SOLES, which would be better left whole. There are surely no better pan-sized fish than Dover Soles when skinned and fried whole à la meunière (dusted with seasoned flour) and finished with a little beurre noisette and lemon (see page 181). An ideal-sized flat fish for eating whole weighs between 300 g and 550 g (10 oz and 1lb 2 oz). Larger Dover soles are cheaper than the single-portion sized ones and produce excellent, firm white fillets. Dover soles are not at their best when eaten immediately after they have been caught as their natural firmness makes them too tough – they need one or two days after catching for the flavour and texture of the flesh to develop. I always think that eating a Dover Sole is like eating a perfect steak. Everything about it is just simple uncomplicated pleasure, even down to the fact that the fillets are easy to lift off, as the skeleton stays intact after cooking. No wonder they are just as popular in New York as in London and Paris.

plaice, flounder and dabs

PLAICE and FLOUNDER have a similar flavour to Dover Sole but, unlike them, are best eaten as soon as possible after being caught, since the fresh 'ozone' flavour of both fish quickly dissipates. Although they can be served on the bone or in fillet form, I think plaice and flounder (also known as FLUKE) are only worth eating whole when no more than a couple of days old. Otherwise they are best filleted, floured, egg-and-breadcrumbed and deep-fried. This cooking method nurtures the flavour of slightly dull fish. Small whole DABS are good cooked like this and served with tartare sauce.

13

The Danish have an appetizing way with whole plaice, flounder or dabs, which they call Bakskuld: they lightly brine the fish, then hot smoke them and fry them in butter. It's a speciality of Esbjerg in West Jutland, and excellent with ice-cold aquavit or beer.

In the USA the name FLOUNDER refers to a number of fish of rather better eating quality than our own flounder, all belonging to the *pleuronectididae* family. The WINTER FLOUNDER (or BLACKBACK), considered to be the best tasting of the US Flounder, has very sweet, fine-flaked, firm, white meat. Although on average they weigh between 450–900 g (1–2 lb), the biggest can weigh about 3 kg (6 lb 8 oz) and are often called sea flounders to distinguish them from the smaller bay fish. The SUMMER FLOUNDER, or FLUKE, also has an excellent flavour and is usually sold on the market weighing between 450 g and 2.25 kg (1 and 5 lb) but can reach up to 9 or 10 kg (19 lb 8 oz or 22 lb 8 oz).

lemon sole

British LEMON SOLE has a longer-lasting flavour than the local flounders, plaice and dabs and is thus a better bet for grilling whole if you buy your fish from the average supermarket fish counter. Other good pan-sized flat fish are MEGRIM SOLE (or WHIFF) and WITCH SOLES or TORBAY SOLES, both of which are rather underrated and are therefore good value.

The name Lemon Sole in the US is a market name for another winter flounder and no more accurate a name than the British name for the fish lemon sole, which is not a true sole at all. It would be more accurate to call it a lemon dab.

brill

Brill is similar in shape to turbot, though without the little hard nodules on the darker side. It tends not to be so big – I've never seen one bigger than 5 kg (11 lb) – and is more oval in shape. It too has a great flavour, although softer and less dense in texture than turbot. Like turbot though, the bigger the fish the better the eating. I tend to cook brill with slightly more complicated accompaniments than turbot because it is not quite as special. I note that in Gilbert and Sullivan's operetta, *HMS Pinafore* turbot is described as 'ambitious brill'.

halibut

Halibut, though a lovely fish, is not quite as fine as turbot. It's the largest of all flat fish and the only one to occur on both sides of the Atlantic and, indeed, in a very similar form in the Pacific too. Whole fish can reach up to 100 kg (250 lb) and are therefore always sold in fillet or steak form. It is a remarkably thick meaty fish, the cooking of which needs to be done with care to avoid dryness. I have

a recipe, (see page 183), which calls for the halibut to be very gently poached in olive oil, which I think gives it a soft and melting texture. This is similar to the method of slow-cooking salmon in the oven, from the famous Japanese Australian chef, Tetsuya Wakuda. An interesting fact about farmed halibut is that in the cold months, the fish tend to go into limbo. Fish farmers have discovered that putting a few cod in the tanks encourages the halibut to start feeding earlier in the year. Presumably the cod that accompany halibut in the wild are harbingers of spring.

groupers, sea bass and barramundi

To those of us living in Europe, groupers represent an exotic family of fish conjuring up an image of the southern states of the USA and the Pacific coast, the Caribbean and Australasia. The reason for this is that this fish does not occur in any significant numbers in European waters, except for the MEDITERRANEAN GROUPER, (the MÉROU), known in the UK as the BLACK GROUPER.

Groupers have slightly squat, deep bodies and tend to be rather round and chunky-looking, They are generally excellent eating and the plus point about them is their versatility. You can barbecue them or bake them whole, but they also lend themselves to being filleted and served with delicate sauces like the cream and caviar sauce on page 145. Or try a simple sauce vierge – a warm olive oil dressing spiked with tomato, olives, anchovy and garlic – as with the red mullet on page 173. These are customer-friendly fish – they look colourful and attractive, they've got plenty of flavour, and you don't need to be a trained chef to cook them with success.

You can now buy very well-flavoured groupers in London – and, with a little notice, probably from good quality fishmongers elsewhere. They come from all over the place and the tip, if you're thinking of what to do with a grouper, is to cook it in exactly the same way as you would a sea bass, to which they are closely related.

By far the biggest variety of groupers live in the USA, the largest of which is the ATLANTIC JEWFISH, which can reach weights of up to 300 kg (675 lb) but these are now seriously under threat from over-fishing. Groupers are most common around coral reefs and the rocky outcrops of the US continental shelf. While not so susceptible to trawling, they have suffered considerably from hook-and-line fishing, being large and therefore prized by amateur anglers. A further twist to their fate is that they are hermaphrodites i.e. they all start life as females and become males as they grow larger. Over-

fishing has led to an acute shortage of males as these are the larger fish and therefore more attractive to anglers. The most popular are the RED GROUPER, SPOTTED CABRILLA and the YELLOWMOUTH GROUPER. The Red Grouper can weigh up to 22.5 kg (50 lb) but the average weight on sale is between 2.25 kg (5 lb) and 6.75 kg (15 lb). But unless you want to feed eight or more people, the most convenient way of buying it is in steak or fillet form. The meat is firm, white and sweet and is comparable with the far more expensive snapper. A great advantage of the flesh is that it is free from intermuscular bones but the skin tends to be tough and strongly flavoured so it is usually removed before cooking. The flesh is also often cubed and deep-fried in batter or used in the fish chowders of the southern states.

The BLACK SEA BASS, closely related to the grouper, is a very popular fish in the USA and is especially popular with the Chinese and Italians. It has firm white meat with a delicate flavour – probably produced by its mainly crustacean diet – and can be cooked using most methods.

In Australia there is a much smaller family of groupers, that inhabits the tropical and sub-tropical waters, and these are generally called ROCK CODS. The most common members are the CORAL COD, COMMON CORAL TROUT, ESTUARY ROCK COD and BLACKTIP ROCK COD, this last being considered one of Australia's best eating fish with a distinctively flavoured, firm white flesh. But all of them are good eating, with wide and thick fillets.

sea bass

The EUROPEAN SEA BASS is the most sought-after perch species for cooking. A very attractive fish, it has beautiful silvery skin but evil spines, which can cause very painful wounds. It has a dense, slightly soft-textured flesh and a very delicate, superior flavour. It's now farmed widely, though most farmed bass are still too small to be at their best. A good-sized fish is 1.5 kg (3 lb 5 oz). If sold intact, remove the guts as soon as possible as the stomach is prone to bursting and this will taint the delicate flesh.

The WRECKFISH (also known as STONE BASS) appears in Cornwall in the summer months. Apparently at that time of year the fish follows floating flotsam towards the north from warmer, more southerly waters. It appears on both sides of the Atlantic but it is a case of feast or famine: you might get two weeks of nothing but Wreckfish, and then not see another one for three years! Its flavour is similar to other bass and I've always found it very good value. The same fish in Australia and New Zealand, HAPUKU, is amongst the most highly priced fish there. What could be a better example of the global nature of so many species of fish?

seafood families

One of the most prized fish in the USA is the STRIPED BASS, (also called ROCKFISH). I once caught a 12 kg (26 lb) Striped Bass in Chesapeake Bay which left me astonished as to how big this excellent fish grows – and apparently it was not a particularly big one! This was testimony to the successful conservation of a fish, the angling for which is far more profitable to the local community than the previous commercial fishery, which hounded the striped bass close to extinction. Like all perches, this is not a particularly oily fish, falling somewhere between cod and salmon, and it's therefore very versatile since it can be cooked in the same way as either.

barramundi

In Australia, the BARRAMUNDI (also called GIANT SEA PERCH) has an idiosyncratic shape, with a head that is disproportionately large in relation to its deep body. As with sea bass, it is now widely farmed but disappointing because of the small size at which the fish are sold. A good-sized fish is 2 kg (4 lb 8 oz). The wild fish are very well flavoured, with thick soft fillets, which are good cooked in any way. Although a marine species, it is also found in the freshwater creeks and rivers of Northern Australia where, presumably, it goes to spawn.

the herring family

herring

The maritime countries of northern Europe have made use of the HERRING in as many diverse culinary ways as the rural people of France have used the pig. Just think of the different ways that herring is served up: kippers, bloaters, buckling, red herrings, roll mops, Bismarck herrings, pickled herrings, matjes herrings. It's a shame though that our taste for oily fish such as herring seems to have disappeared because, fresh out of the sea, there's probably no better tasting fish. It is also becoming increasingly clear that the old adage 'Fish is good for you' is true, The herring is an oily fish which is rich in Omega-3 polyunsaturated fatty acids, which appear to lower the risk of heart disease. Many people think that the increase in heart disease is due to a decrease in oily fish consumption and point out that the Japanese, great fish eaters, have a far lower rate of heart disease than people in the West. It's also believed that Omega-3 is an essential building block for the development of a foetus in the womb.

Though the same species of herring stretches right across the North Atlantic, there are subtle regional differences. NORWEGIAN or ICELANDIC HERRING are those favoured by fish smokers as the larger fish, which weigh about 225 g (8 oz), look more impressive and the greater fat content and bulk leads to a moister product. The BALTIC HERRING is smaller, on average about 150 g (5 oz), than the Atlantic herring, as are the herrings from the North Sea. Wet-cured herrings from the Baltic however, made from smaller, leaner fish, have a distinctive flavour.

There is also an important herring fishery on the Pacific coast of the USA and Canada where the fish can weigh up to 675 g (1 lb 8 oz), though the average is about 300 g (10 oz). This is the main source of our herring milts for which there's a recipe on page 159.

One of the problems with cooking all oily fish is that they smell. When perfectly fresh the smell is very appetizing, but there's no denying that as the fish goes stale the smell is quite off-putting. Assuming you've bought the freshest herrings, I think that grilling them whole is preferable to any other way. But I also like them filleted (it's the bones that so many people find objectionable in herrings), dusted with medium-coarse oatmeal and pan-fried with a little oil and butter and a rasher of bacon.

For a description of the best possible way of eating herrings I found this account of a Lowestoft drift-trawler crew's breakfast – at which the average consumption was nine herrings per person – in an old book called *The Fish Retailer and his Trade* by William Wood, published in 1933. 'There is tea, bread and butter in plenty and a wolfish appetite. The herrings have been taken straight from the net and gutted, beheaded and the tails cut off, then they have been slashed across the back with a large jack knife and this slashing seems to hold the secret of the success of this cooking because it allows the boiling fat, into which the herring is plunged, to get a real hold of the flesh. When the cooking is finished, in a few minutes, there is a huge tin dishful of the herrings, crisped and browned and with a flavour that is never approached on shore.'

cured herrings

These products are more important economically than the fresh fish to the herring fishing countries.

BISMARCK HERRINGS are filleted, unskinned herrings, which are cured in vinegar, brine and sugar and packed with slices of onion.

BLOATERS are whole, ungutted (and therefore plump-looking) salted herrings, which are cold-smoked for just 12 hours, leaving them with a slightly gamey flavour.

BUCKLING are hot-smoked, headless salted herring and can be purchased either gutted or ungutted. This renders them ready-to-eat, like smoked trout, with bread and butter, lemon and horseradish cream.

HARENG SAUR are the French equivalent of kippers, gutted and salted aboard the boat then smoked at a factory close to the landing point

KIPPERS are fat herring, split from head to tail and air-dried then cold-smoked.

MATJES HERRINGS or 'MAIDEN HERRING' are young herring, which have been skinned and hand-filleted, then mild-cured in sugar, salt, vinegar and spices.

PICKLED HERRING is merely the term for gutted herring, which has been dry-salted in barrels.

ROLLMOPS are Bismarck herring fillets rolled around a pickle or onion slices and secured with a wooden skewer.

RED HERRINGS, called GENDARME in French, are little used these days but are salted and long-smoked whole herring, which turn a deep red colour after about three weeks. They were preserved for storing in tropical countries without refrigeration.

sardines and pilchards

Much of what I've said about herring applies to Sardines, Pilchards and Sprats as well. SARDINES have a certain cachet, associated as they are with charcoal grills and robust local wine in the Mediterranean. But PILCHARDS are devilishly difficult to sell in the UK, even though an enterprising pilchard buyer in Cornwall has renamed pilchards, 'Cornish Sardines'. (Pilchards are, in fact, adult sardines). Maybe it's the weather, but the market for sardines for barbecuing is gradually growing. Wouldn't it be nice if there were small beach cafés all along the British coast serving little more than local grilled fish? At Saint Jean-de-Luz near Biarritz, one of France's main sardine ports, there's a restaurant that specializes in only two dishes – grilled sardines or grilled tuna with local Basque wine. It's always packed, you get a salad, sardines and chips. What more could a man ask for?

In my first TV series, I made a film of my son barbecuing sardines on a beach near my house. I drank some red wine and made a tomato, red onion and basil salad to go with them. I still regard it as the epitome of what I like best about eating fish.

anchovies and sprats

It's extremely rare to get fresh ANCHOVIES in fishmongers; they're really all destined for processing. Like SPRATS, they're a bit too small for most people to bother with, and unlike whitebait they can't be eaten whole and are therefore a bit fiddly. There's a technique for eating small oily fish though, which is to nibble along the backbone, then more or less suck the fillets off the bones, almost like a horse nuzzling at oats.

Like all oily fish, anchovies spoil very quickly and should be iced immediately after they are caught. Indeed, the reason that the flesh around the gut cavities of herrings, sardines and anchovies is often disintegrating when you buy them is because the guts have started to ferment on board the trawlers. For perfect condition, the temperature of oily fish like these should never rise above the temperature of the sea. Sprats keep better in this respect than anchovies, herrings and sardines. If you're lucky enough to get fresh anchovies in good condition, cook them in the same way as you would sardines, or try the excellent Italian recipe for marinated anchovies on page 161. There's a suggestion for a dish in Jane Grigson's *Fish Cookery*, Penguin Books 1973, which strikes me as worth seeking out; it's from Ischia in the Bay of Naples. The anchovies are boned and baked in olive oil, flavoured with oregano, then lemon juice is squeezed over just before serving.

shad

The SHAD is a similar fish to the herring but much larger and much more bony. The wild fish in Europe tend to weigh about 1.3 kg (3 lb), but commonly reach 2.25 kg (5 lb) in America. Each fillet has three lines of bones running down it and needs to be dealt with by an accomplished filleter. This can be the only explanation as to why the fish is not more popular than it is because it's taste ranks with the best salmon. The best time to eat shad is in May when it appears in estuaries in Europe and North America, before going upriver to spawn, but you can buy farmed shad in the Garonne region in France. Cook it in any way that you like to eat salmon. If you're lucky enough to get hold of the great roe of the female shad – described by an excellent seafood cook, Mark Bittman, as 'the foie gras of the fish world' – it should be dusted in seasoned flour, gently sautéed, and served still pink.

Though not considered great eating in the North, the TARPON is more esteemed in West Africa. A southern member of the herring family, it can reach up to 2 metres (6 feet) in length and is a great game fish. The roes are much esteemed across the Atlantic in Central America.

jacks, pompanos and trevallys

jacks

The meat of all jacks is dark since they are pelagic (surface swimmers), and travel long distances. Like many other large pelagic fish, such as tuna and swordfish, they should be bled after capture by cutting off or slashing the tail. Jacks are not well represented in Europe, though a species of HORSE MACKEREL (also known as SCAD) occurs all around Britain, and is primarily used as lobster bait. They fetch low prices because of their exterior of bony platelets, however with these platelets removed they are rather good cooked à la meunière (see page 181).

A close relative, the BLUEFISH, swims in the Mediterranean, as well as the Atlantic. In fact, being a long-distance pelagic fish, it also appears in Australia, where it is called TAILOR. This is a great fighting fish and a voracious eater. Although it is very nutritious, Tailor or Bluefish does not have a good shelf-life and like other members of this group, also benefits from having the dark protein line along the fillet removed, since it's rather harsh-tasting. Bluefish is a bit like bonito in flavour. Both have dark and coarse flesh and neither are as fine tasting as tuna. Like bonito too, it is much better undercooked and suits strong accompaniments such as garlic, soy, ginger and chilli.

With the exception of the POMPANO, jacks are not important commercially in America. This is because many of them are not particularly good eating and some of the larger tropical species occasionally suffer from ciguatera poisoning (see page 235). By far the best eating is the Pompano, which is normally sold as a whole fish weighing between 750 g–1.5 kg (1½–3 lb) or as skin-on fillets. Its flesh is white but oily, meaty and sweet with an exquisite flavour. I think it's best grilled, though I once had it braised with tomato, garlic, fish stock and epazote – a rather pungent herb – in Vera Cruz in Mexico, which was startlingly good.

Nevertheless, the AMBERJACK is quite common in the southern states and, when smoked, is quite a delicacy in Florida. Mention too should be made of the CREVALLE JACK, a member of the *Caranx* species, which is found in all tropical and sub-tropical seas in the world and is known in Australian waters as a TREVALLY.

trevally

The fillet of this fish family is dark and the darker meat running along the centre of the fillet, under the skin, is best removed as it is quite overpowering. There are quite a number of species of trevallys in Indo-Pacific waters; the best-tasting for me are the BLACK POMFRET and the YELLOWTAIL KINGFISH.

cobia

The COBIA, also known as the BLACK KINGFISH, is not truly a jack, but in a family all on its own. It is a prime game fish which is also fished for commercially and is very fine-tasting. It has a very tough skin so it is usually sold in fillet form and is also often sold smoked.

dolphinfish

In a class of its own, is the MAHI MAHI, also called the DOLPHIN FISH or DORADO. It's very popular in the Mediterranean as well, where it is known as LAMPUKI in Malta and LAMPUGA in Spain. It is very popular on both the Pacific and Atlantic coasts of the USA too, and my recipe

(see page 138) was inspired by a recent visit to the USA and Mexico. Like all the better quality members of this group, Mahi Mahi is excellent served raw as *sashimi*.

mackerel and tuna

Like the Jacks and Trevallys above, mackerel and tuna are pelagic, long-roaming fish, which have dark oily meat as a result. All species of mackerel and tuna are popular and widely fished commercially, so rather than describe each species, I have grouped them into three broad categories for cooking and eating purposes.

small mackerel

All these small mackerels – the ATLANTIC MACKEREL, CHUB MACKEREL from the Mediterranean and the BLUE MACKEREL from Australian and New Zealand waters – average out at less then 500 g (1 lb 2 oz) in weight, and are the fish of summer holidays all over the world. As with herrings, mackerel have to be jumping fresh and I prefer them grilled or pan-fried. But I do like poached fillets too, and when cooked like this they can take a sauce with some butter in them, as I've suggested for the recipe on page 158. Small mackerel can be cured in many of the ways that herring can – salted or smoked. Try preserving them as Gravlax, page 66, to produce the Swedish Gravad Mackerel. Like all members of the mackerel and tuna family, these small mackerel are excellent sliced and served raw as sashimi. They are also very good used in an escabèche (see page 163).

large mackerel

The next group comprises all the mackerel ranging between 1 and 5 kg (2 lb 4 oz and 12 lb 8 oz). These are the CERO, CHUB MACKEREL, KING MACKEREL (also called KINGFISH), SPANISH MACKEREL, WAHOO, FRIGATE MACKEREL, KAWAKAWA, SPOTTED MACKEREL and the BONITO. These again are all good eating, but the flesh tends to be coarser than that of the tunas and doesn't keep as well. While they can be successfully grilled, I think they are particularly good cooked in olive oil confits (see page 144), or poached in oil (as I've done with the halibut on page 183), tandooried, or used in Goan-style curries.

large tuna

These are the BLUEFIN TUNA, YELLOWFIN TUNA and SKIPJACK TUNA, which fetch high prices for the Japanese sashimi market. They are available in all fish shops as dark red, meaty loins, or steaks that are good for searing and char-grilling as in the recipe on page 119. The ALBACORE, also called LONG-FIN TUNA, is in

seafood families

this category too but its meat is much lighter in colour, and often called the 'chicken of the sea' or WHITE TUNA. It is to my mind a revelation when cooked on a good barbecue and, unlike Bluefin Tuna, is not in danger of being over-fished.

Tuna belly, which is rich in fat, is much esteemed by the Japanese. In sashimi (their elegant presentation of sliced raw fish) or sushi (vinegared rice topped with raw fish) it provides a flavourful contrast to the leaner loin meat. Being an oily fish it also lends itself to various types of curing. It is occasionally smoked, though I don't think this works very well. But, when cured and dried, then very thinly sliced, it makes a great addition to crunchy salads made with vegetables such as fennel and chicory. And the Spanish blocks of dried tuna, called MOJAMA, are excellent.

monkfish and stargazers

Monkfish is in a group of its own – there is no other fish quite like it. Although there is a very similar species called GOOSEFISH or Monkfish in America and another, STARGAZER or Monkfish, in Australia and New Zealand, it's in Europe that the fish is really popular. I'm surprised it hasn't taken off elsewhere because it satisfies a universal desire for firm, meaty, boneless fish. Its flavour is not pronounced, though the small tails have a sweet freshness which, combined with the texture, make it one of my favourite fish. It's particularly suited to char-grilling and is also great in curries because it remains intact after cooking.

Once the fish is skinned, you'll find the fillets are encased in a thin membrane. You need to remove this or it will cause the tails to distort during cooking (see page 62).

WEEVER is an underrated fish in all parts of the world except for the Mediterranean. Weever has an excellent flavour and firm texture, almost on a par with Dover Sole. Maybe its lack of popularity is due to the poisonous spines on the gill covers and the first spine on the dorsal fin, which can give you a sting that's a great deal worse than that of a bee. The pain lasts for about 12 hours, which accounts for the saying 'it's the following tide that takes the pain away'.

mullets

red mullet

There's really no similarity between red and grey mullet except for the name and the fact that they can be cooked in much the same way. Both fish appear all over the world. By far my favourite is the RED MULLET, particularly those species from the Mediterranean. All fish that live on a diet of crustaceans have a flavour somewhat echoing that of shellfish,

but none more so than the red mullet. It has a perfect flake and skin which, when grilled, smells of rock pools. If you are lucky enough to get an ungutted red mullet, the liver is something of a delicacy too. Indeed the first red mullet I ever ate was grilled with its liver intact and in this form is known as becasse de mer. Like the woodcock, it doesn't have a gall bladder, so provided that the intestine is removed, the rest will not taste bitter.

The red mullet has the same name in Australia but is often called GOATFISH there, which is also the most common name for a very similar species of mullet in America. There are five different species on both the Atlantic and Pacific coasts, but they are most commonly found in Florida and the Caribbean.

grey mullet

The GREY MULLET is generally not so well regarded around the world. Unfortunately, they have a reputation for feeding on mud and other undesirable material in estuaries, a habit which is reflected in the flavour. But the mullet in the bays around Padstow, which have a little golden flash on the gill cover, are as good to eat as sea bass.

The grey mullet is either called Grey Mullet or STRIPED MULLET in the USA. *The Encyclopaedia of Fish Cookery* by A. J. McClane, is an excellent book and one that I've referred to a lot when writing this section. In it the author describes an attempt in Florida to increase grey mullet sales as follows: 'The State of Florida chose the seemingly romantic name "Lisa" to promote sales of the fish. This was no more comprehensible than a plague of bullfrogs. The consumer invariably asked, "What is a Lisa?" and when the retailer explained that it was a mullet, nothing was accomplished, except to suggest that the fish had to be disguised'.

Grey mullet is known as MULLET, SEA MULLET, or DIAMOND-SCALE MULLET in Australia and New Zealand.

puffer fish

I must confess that I have never eaten PUFFER FISH but I'd certainly like to. Apparently it's one of the most delicate fish in the sea, the creamy white meat being similar to a plump frog's leg.

Puffers, which are known as SEA SQUABS or BLOWFISH in America, are found from Cape Cod down to Florida, but the largest number of species (38) are found around Japan and it is from here that the fame of the world's most poisonous fish stems. It seems that the more fatalities that are caused by pufferfish, or FUGU, as it is known, the more popular it becomes. There are on average 70 deaths a year, usually in rural areas where people prepare the fish at home. The poison, found in the gut, liver, ovaries and skin of the fish, is

called tetrotoxin. It's similar to curare (the poison used by the Amazonian Indians to tip their arrows), and is 1250 times deadlier than cyanide.

Kitaoji Rosanjin, the famous Japanese potter and gourmet wrote 'The taste of fugu is incomparable; if you eat it three or four times you are enslaved; anyone who declines it for fear of death is a really pitiable person'. A chef must be licensed to prepare fugu and this requires a written and practical examination that includes eating the fugu he has prepared. Prior to that the chef must have completed at least two years experience working under a master. Death by fugu poisoning is described as terrible: although you can think clearly, you cannot speak or move, and soon cannot breathe. But enthusiasts say consumption of the meat produces a pleasant, warm tingling, a faint echo of the poison. Perhaps eating un-prepared fugu is one of the favoured ways of committing hara-kiri (suicide). As the haiku poet Buson wrote:
'I cannot see her tonight.
I have to give her up
So I will eat fugu'

roe fish

Here I've included fish that are most important for their roe (eggs). Some fish, such as LUMPFISH are only valuable for their roe – which is similar to caviar in appearance, but not in taste – while other fish, such as STURGEON, have tasty flesh as well as roe. Sturgeon has very firm flesh with a high oil content. It is sold in North America. as steaks or is preserved in wine vinegar and spices, but it is most often sold smoked.

It is the roe of the BELUGA, OSCIETRA and SEVRUGA STURGEON that forms the world's most luxurious food – CAVIAR. It is only the sturgeon that live in the Caspian Sea and the rivers which flow into it that matter. Caviar from farmed sturgeon is produced near Bordeaux in France, and California in America. Both are good but bear no comparison to Caspian caviar. The flavour of caviar grows on you: the first time most people taste it it's a little disappointing but there's something about the salty, oiliness of it that makes you give it a second try and then – like some fiendish drug – it becomes an expensive obsession. Sevruga is the cheapest caviar and Beluga the most expensive, mainly because it comes from the largest of the sturgeons and the eggs are therefore bigger. I think Oscietra is the perfect compromise.

To make caviar, the master caviar-maker removes the sac of roe from the fish and then rubs it through a fine screen, allowing the eggs to pass through whole but removing blood and membrane. The roe is then rinsed and salted. Adding the right amount of salt – between three and five per cent –

is where the caviar-maker's art lies. The freshest roe requires the least salt and good caviar will always have the label 'molossol' or 'malossol', which means 'little salt'. Caviar is now unbelievably expensive due to over-fishing, pollution and poaching in the Caspian Sea. Let's hope that a recent agreement signed by all the countries that surround the Caspian prohibiting all open-sea sturgeon fishing (i.e. permitting fishing only in the rivers), can be successfully implemented.

Here are a few tips on how best to enjoy caviar.

• Avoid pasteurized caviar. Only buy fresh and allow about 25 g (1 oz) per person.
• As long as it hasn't been opened, caviar will keep for 6–9 months in the coldest part of the fridge but the sooner it's eaten the better.
• Remove the caviar from the fridge half an hour before serving. Nestle the tin in some crushed ice and use a non-metal spoon to serve it – mother of pearl or even plastic are good – as caviar reacts with metal.
• Serve simply with thin wholemeal toast, blinis or good fresh bread.

Some classic accompaniments are blinis brushed with melted butter, or topped with sour cream or crème fraîche. In addition Russians serve caviar accompanied by finely chopped onions and chopped hard-boiled eggs, both of which are said to bring out the flavour of the fish eggs.

other roe
The roes of some other fish are worthy of note. Both the eggs and the milt of HERRING ROE are delicious. The Japanese lightly salt the roe of the female and use it in sashimi, while the Milt, the white seminal fluid of the male, is excellent floured and shallow-fried (see page 159). It's a good idea to disgorge the milt for ten minutes or so in water, to which lots of lemon juice has been added, before drying and coating it for cooking. I've recently been using lightly smoked herring roe with a lot of success, adding half a teaspoon of it to a cream sauce similar to that on page 145 and serving it with salmon escalopes. I've also mentioned Shad Roe, sometimes called the 'foie gras of the sea', under the entry for the herring family.

If you can get hold of the Greek salted and dried GREY MULLET ROE (BOTARGO), it is nice sliced into very thin strips and served with olive oil, pepper and lemon juice as a very pleasant mezze, or added like anchovies to salads to give them piquancy.

SMOKED SALTED COD ROE is now a common substitute for grey mullet roe in the making of the Greek dish, Taramasalata (see page 130).

Lightly salted salmon eggs called KETA are something of a delicacy (see the recipe for Nigiri Sushi on pages 105–6).

salmon and sea trout

There are six species of SALMON native to the northern hemisphere. There are none in the southern hemisphere, although you wouldn't realise it because the farming of salmon in Tasmania means that ATLANTIC SALMON is just as common there. Atlantic Salmon is the fish that is always used for farming. Like it or not, farmed salmon has encouraged more people to eat fish as it is now cheap and readily available. It's got lots of flavour and suits cooking in almost any way, though I'm not sure about the current fish-and-chip-shop trend for deep-frying it in batter; it's too oily a fish for that.

There's a great deal of controversy about the farming of salmon because, when done unscrupulously, it can have a devastating effect on the wild stocks of other fish as well as salmon, due to the build up of parasites, disease and chemicals in an overpopulated environment. Some would like to see all salmon farms banned. But when the fish are kept further out at sea, rather than in the more usual lochs and estuaries, or where the fish densities are kept at a sensible level and the fish are well looked after, far less damage is caused. It is worth paying the price for premium quality farmed salmon, particularly if it is organically farmed. It tastes so much better; the flesh is firmer and not overwhelmingly fatty and you are less likely to be damaging the environment.

My favourite way to cook salmon and sea trout is to poach them whole in salted water and serve them with home-made mayonnaise, new potatoes and a cucumber and mint salad. I'm also particularly fond of seasoning a steak or two of salmon and cooking them gently in butter in a frying pan. I add half a glass of white wine half-way through cooking and let the liquid reduce, then finish the dish off with some chopped parsley.

atlantic salmon
WILD ATLANTIC SALMON are still my favourite but there is a severe shortage, mostly through over-fishing rather than any disasters caused by farming. I mourn the decline of the Wild Atlantic Salmon and get depressed when I hear that the Rhine was once teeming with them. We're lucky that we can still buy some wild salmon from the estuary on which our restaurant stands; the lean taste of the wild fish, which has swum so far, is incomparable. Atlantic salmon was also found on the east Coast of Canada and North America but it has suffered a decline similar to that of the same species in Europe.

pacific salmon
There are six other salmon, all from the Pacific coast which are in much better shape. The biggest of them all is the CHINOOK SALMON, also called the KING SALMON, sometimes reaching as much as 50 kg (125 lb). It's a large flaked fish with a high fat content and soft texture. Next, there's the COHO SALMON, which is smaller – it reaches 15 kg (37 lb 8 oz) – and the fillet is lighter in colour than the Chinook. The SOCKEYE SALMON's name has nothing to do with the eyes but is a corruption of an Indian word. Both the male and female sockeye salmon become bright red on spawning. They have very dark, almost orange flesh, with a firm texture and delicate taste. The CHUM SALMON, that weighs up to 15 kg (37 lb 8 oz) is, along with Pink Salmon, cheaper than the others and somewhat coarse in texture. It probably fetches a lower price because its flesh colour is often more grey than pink, but it takes to smoking well. The PINK SALMON is the smallest Pacific Salmon, never weighing more than 5 kg (11 lb). It is the cheapest salmon of all except the Chum, but has a delicate, distinctive flavour and a good pink colour.

sea trout
I'm almost more fond of WILD SEA TROUT than I am of Atlantic Salmon. The small ones that we get at the restaurant, fresh from the sea during the months of May and June, are one of the great pleasures of early summer, as are the spider crabs that arrive on the rocky beaches just below the low-tide mark (at exactly the same time as the thrift blooms in the stone walls and hedges in the fields above).

A sea trout, also known as SALMON TROUT, SEWIN or OCEAN TROUT, is a freshwater brown trout that has gone to sea. Why some members of the same species should travel down rivers, through the brackish waters of estuaries into the sea to feed on prawns and other crustaceans – which produce the characteristic pink colour of the flesh – is unclear. But something in their genetic make up enables them to develop a silvery sheen and the ability to cope with the osmotic effect of salt in the water. They don't follow the same migratory pattern as salmon but stay in relatively near-coastal waters before returning up-river to spawn. Predictably they have a taste somewhere between trout and salmon, being less rich than salmon and slightly less pink. Incidentally, large sea trout and small salmon look very similar. The only sure way to tell the difference is to look at the eyes: those of a sea trout are slightly higher up the head. If you draw an imaginary line from the mouth through to the centre of the gill cover it will bisect the eye of a salmon, but a salmon trout's eye will be above it.

char and smelt

There are a couple of other members of the salmon family that are worthy of note. There are two types of CHAR or ARCTIC CHAR: those that live most of their lives in their sea and swim up northern rivers to spawn, and landlocked char which can be found in many lakes all over Northern Europe (including Lake Windermere in England), Canada and Alaska. The sea-going variety make by far the best eating and reach up to 13 kg (30 lb) in size. They are fat fish, with firm red flesh when caught in the wild, but less firm or deeply coloured when farmed.

The SMELT (also called RAINBOW SMELT or SPARLING), a small member of the salmon family reaching no more than 27 cm (11 inches) in length, is found in both Northern Europe and North America. The fish have a characteristic smell of cucumbers when very fresh and generally have light green skin, soft flesh and bones. They deteriorate incredibly rapidly and like so many oily fish – herrings, mackerel, sardines – should be cooked the day they're caught. However, as long as they're chilled straight after catching and frozen soon after, then defrosted to a temperature of no more than 1°C and cooked from that temperature, they will be almost as good as fresh ones. The best way to cook the smaller ones is to thread them on to wooden skewers and grill or fry them in clarified butter where, because of their soft open texture they'll take no more than 2–3 minutes. They are also particularly nice whole, coated in tempura batter and deep-fried.

smoked salmon

All members of the salmon family can be smoked successfully but none more so than salmon itself. Cold smoked salmon, where the fish is subjected to smoke without heat, is now so popular that its luxury status has all but disappeared and much of the cheap, pre-sliced stuff that you can buy is just pink, flabby and boring. However, a side of salmon, not necessarily wild, but with a good high fat content, cured maybe with salt and brown sugar and smoked over oak chippings, beech or whisky barrels for at least eight hours is still something very special. Hot-smoked salmon called BRADAN ROST is good served on lightly griddled slices of sour-dough bread with mixed, small salad leaves and a chive, caper and crème fraîche dressing.

sea bream, porgies and snappers

This section looks just at SEA BREAM, not freshwater bream. There are many species, but all bream are firm-fleshed fish with medium oil content, although smaller ones tend to be a bit bony. They are well-flavoured, thanks to a diet of crustaceans, and have a pleasing, compact body shape, which makes them ideal for steaming, grilling or cooking on a barbecue. One of the unifying features of all bream is that they generally come in one or two portion sizes i.e. 500 g–1 kg (1 lb 2 oz–2 lb 4 oz). However, there are plenty of exceptions. I've seen snappers as big as 4 kg (9 lb). Once, whilst on holiday in Cephalonia, six of us dined on a sumptuous Synagrida (the Greek word for the DENTEX), served with Greek salad and chips fried in olive oil, and washed down with copious quantities of Robola, a very good local white wine.

red bream

In Padstow in the 1970s and 80s, we used to have regular landings of RED BREAM caught very close to the coast near Newquay. They are firm-textured and sweet with a thick skin and amazingly large scales. Their subtle red colour and enormous eyes also make them one of the most attractive fish. I used to serve them baked on a bed of haricot beans with chilli, bay leaf, garlic, olive oil, orange juice and zest. I recall having a boy working in the kitchen for the summer holiday once. When I asked him to gut the fish he cut off all their heads which, owing to the round shape of a bream and his inexperience, meant that half the fillet went with it too. He's now a successful surgeon, I'm still a chef and every time I see him he recalls with acute embarrassment the beheading of the red bream. I wish I could go back to those days because there are no red bream left and they were one of my favourite fish.

In fact all the bream and the closely related PORGY from America are good eating, but the Red Bream and the most highly esteemed GILT-HEAD BREAM (Daurade in French) are the best in Europe. We buy a lot of local BLACK SEA BREAM, which is reasonably good eating. I like them steamed whole with garlic and ginger, as I've done for the recipe with grey mullet on page 171. And although the scales on bream are always plate-like, once they're removed the skin is often soft and pleasing to eat, particularly when steamed in this way.

In America, the most highly regarded Porgies are the SHEEPSHEAD BREAM and the SCUP which, when whole, weigh from 350 g (12 oz) to 1.5 kg (3 lb), and have flaky, tender and very tasty flesh. Interestingly, the EUROPEAN SEA BREAM and the AMERICAN RED PORGY appear to be one and the same fish. As a result of a relatively comprehensive study of the migration of these fish, it is clear that fish appear in different far-flung parts of the world not generally through a sort of Viking migratory habit, but rather through the eggs drifting on the ocean currents. How else might we explain the presence in Australian and New Zealand waters of the same group of fish, the *Sparidae*? The best-flavoured examples of these are the BLACK BREAM, the YELLOWFIN BREAM, the SWEETLIP BREAM, the FRYPAN BREAM and the SNAPPER. In fact this snapper, which is one of Australia's most highly regarded fish, is not a true snapper but a bream. Then again, there is another group of fish in Australasia called THREADFIN BREAM, which are not true bream. How confusing!

There is a small group of fish called bream, which are actually more closely related to Pomfret, (see Thin-Bodied fish, page 246). These are the wide-ranging RAY'S BREAM, the *Brama brama*, which appear in the southern oceans off New Zealand and yet have also been landed on the beaches of Sussex.

snappers

Snappers are a very important fish family in tropical waters and provide one of the best tasting fish the sea has to offer, with their succulent, fantastically flavoured white meat. Owing to the wonders of airfreight we can now buy them here, almost as fresh and lively as fish from the quayside, though I have this rather depressed feeling that the quality could sometimes be better on a lot of supermarket counters. One of my favourites is the RED EMPEROR also known as BOURGEOIS, EMPEROR or SNAPPER from Australia and this is possibly the best fish I know for barbecuing. I've had great success char-grilling large fillets of red emperor. I make a marinade of olive oil, lemon zest, bay leaves, thyme, chilli flakes and salt, then I grill the fish, brushing it constantly with the same marinade.

A closely related species, from the Indian Ocean and Australia, which is also easy to get in the UK is the SPANGLED EMPEROR, known as CAPITAINE or BLUE EMPEROR. I cooked this once at a barbecue on Mauritius and served it with the prawn and mango salsa on page 147. Unfortunately, it happened to coincide with the only tropical rainstorm of the two-week trip.

In America the most sought-after fish in this family is the RED SNAPPER; others with good eating qualities are the MUTTON SNAPPER and YELLOWTAIL SNAPPER. But it's the Red Snapper that's the snapper for me. When I was twenty, I spent two years travelling around the world between school and university. I was in Acapulco, Mexico for a couple of months, living, as was the custom then, on five dollars a day (actually more like two dollars, five was luxury!) Such economy meant eating canned frankfurters and sweet American bread from the supermarket but, with my growing interest in food, also the

13

enchiladas, tamales and tacos from the street vendors in the back streets around the market. (It also meant sleeping on the beach – at least until I was robbed of all my possessions. Served me right I suppose.) Every day, what seemed then like absurdly well-off Americans sat at the beachside restaurants eating whole grilled red snapper with tortillas, tomato and chilli. I can remember to this day the smell of those chunky grilled fish and the sight of lots of chilled Mexican beer slipping down to a hungry youth … If you want fillets, the ideal weight to buy would be between 3.5 kg (8 lb) and 5.5 kg (12 lb) but whole fish weighing between 450 g (1 lb) and 1.5 kg (3 lb) are also great for cooking whole.

grunters

The first thing you'd want to know about a fish called a GRUNTER is … why? Well, it's because when they're caught they grind their teeth in panic and the sound is then amplified by their air bladder to make a grunt-like noise. The fish are related to snappers; they have a delicate white flesh but with a slightly softer texture and finer white flake. They tend to be small fish, no more than 500 g (1 lb 2 oz) in size, and are ideal for cooking whole on a barbecue. Particularly good is the PORKFISH.

sea catfish

Closely related to the freshwater catfish of the Mississippi, the Danube and other large rivers of Eastern Europe, SEA CATFISH, *Galeichthys felis* has well-flavoured white, medium-firm flesh, which keeps well. The skins of all catfish are thick, slippery and strong like that of an eel and they therefore have to be skinned in the same way, but it is unusual to buy it in any form other than fillets.

The name catfish is also given to an unrelated species in northern Europe called the WOLF FISH, *Anarhichas lupus*, which is also called SEACAT, OCEAN CATFISH or ROCK TURBOT, and is of excellent quality. There is a recipe using this fish on page 138. It has particularly firm white fillets and the first time I ate it I thought it tasted a bit like Dover sole, but it deteriorates much more quickly.

In America, by far the most popular way of cooking catfish is to coat it in cornmeal, often flavoured with things such as curry powder, chilli and even five-spice powder, and to fry it until crisp and golden. It is traditionally served with hush puppies (onion-flavoured cornmeal fritters) and lemon wedges. Interestingly, though the name catfish refers to the 'whiskers' or barbels situated near the mouth, the most striking feature of the US GAFFTOPSAIL CATFISH is the enormous Arabic dhow-sail-like dorsal fin.

The similar species in Australia and New Zealand, CATFISH and COBBLER, though just as good in quality, are not as well appreciated as the American and European fish. However there is a growing market in Western Australia for Cobbler fillets also known, inevitably, as catfish fillets.

sea creatures

Most of the species in this section are pretty esoteric, and not even known to many people, but they have their enthusiasts. Get talking to a Galician about *Percebes*, or a Chinese about sea slugs and you'd think you were talking about a delicacy waiting to take the world by storm. But I think the seafood lover should be familiar with all of these and most of the time they are very good to eat.

percebes or goose neck barnacles

The Galicians of Northern Spain are mad about these strange brown barnacles, which are correctly classified as crustaceans. They look a bit like the legs of a tortoise, a bit shorter and stumpier than your little finger. They taste something like the claw meat of lobster and are boiled in salted water and eaten plain, often with Albarino, the local wine of Galicia. Percebes fetch big money in Spain because the fishing of them is very dangerous. The fishermen, called 'mariscadores', prise them off the rocks at low tide and often risk being swept away by an extra large wave.

jellyfish

Although we don't eat JELLYFISH in the West, the Chinese dry the umbrella part of certain species. They are then re-hydrated, cut into strips and served in a classic Chinese dish, with strips of chicken, cucumber, coriander and soy. The jellyfish doesn't have much taste; it's more the texture that is valued. The edible species are *Rhopilema esculenta* and *Stomolophus nomurai* and, from Australian waters, *Aurelia aurita*, also known as the BLUE JELLYFISH.

sea urchin

The only edible part of a SEA URCHIN is the cluster of creamy or orange coloured roe, also known as corals. Though not common in fishmongers, urchins have many fans. They have a beautiful, fragrant flavour and are to be enjoyed spooned out of the opened and cleaned shell (see page 97) and eaten raw, folded into hot pasta (see page 218) or used to thicken a fine sauce. The best eating is the MEDITERRANEAN SEA URCHIN, *Paracentrotus lividus*. This is the one with long black or dark brown spines. The urchin of Northern Europe and North America, the GREEN SEA URCHIN, has a much bigger 'test' (shell). In Orkney they are known as a 'Scarrimans Heid',

meaning a street child with unruly spiky hair. This same urchin is present in the Northern Pacific as well, but there's a bigger species in Northern California, which reaches as much as 12.5 cm (5 inches) in diameter. In Australia and New Zealand, the BLACK SEA URCHIN is more like the Mediterranean in shape but the roe is mostly exported to Asia.

violets

This is a knobbly creature with leathery skin, that lives anchored to rocks or the sea bed in the Mediterranean. You cut them in half – the skin is violet in colour as you are cutting through it, hence the name. The inside, the bit you eat, is bright yellow. It's very soft, like scrambled egg, with a taste of ozone but quite bitter, as raw mussels can sometimes be. Shallot vinegar can offset this.

I've eaten the same sort of creature in New South Wales in Australia, but I haven't been able to track down the name of it in any book. Local fishermen put me on to them. They were nicer than Mediterranean violets, being less bitter.

sea cucumbers

The Chinese hold SEA CUCUMBERS in great esteem. They look like fat slugs lying on the sea bed, about 25–35 cm (10–14 inches) in length and weighing up to 2 kg (4 lb 8 oz) when alive. Once harvested, they are gutted, boiled and dried and sometimes smoked. They are then reconstituted in water before cooking. Sea cucumbers have strong longitudinal muscles and therefore need to be cut thinly crossways to make them edible. As with jellyfish, the Chinese enjoy their rubbery texture, liking a more comprehensive range of textures in their food than we do in the West.

sea perch

This is a collection of similarly shaped fish with round, deep-bodies, tough skins and large scales, and with the first and second dorsal fins joined, the first fin always being spiny. Their flesh is generally pinkish-white in colour, firm but open-textured and therefore slightly flaky when cooked. Because of their medium oil content, they suit every type of cooking, particularly barbecues, hence the popularity of Surfperch in America and Dhufish in Australia at convivial *al fresco* meetings.

There are 20 types of SURFPERCH on the Pacific coast of America, ranging from Alaska down to the Baja, California. These are not true perch but are similar in texture and for cooking purposes we can treat them the same. The best eating are the REDTAIL, the BARRED and the CALICO SURFPERCH. All are what you might call pan fish as they are never much bigger than 1–2 kg (2 lb 4 oz–4 lb 8 oz), thus they can be pan fried or cooked whole. The OPALEYE is also sold as Perch, being very similar in size and shape.

DRUMMERS are a group of fish in Australia which have a general perch-like appearance. One is the LUDERICK, the other best known fish in this family is the SWEEP. These fish are essentially vegetarian and mainly feed on seaweed. Though they are good table fish, they can be tainted by iodine from eating too much seaweed.

The DHUFISH, also known as JEWFISH, is one of the most sought-after Indian Ocean fish in Western Australia, so next time you're in Perth you'll know what to order at Fraser's fish restaurant overlooking the Swan River. Dhufish, and the closely related PEARL PERCH, which is available on the East Coast, have excellent flavour and texture and are among the best fish on the continent.

sea vegetables

carragheen (irish moss)

A red or greenish-brown seaweed which grows in short, frilly tufts on the coastlines of Europe and America. It is dried in the open air and bleaches to a creamy pink colour. It's traditionally used in Ireland to thicken milk puddings, and to make a vegetarian-friendly alternative to gelatine.

dulse

An edible red seaweed that occurs in both the northern and southern hemispheres. It's most popular in Ireland where dried dulse is sold in the pubs of Belfast in little packets, as snacks.

laver

Found around the coast of Northern America and Europe, laver is green when young, becoming purple, then dark brown as it ages. It is particularly popular in South Wales where, after harvesting, it is boiled to a purée. I think this goes extremely well with the cockles that would often have come from the same beach. (See the recipe on page 207). Laver is also known as NORI in Japan and in its dried form, pressed into thin sheets it is used as the outer wrapping in Nori Sushi.

kelp

This name is given to several large varieties of brown seaweed which grow in the Atlantic and are used by local people in their traditional dishes.

kombu

This name is given to a group of brown seaweeds, of which *Laminaria japonica* is the most common. When dried it is very important in Japanese cooking. Kombu and dried bonito flakes (*katsuo-bushi*) – a fish from the same family and tuna and mackerel – are the two ingredients needed for making dashi, the classic Japanese stock, which is used in many dishes. Kombu, which is very similar to the Kelps, which grow in the Atlantic, is very rich in monosodium glutamate.

wakame

By far and away the most popular seaweed in Japan, it's a green, frilly-fronded seaweed, which is easy to buy dried and can be used raw in salads or cooked in soups such as the Miso soup on page 104–5.

sea lettuce

The most widely distributed of edible seaweeds in the world, this is used in salads and soups.

sea kale

This member of the cabbage family, which normally grows wild on the pebbly beaches of Europe, is bitter and inedible unless it has grown under sand. These days the young shoots of the new season's sea kale are covered and forced like rhubarb to present an early spring delicacy, which is excellent boiled and served like asparagus, with hollandaise sauce.

marsh samphire

As its name suggests, this grows in muddy estuaries and tidal salt marshes around Europe. It's easy to identify, having unusual light green branches rather than leaves and growing little more than 20 cm (8 inches) off the mud. It is harvested in Britain between May and September, though earlier in more southern countries. Contrary to what many think, picking the whole plant out of the mud will not endanger stocks, as the plants grow from seed and not from regeneration of the roots. It has a delicious salty fresh taste, making it an ideal vegetable for serving with fish, and is particularly delicious when served with hollandaise sauce. It should be boiled – without salt in the water – until only just tender.

rock samphire

Gatherers of this variety of samphire are described in King Lear as plying a 'dangerous trade', presumably referring to the need to scramble over the face of high cliffs to collect it. In my part of the world, it grows conveniently out of Cornish stone walls and low rocks by the beach. It has a pungent, aromatic smell, slightly reminiscent of fennel, and in fact belongs to the same family, the *Umbelliferae*. Traditionally it was always pickled. I have had some success in using it as a herb for flavouring a cream sauce, but you have to be very parsimonious with it. To me it is the most evocative of plants, recalling childhood summer holidays strolling down sandy Cornish lanes.

sharks and rays

Here I've grouped all those shark and shark-like fish that have cartilage rather than bones. There are a few other fish with cartilage rather than bone – notably the sturgeon and the lamprey – but these are not related to sharks and rays.

sharks and rays

The great plus of all sharks is that there are no bones in the flesh. All have lots of flavour, many with a slight tartness, particularly the Atlantic sharks – the PORBEAGLE and MAKO – which are excellent eating. Part of the assertive flavour of shark comes from the presence of urea in their flesh. All fish are less salty than the sea around them so, to avoid dehydration, they have to counteract osmosis (the tendency of salt to attract water). Sharks do this by producing urea, which is perfectly acceptable in fresh fish; however after death urea gradually breaks down into ammonia and becomes repulsive in stale fillets. The advantage of this breakdown is that while quite a few sharks – notably skates and rays – are inedible when just caught, being incredibly tough, the subsequent break up of the urea tenderizes the fish. Skate and ray are at their best about 2–5 days old: after that point, the smell of the ammonia becomes most unpleasant and no amount of cooking will remove it.

In Britain most shark appears as PORBEAGLE, if named at all. I wonder sometimes if it's not BLUE SHARK, which is not as nice, being coarser and darker meat with rather an assertive flavour similar to TOPE. Both these are good for soups and curries but too powerful for my taste for simple grilling. Most sharks that we can buy in the UK would be between 4–20 kg (9–45 lb). The larger ones are sold in filleted form, the smaller ones as steaks.

The BLACKTIP SHARK from Florida and the Caribbean has very white meat, a bit drier than MAKO and TIGER SHARK but in America most shark gets marketed as mako and sometimes mako gets marketed as swordfish, since the fillet is very similar. Other fine-tasting sharks in the Atlantic are the HAMMERHEAD SHARK, which also swim in Indo-Pacific waters and are the favoured shark in Goan Shark Vindaloo (see page 120).

In Australia the most popular eating sharks are the GUMMY SHARK, the WHISKERY SHARK and SCHOOL SHARK. The school and gummy sharks are sold in fish-and-chip shops as FLAKE. Australia and New Zealand also have a number of dogfish, skates and rays very similar to our own. They also have the ANGEL SHARK as do we, but this is confusingly also called monkfish both there and here. It looks similar to monkfish but its flavour is more like that of skate or ray, and it has small wings like they do, but without the long fibrous strands of flesh.

rays

The naming of SKATE and RAY is a little confusing. Alan Davidson, perhaps the world's greatest culinary ichthyologist, suggests that the old distinction should stand, whereby we call skates the bigger fish with long snouts, and rays the smaller fish with rounded heads. In Britain the best ray for eating is the THORNBACK RAY. The BLONDE RAY is also good.

dogfish

Dogfish are small relatives of the shark family. The best DOGFISH is the SPUR-DOG though the LESSER SPOTTED DOGFISH, also called the ROUGH HOUND, MURGY or MORGAY is good. The NURSEHOUND and SMOOTH HOUND are also perfectly enjoyable and are used for the fish-and-chip trade as rock salmon or rock eel. All dogfish are also good with Indian masalas, as with the recipe on page 103, but above all I regard them as a vital ingredient in fish soup. Other popular names for dogfish are HUSS and ROCK SALMON, or Saumonette in French, probably due to the pinkish-white colour of the flesh.

shellfish – bivalves and univalves

bivalves

These are the shellfish that live in two, hinged shells. Unlike fish, there is little difference in the taste of CLAMS, MUSSELS or OYSTERS around the world. Some experts swear that they can taste the water in which they grow. A friend of mine, Johnny Noble, owns Loch Fyne Oysters in Argyllshire in Scotland. He swears that when he's far away from home, say at the Mandarin Hotel in Hong Kong, which stocks his oysters, just one taste takes him back to the bonny banks of the loch. It's a lovely thought and I earnestly believe it to be true. If it is, it rather confounds the idea of a difference between, say 20 types of oyster, in a big oyster bar I know in New York, where I'm told all the oysters are stored in the same tank.

Because of their similarity in taste, I have grouped all the bivalves by size: small, medium, large.

small bivalves

I use small clams for several first courses, including Mussel, Cockle and Clam Masala (see page 103)

and Linguine alle Vongole (page 205) and I find generally that MUSSELS and COCKLES can be used in the same way. The CARPETSHELL CLAM, called Vongole in Italian, and Palourde in France, is the best one for Linguine alle Vongole, although I've made it with PIPIS in Australia and been well pleased with it. Clams can be used instead of mussels for Moules Marinière (see page 213), if you prefer, although I do think that mussels have the edge for this dish. Though I have a nostalgic affection for the small beach mussels from around Padstow, we find that the best mussels to use for all our dishes are rope-grown farmed ones. Suspended in mid-water in estuaries rich in plankton, rope mussels grow very quickly and are not attacked by predators such as crabs and starfish living on the bottom. Because they are always covered with water they are constantly feeding and develop a thinner shell than mussels that live on the shore and have to withstand the attrition of waves. The thin shell ensures that they cook quickly and uniformly, which is particularly advantageous in stir-fries such as the garlic and ginger dish, on page 206.

The technique of opening small clams for serving raw on ice is illustrated on page 89, but you can also steam them open carefully in a covered pan, if you prefer, with a splash of water or wine. The trick is to take them out as soon as the shells pop open so don't try to do too many at once – just enough to cover the base of the pan. You can open cockles by pushing the knuckle end (the hinge of the cockle) against the knuckle of another one and twisting. It's rather satisfying; particularly if, like me, you enjoy gathering cockles and eating the odd one as you do so – only when the beds are pollution free, of course.

medium bivalves

I wouldn't tend to use the American MEDIUM QUAHOGS, LITTLENECKS, STEAMERS or CHERRYSTONES on a fruits de mer or in a pasta dish. I think of them more as a delicacy to be served on their own. I love a bowl of steamers with just drawn butter and the cooking liquor.

large bivalves

I prefer to stuff larger mussels such as the NEW ZEALAND GREENLIP MUSSEL, with garlic breadcrumbs as for Moules Farcies on page 212. And I find that the larger the clam, the more the resistance to eating it whole. I persist in serving RAZOR CLAMS whole – with their fantastic-looking shells that look like an old cut-throat razor – but some people have an aversion to eating something that looks like it has come out of the film Alien. Razor clams have a wonderful sweet flavour, which is slightly peppery, I think.

Large clams such as QUAHOGS (known as CHOWDERS), SURF CLAMS and GEODUCKS are best taken out of the shells (see how, page 89), sliced and used in chowders and stir-fries.

scallops

At our restaurant, we use SMALL SCALLOPS (or QUEENS), or sometimes BAY SCALLOPS from North America, raw on the fruits de mer. Scallops are also great thinly sliced and served for sashimi, (see page 105), where their sweetness makes a delightful contrast to the oiliness of the sea trout and texture of the brill. One of our most successful dishes is grilled queenies with noisette butter (nut-brown butter) with lemon juice and parsley. You can't get much simpler than that, but I think it's the combination of nutty butter and the smell of hot shells (which I always think smell like hot beaches on a sunny day), that gets customers excited.

In America, it's customary to remove the coral of scallops, which is a bit of a shame – a bit like removing the yolk from eggs. Not only are they lovely to eat but they can also be used to thicken sauces, just like an egg yolk.

oysters

To me the perfect sized Oyster is what we in Britain call a number 3 – not too big and not too small, weighing about 90 g (3½ oz). There's a big price premium for the larger oysters (2s or 1s). In Europe we have 2 types of oyster, the NATIVE OYSTER, Ostrea edulis and the PACIFIC OYSTER, Crassostrea gigas. The Native Oyster is considered the best: the most famous and revered beds are Colchester, Whitstable and Helford in England; Galway and Cork in Ireland; Belon and Arachon in France; Ostend in Belgium; Zeeland in Holland; and Limfjord in Denmark.

PACIFIC OYSTERS are much cheaper because they grow faster. They are the variety favoured for farming and crop up everywhere – favourites of mine are from Loch Fyne in Scotland and Fowey in Cornwall. The PORTUGESE OYSTER, once considered a separate species, is now acknowledged to be the same as the Pacific. It just got to Portugal a bit earlier.

In the States the native eastern AMERICAN OYSTER, the Crassostrea virginica, is larger than the European oyster and ranges from New Brunswick in Canada right down to the Gulf of Mexico. Those from the colder northern waters are held to be the best – they grow more slowly and their shells are more uniform. The most famous beds for these are at Long Island where grow such evocatively named oysters as Blue Points, and Cape Cod where Wellfleet Oysters come from.

In Australia and New Zealand, there is the ubiquitous PACIFIC OYSTER and the SYDNEY

ROCK OYSTER, *Saccostrea glomerata*. The European native oyster has also been grown in South Australia and Victoria for over 100 years. In NW Australia you'll find pearl meat, a by-product of the pearl oyster fishery there. The adductor muscle of the PEARL LIP OYSTER, has a white, sweet and soft texture, much sought after by Perth restaurants.

univalves

Univalves are all those molluscs that live in one shell (unlike bivalves, which live in two shells).

There's the WINKLE or PERIWINKLE, which is held in much affection by serious seafood lovers. They don't have a great taste but picking out a bowl of winkles with your winkle picker and some shallot vinegar provides an enjoyable diversion along with a glass or two of Muscadet. WHELKS too are greatly enjoyed by some. I think the small ones have the best flavour. I like them boiled and served with a choice of mayonnaise or shallot vinegar or in the English fashion, with pepper, malt vinegar and a pint of beer. I've had success by breaking open the shells, removing the meats and stir-frying them or turning them into fritters. The MUREX is another tough, whelk-like sea snail from the Mediterranean. The attractive shell is much sought after and the TOP-SHELL, known as Bodolletti, is popular in Venice, where it is cooked in a fireproof dish with olive oil, bay leaves and salt for about 20 minutes.

LIMPETS are reasonable eating in the same way as abalone if slow-cooked. They must have been very popular in the long past, the house I lived in on Trevose Head seems to have been built on a midden of them. There's also a univalve called the SLIPPER LIMPET, which has become a bit of a pest in Britain. It came originally from America (probably on the keel of a ship), and has since invaded a number of oyster beds, where they smother the oysters in their fight for food. But they're actually good to eat when steamed with a bit of white wine, stuffed like snails with garlic butter, and briefly grilled.

Deal with CONCH, which are found in the waters off the Florida Keys and the Caribbean, in the same way I've described for whelks, either stir-frying them or using them in fritters.

abalone

By far the most sought after univalve is the ABALONE, (or PAUA as it's known in New Zealand, ORMER in the Channel Islands, and ORMEAU in France). But it is in the Pacific that the abalone are most prolific. There are three ways of dealing with the toughness of abalone. Slice it very thinly when raw and drop it into hot stock as the Chinese do. Bash it for a minute or so with a mallet and then fry it (for example, in

breadcrumbs) or slow-cook it with oil and aromatics in a low oven for 2–3 hours, (see page 207). It has a similar flavour and texture to cuttlefish or octopus. The BAILER SHELL from Australia and New Zealand, sought after for its ornamental shell, is now gaining in popularity for its meat as well, which is used in the same way as abalone.

small fry

Here I've grouped together those immature fish that are caught for cooking and eating whole, but I've also included a few tiny adult fish too.

whitebait

The general term for tiny frying fish in English is WHITEBAIT, which can actually be the fry of any number of species – although they tend to be those oily members of the herring family. In Tasmania and New Zealand they are normally tiny trout, while in the Indian Ocean a similar harvest of tiny fish is called INDIAN BAIT. In the West Indies they're PISQUETTES and on the French Mediterranean coast, NONNATS.

Deep-fried whitebait, freshly caught, served with a little cayenne pepper and lemon are one of the joys of fish cookery. Curiously the Americans haven't caught on to this delight yet. It's quite easy to get frozen whitebait but more often than not they seem to have an overpowering and unpleasant flavour, probably because they've been frozen for too long.

sprats, blennys, capelin, gobys, sand eels, silversides and sand smelts

These small fish are excellent either floured and deep-fried, made into fritters, or skewered, grilled and sprinkled with chopped herbs as for the recipe on page 160. SAND EELS in particular are good when floured and deep-fried. The larger ones though, known locally as LANCES, need gutting, weigh 50 g (2 oz) or more and are better cooked like sprats. It's a matter of taste whether you remove the guts in small fish, which is a laborious procedure with something like a sprat or anchovy, but there are instructions on how to do it on page 57 if you wish to. A lot will depend on the cleanliness of the water in which they were caught.

thin-bodied fish

Nothing in the naming of fish is perfect and a family containing a number of thin-bodied fish is clearly not a collection of related species, but rather a group selected by appearance and similar cooking qualities. Round fish have an eye on each side of their head, i.e. on each flank, while flat fish have both eyes on their top flank. The fish I've described here as flat round fish have very thin but deep

bodies. Their design is perfect for concealment, whether for predatory reasons or defence, since they become almost invisible when seen head on.

john dory

The fish that embodies this shape is the JOHN DORY, which is found both in the Atlantic and the Pacific, as far south as New Zealand. Some people refer to this lugubrious-looking, big-jawed fish as ugly, but I regard it as splendid with its expressive face, fierce eyes and astonishing array of long fins.

It's also a great fish to cook, having very firm dense white fillets with a good fresh flavour, ideal for pan-frying, grilling and char-grilling whole. It also takes a classic French cream sauce and we use it in a Mediterranean combination with olives, capers, tomato, rosemary and new potatoes. (See the recipe on page 168.)

pomfret

Perhaps even better known worldwide than the John Dory is the WHITE POMFRET, which is part of a small family of thin-bodied fish, which also includes RAY'S BREAM and BUTTERFISH. These are all very good eating. The pomfret is becoming increasingly popular in the UK. William Black, in the very good seafood book, *Fish* says, 'Supplies of pomfret from the Indian Ocean will almost certainly increase over the coming years, as it's deemed to be one of the under-exploited species, God help it!' Notwithstanding that, the fillets are close-textured and white and it's great stuffed with a masala paste, like that on page 226, and grilled. Ray's Bream is of a very fine quality too; the fish is tinged with pink and formed of long strands, rather like skate.

opah or moonfish

Finally, mention must be made of the OPAH or MOONFISH, a giant, thin-bodied fish which can reach 25 kg (55 lb). I bought some once in Woy Woy in Australia, took it back to where I was staying and pan-fried the fillets with a lick of olive oil. The flesh was pink and firm. I ate it slightly undercooked and I could have sworn I was eating scallops, it was that good. Opah, *Lampris guttatus*, can be found in both the Pacific and the Atlantic but should not be confused with the SUNFISH, which is sometimes also called moonfish, or MOLA MOLA. Sunfish is a thick-skinned, thin, gelatinous-fleshed fish found flopping around on the surface of the seas around Cornwall in the summer months and often gaffed by lobster fisherman and dragged aboard. It's of no culinary value and so much better left where it is, in the sea.

leatherjacket and trigger-fish

These two fish, the LEATHERJACKET from Australia and New Zealand and the TRIGGER-

FISH from the Atlantic, closely resemble the John Dory, They have thick, leather-like skins and sharp spines just behind the eyes. Both are sold as skinned fillets and have firm flesh like that of John Dory. Trigger-fish are quite rare in Britain, normally being caught in lobster pots, but I once picked up half a dozen flapping on the beach in Trevose where I live, flung ashore out of the surf during a winter storm.

usa catchall

Here are a few fish unique to the United States, which didn't fit into any other category.

There are nine types of GREENLING found along the Pacific coast of North America, the most popular of which is the LINGCOD, which can grow as large as 30 kg (65 lb). It is not related to the cod, unsurprisingly, but is a bottom-feeding fish usually caught by long line fishing, and produces good, tasty fillets.

There is also the TILEFISH, a member of a small family of fish on both the Atlantic and Pacific Oceans. The main Atlantic species is the BLACKLINE TILEFISH. In the Pacific these are just known as OCEAN WHITEFISH and are much sought after. They eat crabs and other crustacea and this is reflected in their flavour, which is something like lobster or scallop meat. The FLYING FISH is considered a delicacy in some parts of the world, especially in the West Indies and in Japan where their eggs are served in sashimi. They are also extremely nice just dusted with flour and deep-fried.

Finally, from South America, there's something of an ichthyophile's treasure, which somewhat resembles caviar in appearance but not in taste. The ICEFISH, called GUNNARI in French, is fished off Kerguelen Island in the deeply cold water south of Tierra del Fuego. This fish is often confused with the CHILEAN SEA BASS (Patagonian Toothfish), but is quite different from it as it has no haemoglobin, the component of blood that carries oxygen around the body. Instead, the fluid in its body is more like anti-freeze and the fish has few innards so it doesn't go off quickly. It has very firm, lean white flesh, with no bones, apart from a central spine, like a monkfish. According to those lucky enough to have tasted it, it is delicious. I've seen it on sale in France and it's very popular in Southern Argentina and Chile.

wrasse

Unfortunately the BALLAN WRASSE that swims off the coast of Great Britain, though of astonishingly beautiful hues of red, green and gold (and easy to catch from the rocks) is really rather tasteless. As always with fish such as this, it's good for fish soup or fish stews. However, across the world, there are much better flavoured members of this family, *Labridae*.

In the USA the TAUTOG, HOGFISH, CUNNER and CALIFORNIA SHEEPHEAD are much better eating, particularly the tautog, which has very firm white meat and is especially suitable for chowders and fish stews because it doesn't break up during cooking. The California sheephead feeds on lobster and abalone and therefore has a good flavour.

parrotfish, maori wrasse and pigfish

Closely related to the wrasse are the PARROTFISH of the Indian Ocean, which resemble the birds in both colour and shape. They appear to have a beak and their teeth are configured somewhat like a parrot's beak in order to crush coral from which they filter out the algae they eat. If you've ever been diving on a coral reef, the sound that fills your ears underwater might well be that of grazing parrotfish. They are extremely highly regarded with firm, white and delicate tasting fish. The parrotfish is also present in Australian waters, along with a number of other wrasse, in particular the MAORI WRASSE, much favoured by the Chinese for inclusion in the live fish tanks of their restaurants. Have you ever noticed the fish swim to the back of the tank as the chef approaches? There is also the PIGFISH, which has firm, white flaky flesh and is in great demand by the Asian community. Prices for Pigfish in Sydney are amongst the highest for any Australian fish.

identifying seafood

SHARKS AND RAYS

1 PORBEAGLE SHARK
Lamna nasus

2 DOGFISH
Scyliorhinus canicula

3 THORNBACK RAY
Raja clavata

ROEFISH

4 STURGEON HYBRID
Huso huso x Acipenser ruthenus

EELS AND EEL-LIKE FISH

5 FRESHWATER EEL
Anguilla anguilla

6 CONGER EEL
Conger conger

MONKFISH AND STARGAZERS

7 MONKFISH
Lophius piscatorius

8 ATLANTIC STARGAZER
Uranoscopus scaber

9 GREATER WEEVER
Trachinus draco

SMALL FRY

10 ATLANTIC SMELT
Osmerus eperlanus

11 ANCHOVY
Engraulis encrasicolus

12 WHITEBAIT
Clupea harengus

HERRING

13 PILCHARD AND SARDINE
Sardina pilchardus

14 HERRING
Clupea harengus

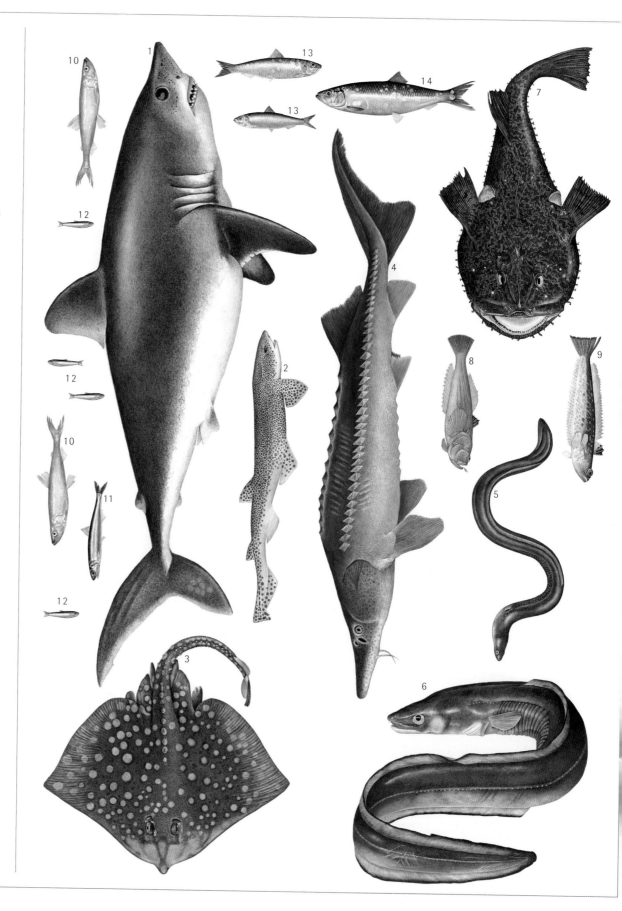

13

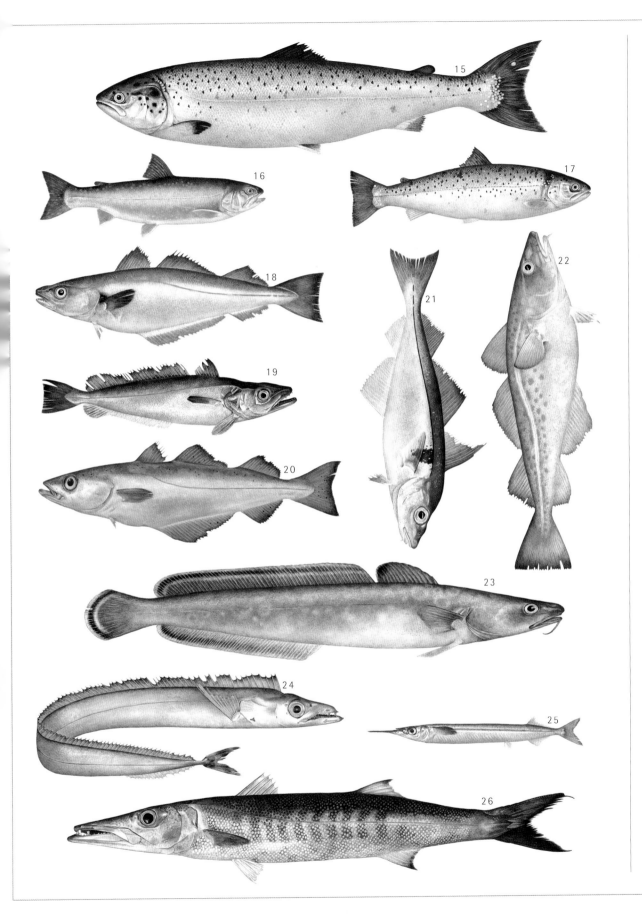

SALMON

15 ATLANTIC SALMON
Salmo salar

16 ARCTIC CHAR
Salvelinus alpinus

17 SEA TROUT
Salmo trutta

COD AND COD-LIKE FISH

18 WHITING
Merlangius merlangus

19 HAKE
Merluccius merluccius

20 POLLACK
Pollachius pollachius

21 HADDOCK
Melanogrammus aeglefinus

22 COD
Gadus morhua

23 LING
Molva molva

ELONGATED FISH

24 SILVER SCABBARD
Lepidopus caudatus

25 EASTERN SEA GARFISH
Hyporhamphus australis

26 EUROPEAN BARRACUDA
Sphyraena sphyraena

identifying seafood

BONY-CHEEKED/ SCORPION-LIKE FISH

1 REDFISH
Sebastes marinus

2 RED GURNARD
Aspitrigla cuculus

3 SAND FLATHEAD
Platycephalus bassensis

GROUPERS, SEA BASS AND BARRAMUNDI

4 STRIPED BASS
Morone saxatilis

5 SEA BASS
Dicentrarchus labrax

6 LEOPARD CORAL TROUT
Plectropomus leopardus

7 BARRAMUNDI
Lates calcarifer

JACKS, POMPANOS AND TREVALLYS

8 DOLPHIN FISH
Coryphaena hippurus

9 BLUEFISH
Pomatomus saltatrix

10 POMPANO
Trachinotus carolinus

SEA BREAM, PORGIES AND SNAPPERS

11 DENTEX
Dentex maroccanus

12 KEY WEST PORGY
Calamus nodosus

13 SHEEPSHEAD
Archosargus probatocephalus

14 GILT-HEAD BREAM
Sparus aurata

15 RED EMPEROR
Lutjanus sebae

16 SILK SNAPPER
Lutjanus vivanus

DRUMS

17 GREY WEAKFISH
Cynoscion regalis

18 MULLOWAY
Argyrosomus hololepidotus

MULLETS

19 RED MULLET
Mullus surmuletus

20 THICK-LIPPED GREY MULLET
Chelon labrosus

WRASSE

21 PARROTFISH
Scarus ghobban

identifying seafood

SEA CATFISH

1 WOLF FISH
Anarhichas lupus

DEEP-SEA FISH

2 ORANGE ROUGHY
Hoplostethus atlanticus

PUFFERS

3 NORTHERN PUFFER
Spheroides maculatus

MACKEREL AND TUNA

4 NARROW-BARRED SPANISH MACKEREL
Scomberomorus commerson

5 SPANISH MACKEREL
Scomberomorus maculatus

6 MACKEREL
Scomber scombrus

7 ATLANTIC BONITO
Sarda sarda

8 BLUEFIN TUNA
Thunnus thynnus

BILLFISH

9 SWORDFISH
Xiphias gladius

OZ CATCHALL

10 BLUE-EYE COD
Hyperoglyphe antarctica

11 SAND WHITING
Sillago ciliata

USA CATCHALL

12 TILEFISH
Lopholatilus chamaeleonticeps

13

THIN-BODIED FISH

13 JOHN DORY
Zeus faber

14 WHITE POMFRET
Pampus argenteus

15 VELVET LEATHERJACKET
Parika scaber

FLAT FISH

16 LEMON SOLE
Microstomus kitt

17 TURBOT
Psetta maxima

18 PLAICE
Pleuronectes platessa

19 HALIBUT
Hippoglossus hippoglossus

20a DAB (UNDERSIDE)
20b and 20c DAB (TOP)
Limanda limanda

21 STARRY FLOUNDER
Platichthys stellatus

22 DOVER SOLE
Solea solea

23 BRILL
Scophthalmus rhombus

CRUSTACEANS

1 LOBSTER
Homarus gammarus

2 SQUAT LOBSTER
Galathea squamifera

**3 SPINY ATLANTIC
LOBSTER**
Palinurus elephas

4 DUBLIN BAY PRAWN
Nephrops norvegicus

5 MORETON BAY BUG
Thenus orientalis

6 DEEP-WATER PRAWNS
Pandalus borealis

**7 BLACK TIGER PRAWN,
UNCOOKED AND COOKED**
Penaeus monodon

**8 BROWN SHRIMPS,
COOKED AND UNCOOKED**
Crangon crangon

9 BLUE CRAB
Callinectes sapidus

10 VELVET CRAB
Liocarcinus puber

11 BLUE SWIMMER CRAB
Portunus pelagicus

12 MUD CRAB
Scylla serrata

13 SPIDER CRAB
Maia squinado

14 BROWN CRAB
Cancer pagurus

OPPOSITE PAGE

SHELLFISH (BIVALVES)

15 STEAMER CLAM
Mya arenaria

16 POD RAZOR
Ensis siliqua

17 PIPI
Donax deltoides

**18 VENUS WARTY, OPEN
AND CLOSED**
Venus verrucosa

**19 SMOOTH VENUS,
CLOSED AND OPEN**
Callista chione

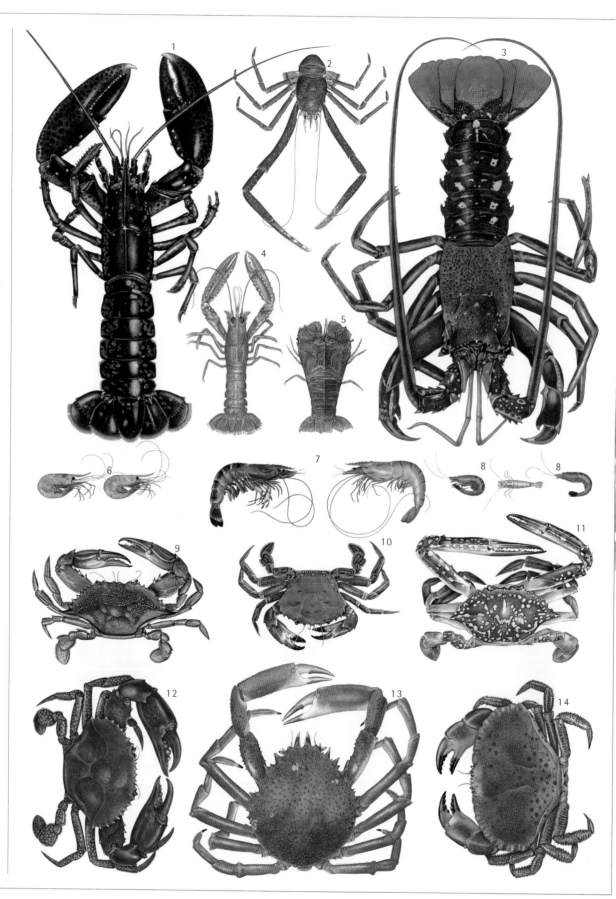

20a BLUE MUSSEL, OPEN
20b BLUE MUSSEL, CLOSED
Mytilus edulis

21 EUROPEAN OR NATIVE
OYSTER
Ostrea edulis

22 COCKLE, CLOSED AND
OPEN
Cerastoderma edule

23 CARPETSHELL CLAM,
OPEN AND CLOSED
Venerupis decussata

24a GREAT SCALLOP, CLOSED
24b GREAT SCALLOP, OPEN
Pecten maximus

25 CHERRYSTONE CLAM
Mercenaria mercenaria

26 LITTLE NECK CLAM,
OPEN AND CLOSED
Mercenaria mercenaria

27 QUAHOG CLAM
Mercenaria mercenaria

28a PACIFIC OYSTER, CLOSED
28b PACIFIC OYSTER, OPEN
Crassostrea gigas

SHELLFISH (UNIVALVES)

29 WHELK
Buccinum undatum

30 WINKLE
Littorina littorea

31 ORMER
Haliotis tuberculata

CEPHALOPODS

32 OCTOPUS
Octopus vulgaris

33 SQUID
Loligo forbesi

34 CUTTLEFISH
Sepia officinalis

SEA CREATURES

35 GREEN SEA URCHIN
Strongylocentrotus droebachiensis

36 RED SEA URCHIN,
OPEN AND CLOSED
Paracentrotus lividus

37 GOOSE-NECKED
BARNACLES
Pollicipes cornucopia

38 SEA CUCUMBERS
Holothuria scabra

classifying seafood

COMMON NAME	REGION	LATIN NAME	A–Z FAMILY	LATIN FAMILY
Abalone, Atlantic	Eur	Haliotis tuberculata	Shellfish (Univalves)	Haliotidae
Abalone, Green Lip	Anz	Haliotis laevigata	Shellfish (Univalves)	Haliotidae
Albacore, False	USA Atl	Euthynnus alletteratus	Mackerel & Tuna	Scombridae
Alewife	USA Atl	Alosa pseudoharengus	Herring	Clupeidae
Alfonsino	Anz	Beryx splendens	Deep-sea Fish	Berycidae
Amande	Eur	Glycymeris glycemeris	Shellfish (Bivalves)	Glycymeridae
Amberjack, Greater	Eur/USA Atl	Seriola dumerili	Jacks, Pompanos & Trevallys	Carangidae
Amberjack, Lesser	USA Atl	Seriola fasciata	Jacks, Pompanos & Trevallys	Carangidae
Amberjack, Pacific	USA Pac	Seriola colburni	Jacks, Pompanos & Trevallys	Carangidae
Anchovy, Australian	Anz	Engraulis australis	Small Fry	Engraulidae
Anchovy, European	Eur	Engraulis encrasicolus	Small Fry	Engraulidae
Anchovy, North American	USA Atl	Anchoa hepsetus	Small Fry	Engraulidae
Angler Fish	Eur	Lophius piscatorius	Monkfish & Stargazers	Lophiidae
Argentine	Eur/USA Atl	Argentina silus	Salmon	Argentinidae
Bailer Shell	Anz	Livonia mamilla	Shellfish (Univalves)	Volutidae
Baloonfish	Anz	Contusus richei	Puffer Fish	Tetraodontidae
Barnacle, Goose-Necked	Eur	Pollicipes cornucopia	Sea Creature	Pollicipidae
Barracouta	Anz	Thyrsites atun	Elongated fish	Gempylidae
Barracuda, European	Eur	Sphyraena sphyraena	Elongated fish	Sphyraenidae
Barracuda, Great	USA/Anz	Sphyraena barracuda	Elongated Fish	Sphyraenidae
Barracuda, Pacific	USA Pac	Sphyraena argentea	Elongated Fish	Sphyraenidae
Barracuda, Slender	Anz	Sphyraena jello	Elongated Fish	Sphyraenidae
Barracuda, Yellowtail	USA Atl	Sphyraena flavicauda	Elongated Fish	Sphyraenidae
Barramundi	Anz	Lates calcarifer	Groupers, Sea Bass & Barramundi	Centropomidae
Bass, Antarctic Sea	Anz	Dissostichus eleginoides	Deep-sea Fish	Nototheniidae
Bass, Black Sea	USA Atl	Centropristes striatus	Groupers, Sea Bass & Barramundi	Serranidae
Bass, Channel	USA Atl	Sciaenops ocellatus	Drums	Sciaenidae
Bass, Chilean Sea	Anz	Dissostichus eleginoides	Deep-sea Fish	Nototheniidae
Bass, European Sea	Eur	Dicentrarchus labrax	Groupers, Sea Bass & Barramundi	Serranidae
Bass, Kelp	USA Pac	Paralabrax clathratus	Groupers, Sea Bass & Barramundi	Serranidae
Bass, Rock	USA Pac	Paralabrax clathratus	Sea Bream, Porgies & Snappers	Sparidae
Bass, Spotted Sea	Eur	Dicentrarchus punctatus	Groupers, Sea Bass & Barramundi	Serranidae
Bass, Stone	Eur/USA Atl	Polyprion americanus	Groupers, Sea Bass & Barramundi	Serranidae
Bass, Striped	USA Atl	Morone saxatilis	Groupers, Sea Bass & Barramundi	Serranidae
Bergall	USA Atl	Tautogolabrus adspersus	Wrasse	Labridae
Biddy, Silver	Anz	Gerres subfasciatus	Small Fry	Gerridae
Blackback	USA Atl	Pseudopleuronectes americanus	Flatfish	Pleuronectidae
Blackfish	USA Atl	Tautoga onitis	Wrasse	Labridae
Blenny	Eur	Blennius gattorugine	Small Fry	Blenniidae
Blowfish	USA Atl	Spheroides maculatus	Puffer Fish	Tetraodontidae
Blue-Eye	Anz	Hyperoglyphe antarctica	Australian Catchall	Centrolophidae
Blue-Mouth	Eur	Helicolenus dactylopterus	Bony-Cheeked Fish	Scorpaenidae
Blue-nose	Anz	Sillago ciliata	Australian Catchall	Sillaginidae
Bluefish	USA Atl/Anz	Pomatomus saltatrix	Jacks, Pompanos & Trevallys	Pomatomidae
Bogue	Eur	Boops boops	Sea Bream, Porgies & Snappers	Sparidae
Bonefish	USA Atl	Albula vulpes	Herring	Albulidae
Bonito, Arctic	USA Pac	Euthynnus pelamis	Mackerel & Tuna	Scombridae
Bonito, Atlantic	Eur	Sarda sarda	Mackerel & Tuna	Scombridae
Bonito, Australian	Anz	Sarda australis	Mackerel & Tuna	Scombridae
Bonito, Black	USA Atl/Anz	Sarda sarda	Jacks, Pompanos & Trevallys	Scombridae
Bonito, Oceanic	USA Pac	Euthynnus pelamis	Mackerel & Tuna	Scombridae
Bonito, Pacific	USA Pac	Sarda chiliensis	Mackerel & Tuna	Scombridae
Bonito, Striped	USA Pac	Euthynnus pelamis	Mackerel & Tuna	Scombridae
Bourgeois	Anz	Lutjanus sebae	Sea Bream, Porgies & Snappers	Lutjanidae
Bream, Annular	Eur	Diplodus annularis	Sea Bream, Porgies & Snappers	Sparidae
Bream, Black	Anz	Acanthopagrus butcheri	Sea Bream, Porgies & Snappers	Sparidae
Bream, Black Sea	Eur	Spondyliosoma cantharus	Sea Bream, Porgies & Snappers	Sparidae
Bream, Bronze	Eur	Pagellus acarne	Sea Bream, Porgies & Snappers	Sparidae
Bream, European Sea	Eur	Pagrus pagrus	Sea Bream, Porgies & Snappers	Sparidae
Bream, Frypan	Anz	Argyrops spinifer	Sea Bream, Porgies & Snappers	Sparidae
Bream, Gilt-Head	Eur	Sparus aurata	Sea Bream, Porgies & Snappers	Sparidae
Bream, Grunter	Anz	Pomadasys kaakan	Sea Bream, Porgies & Snappers	Sparidae
Bream, Pikey	Anz	Acanthopagrus berda	Sea Bream, Porgies & Snappers	Sparidae
Bream, Ray's	Eur/Anz	Brama brama	Sea Bream, Porgies & Snappers	Sparidae
Bream, Red	Eur	Beryx decadactylus	Sea Bream, Porgies & Snappers	Sparidae
Bream, Red	Eur	Pagellus bogaraveo	Sea Bream, Porgies & Snappers	Sparidae
Bream, Red Sea	Eur	Pagellus centrodontus	Sea Bream, Porgies & Snappers	Sparidae
Bream, Royal	Eur	Sparus aurata	Sea Bream, Porgies & Snappers	Sparidae
Bream, Saddled	Eur	Oblada melanura	Sea Bream, Porgies & Snappers	Sparidae
Bream, Sea (UK)	Eur	Pagrus pagrus	Sea Bream, Porgies & Snappers	Sparidae
Bream, Sheepshead	Eur	Puntazzo puntazzo	Sea Bream, Porgies & Snappers	Sparidae
Bream, Spanish	Eur	Pagellus acarne	Sea Bream, Porgies & Snappers	Sparidae
Bream, Striped	Eur	Lithognathus mormyrus	Sea Bream, Porgies & Snappers	Sparidae
Bream, Sweetlip	Anz	Diagramma labiosum	Sea Bream, Porgies & Snappers	Haemulidae
Bream, Threadfin	Anz	Nemipterus furcosus	Sea Bream, Porgies & Snappers	Nemipteridae
Bream, Two-Banded	Eur	Diplodus vulgaris	Sea Bream, Porgies & Snappers	Sparidae
Bream, White	Eur	Diplodus sargus	Sea Bream, Porgies & Snappers	Sparidae
Bream, Yellowfin	Anz	Acanthopagrus australis	Sea Bream, Porgies & Snappers	Sparidae
Brill	Eur	Scopthalmus rhombus	Flatfish	Bothidae
Bug, Balmain	Anz	Ibacus peronii	Crustacean	Scyllaridae
Bug, Moreton Bay	Anz	Thenus orientalis	Crustacean	Scyllaridae
Butterfish	Anz	Scatophagus multifasciatus	Thin-bodied fish	Scatophagidae
Butterfish	USA Atl	Peprilus triacanthus	Thin-bodied fish	Stromateidae
Butterfish	Anz	Coridodax pullus	Thin-bodied fish	Odacidae
Cabezon	USA Pac	Scorpaenichtys marmoratus	Bony-Cheeked Fish	Scorpaenidae
Cabio	USA Atl/Anz	Rachycentron canadum	Jacks, Pompanos & Trevallys	Rachycentridae
Cabrilla, Spotted	USA Pac	Epinephelus analogus	Groupers, Sea Bass & Barramundi	Serranidae
Calamari, Northern	Anz	Sepioteuthis lessoniana	Cephalapods	Loliginidae
Calamari, Southern	Anz	Sepioteuthis australis	Cephalapods	Loliginidae
Candlefish	USA Pac	Thaleichthys Pacificus	Small Fry	Osmeridae
Capelin	Eur	Mallotus villosus	Small Fry	Osmeridae
Capitaine	Anz	Lethrinus nebulosus	Sea Bream, Porgies & Snappers	Lethrinidae
Cardinal Fish	Anz	Epigonus telescopus	Australian Catchall	Apogonidae
Carrageen Moss	Eur/USA Atl	Chrondrus crispus	Seaweed	Rhodophyceae
Catfish, Australian	Anz	Arius thalassinus	Sea Catfish	Arriidae
Catfish, Gafftopsail	USA Atl	Bagre marinus	Sea Catfish	Ariidae
Catfish, Hardhead	USA Atl	Arius felis	Sea Catfish	Arridae
Catfish, Ocean	Eur/USA Atl	Anarhichas lupus	Sea Catfish	Anarhichadidae
Catfish, Sea	USA Atl	Galeichthys felis	Sea Catfish	Arridae
Cavalla	USA Atl	Scomberomorus cavalla	Mackerel & Tuna	Scombridae
Cero	USA Atl	Scomberomorus regalis	Mackerel & Tuna	Scombridae
Char, Arctic	Eur & N. USA	Salvelinus alpinus	Salmon	Salmonidae
Char	Eur	Salvelinus alpinus	Salmon	Salmonidae
Clabbydoo/Clappydoo	Eur/USA Atl	Modiolus modiolus	Shellfish (Bivalves)	Mytilidae
Clam, Bar	USA Atl	Spisula solidissima	Shellfish (Bivalves)	Mactridae
Clam, Butter	USA Atl	Saxidomus giganteus	Shellfish (Bivalves)	Veneridae
Clam, Carpetshell	Eur	Venerupis decussata	Shellfish (Bivalves)	Veneridae
Clam, Cherrystone	USA Atl	Mercenaria mercenaria	Shellfish (Bivalves)	Veneridae
Clam, Clovisse	Eur	Venerupis decussata	Shellfish (Bivalves)	Veneridae
Clam, Coquina	Eur	Donax vitttatus	Shellfish (Bivalves)	Donacidae
Clam, Eastern Razor	USA Atl	Ensis directus	Shellfish (Bivalves)	Solenidae
Clam, Gaper	USA Atl	Mya arenaria	Shellfish (Bivalves)	Myacidae
Clam, Geoduck	USA Pac	Panope geodosa	Shellfish (Bivalves)	Hiatellidae
Clam, Giant Callista	USA Atl	Macrocallista nimbosa	Shellfish (Bivalves)	Veneridae
Clam, Hard	USA Atl	Mercenaria mercenaria	Shellfish (Bivalves)	Veneridae
Clam, Hardshell	USA Atl	Mercenaria mercenaria	Shellfish (Bivalves)	Veneridae
Clam, Hen	USA Atl	Spisula solidissima	Shellfish (Bivalves)	Mactridae
Clam, Little Neck	USA Atl	Mercenaria mercenaria	Shellfish (Bivalves)	Veneridae
Clam, Littleneck	USA Atl	Protothaca stamina	Shellfish (Bivalves)	Veneridae
Clam, Longneck	USA Atl	Mya arenaria	Shellfish (Bivalves)	Myacidae
Clam, Palourde	Eur	Venerupis decussata	Shellfish (Bivalves)	Veneridae
Clam, Praire	Eur	Venus vericosa	Shellfish (Bivalves)	Veneridae
Clam, Quahog	USA Atl	Mercenaria mercenaria	Shellfish (Bivalves)	Veneridae
Clam, Razor	Eur	Ensis ensis	Shellfish (Bivalves)	Solenidae
Clam, Skimmer	USA Atl	Spisula solidissima	Shellfish (Bivalves)	Mactridae
Clam, Smooth Venus	Eur	Callista chione	Shellfish (Bivalves)	Veneridae
Clam, Softshell	USA Atl	Mya arenaria	Shellfish (Bivalves)	Myacidae
Clam, Steamer	USA Atl	Mya arenaria	Shellfish (Bivalves)	Myacidae
Clam, Sunray	USA Atl	Macrocallista nimbosa	Shellfish (Bivalves)	Veneridae
Clam, Sunray Venus	USA Atl	Macrocallista nimbosa	Shellfish (Bivalves)	Veneridae
Clam, Surf	USA Atl	Spisula solidissima	Shellfish (Bivalves)	Mactridae
Clam, Surf	Anz	Dosinia caerulea	Shellfish (Bivalves)	Veneridae
Clam, Thin Tellin	Eur	Tellina tenuis	Shellfish (Bivalves)	Scrobiculariidae
Clam, Verni	Eur	Callista chione	Shellfish (Bivalves)	Veneridae
Clam, Vongole	Eur	Venerupis decussata	Shellfish (Bivalves)	Veneridae
Clam, Warty Venus	Eur	Venus verrucosa	Shellfish (Bivalves)	Veneridae
Clam, Wedge Shell	Eur	Donax vitttatus	Shellfish (Bivalves)	Donacidae
Coalfish	Eur	Pollachius virens	Cod & Cod-like	Gadidae
Cobbler	Anz	Cnidoglanis macrocephalus	Sea Catfish	Plotosidae
Cobia	USA Atl/Anz	Rachycentron canadum	Jacks, Pompanos & Trevallys	Rachycentridae
Cockle, Australian	Anz	Katelysia scalarina	Shellfish (Bivalves)	Veneridae
Cockle, Dog	Eur	Glycymeris glycemeris	Shellfish (Bivalves)	Glycymeridae
Cockle, European	Eur	Cerastoderma edule	Shellfish (Bivalves)	Cardiidae
Cockle, Heart	Eur	Glossus humanus	Shellfish (Bivalves)	Glossidae
Cockle, Spiny	Eur	Acanthocardia aculeata	Shellfish (Bivalves)	Cardiidae
Cod, Atlantic	Eur	Gadus morhua	Cod & Cod-like	Gadidae
Cod, Barramundi	Anz	Cromileptes altivelis	Groupers, Sea Bass & Barramundi	Serranidae
Cod, Black	Eur	Pollachius virens	Cod & Cod-like	Gadidae
Cod, Black	USA Atl	Anopoploma fimbria	Thin-bodied fish	Anopoplomatidae
Cod, Blue-Eye	Anz	Hyperoglyphe antarctica	Australian Catchall	Centrolophidae
Cod, Coral	Anz	Cephalopholis cyanostigma	Groupers, Sea Bass & Barramundi	Serranidae
Cod, Deep Sea	Anz	Mora moro	Deep-sea Fish	Moridae

COMMON NAME	REGION	LATIN NAME	A-Z FAMILY	LATIN FAMILY
Cod, Pacific	USA Pac	Gadus macrocephalus	Cod & Cod-like	Gadidae
Cod, Southern Rock	Anz	Pseudophycis bachus	Cod & Cod-like	Ophidiidae
Coley	Eur	Pollachius virens	Cod & Cod-like	Gadidae
Conch	USA Pac	Strombus gigas	Shellfish (Univalves)	Strombidae
Coney	USA Atl	Cephalopholis fulva	Groupers, Sea Bass & Barramundi	Serranidae
Coquille Saint-Jacques	Eur	Pecten maximus	Shellfish (Bivalves)	Pectinidae
Coral Hind	Anz	Cephalopholis miniata	Groupers, Sea Bass & Barramundi	Serranidae
Corvina, Californian	USA Pac	Menticirrhus undulatas	Drums	Sciaenidae
Crab, Alaskan King	USA Pac	Paralithodes camtschatica	Crustacean	Lithodidae
Crab, Blue	USA Atl	Callinectes sapidus	Crustacean	Portunidae
Crab, Blue Swimmer	Anz	Portunus pelagicus	Crustacean	Portunidae
Crab, Brown	Eur	Cancer pagurus	Crustacean	Cancridae
Crab, Coral	Anz	Charybdis feriata	Crustacean	Portunidae
Crab, Dungeness	USA Pac	Cancer magister	Crustacean	Cancridae
Crab, Frog	Anz	Ranina ranina	Crustacean	Raninidae
Crab, Giant Tasmanian	Anz	Pseudocarcinus gigas	Crustacean	Portunidae
Crab, Green	Eur	Carcinus maenas	Crustacean	Portunidae
Crab, Horseshoe	USA Atl	Limulus polyphemus	Crustacean	Limulidae
Crab, Jonah	USA Atl	Cancer borealis	Crustacean	Cancridae
Crab, Lady	Eur	Ovalipes ocellatus	Crustacean	Portunidae
Crab, Mangrove	Anz	Scylla serrata	Crustacean	Portunidae
Crab, Mud	Anz	Scylla serrata	Crustacean	Portunidae
Crab, Oyster	Eur	Pinnotheres ostreum	Crustacean	Pinnotheridae
Crab, Pea	Eur	Pinnotheres ostreum	Crustacean	Pinnotheridae
Crab, Queen	USA Atl	Chionocoetes opilio	Crustacean	Majidae
Crab, Red	USA Atl	Geryon quinquedens	Crustacean	Geryyonidae
Crab, Rock	USA Atl	Cancer irroratus	Crustacean	Cancridae
Crab, Sand	Anz	Ovalipes australiensis	Crustacean	Portunidae
Crab, Shore	Eur	Carcinus maenas	Crustacean	Portunidae
Crab, Snow	USA Atl	Chionocoetes opilio	Crustacean	Majidae
Crab, Spanner	Anz	Ranina ranina	Crustacean	Raninidae
Crab, Spider	Eur & USA Atl	Maia squinado	Crustacean	Majidae
Crab, Stone	USA Atl	Menippe mercenaria	Crustacean	Xanthidae
Crab, Tanner	USA Atl	Chionocoetes opilio	Crustacean	Majidae
Crab, Tasmanian King	Anz	Pseodocarcinus gigas	Crustacean	Portunidae
Crab, Velvet	Eur	Liocarcinus puber	Crustacean	Portunidae
Crabeater	USA Atl/Anz	Rachycentron canadum	Jacks, Pompanos & Trevallys	Rachycentridae
Crawfish	Eur/USA Atl	Palinurus argus	Crustacean	Palinuridae
Crayfish, Seawater	Eur/USA Atl	Palinurus argus	Crustacean	Palinuridae
Creamfish	Anz	Parika scaber	Thin-bodied fish	Balistidae
Crevette Royale	Eur	Aristeus antennatus	Crustacean	Penaeidae
Crevette, Mediterranean	Eur	Penaeus kerathurus	Crustacean	Penaeidae
Crevette, Mediterranean	Eur	Parapenaeus longirostris	Crustacean	Penaeidae
Croaker, Atlantic	USA Atl	Micropogon undulatus	Drums	Sciaenidae
Croaker, White	USA Pac	Genyonemus lineatus	Drums	Sciaenidae
Croaker, Yellowfin	USA Pac	Umbrina roncador	Drums	Sciaenidae
Cunner	USA Atl	Tautogolabrus adspersus	Wrasse	Labridae
Cusk	USA Atl	Brosme brosme	Cod & Cod-like	Gadidae
Cutlass Fish	Eur	Aphanopus carbo	Elongated Fish	Trichiuridae
Cuttlefish	Eur	Sepia officinalis	Cephalapods	Sepiidae
Cuttlefish	Anz	Sepia rex	Cephalapods	Sepiidae
Cuttlefish	Anz	Sepia apama	Cephalapods	Sepiidae
Cuttlefish, Little	Eur	Sepiola rondeleti	Cephalapods	Sepiidae
Cuttlefish, Little	Eur	Sepiola rondeletti	Cephalapods	Sepiidae
Dab	Eur	Limanda limanda	Flat fish	Bothidae
Dab, Long Rough	USA Atl	Hippoglossoides platessoides	Flat fish	Pleuronectidae
Dab, Sand	USA Atl	Hippoglossoides platessoides	Flat fish	Pleuronectidae
Dab, Yellowtail	USA Atl	Limanda ferruginea	Flat fish	Pleuronectidae
Dart	Anz	Trachinotus botla	Jacks, Pompanos & Trevallys	Carangidae
Daurade Royale	Eur	Sparus auratus	Sea Bream, Porgies & Snappers	Sparidae
Dentex	Eur	Dentex maroccanus	Sea Bream, Porgies & Snappers	Sparidae
Dentex	Eur	Dentex dentex	Sea Bream, Porgies & Snappers	Sparidae
Dhufish	Anz	Glaucosoma hebraicum	Sea Perch	Glaucosomatidae
Dogfish	Eur	Scyliorhinus canicula	Sharks & Rays	Scyliorhinidae
Dogfish, Endeavour	Anz	Centrophorus harrissoni	Sharks & Rays	Squalidae
Dogfish, Greeneye	Anz	Squalus megalops	Sharks & Rays	Squalidae
Dogfish, Lesser-Spotted	Eur	Scyliorhinus canicula	Sharks & Rays	Scyliorhinidae
Dogfish, Spikey	Anz	Squalus megalops	Sharks & Rays	Squalidae
Dogfish, White-Spotted	Anz	Squalus acanthias	Sharks & Rays	Squalidae
Dolphin Fish	Eur/USA Atl/Anz	Coryphaena hippurus	Jacks, Pompanos & Trevallys	Coryphaenidae
Dorado	Eur/USA Atl/Anz	Coryphaena hippurus	Jacks, Pompanos & Trevallys	Coryphaenidae
Drum, Banded	USA Atl	Larimus fasciatus	Drums	Sciaenidae
Drum, Black	USA Atl	Pogonias cromis	Drums	Sciaenidae
Drum, Red	USA Atl	Sciaenops ocellatus	Drums	Sciaenidae
Dulse	Eur/USA Atl	Palmaria palmata	Seaweed	Rhodophyceae
Eel, American	USA Atl	Anguilla rostrata	Eel & Eel-like	Anguillidae
Eel, Australian Conger	Anz	Conger verreauxi	Eel & Eel-like	Congridae
Eel, Californian Moray	USA Pac	Gymnothorax mordax	Eel & Eel-like	Muraenidae
Eel, Conger	Eur	Conger conger	Eel & Eel-like	Congridae
Eel, Conger	USA Atl	Conger oceanicus	Eel & Eel-like	Congridae
Eel, European	Eur	Anguilla anguilla	Eel & Eel-like	Anguillidae
Eel, Freshwater	Eur	Anguilla anguilla	Eel & Eel-like	Anguillidae
Eel, Longfin	Anz	Anguilla reinhardtii	Eel & Eel-like	Anguillidae
Eel, Monkeyface	USA Pac	Cebidichthys violaceus	Elongated fish	Stichaeidae
Eel, Moray	Eur	Muraena helena	Eel & Eel-like	Muraenidae
Eel, Rock	USA Pac	Xiphister mucosus	Elongated fish	Stichaeidae
Eel, Shortfin	Anz	Anguilla australis	Eel & Eel-like	Anguillidae
Elephant Fish	Anz	Callorhincus milii	Sharks & Rays	Callorhinchidae
Emperor, Blue	Anz	Lethrinus nebulosus	Sea Bream, Porgies & Snappers	Lethrinidae
Emperor, Longtail	Anz	Lethrinus olivaceus	Sea Bream, Porgies & Snappers	Lethrinidae
Emperor, Red	Anz	Lutjanus sebae	Sea Bream, Porgies & Snappers	Lutjanidae
Emperor, Redspot	Anz	Lethrinus lentjan	Sea Bream, Porgies & Snappers	Lethrinidae
Emperor, Redthroat	Anz	Lethrinus miniatus	Sea Bream, Porgies & Snappers	Lethrinidae
Emperor, Sky	Anz	Lethrinus mahsena	Sea Bream, Porgies & Snappers	Lethrinidae
Emperor, Snubnose	Anz	Lethrinus borbonicus	Sea Bream, Porgies & Snappers	Lethrinidae
Emperor, Spangled	Anz	Lethrinus nebulosus	Sea Bream, Porgies & Snappers	Lethrinidae
Emperor, Yellowtail	Anz	Lethrinus mahsena	Sea Bream, Porgies & Snappers	Lethrinidae
Escolar	Anz	Lepidocybium flavobrunneum	Elongated fish	Gempylidae
Espada	Eur/USA Atl	Lepidopus caudatus	Elongated Fish	Trichiuridae
Eulachon	USA Pac	Thaleichthys Pacificus	Small Fry	Osmeridae
Flake	Anz	Galeorhinus galeus	Sharks & Rays	Carcharhinidae
Flathead	Anz	Platycephalus longispinis	Bony-Cheeked Fish	Platycephalidae
Flathead, Deepwater	Anz	Platycephalus conatus	Bony-Cheeked Fish	Platycephalidae
Flathead, Dusky	Anz	Platycephalus fuscus	Bony-Cheeked Fish	Platycephalidae
Flathead, Rock	Anz	Platycephalus laevigatus	Bony-Cheeked Fish	Platycephalidae
Flathead, Sand	Anz	Platycephalus bassensis	Bony-Cheeked Fish	Platycephalidae
Flathead, Southern	Anz	Platycephalus speculator	Bony-Cheeked Fish	Platycephalidae
Flathead, Tiger	Anz	Neoplatycephalus richardsoni	Bony-Cheeked Fish	Platycephalidae
Flounder	Anz	Pseudorhombus spinosus	Flat fish	Pleuronectidae
Flounder	Eur	Platichthys flesus	Flat fish	Pleuronectidae
Flounder, Bay	Anz	Ammotretis rostratus	Flat fish	Pleuronectidae
Flounder, Greenback	Anz	Rhombosolea tapirina	Flat fish	Pleuronectidae
Flounder, Pacific	USA Pac	Microstomus Pacificus	Flat fish	Pleuronectidae
Flounder, Rusty	USA Atl	Limanda ferruginea	Flat fish	Pleuronectidae
Flounder, Southern	USA Atl	Paralichthys lethostigmus	Flat fish	Bothidae
Flounder, Starry	USA Pac	Platichthys stellatus	Flat fish	Pleuronectidae
Flounder, Summer	USA Atl	Paralichthys dentatus	Flat fish	Bothidae
Flounder, Winter	USA Atl	Pseudopleuronectes americanus	Flat fish	Pleuronectidae
Fluke	Eur	Platichthys flesus	Flat fish	Pleuronectidae
Fluke, Northern	USA Atl	Paralichthys dentatus	Flat fish	Bothidae
Flying fish	USA Atl	Exocoetus volitans	USA Catchall	Exocetidae
Forkbeard	Eur	Phycis blennoides	Cod & Cod-like	Gadidae
Frostfish, Southern	Anz	Lepidopus caudatus	Elongated fish	Trichiuridae
Fugu Fish	Anz	Takifugu rubripes	Puffer Fish	Tetraodontidae
Fugu Fish	Anz	Takifugu porphyreus	Puffer Fish	Tetraodontidae
Garfish	Eur	Belone belone	Elongated Fish	Belonidae
Garfish, Eastern Sea	Anz	Hyporhamphus australis	Elongated fish	Hemiramphidae
Garfish, River	Anz	Hyporhamphus regularis	Elongated fish	Hemiramphidae
Garfish, Shortnosed	Anz	Hyporhamphus quoyi	Elongated Fish	Hemiramphidae
Garfish, Snubnose	Anz	Arrhamphus sclerolepis	Elongated Fish	Hemiramphidae
Garfish, Southern	Anz	Hyporhamphus melanochir	Elongated fish	Hemiramphidae
Garfish, Tropical	Anz	Hyporhamphus affinis	Elongated fish	Hemiramphidae
Gemfish	Anz	Rexea solandri	Elongated fish	Gempylidae
Globefish	USA Atl	Spheroides maculatus	Puffer Fish	Tetraodontidae
Goatfish	USA Atl	Mullus auratus	Mullets	Mullidae
Goatfish, Goldband	Anz	Upeneus moluccensis	Mullets	Mullidae
Goatfish, Indian	Anz	Parupeneus indicus	Mullets	Mullidae
Goatfish, Yellowspot	Anz	Parupeneus indicus	Mullets	Mullidae
Goby	Eur	Gobius niger	Small Fry	Gobiidae
Goosefish	USA Atl	Lophius americanus	Monkfish & Stargazers	Lophiidae
Greenbone	Anz	Coridodax pullus	Thin-bodied fish	Odacidae
Grenadier	Eur/USA Atl	Macrourus berglax	Deep-sea Fish	Macrouridae
Grenadier, Blue	Anz	Macruronus novaezelandiae	Deep-sea Fish	Macrouridae
Grenadier, Roughhead	Eur/USA Atl	Macrourus berglax	Deep-sea Fish	Macrouridae
Grenadier, Roundnose	Eur/ Usa Atl	Coryphaenoides rupestris	Deep-sea Fish	Macrouridae
Groper, Baldchin	Anz	Choerodon rubescens	Wrasse	Labridae
Groper, Blue	Anz	Achoerodus gouldii	Wrasse	Labridae
Grouper	Eur	Epinephelus guaza	Groupers, Sea Bass & Barramundi	Serranidae
Grouper, Black	USA Atl	Epinephelus marginatus	Groupers, Sea Bass & Barramundi	Serranidae
Grouper, Blue Spotted	USA Atl	Cephalopholis taeniops	Groupers, Sea Bass & Barramundi	Serranidae
Grouper, Malabar	USA Atl	Epinephelus malabaricus	Groupers, Sea Bass & Barramundi	Serranidae
Grouper, Nassau	USA Atl	Epinephelus striatus	Groupers, Sea Bass & Barramundi	Serranidae
Grouper, Red	USA Atl	Epinephelus morio	Groupers, Sea Bass & Barramundi	Serranidae
Grouper, Red	USA Atl	Cephalopholis taeniops	Groupers, Sea Bass & Barramundi	Serranidae
Grouper, Warsaw	USA Atl	Epinephelus nigritus	Groupers, Sea Bass & Barramundi	Serranidae
Grouper, Yellowmouth	USA Atl	Mycteroperca interstitialis	Groupers, Sea Bass & Barramundi	Serranidae
Grunt, White	USA Atl	Haemulon plumieri	Sea Bream, Porgies & Snappers	Pomadasyidae
Gurnard, Butterfly	Anz	Lepidotrigla vanessa	Bony-Cheeked Fish	Triglidae

classifying seafood (continued)

COMMON NAME	REGION	LATIN NAME	A–Z FAMILY	LATIN FAMILY
Gurnard, Grey	Eur	Eutrigla gurnardus	Bony-Cheeked Fish	Triglidae
Gurnard, Red	Eur	Aspitrigla cuculus	Bony-Cheeked Fish	Triglidae
Gurnard, Red	Anz	Chelidonichthys kumu	Bony-Cheeked Fish	Triglidae
Gurnard, Tub	Eur	Trigla lucerna	Bony-Cheeked Fish	Triglidae
Haddock	Eur/USA Atl	Melanogrammus aeglefinus	Cod & Cod-like	Gadidae
Hake	Eur	Merluccius merluccius	Cod & Cod-like	Gadidae
Hake, Blue	Anz	Macruronus novaezelandiae	Deep-sea Fish	Macrouridae
Hake, Pacific	USA Pac	Merluccius productus	Cod & Cod-like	Gadidae
Hake, Red	USA Atl	Urophycis chuss	Cod & Cod-like	Gadidae
Hake, Silver	USA Atl	Merluccius bilinearis	Cod & Cod-like	Gadidae
Hake, South African	Anz/South Africa	Merluccius capensis	Cod & Cod-like	Gadidae
Hake, Southern	Anz	Merluccius australis	Cod & Cod-like	Gadidae
Hake, Squirrel	USA Atl	Urophycis tenuis	Cod & Cod-like	Gadidae
Hake, White	USA Atl	Urophycis tenuis	Cod & Cod-like	Gadidae
Halibut	USA Atl	Hippoglossus hippoglossus	Flat fish	Pleuronectidae
Halibut, Australian	Anz	Psettodes erumei	Flat fish	Psettodidae
Halibut, Californian	USA Pac	Paralichthys californicus	Flat fish	Bothidae
Halibut, Greenland	Usa Atl	Reinhardtius hippoglossoides	Flat fish	Pleuronectidae
Halibut, Pacific	USA Pac	Hippoglossus stenolepis	Flat fish	Pleuronectidae
Hapuku	Anz	Polyprion oxygeneios	Groupers, Sea Bass & Barramundi	Serranidae
Hardhead	USA Atl	Micropogon undulatus	Drums	Sciaenidae
Hardtail	USA Atl	Caranx crysos	Jacks, Pompanos & Trevallys	Carangidae
Harvestfish	USA Atl	Peprilus alepidotus	Thin-bodied fish	Stromateidae
Heart Shell	Eur	Glossus humanus	Shellfish (Bivalves)	Glossidae
Herring	Eur/USA Atl	Clupea harengus	Herring	Clupeidae
Herring, Australian	Anz	Arripis georgianus	Herring	Clupeidae
Herring, Pacific	USA Pac	Clupea harengus pallasii	Herring	Clupeidae
Hind, Red	USA Atl	Epinephelus guttatus	Groupers, Sea Bass & Barramundi	Serranidae
Hind, Speckled	USA Atl	Epinephelus drummondhayi	Groupers, Sea Bass & Barramundi	Serranidae
Hins, Rock	USA Atl	Epinephelus adscensionis	Groupers, Sea Bass & Barramundi	Serranidae
Hogfish	USA Atl	Lachnolaimus maximus	Wrasse	Labridae
Hoki	Anz	Macruronus novaezelandiae	Deep-sea Fish	Macrouridae
Hussar	Anz	Lutjanus adetii	Sea Bream, Porgies & Snappers	Lutjanidae
Icefish	Anz	Chamsocephalus gunnari	Deep-sea Fish	Channichthyidae
Imperador	Anz	Beryx decadactylus	Bony-Cheeked Fish	Berycidae
Inanga	Anz	Galaxias maculatus	Small Fry	Galaxiidae
Inkfish	USA Pac	Loligo opalescens	Cephalapods	Loliginidae
Jack, Almaco	USA/Anz	Seriola rivoliana	Jacks, Pompanos & Trevallys	Carangidae
Jack, Common	Eur	Caranx hippos	Jacks, Pompanos & Trevallys	Carangidae
Jack, Crevalle	USA Atl	Caranx hippos	Jacks, Pompanos & Trevallys	Carangidae
Jack, Mangrove	Anz	Lutjanus argentimaculatus	Sea Bream, Porgies & Snappers	Lutjanidae
Jack, Silver	Anz	Lutjanus argentimaculatus	Sea Bream, Porgies & Snappers	Lutjanidae
Jack, Yellow	USA Atl	Caranx bartholomaei	Jacks, Pompanos & Trevallys	Carangidae
Jackmackerel	USA Atl	Trachurus symmetricus	Jacks, Pompanos & Trevallys	Carangidae
Jackmackerel	Anz	Trachurus declivis	Jacks, Pompanos & Trevallys	Carangidae
Jacknife, Atlantic	USA Atl	Ensis directus	Shellfish (Bivalves)	Solenidae
Jellyfish	Anz	Aurelia aurita	Sea Creature	Schyphoza
Jellyfish, Blue	Eur/Anz	Aurelia aurita	Sea Creature	Ulmariidae
Jewfish	Anz	Johnius borneensis	Drums	Sciaenidae
Jewfish	USA Atl	Epinephelus itajara	Groupers, Sea Bass & Barramundi	Serranidae
Jewfish, Atlantic	Eur	Epinephelus guaza	Groupers, Sea Bass & Barramundi	Serranidae
Jewfish, Black	Anz	Protonibea diacanthus	Drums	Sciaenidae
Jobfish	Anz	Aprion virescens	Sea Bream, Porgies & Snappers	Lutjanidae
John Dory	Eur/Anz	Zeus faber	Thin-bodied fish	Zeidae
Kahawai	Anz	Arripis trutta	Sea Bream, Porgies & Snappers	Arripidae
Kawakawa	USA Pac/Anz	Euthynnus affinis	Mackerel & Tuna	Scombridae
Kelp, Japanese	Anz	Laminaria japonica	Seaweed	Laminariacea
Kingfish	Anz	Seriola dorsalis	Jacks, Pompanos & Trevallys	Carangidae
Kingfish	USA Atl	Scomberomorus cavalla	Mackerel & Tuna	Scombridae
Kingfish, Black	USA Atl/Anz	Rachycentron canadum	Jacks, Pompanos & Trevallys	Rachycentridae
Kingfish, Northern	USA Atl	Menticirrhus saxatilis	Drums	Sciaenidae
Kingfish, Southern	USA Atl	Menticirrhus americanus	Drums	Sciaenidae
Kingfish, Yellowtail	Anz	Seriola lalandi	Jacks, Pompanos & Trevallys	Carangidae
Knifejaw	Anz	Oplegnathus woodwardi	Thin-bodied fish	Oplegnathidae
Kombu	Anz	Laminaria japonica	Seaweed	Laminariacea
Lamprey	Eur/USA Atl	Petromyzon marinus	Eel & Eel-like	Petromyzonidae
Langoustine	Eur	Nephrops norvegicus	Crustacean	Nephropidae
Latchet	Anz	Pterygotrigla polyommata	Bony-Cheeked Fish	Triglidae
Laver	Eur	Porphyra purpurea	Seaweed	Rhodophyceae
Leatherjacket, Potbelly	Anz	Pseudomonacanthus peroni	Thin-bodied fish	Monacanthidae
Leatherjacket, Velvet	Anz	Parika scaber	Thin-bodied fish	Balistidae
Lemonfish	Anz	Mustelus lenticulatus	Sharks & Rays	Triakidae
Limpet	Eur	Patella vulgata	Shellfish (Univalves)	Patellidae
Limpet, Slipper	Eur	Crepidula fornicata	Shellfish (Univalves)	Calyptraeidae
Ling	Eur	Molva molva	Cod & Cod-like	Gadidae
Ling, Boston	USA Atl	Urophycis tenuis	Cod & Cod-like	Gadidae
Ling, Pink	Anz	Genypterus blacodes	Cod & Cod-like	Ophidiidae
Ling, Rock	Anz	Genypterus tigerinus	Cod & Cod-like	Ophidiidae
Lingcod	USA Pac	Ophiodon elongatus	USA Catchall	Hexagramidae
Lobster, American	USA Atl	Homarus americanus	Crustacean	Nephropidae
Lobster, Bay	Anz	Thenus orientalis	Crustacean	Scyllaridae
Lobster, Eastern Rock	Anz	Jasus verreauxi	Crustacean	Palinuridae
Lobster, European	Eur	Homarus gammarus	Crustacean	Nephropidae
Lobster, European	Eur	Homarus vulgaris	Crustacean	Nephropidae
Lobster, Flat	Eur	Scyllarus arctus	Crustacean	Scyllaridae
Lobster, Norway	Eur	Nephrops norvegicus	Crustacean	Nephropidae
Lobster, Pink Spiny	Africa	Palinurus mauritanicus	Crustacean	Palinuridae
Lobster, Rock	Eur	Palinurus elephas	Crustacean	Palinuridae
Lobster, Shovel-nosed	USA Atl	Scyllarides nodifer	Crustacean	Scyllaridae
Lobster, Slipper	Eur	Scyllarus arctus	Crustacean	Scyllaridae
Lobster, Slipper	Eur	Scyllarus latus	Crustacean	Scyllaridae
Lobster, Slipper	USA Atl	Scyllarides nodifer	Crustacean	Scyllaridae
Lobster, Slipper	USA Atl	Scyllarides aequinoctialis	Crustacean	Scyllaridae
Lobster, Slipper	USA Atl	Scyllarides depressus	Crustacean	Scyllaridae
Lobster, Slipper	Anz	Scyllarides squammosus	Crustacean	Scyllaridae
Lobster, Southern Rock	Anz	Jasus edwardsii	Crustacean	Palinuridae
Lobster, Spanish	USA Atl	Scyllarides nodifer	Crustacean	Scyllaridae
Lobster, Spiny	Eur	Palinurus elephas	Crustacean	Palinuridae
Lobster, Spiny	USA Atl	Palinurus argus	Crustacean	Palinuridae
Lobster, Squat	Eur	Galathea squamifera	Crustacean	Scyllaridae
Lobster, Tropical Rock	Anz	Panulirus ornatus	Crustacean	Palinuridae
Lobster, Western Rock	Anz	Panulirus cygnus	Crustacean	Palinuridae
Lobsterette	USA Atl	Metanephrops binghami	Crustacean	Nephropidae
Longfin	Anz	Caprodon longimanus	Groupers, Sea Bass & Barramundi	Serranidae
Longtom, Stout	Anz	Tylosurus gavialoides	Elongated fish	Belonidae
Lookdown	USA Atl/Anz	Alectis indicus	Jacks, Pompanos & Trevallys	Carangidae
Lotte	Eur	Lophius piscatorius	Monkfish & Stargazers	Lophiidae
Luderick	Anz	Girella tricuspidata	Sea Perch	Kyphosidae
Lumpfish	Eur/USA Atl	Cyclopterus lumpus	Roe-Fish	Cyclopteridae
Mackerel, School	Anz	Scomberomorus queenslandicus	Mackerel & Tuna	Scombridae
Mackerel, Atlantic	Eur/USA Atl	Scomber scombrus	Mackerel & Tuna	Scombridae
Mackerel, Blue	Anz	Scomber australasicus	Mackerel & Tuna	Scombridae
Mackerel, Bullet	Eur	Auxis rochei	Mackerel & Tuna	Scombridae
Mackerel, Chub	Eur	Scomber colias	Mackerel & Tuna	Scombridae
Mackerel, Chub	USA Pac	Scomber japonicus	Mackerel & Tuna	Scombridae
Mackerel, Frigate	Anz	Auxis thazard	Mackerel & Tuna	Scombridae
Mackerel, Frigate	Eur	Auxis rochei	Mackerel & Tuna	Scombridae
Mackerel, Grey	Anz	Scomberomorus semifasciatus	Mackerel & Tuna	Scombridae
Mackerel, Horse	Eur	Trachurus mediterraneus	Jacks, Pompanos & Trevallys	Carangidae
Mackerel, Narrow-Barred Spanish	Anz	Scomberomorus commerson	Mackerel & Tuna	Scombridae
Mackerel, Painted	USA Atl	Scomberomorus regalis	Mackerel & Tuna	Scombridae
Mackerel, Shark	Anz	Grammatorcynus bicarinatus	Mackerel & Tuna	Scombridae
Mackerel, Snake	Eur	Ruvettus pretiosus	Elongated fish	Gempylidae
Mackerel, Spotted	Anz	Scomberomorus munroi	Mackerel & Tuna	Scombridae
Mackerel, Spanish	USA Atl	Scomberomorus maculatus	Mackerel & Tuna	Scombridae
Mahi Mahi	Eur/USA Atl/Anz	Coryphaena hippurus	Jacks, Pompanos & Trevallys	Coryphaenidae
Mackerel, King	USA Atl	Scomberomorus cavalla	Mackerel & Tuna	Scombridae
Maomao, Blue	Anz	Scorpis aequipinnis	Sea Perch	Kyphosidae
Maomao, Pink	Anz	Caprodon longimanus	Groupers, Sea Bass & Barramundi	Serranidae
Marbré	Eur	Lithognathus mormyrus	Sea Bream, Porgies & Snappers	Sparidae
Marlin, Black	USA Pac/Anz	Makaira indica	Billfish	Istiophoridae
Marlin, Blue	USA Atl	Makaira nigricans	Billfish	Istiophoridae
Marlin, Blue	Anz	Makaira mazara	Billfish	Istiophoridae
Marlin, Striped	USA Pac/Anz	Tetrapturus audax	Billfish	Istiophoridae
Marlin, White	USA Atl	Makaira albida	Billfish	Istiophoridae
Meagre	Eur	Argyrosomus regius	Drums	Sciaenidae
Mérou	Eur	Epinephelus guaza	Groupers, Sea Bass & Barramundi	Serranidae
Mirror Dory	Anz	Zenopsis nebulosus	Thin-bodied fish	Zeidae
Moki	Anz	Latridopsis ciliaris	Australian Catchall	Latrididae
Moki, Blue	Anz	Latridopsis ciliaris	Australian Catchall	Latrididae
Monkfish	Eur	Lophius piscatorius	Monkfish & Stargazers	Lophiidae
Moonfish	Eur/Anz	Lampris guttatus	Thin-bodied fish	Lampridae
Morgay	Eur	Scyliorhinus canicula	Sharks & Rays	Scyliorhinidae
Morwong	Anz	Nemadactylus macropterus	Australian Catchall	Cheilodactylidae
Morwong, Banded	Anz	Cheilodactylus spectabilis	Australian Catchall	Cheilodactylidae
Morwong, Blue	Anz	Nemadactylus valenciennesi	Australian Catchall	Cheilodactylidae
Morwong, Grey	Anz	Nemadactylus douglasii	Australian Catchall	Cheilodactylidae
Morwong, Red	Anz	Cheilodactylus fuscus	Australian Catchall	Cheilodactylidae
Mullet, Diamond-Scale	Anz	Liza vaigiensis	Mullets	Mugilidae
Mullet, Golden Grey	Eur	Liza aurata	Mullets	Mugilidae
Mullet, Green-Backed Grey	USA Pac	Liza subviridis	Mullets	Mugilidae
Mullet, Grey	Eur/USA Atl	Mugil cephalus	Mullets	Mugilidae
Mullet, Red	Eur	Mullus surmuletus	Mullets	Mullidae
Mullet, Red	Eur	Mullus barbatus	Mullets	Mullidae

COMMON NAME	REGION	LATIN NAME	A-Z FAMILY	LATIN FAMILY
Mullet, Red	Anz	Parupeneus indicus	Mullets	Mullidae
Mullet, Sea	Anz	Mugil cephalus	Mullets	Mugilidae
Mullet, Southern Red	Anz	Upeneichthys vlamingii	Mullets	Mullidae
Mullet, Striped	USA Atl	Mugil cephalus	Mullets	Mugilidae
Mullet, Thick-Lipped Grey	Eur	Chelon labrosus	Mullets	Mugilidae
Mullet, Thin-Lipped Grey	Eur	Liza ramada	Mullets	Mugilidae
Mullet, White	USA Atl	Mugil curema	Mullets	Mugilidae
Mullet, Yelloweye	Anz	Aldrichetta forsteri	Mullets	Mugilidae
Mulloway	Anz	Argyrosomus hololepidotus	Drums	Sciaenidae
Murex	Eur	Murex brandaris	Shellfish (Univalves)	Muricidae
Murgy	Eur	Scyliorhinus canicula	Sharks & Rays	Scyliorhinidae
Mussel	Eur/USA At/Anz	Mytilus edulis	Shellfish (Bivalves)	Mytilidae
Mussel, Blue	USA Atl	Mytilus edulis	Shellfish (Bivalves)	Mytilidae
Mussel, Californian	USA Pac	Mytilus californianus	Shellfish (Bivalves)	Mytilidae
Mussel, Fan	Eur	Pinna fragilis	Shellfish (Bivalves)	Pinnidae
Mussel, Greenlip	Anz	Perna canaliculus	Shellfish (Bivalves)	Mytilidae
Mussel, Horse	Eur/USA Atl	Modiolus modiolus	Shellfish (Bivalves)	Mytilidae
Mussel, Mediterranean	Eur	Mytilus galloprovincialis	Shellfish (Bivalves)	Mytilidae
Mutton-Fish	USA Atl	Macrozoarces americanus	Cod & Cod-like	Gadidae
Needlefish	Eur	Scomberesox saurus	Elongated fish	Scomberesocidae
Norway Haddock	Eur	Sebastes viviparus	Bony-Cheeked Fish	Scorpaenidae
Nursehound	Eur	Scyliorhinus stellaris	Sharks & Rays	Scyliorhinidae
Oblade	Eur	Oblada melanura	Sea Bream, Porgies & Snappers	Sparidae
Ocean Perch	USA	Sebastes marinus	Bony-Cheeked Fish	Scorpaenidae
Octopus	Eur	Octopus macropus	Cephalapods	Octopodidae
Octopus, Common	Eur/USA Atl	Octopus vulgaris	Cephalapods	Octopodidae
Octopus, Curled	Eur	Eledone cirrosa	Cephalapods	Octopodidae
Octopus, Gloomy	Anz	Octopus tetricus	Cephalapods	Octopodidae
Octopus, Lesser	Eur	Eledone cirrosa	Cephalapods	Octopodidae
Octopus, Maori	Anz	Octopus maorum	Cephalapods	Octopodidae
Octopus, Pacific	USA Pac	Octopus dofleini	Cephalapods	Octopodidae
Octopus, Pale	Anz	Octopus pallidus	Cephalapods	Octopodidae
Octopus, Southern	Anz	Octopus australis	Cephalapods	Octopodidae
Opah	Eur	Lampris guttatus	Thin-bodied fish	Lampridae
Opaleye	USA Pac	Girella nigricans	Sea Perch	Kyphosidae
Oreo, Black	Anz	Allocyttus niger	Thin-bodied fish	Zeidae
Oreo, Smooth	Anz	Pseudocyttus maculatus	Thin-bodied fish	Zeidae
Ormer	Eur	Haliotis tuberculata	Shellfish (Univalves)	Haliotidae
Oyster, American Blue Point	USA Atl	Crassostrea virginica	Shellfish (Bivalves)	Ostreidae
Oyster, European	Eur	Ostrea edulis	Shellfish (Bivalves)	Ostreidae
Oyster, Japanese	USA Pac	Ostrea lurida	Shellfish (Bivalves)	Ostreidae
Oyster, New Zealand	Anz	Saccostrea glomerata	Shellfish (Bivalves)	Ostreidae
Oyster, Olympia	USA Pac	Ostrea lurida	Shellfish (Bivalves)	Ostreidae
Oyster, Pacific	USA Pac/Anz	Crassostrea gigas	Shellfish (Bivalves)	Ostreidae
Oyster, Portuguese	Eur	Crassostrea angulata	Shellfish (Bivalves)	Ostreidae
Oyster, Sydney Rock	Anz	Saccostrea glomerata	Shellfish (Bivalves)	Ostreidae
Pageot	Eur	Pagellus erythrinus	Sea Bream, Porgies & Snappers	Sparidae
Pagre	Eur	Pagrus pagrus	Sea Bream, Porgies & Snappers	Sparidae
Pandora	Eur	Pagellus erythrinus	Sea Bream, Porgies & Snappers	Sparidae
Pandora, Common	Eur	Pagellus erythrinus	Sea Bream, Porgies & Snappers	Sparidae
Parore	Anz	Girella tricuspidata	Sea Perch	Kyphosidae
Parrotfish	Anz	Scarus ghobban	Wrasse	Scaridae
Paua	Anz	Haliotis iris	Shellfish (Univalves)	Haliotidae
Pen Shell	Eur	Pinna fragilis	Shellfish (Bivalves)	Pinnidae
Percebes	Eur	Pollicipes cornucopia	Sea Creature	Pollicipidae
Perch, Coral	Anz	Scorpaena cardinalis	Bony-Cheeked Fish	Scorpaenidae
Perch, Crimson Sea	Anz	Lutjanus erythropterus	Sea Bream, Porgies & Snappers	Lutjanidae
Perch, Giant Sea	Anz	Lates calcarifer	Groupers, Sea Bass & Barramundi	Centropomidae
Perch, Longfin	Anz	Caprodon longimanus	Groupers, Sea Bass & Barramundi	Serranidae
Perch, Ocean	Anz	Helicolenus barathri	Bony-Cheeked Fish	Scorpaenidae
Perch, Pacific Ocean	USA Pac	Sebastes alutus	Bony-Cheeked Fish	Scorpaenidae
Perch, Pearl	Anz	Glaucosoma scapulare	Sea Perch	Glaucosomatidae
Perch, Saddletail Sea	Anz	Lutjanus malabaricus	Sea Bream, Porgies & Snappers	Lutjanidae
Perch, Sea	USA Atl	Morone americanus	Groupers, Sea Bass & Barramundi	Serranidae
Perch, Silver	USA Atl	Bairdiella chrysura	Drums	Sciaenidae
Perch, White	USA Atl	Morone americanus	Groupers, Sea Bass & Barramundi	Serranidae
Periwinkle	Anz	Turbo undulatus	Shellfish (Univalves)	Turbinidae
Periwinkle	Eur	Littorina littorea	Shellfish (Univalves)	Lacunidae
Permit	USA Atl	Trachinotus falcatus	Jacks, Pompanos & Trevallys	Carangidae
Petoncle	Eur	Pecten opercularis	Shellfish (Bivalves)	Pectinidae
Piddock	Eur	Pholas dactylus	Shellfish (Bivalves)	Pholadidae
Pigfish	USA Atl	Orthopristis chrysoptera	Sea Bream, Porgies & Snappers	Pomadasyidae
Pigfish	Anz	Bodianus unimaculatus	Wrasse	Labridae
Pike	Anz	Sphyraena novaehollandiae	Elongated Fish	Sphyraenidae
Pilchard	Anz	Sardinops neopilchardus	Herring	Clupeidae
Pilchard	Eur	Sardina pilchardus	Herring	Clupeidae
Pilot Fish	Eur	Naucrates ductor	Jacks, Pompanos & Trevallys	Carangidae
Piper	Eur	Trigla lyra	Bony-Cheeked Fish	Scorpaenidae

COMMON NAME	REGION	LATIN NAME	A-Z FAMILY	LATIN FAMILY
Piper	Anz	Hyporhamphus ihi	Elongated fish	Hemiramphidae
Pipi	Anz	Donax deltoides	Shellfish (Bivalves)	Donacidae
Plaice	Eur	Pleuronectes platessa	Flat fish	Pleuronectidae
Plaice, American	USA Atl	Hippoglossoides platessoides	Flat fish	Pleuronectidae
Plaice, Canadian	USA Atl	Hippoglossoides platessoides	Flat fish	Pleuronectidae
Pod Razor	Eur	Ensis siliqua	Shellfish (Bivalves)	Solenidae
Pollack	Eur	Pollachius pollachius	Cod & Cod-like	Gadidae
Pollock	USA Atl	Pollachius virens	Cod & Cod-like	Gadidae
Pomfret, Atlantic	Eur/Anz	Brama brama	Thin-bodied fish	Bramidae
Pomfret, Black	Anz	Parastromateus niger	Jacks, Pompanos & Trevallys	Carangidae
Pomfret, White	USA Atl	Pampus argenteus	Thin-bodied fish	Stromateidae
Pompano, African	USA Atl/Anz	Alectis ciliaris	Jacks, Pompanos & Trevallys	Carangidae
Pompano, Californian	USA Pac	Peprilus simillimus	Jacks, Pompanos & Trevallys	Carangidae
Pompano, Florida	USA Atl	Trachinotus carolinus	Jacks, Pompanos & Trevallys	Carangidae
Pompano, Pacific	USA Pac	Peprilus simillimus	Jacks, Pompanos & Trevallys	Carangidae
Pompano, Round	Eur/USA Atl	Trachinotus ovatus	Jacks, Pompanos & Trevallys	Carangidae
Porae	Anz	Nemadactylus douglasii	Australian Catchall	Cheilodactylidae
Porgy, European	Eur	Sparus pagrus	Sea Bream, Porgies & Snappers	Sparidae
Porgy, Jolthead	USA Atl	Calamus bajonado	Sea Bream, Porgies & Snappers	Sparidae
Porgy, Key West	USA Atl	Calamus nodosus	Sea Bream, Porgies & Snappers	Sparidae
Porgy, Knobbed	USA Atl	Calamus nodosus	Sea Bream, Porgies & Snappers	Sparidae
Porgy, Northern	USA Atl	Stenotomus chrysops	Sea Bream, Porgies & Snappers	Sparidae
Porgy, Red	USA Atl	Stenotomus chrysops	Sea Bream, Porgies & Snappers	Sparidae
Porgy, Red	USA Atl/Eur	Pagrus pagrus	Sea Bream, Porgies & Snappers	Sparidae
Porgy, Whitebone	USA Atl	Calamus leucosteus	Sea Bream, Porgies & Snappers	Sparidae
Porkfish	USA Atl	Anisotremus virginicus	Sea Bream, Porgies & Snappers	Pomadasyidae
Pout, Eel	Eur	Zoarces viviparus	Cod & Cod-like	Zoarcidae
Pout, Ocean	USA Atl	Macrozoarces americanus	Cod & Cod-like	Zoarcidae
Prawn, Banana	Anz	Fenneropenaeus merguiensis	Crustacean	Penaeidae
Prawn, Bay	Anz	Metapenaeus bennettae	Crustacean	Penaeidae
Prawn, Black Tiger	Anz	Penaeus monodon	Crustacean	Penaeidae
Prawn, Common	Eur	Palaemon serratus	Crustacean	Palaemonidae
Prawn, Deep-water	Eur/USA Atl	Pandalus borealis	Crustacean	Pandalidae
Prawn, Dublin Bay	Eur	Nephrops norvegicus	Crustacean	Nephropidae
Prawn, Endeavour	Anz	Metapenaeus ensis	Crustacean	Penaeidae
Prawn, Giant Tiger	Anz	Penaeus monodon	Crustacean	Penaeidae
Prawn, Indian White	Anz	Penaeus indicus	Crustacean	Penaeidae
Prawn, King	Anz	Melicertus latisulcatus	Crustacean	Penaeidae
Prawn, Kuruma	Anz	Marsupenaeus japonicus	Crustacean	Penaeidae
Prawn, Mediterranean	Eur	Aristeus antennatus	Crustacean	Penaeidae
Prawn, Redspot King	Anz	Melicertus longistylus	Crustacean	Penaeidae
Prawn, Royal Red	Anz	Haliporoides sibogae	Crustacean	Solenoceridae
Prawn, School	Anz	Metapenaeus macleayi	Crustacean	Penaeidae
Prawn, Tiger	Anz	Penaeus esculentus	Crustacean	Penaeidae
Puffer Fish	USA Atl	Spheroides maculatus	Puffer Fish	Tetraodontidae
Rabbitfish	Eur/USA Atl	Chimaera monstosa	Deep-sea Fish	Siganidae
Rabbitfish	Eur	Siganus rivulatus	Puffer Fish	Siganidae
Rabbitfish	Anz	Siganus nebulosus	Puffer Fish	Siganidae
Rajafish	USA	Raja batis	Sharks & Rays	Rajidae
Rascasse	Eur	Scorpaena scrofa	Bony-Cheeked Fish	Scorpaenidae
Rat-Tail	Eur/USA Atl	Macrourus berglax	Deep-sea Fish	Macrouridae
Ray, Blonde	Eur	Raja brachyura	Sharks & Rays	Rajidae
Ray, Spotted	Eur	Raja montagui	Sharks & Rays	Rajidae
Ray, Starry	USA Atl	Raja radiata	Sharks & Rays	Rajidae
Ray, Thornback	Eur	Raja clavata	Sharks & Rays	Rajidae
Redfish	Eur/USA Atl	Sebastes marinus	Bony-Cheeked Fish	Scorpaenidae
Redfish	Anz	Centroberyx affinis	Bony-Cheeked Fish	Berycidae
Redfish, Bight	Anz	Centroberyx gerrardi	Bony-Cheeked Fish	Berycidae
Ribaldo	Anz	Mora moro	Deep-sea Fish	Moridae
Ribbonfish	Anz	Lepidopus caudatus	Elongated Fish	Trichiuridae
River Roman	Anz	Lutjanus argentimaculatus	Sea Bream, Porgies & Snappers	Lutjanidae
Rock Cod, Blacktip	Anz	Epinephelus fasciatus	Groupers, Sea Bass & Barramundi	Serranidae
Rock Cod, Estuary	Anz	Epinephelus coioides	Groupers, Sea Bass & Barramundi	Serranidae
Rock Cod, Red	Anz	Scorpaena cardinalis	Bony-Cheeked Fish	Scorpaenidae
Rock Cod, White-spotted	Anz	Epinephelus multinotatus	Groupers, Sea Bass & Barramundi	Serranidae
Rock Cod, Yellow-spotted	Anz	Epinephelus areolatus	Groupers, Sea Bass & Barramundi	Serranidae
Rock Turbot	Eur/USA Atl	Anarhichas lupus	Sea Catfish	Anarhichadidae
Rockcod, Coral	Anz	Cephalopholis miniata	Groupers, Sea Bass & Barramundi	Serranidae
Rockfish, Brown	USA Pac	Sebastes auriculatus	Bony-Cheeked Fish	Scorpaenidae
Rockfish, Golden Eye	USA Pac	Sebastes ruberrimus	Bony-Cheeked Fish	Scorpaenidae
Rockfish, Olive	USA Atl	Morone saxatilis	Groupers, Sea Bass & Barramundi	Serranidae
Rockling	Eur/USA Atl	Gaidropsarus vulgaris	Cod & Cod-like	Gadidae
Roker	Eur	Raja clavata	Sharks & Rays	Rajidae
Roosterfish	USA Pac	Nematistius pectoralis	USA Catchall	Nematistiidae
Rouget (de roche)	Eur	Mullus surmuletus	Mullets	Mullidae
Rough Hound	Eur	Scyliorhinus canicula	Sharks & Rays	Scyliorhinidae
Roughjacket	USA Pac	Platichthys stellatus	Flat fish	Pleuronectidae
Roughy, Darwin's	Anz	Gephyroberyx darwinii	Deep-sea Fish	Trachichthyidae

classifying seafood (continued)

COMMON NAME	REGION	LATIN NAME	A-Z FAMILY	LATIN FAMILY
Roughy, Orange	Anz	Hoplostethus Atlanticus	Deep-sea Fish	Trachichthyidae
Rudderfish	Anz	Centrolophus niger	Australian Catchall	Centrolophidae
Rudderfish	Eur/USA Atl	Seriola dumerili	Jacks, Pompanos & Trevallys	Carangidae
Rudderfish, Banded	Anz	Seiola zouata	Australian Catchall	Centrolophidae
Runner, Blue	USA Atl	Caranx crysos	Jacks, Pompanos & Trevallys	Carangidae
Runner, Rainbow	USA Atl	Elagatis bipinnulatus	Jacks, Pompanos & Trevallys	Carangidae
Sablefish	USA Atl/Pac	Anopoploma fimbria	Thin-bodied fish	Anopoplomatidae
Sabre Fish	Eur/USA Atl	Lepidopus caudatus	Elongated Fish	Trichiuridae
Sailfish	Eur/USA/Anz	Istiophorus platypterus	Billfish	Istiophoridae
Saithe	Eur	Pollachius virens	Cod & Cod-like	Gadidae
Salema	Eur	Sarpa salpa	Sea Bream, Porgies & Snappers	Sparidae
Salmon, Atlantic	Eur	Salmo salar	Salmon	Salmonidae
Salmon, Australian	Anz	Arripis trutta	Sea Bream, Porgies & Snappers	Arripidae
Salmon, Blueback	USA Pac	Oncorhynchus nerka	Salmon	Salmonidae
Salmon, Chinook	USA Pac	Oncorhynchus tshawytscha	Salmon	Salmonidae
Salmon, Chum	USA Pac	Oncorhynchus keta	Salmon	Salmonidae
Salmon, Coho	USA Pac	Oncorhynchus kisutch	Salmon	Salmonidae
Salmon, King	USA Pac	Oncorhynchus tshawytscha	Salmon	Salmonidae
Salmon, Pink	USA Pac	Oncorhynchus gorbuscha	Salmon	Salmonidae
Salmon, Rock	Eur	Scyliorhinus canicula	Sharks & Rays	Scyliorhinidae
Salmon, Silver	USA Pac	Oncorhynchus kisutch	Salmon	Salmonidae
Salmon, Sockeye	USA Pac	Oncorhynchus nerka	Salmon	Salmonidae
Samphire, Marsh	Eur	Salicornia europea	Seaweed	Chenopodiaceae
Samphire, Rock	Eur	Crithmum maritimum	Seaweed	Umbelliferae
Samson Fish	Anz	Seriola hippos	Jacks, Pompanos & Trevallys	Carangidae
Sand Gaper	USA Atl	Mya arenaria	Shellfish (Bivalves)	Myacidae
Sand-eel	USA Atl	Ammodytes americanus	Small Fry	Ammodytidae
Sand-eel	Eur	Ammodytes tobianus	Small Fry	Ammodytidae
Sand-Lance	Eur	Ammodytes tobianus	Small Fry	Ammodytidae
Sardine	Eur	Sardina pilchardus	Herring	Clupeidae
Saupe	Eur	Sarpa salpa	Sea Bream, Porgies & Snappers	Sparidae
Saury, Atlantic	Eur	Scomberesox saurus	Elongated Fish	Scomberesocidae
Scabbard Fish, Black	Eur	Aphanopus carbo	Elongated fish	Trichiuridae
Scabbard Fish, White/Silver	Eur/USA Atl	Lepidopus caudatus	Elongated Fish	Trichiuridae
Scad	Eur	Trachurus trachurus	Jacks, Pompanos & Trevallys	Carangidae
Scad, Yellowtail	Anz	Trachurus novaezelandiae	Jacks, Pompanos & Trevallys	Carangidae
Scaldfish	Eur	Arnoglossus laterna	Flat fish	Bothidae
Scallop, Atlantic Deep-sea	USA Atl	Placopecten magellicanus	Shellfish (Bivalves)	Pectinidae
Scallop, Ballot's Saucer	Anz	Amusium balloti	Shellfish (Bivalves)	Pectinidae
Scallop, Bay	USA Atl	Argopecten irradians	Shellfish (Bivalves)	Pectinidae
Scallop, Calico	USA Atl	Argopecten gibbus	Shellfish (Bivalves)	Pectinidae
Scallop, Commercial	Anz	Pecten fumatus	Shellfish (Bivalves)	Pectinidae
Scallop, Doughboy	Anz	Mimachlamys asperrima	Shellfish (Bivalves)	Pectinidae
Scallop, Fan	Anz	Annachlamys flabellata	Shellfish (Bivalves)	Pectinidae
Scallop, Great	Eur	Pecten maximus	Shellfish (Bivalves)	Pectinidae
Scallop, Mediterranean	Eur	Pecten jacobaeus	Shellfish (Bivalves)	Pectinidae
Scallop, Northern Saucer	Anz	Amusium pleuronectes	Shellfish (Bivalves)	Pectinidae
Scallop, Queen	Eur	Chlamys opercularis	Shellfish (Bivalves)	Pectinidae
Scallop, Queen	Anz	Equichlamys bifrons	Shellfish (Bivalves)	Pectinidae
Scallop, Rock	USA Pac	Hinnites giganteus	Shellfish (Bivalves)	Pectinidae
Scampi	Anz	Metanephrops boschmai	Crustacean	Nephropidae
Scampi	Eur	Nephrops norvegicus	Crustacean	Nephropidae
Scorpion Fish	Eur	Scorpaena scrofa	Bony-Cheeked Fish	Scorpaenidae
Scorpion Fish, Californian	USA Pac	Scorpaena guttata	Bony-Cheeked Fish	Scorpaenidae
Scorpion Fish, Spotted	USA Atl	Scorpaena plumieri	Bony-Cheeked Fish	Scorpaenidae
Scourer	Eur	Ruvettus pretiosus	Elongated Fish	Gempylidae
Sculpin	USA Atl	Myoxocephalus scorpius	Bony-Cheeked Fish	Scorpaenidae
Sculpin, Longhorn	USA Atl	Myoxocephalus octodecemspinosus	Bony-Cheeked Fish	Scorpaenidae
Scup	USA Atl	Stenotomus chrysops	Sea Bream, Porgies & Snappers	Sparidae
Sea Cucumber	Anz	Holothuria scabra	Sea Creature	Holothuriidae
Sea Devil	Eur	Lophius piscatorius	Monkfish & Stargazers	Lophiidae
Sea Lettuce	Eur	Ulva lactuca	Seaweed	Chlorophyceae
Sea Robin	USA Atl	Prionotus carolinus	Bony-Cheeked Fish	Triglidae
Sea Scorpion	USA Atl	Myoxocephalus scorpius	Bony-Cheeked Fish	Scorpaenidae
Sea Squab	USA Atl	Spheroides maculatus	Puffer Fish	Tetraodontidae
Sea Urchin	Anz	Heliocidaris erythrogramma	Sea Creature	Echinoidea
Sea Urchin, Black	Eur	Arbacia lixula	Sea Creature	Echinoidea
Sea Urchin, Green	Eur/USA Atl	Strongylocentrotus droebachiensis	Sea Creature	Strongylocentrotidae
Sea Urchin, Mediterranean	Eur	Paracentrotus lividus	Sea Creature	Echinoidea
Sea-wing	Eur	Pinna fragilis	Shellfish (Bivalves)	Pinnidae
Seabass, White	USA Pac	Atractoscion nobilis	Drums	Sciaenidae
Seabass, White	USA Atl	Sciaenops ocellatus	Drums	Sciaenidae
Seacat	Eur/USA Atl	Anarhichas lupus	Sea Catfish	Anarhichadidae
Seaperch, Brownband	Anz	Lutjanus vitta	Sea Bream, Porgies & Snappers	Lutjanidae
Seaperch, Darktail	Anz	Lutjanus lemniscatus	Sea Bream, Porgies & Snappers	Lutjanidae
Seaperch, Fingermark	Anz	Lutjanus johnii	Sea Bream, Porgies & Snappers	Lutjanidae
Seaperch, Moses	Anz	Lutjanus russelli	Sea Bream, Porgies & Snappers	Lutjanidae

COMMON NAME	REGION	LATIN NAME	A-Z FAMILY	LATIN FAMILY
Seaperch, Stripey	Anz	Lutjanus carponotatus	Sea Bream, Porgies & Snappers	Lutjanidae
Seapike	Anz	Sphyraena barracuda	Elongated Fish	Sphyraenidae
Seapike, Striped	Anz	Sphyraena obtusata	Elongated Fish	Sphyraenidae
Seatrout, Spotted	USA Atl	Cynoscion nebulosus	Drums	Sciaenidae
Sergeant Fish	USA Atl/Anz	Rachycentron canadum	Jacks, Pompanos & Trevallys	Rachycentridae
Sewin	Eur	Salmo trutta	Salmon	Salmonidae
Shad, Allis (Allice)	Eur	Alosa alosa	Herring	Clupeidae
Shad, American	USA Atl	Alosa sapidissima	Herring	Clupeidae
Shad, Hickory	USA Atl	Pomolobus mediocris	Herring	Clupeidae
Shad, Twaite	Eur	Alosa fallax	Herring	Clupeidae
Shark, Australian Angel	Anz	Squatina australis	Sharks & Rays	Squatinidae
Shark, Blacktip	USA Atl	Carcharhinus limbatus	Sharks & Rays	Carcharhinidae
Shark, Blacktip	Anz	Carcharhinus dussumieri	Sharks & Rays	Carcharhinidae
Shark, Blue	Eur.Anz	Prionace glauca	Sharks & Rays	Carcharhinidae
Shark, Blue Whaler	Anz	Prionace glauca	Sharks & Rays	Carcharhinidae
Shark, Bronze Whaler	Anz	Carcharhinus obscurus	Sharks & Rays	Carcharhinidae
Shark, European Angel	Eur	Squatina squatina	Sharks & Rays	Squatinidae
Shark, Gummy	Anz	Mustelus antarcticus	Sharks & Rays	Triakidae
Shark, Hammerhead	Eur/USA Atl	Sphyrna zygaena	Sharks & Rays	Sphyrnidae
Shark, Mako	Eur/USA Atl	Isurus oxyrinchus	Sharks & Rays	Lamnidae
Shark, North American Angel	USA Atl	Squatina dumerili	Sharks & Rays	Squatinidae
Shark, Porbeagle	Eur/USA Atl	Lamna nasus	Sharks & Rays	Lamnidae
Shark, Sand	USA Atl	Mustelus canis	Sharks & Rays	Triakidae
Shark, School	Anz	Galeorhinus galeus	Sharks & Rays	Carcharhinidae
Shark, Shortfin Mako	Eur/USA Atl	Isurus oxyrinchus	Sharks & Rays	Lamnidae
Shark, Tiger	USA Atl/Pac	Galeocerdo cuvieri	Sharks & Rays	Carcharhinidae
Shark, Whiskery	Anz	Furgaleus macki	Sharks & Rays	Triakidae
Sheephead, California	USA Pac	Pimelometopon pulchrum	Wrasse	Labridae
Sheepshead	USA Atl	Archosargus probatocephalus	Sea Bream, Porgies & Snappers	Sparidae
Shrimp, Brown	USA Atl	Penaeus aztecus aztecus	Crustacean	Penaeidae
Shrimp, Brown	Eur	Crangon crangon	Crustacean	Crangonidae
Shrimp, Caribbean White	USA Atl	Penaeus schmitti	Crustacean	Penaeidae
Shrimp, Coon-Stripe	USA Pac	Pandalus danae	Crustacean	Pandalidae
Shrimp, Pink	Eur/USA Atl/Pac	Pandalus borealis	Crustacean	Pandalidae
Shrimp, Rock	USA Atl	Sicyonia brevirostris	Crustacean	Scyoniidae
Shrimp, Royal Red	USA Atl	Hymenopenaeus robustus	Crustacean	Penaeidae
Shrimp, Side-Stripe	USA Pac	Pandalopsus dispar	Crustacean	Pandalidae
Shrimp, Spot	USA Pac	Pandalus platyceros	Crustacean	Pandalidae
Shrimp, White	USA Atl	Penaeus setiferus	Crustacean	Penaeidae
Silverside	USA Atl	Menidia menidia	Small Fry	Atherinidae
Silverside	Eur	Atherina presbyter	Small Fry	Atherinidae
Skate & Ray	Anz	Raja batis	Sharks & Rays	Rajidae
Skate, Barndoor	USA Atl	Raja laevis	Sharks & Rays	Rajidae
Skate, Big/Large	USA Pac	Raja binoculata	Sharks & Rays	Rajidae
Skate, California	USA Pac	Raja inornata	Sharks & Rays	Rajidae
Skate, Common	Eur	Raja batis	Sharks & Rays	Rajidae
Skate, Clearnose	USA Atl	Raja eglanteria	Sharks & Rays	Rajidae
Skate, Thorny	USA Atl	Raja radiata	Sharks & Rays	Rajidae
Skipjack	USA Pac	Euthynnus pelamis	Mackerel & Tuna	Scombridae
Skipper	Eur	Scomberesox saurus	Elongated fish	Scomberesocidae
Smelt, Atlantic	Eur	Osmerus eperlanus	Small Fry	Osmeridae
Smelt, Rainbow	USA Atl	Osmerus mordax	Small Fry	Osmeridae
Smelt, Sand	Eur	Atherina presbyter	Small Fry	Atherinidae
Smelt, Silver	Eur/USA Atl	Argentina silus	Salmon	Argentinidae
Smelt, Surf	USA Pac	Hypomesus pretiosus	Small Fry	Osmeridae
Smooth Hound	Eur	Mustelus mustelus	Sharks & Rays	Triakidae
Smooth Hound	Anz	Mustelus lenticulatus	Sharks & Rays	Triakidae
Snapper	Anz	Pagrus auratus	Sea Bream, Porgies & Snappers	Sparidae
Snapper, American Red	USA Atl	Lutjanus campechanus	Sea Bream, Porgies & Snappers	Lutjanidae
Snapper, Cubera	USA Atl	Lutjanus cyanopterus	Sea Bream, Porgies & Snappers	Lutjanidae
Snapper, Emperor	Anz	Lutjanus sebae	Sea Bream, Porgies & Snappers	Lutjanidae
Snapper, Goldband	Anz	Pristipomoides multidens	Sea Bream, Porgies & Snappers	Lutjanidae
Snapper, Gray	USA Atl	Lutjanus griseus	Sea Bream, Porgies & Snappers	Lutjanidae
Snapper, Humpback Red	Anz	Lutjanes gibbus	Sea Bream, Porgies & Snappers	Lutjanidae
Snapper, King	Anz	Pristipomoides filamentosus	Sea Bream, Porgies & Snappers	Lutjanidae
Snapper, Lane	USA Atl	Lutjanus synagris	Sea Bream, Porgies & Snappers	Lutjanidae
Snapper, Mangrove	USA Atl	Lutjanus griseus	Sea Bream, Porgies & Snappers	Lutjanidae
Snapper, Mutton	USA Atl	Lutjanus analis	Sea Bream, Porgies & Snappers	Lutjanidae
Snapper, Red	USA Atl	Lutjanus campechanus	Sea Bream, Porgies & Snappers	Lutjanidae
Snapper, Ruby	Anz	Etelis coruscans	Sea Bream, Porgies & Snappers	Lutjanidae
Snapper, Schoolmaster	USA Atl	Lutjanus apodus	Sea Bream, Porgies & Snappers	Lutjanidae
Snapper, Silk	USA Atl	Lutjanus vivanus	Sea Bream, Porgies & Snappers	Lutjanidae
Snapper, Two-Spot	Anz	Lutjanes bohar	Sea Bream, Porgies & Snappers	Lutjanidae
Snapper, Vermillion	USA Atl	Rhomboplites aurorubens	Sea Bream, Porgies & Snappers	Lutjanidae
Snapper, Yellowtail	USA Atl	Ocyurus chrysurus	Sea Bream, Porgies & Snappers	Lutjanidae
Snoek	Anz	Thyrsites atun	Elongated fish	Gempylidae
Snook	Anz	Sphyraena novaehollandiae	Elongated Fish	Sphyraenidae

COMMON NAME	REGION	LATIN NAME	A–Z FAMILY	LATIN FAMILY
Snook	USA Atl	Centropomus undecimalis	Groupers, Sea Bass & Barramundi	Centropomidae
Snook, Black	USA Pac	Centropomus nigrescens	Groupers, Sea Bass & Barramundi	Centropomidae
Sole	Anz	Synaptura nigra	Flat fish	Pleuronectidae
Sole, Butter	USA Pac	Isopsetta isolepis	Flat fish	Pleuronectidae
Sole, California	USA Pac	Parophrys ventulus	Flat fish	Pleuronectidae
Sole, Dover	Eur	Solea solea	Flat fish	Soleidae
Sole, English	USA Pac	Parophrys ventulus	Flat fish	Pleuronectidae
Sole, French	Eur	Solea lascaris	Flat fish	Soleidae
Sole, Lemon	Eur	Microstomus kitt	Flat fish	Pleuronectidae
Sole, Megrim	Eur	Lepidorhombus whiffiagonis	Flat fish	Bothidae
Sole, Petrale	USA Pac	Eopsetta jordani	Flat fish	Pleuronectidae
Sole, Thickback	Eur	Microchirus variegatus	Flat fish	Soleidae
Sole, Torbay	Eur	Glyptocephalus cynoglossus	Flat fish	Pleuronectidae
Sole, Witch	Eur	Glyptocephalus cynoglossus	Flat fish	Pleuronectidae
Sparling	Eur	Osmerus eperlanus	Small Fry	Osmeridae
Spearfish, Mediterranean	Eur	Tetrapturus albidus	Billfish	Istiophoridae
Spearfish, Shortbill	USA Pac	Tetrapturus angustirostris	Billfish	Istiophoridae
Spot	USA Atl	Leiostomus xanthurus	Drums	Sciaenidae
Sprat	Eur	Sprattus sprattus	Herring	Clupeidae
Sprat	Anz	Sprattus antipodum	Herring	Clupeidae
Sprat, Sandy	Anz	Hyperlophus vittatus	Herring	Clupeidae
Spur-Dog	Eur/USA/Anz	Squalus acanthias	Sharks & Rays	Squalidae
Squeteague, Spotted	USA Atl	Cynoscion nebulosus	Drums	Sciaenidae
Squid, Arrow	Anz	Nototodarus gouldi	Cephalapods	Loliginidae
Squid, Bone	USA Atl	Loligo pealei	Cephalapods	Loliginidae
Squid, California	USA Pac	Loligo opalescens	Cephalapods	Loliginidae
Squid, Common	Eur	Loligo forbesi	Cephalapods	Loliginidae
Squid, European	Eur	Loligo vulgaris	Cephalapods	Loliginidae
Squid, Flying	Eur	Todarodes saggittatus	Cephalapods	Loliginidae
Squid, Flying	USA Pac	Todarodes Pacificus	Cephalapods	Loliginidae
Squid, Long-finned	USA Atl	Loligo pealei	Cephalapods	Loliginidae
Squid, Mitre	Anz	Loligo chinensis	Cephalapods	Loliginidae
Squid, Winter	USA Atl	Loligo pealei	Cephalapods	Loliginidae
St Peter's Fish	Eur	Zeus faber	Thin-bodied fish	Zeidae
Stargazer	Eur	Uranoscopus scaber	Monkfish & Stargazers	Uranoscopidae
Stargazer	Anz	Kathetostoma canaster	Monkfish & Stargazers	Uranoscopidae
Stargazer, Giant	Anz	Kathetostoma giganteum	Monkfish & Stargazers	Uranoscopidae
Sturgeon	Eur	Acipenser sturio	Roe-Fish	Acipenseridae
Sturgeon	Eur	Acipenser gueldenstaedti colchicus	Roe-Fish	Acipenseridae
Sturgeon	USA Atl	Acipenser oxyrhynchus	Roe-Fish	Acipenseridae
Sturgeon, Beluga	Eur	Huso huso	Roe-Fish	Acipenseridae
Sturgeon, Sevruga	Eur	Acipenser stellatus	Roe-Fish	Acipenseridae
Sunfish	Eur/USA	Mola mola	Thin-bodied fish	Molidae
Surfperch, Barred	USA Pac	Amphistichus argenteus	Sea Perch	Embiotocidae
Surfperch, Calico	USA Pac	Amphistichus koelzi	Sea Perch	Embiotocidae
Surfperch, Redtail	USA Pac	Amphistichus rhodoterus	Sea Perch	Embiotocidae
Swallowtail	Anz	Centroberyx lineatus	Bony-Cheeked Fish	Berycidae
Sweep	Anz	Scorpis lineolatus	Sea Perch	Scorpididae
Swellfish	USA Atl	Spheroides maculatus	Puffer Fish	Tetraodontidae
Swordfish	Eur/USA Atl/Anz	Xiphias gladius	Billfish	Xiphiidae
Tailor	Anz	Pomatomus saltatrix	Jacks, Pompanos & Trevallys	Pomatomidae
Tarpon	USA Atl	Megalops Atlanticus	Herring	Elopidae
Tarwhine	Anz	Rhabdosargus sarba	Sea Bream, Porgies & Snappers	Sparidae
Tautog	USA Atl	Tautoga onitis	Wrasse	Labridae
Tellin	Eur	Scrobicularia plana	Shellfish (Bivalves)	Scrobiculariidae
Teraglin	Anz	Atractoscion aequidens	Drums	Sciaenidae
Terakihi	Anz	Nemadactylus macropterus	Australian Catchall	Cheilodactylidae
Threadfin, Blue	Anz	Eleutheronema tetradactylum	Sea Bream, Porgies & Snappers	Sparidae
Threadfin, Indian	USA Atl/Anz	Alectis indicus	Jacks, Pompanos & Trevallys	Carangindae
Threadfin, King	Anz	Polydactylus sheridani	Sea Bream, Porgies & Snappers	Sparidae
Threadfin, Pacific	Anz	Polydactylus approximans	Sea Bream, Porgies & Snappers	Sparidae
Tilefish	USA Atl	Lopholatilus chamaeleonticeps	USA Catchall	Branchiostegidae
Tilefish, Blackline	USA Atl	Caulotilus cyanops	USA Catchall	Branchiostegidae
Tilefish, Sand	USA Atl	Malacanthus plumieri	USA Catchall	Branchiostegidae
Tomcod	USA Atl	Microgadus tomcod	Cod & Cod-like	Gadidae
Toothfish, Patagonian	Anz	Dissostichus eleginoides	Deep-sea Fish	Nototheniidae
Top-Shell	Eur	Monodonta turbinata	Shellfish (Univalves)	Trochidae
Tope	Eur	Galeorhinus galeus	Sharks & Rays	Carcharhinidae
Topknot	Eur	Zeugopterus punctatus	Flat fish	Bothidae
Torsk	Eur/USA	Brosme brosme	Cod & Cod-like	Gadidae
Totuava	USA Pac	Cynoscion macdonaldi	Drums	Sciaenidae
Trevalla, Blue-Eye	Anz	Hyperoglyphe antarctica	Australian Catchall	Centrolophidae
Trevally	Anz	Carangoides gymnostethus	Jacks, Pompanos & Trevallys	Carangidae
Trevally, Bigeye	Anz	Caranx sexfasciatus	Jacks, Pompanos & Trevallys	Carangidae
Trevally, Blue-Spotted	Anz	Caranx bucculentus	Jacks, Pompanos & Trevallys	Carangidae
Trevally, Bluefin	Anz	Caranx melampygus	Jacks, Pompanos & Trevallys	Carangidae
Trevally, Giant	Anz	Caranx ignobilis	Jacks, Pompanos & Trevallys	Carangidae
Trevally, Orange-spotted	Anz	Carangoides bajad	Jacks, Pompanos & Trevallys	Carangidae
Trevally, Silver	Anz	Pseudocaranx dentex	Jacks, Pompanos & Trevallys	Carangidae
Trigger-Fish	Eur/USA Atl	Balistes carolinensis	Thin-bodied fish	Balistidae
Trout, Bar-Cheeked Coral	Anz	Plectropomus maculatus	Groupers, Sea Bass & Barramundi	Serranidae
Trout, Bluespot	Anz	Plectropomus laevis	Groupers, Sea Bass & Barramundi	Serranidae
Trout, Common Coral	Anz	Plectropomus leopardus	Groupers, Sea Bass & Barramundi	Serranidae
Trout, Coronation	Anz	Variola louti	Groupers, Sea Bass & Barramundi	Serranidae
Trout, Leopard Coral	Anz	Plectropomus leopardus	Groupers, Sea Bass & Barramundi	Serranidae
Trout, Ocean	Eur	Salmo trutta	Salmon	Salmonidae
Trout, Salmon	Eur	Salmo trutta	Salmon	Salmonidae
Trout, Sea	Eur	Salmo trutta	Salmon	Salmonidae
Trout, Silver	Eur	Salmo trutta	Salmon	Salmonidae
Trumpeter	Anz	Latridopsis forsteri	Australian Catchall	Latrididae
Trumpeter, Bastard	Anz	Latridopsis forsteri	Australian Catchall	Latrididae
Trumpeter, Striped	Anz	Latris lineata	Australian Catchall	Latrididae
Tuna	Anz	Cybiosarda elegans	Mackerel & Tuna	Scombridae
Tuna, Albacore	Eur/USA At/Anz	Thunnus alalunga	Mackerel & Tuna	Scombridae
Tuna, Bigeye	Eur/USA At/Anz	Thunnus obesus	Mackerel & Tuna	Scombridae
Tuna, Blackfin	USA Atl	Thunnus Atlanticus	Mackerel & Tuna	Scombridae
Tuna, Bluefin	Eur, USA Atl	Thunnus thynnus	Mackerel & Tuna	Scombridae
Tuna, Bullet	Eur	Auxis rochei	Mackerel & Tuna	Scombridae
Tuna, Long-Fin	Eur/USA Atl	Thunnus alalunga	Mackerel & Tuna	Scombridae
Tuna, Skipjack	USA Pac	Euthynnus pelamis	Mackerel & Tuna	Scombridae
Tuna, Skipjack	Anz	Katsuwonus pelamis	Mackerel & Tuna	Scombridae
Tuna, Slender	Anz	Allothunnus fallai	Mackerel & Tuna	Scombridae
Tuna, Southern Bluefin	Anz	Thunnus maccoyii	Mackerel & Tuna	Scombridae
Tuna, White	Eur/USA Atl/Anz	Thunnus alalunga	Mackerel & Tuna	Scombridae
Tuna, Yellowfin	Eur/USA/Anz	Thunnus albacares	Mackerel & Tuna	Scombridae
Tunny, Little	USA Atl	Euthynnus alletteratus	Mackerel & Tuna	Scombridae
Turban Shell	Anz	Turbo undulatus	Shellfish (Univalves)	Turbinidae
Turbot	Eur	Psetta maxima	Flat fish	Bothidae
Turbot, Diamond	USA Pac	Hypsopsetta guttulata	Flat fish	Pleuronectidae
Turrum	Anz	Carangoides fulvoguttatus	Jacks, Pompanos & Trevallys	Carangidae
Tusk	Eur	Brosme brosme	Cod & Cod-like	Gadidae
Tusk	Anz	Dannevigia tusca	Cod & Cod-like	Ophidiidae
Tuskfish	Anz	Choerodon venustus	Wrasse	Labridae
Violet	Eur	Microcosmus suculatus	Sea Creature	Pyuridae
Wahoo	USA Atl/Anz	Acanthocybium solanderi	Mackerel & Tuna	Scombridae
Wakame	Anz	Undaria pinnatifida	Seaweed	Laminariacea
Warehou, Blue	Anz	Seriolella brama	Australian Catchall	Centrolophidae
Warehou, Silver	Anz	Seriolella punctata	Australian Catchall	Centrolophidae
Warehou, White	Anz	Seriolella caerulea	Australian Catchall	Centrolophidae
Weakfish, Grey	USA Atl	Cynoscion regalis	Drums	Sciaenidae
Weever	Eur	Trachinus draco	Monkfish & Stargazers	Trachinidae
West Australian Jewfish	Anz	Glaucosoma hebraicum	Sea Perch	Glaucosomatidae
Westralian Jewfish	Anz	Glaucosoma hebraicum	Sea Perch	Glaucosomatidae
Whelk	Eur/USA Atl	Buccinum undatum	Shellfish (Univalves)	Buccinidae
Whelk, Channeled	USA Atl	Busycon canaliculatum	Shellfish (Univalves)	Melongenidae
Whelk, Knobbled	USA Atl	Busycon carica	Shellfish (Univalves)	Melongenidae
Whiff	Eur	Lepidorhombus whiffiagonis	Flat fish	Bothidae
Whiptail	Anz	Macruronus novaezelandiae	Deep-sea Fish	Macrouridae
Whitebait	Eur	Clupea harengus	Small Fry	Clupeidae
Whitebait	Anz	Lovettia sealii	Small Fry	Galaxiidae
Whitefish	Eur	Coregonus lavaretus	Salmon	Coregonidae
Whitefish, Ocean	USA Pac	Caulotilus princeps	USA Catchall	Branchiostegidae
Whiting	Eur	Merlangius merlangus	Cod & Cod-like	Gadidae
Whiting, Blue	Eur/USA Atl	Micromesistius poutassou	Cod & Cod-like	Gadidae
Whiting, Eastern School	Anz	Sillago flindersi	Australian Catchall	Sillaginidae
Whiting, King George	Anz	Sillaginodes punctata	Australian Catchall	Sillaginidae
Whiting, Sand	Anz	Sillago ciliata	Australian Catchall	Sillaginidae
Whiting, Stout	Anz	Sillago robusta	Australian Catchall	Sillaginidae
Whiting, Trumpeter	Anz	Sillago maculata	Australian Catchall	Sillaginidae
Whiting, Western School	Anz	Sillago bassensis	Australian Catchall	Sillaginidae
Whiting, Yellowfin	Anz	Sillago schomburgkii	Australian Catchall	Sillaginidae
Winkle	Eur	Littorina littorea	Shellfish (Univalves)	Lacunidae
Wolf Fish	Eur/USA Atl	Anarhichas lupus	Sea Catfish	Anarhichadidae
Wrasse, Ballan	Eur	Labras bergylta	Wrasse	Labridae
Wrasse, Crimsonband	Anz	Notolabrus gymnogenis	Wrasse	Labridae
Wreckfish	Eur/USA Atl	Polyprion americanus	Groupers, Sea Bass & Barramundi	Serranidae
Yellowtail	Anz	Seriola lalandi	Jacks, Pompanos & Trevallys	Carangidae
Yellowtail, California	USA Pac/Anz	Seriola dorsalis	Jacks, Pompanos & Trevallys	Carangidae
Yellowtail, Japanese	Japan	Seriola guigueradiata	Jacks, Pompanos & Trevallys	Carangidae
Yellowtail, Southern	Anz	Seriola grandis	Jacks, Pompanos & Trevallys	Carangidae

key to abbreviations

Anz – Australia/New Zealand; Eur – Europe; USA Atl – USA east coast; USA Pac – USA west coast

index

Illustrations are shown by *italic* numbers.

acknowledgements

I would like to thank Debbie Major who helped me put this book together, James Murphy who took the wonderful pictures and Paul Welti and Lisa Pettibone for their inspired design work. Thanks to Charlotte Knox for her beautiful illustrations, to my Commissioning Editor Viv Bowler for her quiet insistence and Rachel Copus for her accurate editing. I would also like to thank Myrtle Allen, Betsy Apple, Simon Hopkinson, Tetsuya Wakuda and Patricia Wells for allowing me to use their recipes in this book. Lastly, a big thanks to our fishmonger, Nick Jenkins, for help with the fish preparation techniques – he's the one with the tough hands!